DRIVEN TO THEIR KNEES

Driven to Their Knees

HUMILIATION IN CONTEMPORARY POLITICS

ROXANNE L. EUBEN

PRINCETON UNIVERSITY PRESS
PRINCETON & OXFORD

Published by Princeton University Press
41 William Street, Princeton, New Jersey 08540
99 Banbury Road, Oxford OX2 6JX

press.princeton.edu

GPSR Authorized Representative: Easy Access System Europe - Mustamäe tee 50, 10621 Tallinn, Estonia, gpsr.requests@easproject.com

Library of Congress Cataloging-in-Publication Data

Names: Euben, Roxanne Leslie, 1966- author
Title: Driven to their knees: humiliation in contemporary politics / Roxanne L. Euben.
Description: Princeton: Princeton University Press, 2025. | Includes bibliographical references and index.
Identifiers: LCCN 2024053796 (print) | LCCN 2024053797 (ebook) | ISBN 9780691183688 paperback | ISBN 9780691276045 hardback | ISBN 9780691275154 ebook
Subjects: LCSH: Power (Social sciences) | Humiliation—Political aspects | Rhetoric—Political aspects | Political culture | BISAC: POLITICAL SCIENCE / History & Theory | POLITICAL SCIENCE / World / Middle Eastern
Classification: LCC JC330.E93 2025 (print) | LCC JC330 (ebook) | DDC 303.3—dc23/eng/20250506
LC record available at https://lccn.loc.gov/2024053796
LC ebook record available at https://lccn.loc.gov/2024053797

British Library Cataloging-in-Publication Data is available

Editorial: Fred Appel, James Collier, and Tara Dugan
Production Editorial: Theresa Liu
Jacket/Cover Design: Karl Spurzem
Production: Lauren Reese
Publicity: William Pagdatoon
Copyeditor: Hank Southgate

Jacket image: School of Guercino (Giovanni Francesco Barbieri), *Prisoner or Martyr: Kneeling Man with Wrists Bound*, Italy. Courtesy of Princeton University Art Museum. Gift of Frank Jewett Mather Jr.

This book has been composed in Minion Pro

10 9 8 7 6 5 4 3 2 1

For Asha Fiker

CONTENTS

ACKNOWLEDGMENTS

THIS BOOK has been well over a decade in the making, and its focus and arguments have shifted considerably in that time. When I began, I took this to be a study of humiliation in Islamic thought and the Islamic tradition. The book decided otherwise. With belated clarity, I came to recognize that this is not an inquiry into things Islamic but about language, about how people actually express humiliation, and about what those expressions say and how they work.

When a book has been this long in gestation, the debts of gratitude multiply. Murad Idris, Anne Norton, and Keith Topper have been constant friends and fellow travelers. I am deeply appreciative of Murad's close reading of the entire manuscript; it has benefitted immeasurably from his generous but always incisive comments. Much of my thinking about rhetoric comes from reading Keith's work and his comments on my own. But I have learned even more from his apparently limitless erudition and exemplary collegiality. Anne has been a steadfast champion and inspiration. The book bears the stamp, if indirectly, of our many and varied conversations about writing, political theory, and intellectual heterodoxy.

There are many colleagues and friends who have helped bring this project to fruition, in ways large and small. I owe a singular debt of gratitude to Fred Appel of Princeton University Press for his unflagging commitment to this book and patient willingness to wait for it. Wendy Brown and Bruce Lawrence provided crucial support early in the project. Yasmeen Daifallah, Jill Frank, and Humeira Iqtidar have read parts or all of the manuscript, offering invaluable encouragement and sharp insight that enabled me to think freshly about fine-tuning the argument in the final stretch. For their engagement and suggestions along the way, I thank Asma Afsaruddin, Lawrie Balfour, P. J. Brendese, Lee Cuba, Noah Feldman, Jennifer Gaboury, Lene Hansen, Jeff Isaac, David Johnston, Peter Katzenstein, Louise Marlow, Takis Metaxis, Davide Panagia, Mark Reinhardt, Omar Safadi, Diane Singerman, Cristina Tarnopolsky, Muhammad Qasim Zaman, and Malika Zeghal.

I am grateful for the support, solidarity, and humor my Wellesley College friends have provided over the years, especially Pat Byrne, Stacie Goddard, Hahrie Han, Rachel Isaacs, Kathy Moon, and Anjali Prabhu. More recently, I have been sustained by the conversations and camaraderie among the stellar group of faculty and graduate students in political theory, Near Eastern Studies, Africana Studies and History at the University of Pennsylvania, particularly Abdulaziz Alotaibi, Chris Chambers, Paul Cobb, Yara Damaj, Christy Dickman, Arahi Fletcher, Loren Goldman, Jeff Green, Michael Hanchard, Derek Kennedy, Joe Lowry, Clancy Murray, Thomas (Hank) Owings, Eve Troutt Powell, Nora Reikosky, Miranda Sklaroff, Rogers Smith and Lex von Klark. The graduate students in my Politics, Power, and Affect seminar pushed me to think more clearly and less abstractly about the role of affect in the theory of humiliation I develop in the book. They did so, moreover, over Zoom in the spring of 2020, at the height of the Covid-19 pandemic.

It has been my good fortune to work with Nick Harris and Salma Moustafa Khalil, research assistants who have become invaluable interlocutors and friends. Nick has been there from the very beginning; for too many years to count, he has given generously of his time and linguistic acumen. His meticulous attention to detail is matched only by his relentless curiosity and resilient good humor. Over the course of two very difficult years that spanned the pandemic, Salma brought exemplary dedication, organizational skill, and sensitivity to the research for chapter 4. This chapter, in this form, would not have come together without her. The richness of it is a product of our collaboration; the mistakes are mine alone.

My thanks also to the many students who have helped gather research materials for this book over the years, especially Yara Damaj and Tala Nashawati, but also Yakein Abdelmagid, Adburahman Adan, Ali Asgar Alibhai, Christina Costello, Andrew Halliday, Chayva Lehrman, Rachel Mattson, David K. Owen, Rose Owen, Maliha Rahman, Anne-Sophie Tome, Aseel Najib, Imen Neffati, and Yassine Sboui. For the occasional foray into less familiar linguistic territory, I am indebted to several scholars willing to lend me their expertise: Paul A. Cohen was a great help with Mandarin, Jill Frank with ancient Greek, Rachel Isaacs with Hebrew, Loren Goldman and Jens Kruse with German. Theresa Liu at Princeton University Press, Hank Southgate, Josh Stanfield, and Thomas (Hank) Owings were a great help in bringing the final form of the manuscript into print.

I have had the privilege of presenting parts of this research at different stages in a variety of venues, including Columbia University; Harvard University; Hunter College; Johns Hopkins University; Kings College, London; Trinity College; the University of California at Irvine; the University of Chicago; the

University of Pennsylvania; the University of Virginia; Vanderbilt University; Yale University; and the Middle East Studies Association and APSA annual conferences. The many questions, comments, and conversations in and around these occasions significantly sharpened and enriched the arguments of the book, and I thank the organizers, sponsors, audiences, and participants.

Institutional support for this book has come from several sources. The research has benefitted from the financial support of fellowships from the John Simon Guggenheim Memorial Foundation (2016–17) and the National Endowment for the Humanities (2012–13). Both Wellesley College and the University of Pennsylvania have been generous with resources for the research along with the academic leaves required to conduct it. I am indebted to Humeira Iqtidar and King's College, London for making it possible to continue my work with Salma in the UK. Last but not least, I am most appreciative of the library staff at Wellesley College, particularly the Interlibrary Loan librarians, who were endlessly resourceful and patient.

Portions of the book appeared in previous forms. Earlier versions of sections from chapter 3 were originally published as "Visual Rhetoric, Retaliatory Humiliation: ISIS Executions, Performative Violence, and Sovereign Power," in *The Oxford Handbook of Rhetoric and Political Theory* (Oxford: Oxford University Press, 2023); "Spectacles of Sovereignty in Digital Time: ISIS Executions, Visual Rhetoric, and Sovereign Power," in *Perspectives on Politics* 15, issue 4 (December 2017): 1007–1033. © Cambridge University Press; and "ISIL and the armchair Islamist: How execution videos sell a fantasy of masculinity." Quartz.com, August 13, 2015. Http://qz.com/477063/isil-and-the-armchair-islamist-how-execution-videos-sell-a-fantasy-of-masculinity/. A much earlier version of the argument from chapter 2 was originally published as "Humiliation and the Political Mobilization of Masculinity," in *Political Theory* 43, issue 4 (July 2015): 500–532. © Sage Publications.

In the course of writing this book, I lost my father, J. Peter Euben (1939–2018). He brought tremendous intellectual energy and infamously bad puns to our conversations about this project, along with an unwavering confidence that it would be, in his words, an important book. That confidence was a gift he continually gave me, and it has taken me some time to not just mourn its absence but recognize my great fortune in having had it for so long. I am profoundly grateful to him for it and for much besides. He exemplified and modeled a passion for political theory and sense of its political significance reinforced by the collection of unlikely California transplants—John Schaar, Hanna Pitkin, and Sheldon Wolin—who frequented our house like an uncommonly intense and affectionately argumentative extended family. With Hanna's recent passing, all four are now gone. Many colleagues and former students have eloquently commemorated who and what these remarkable people were to political theory, individually and together. Perhaps this book honors their intellectual and political commitments in some small way, but it is really to the memory of that extended family that I pay tribute here.

In this decade of dramatic change and loss, I have been sustained by cherished friends and family, foremost among them Cristina Beltrán, Donna Euben, Lisa Kohnhorst, Judy Kelliher, Ann and Warren Lane, Hilary Persky, Lee Phenner and Mary Taylor. I want but cannot adequately express my deepest gratitude to Jonathan Perry and Asha Euben-Perry. Without Jonathan, this book could not have come to fruition. He is both ballast and inspiration, lending steadiness and strength, furnishing perspective and patience. Appreciation or gratitude are words too weak to serve. Asha is, very simply, my joy. As she will be fourteen years old at the time of publication, this will be embarrassing enough, so I leave it at that. This book is dedicated to her.

A NOTE ON TRANSLITERATION AND SPELLING

THROUGHOUT THIS BOOK, I have used the system of transliteration for Arabic set by the *International Journal of Middle East Studies*, with the exception of chapters 4 and 5, where the primary texts are a mix of Modern Standard Arabic (MSA) and Egyptian colloquial. When the source material is in MSA, I have followed the IJMES system used in the rest of the book. When the source material is in colloquial, I have followed three primary conventions of spelling and speech associated with the Egyptian dialect. First, I have translated the letter "*jīm*" using the hard "g" sound rather than the "j" of MSA (e.g., the poem from which the title of chapter 5 is taken is transliterated as "*Guḥā*," not "*Juḥā*," as in MSA). Second, I have used "*el-*" for the definite article rather than the "*al-*" of MSA. Third, I have transliterated the "*yā*" at the end of Egyptian names with a "y" rather than an "i." When it comes to proper names, places, and titles that already have an established Romanized spelling, I have sought to follow those conventions whenever possible; otherwise, I have transliterated the names with diacritics.

DRIVEN TO THEIR KNEES

1

Introduction

WHAT'S IN A WORD?

> [Our citizens] have lived through one international humiliation after another. One after another. We all remember the images of our sailors being forced to their knees by their Iranian captors at gunpoint. . . . Another humiliation came when President Obama drew a red line in Syria and the whole world knew it meant absolutely nothing. In Libya, our consulate, the symbol of American prestige around the globe was brought down in flames. . . . This is the legacy of Hillary Clinton: Death, destruction . . . terrorism and weakness. . . . Americanism, not globalism, will be our credo. As long as we are led by politicians who will not put America first, then we can be assured that other nations will not treat America with respect. The respect that we deserve. . . . [This also requires defeating] the barbarians of ISIS. And we are going to defeat them bad. . . . We're going to win. We're going to win fast. . . . It is time to show the whole world that America is back, bigger and better and stronger than ever before.

> [A]fter some minor skirmishes, in which dozens of your soldiers were killed and an American pilot was dragged through the streets of Mogadishu, you left defeated, repelled back, taking your dead, dragging the tails of failure, defeat, and humiliation. Clinton appeared in front of the world threatening to take revenge, but this threat was only a pretext for retreat. God has humiliated you and you withdrew. The extent of your impotence and weakness has become clear. The spectacle of you being defeated in three Islamic cities [Beirut, Aden, and Mogadishu] has brought joy to the heart of every Muslim and "healed the breasts of a believing people."

THESE SALVOS ARE from two of the most infamous public figures in recent decades. The first is an excerpt from Donald Trump's speech at the 2016 Republican National

Convention in Cleveland, Ohio, accepting the nomination as the party's candidate for US President.[1] The second is from Usama bin Laden's 1996 "Declaration of Jihad against the Americans Occupying the Land of the Two Holy Sites," an announcement of war against the United States, the Saudi monarchy, and their allies.[2]

Aside from great wealth and an infamy rooted in a bizarre blend of violence and entertainment, it's hard to imagine two prominent men with less in common. Bin Laden (1957–2011) was the primary founder and financier of al-Qaʿida (Arabic for "the base"), the fluid network of Islamists linked to attacks on military and civilian targets across the globe, including September 11, 2001, the most destructive attack on American territory since Pearl Harbor. Bin Laden was assassinated by US Special Forces in a 2011 raid on his Pakistan compound, an operation that quickly became the subject of a Hollywood movie.[3] Trump (b. 1946) is the New York real estate businessman and TV personality who was elected the forty-fifth and forty-seventh president of the United States. Having campaigned on the slogan "Make America Great Again," Trump's first term in office (2016–20) was marked by greater corruption and abuse of power than any of his predecessors, and he is the only president in American history to be impeached twice by Congress.[4]

At first glance, these passages seem just as mismatched as these men. Separated by two decades, they are in different languages, address disparate audiences, and serve very distinct purposes. But it's precisely the differences that make the commonalities here so striking. Humiliation is central to both and is articulated as a relation of power and powerlessness in which the protagonists are virtually identical: the humiliators and humiliated are Americans and Muslims.[5]

Each depicts defeat as a symbolic emasculation, victory a measure of virility, and virility a means to victory. But here, victory is less a matter of numbers,

1. Trump, "Donald Trump's Complete Convention Speech, Annotated." Trump said something very similar in a speech in October of the same year: "The humiliation for our country never seems to end." "Remarks at the Collier County Fairgrounds."

2. Bin Laden, "Iʿlān al-jihād ʿalā al-Amrīkiyyīn al-Muḥtallīn li-bilād al-Ḥaramayn" [Declaration of Jihad against the Americans Occupying the Land of the Two Holy Sites]. The final phrase in the Bin Laden excerpt is from the Qur'ān (9:14): "Fight them, [and] God shall punish them at your hands and disgrace them and bring you victory over them and heal the breasts of a believing people."

3. Bigelow, *Zero Dark Thirty*.

4. While Trump lost his bid for a second term to Joe Biden in 2020, he was re-elected to a second term in 2024.

5. As the "Declaration of War" is in Arabic, this is my translation of the terms Bin Laden uses: *hawān* and *akhzākum*.

matériel, or battle strategies than a performance in which the enemy is literally or symbolically driven to his knees, witnessed by everyone: humiliation is a "spectacle" for Bin Laden, just as victory over it must be, in Trump's phrase, "shown to the whole world."[6] This public posture of utter subjugation is dictated by the rightful hierarchy of power. The capacity of the intrinsically base to dominate those whose natural superiority grants them dominion over others is an unendurable corruption of the proper order of things. It demands immediate redress, a restoration in which the dominance of the deserving is accomplished by driving the lowly back where they belong, on their knees and in the dirt.

As men inhabit the roles of humiliators and humiliated, this violent contest plays out on and through male bodies. For Bin Laden, the dead, stripped US soldier dragged literally through the dirt of the Mogadishu streets enacts rather than merely symbolizes American abjection.[7] Triumph and defeat are instantaneous here, the satisfactions for the victor and the ignominy of the loser immediate rather than deferred. For Trump, it's not just US sailors kneeling, hands behind their heads, at the feet of their Iranian captors; their families and country have also been driven to their knees.[8] Such an intolerable demonstration of US impotence demands not considered policy proposals but action verbs that deliver American muscularity in speech. Fight. Build. Protect. Win. Win fast.

These salvos are far from anomalous. Trump has a well-earned reputation as a master humiliator who's dangerously thin-skinned when there's a whiff of

6. Trump, "Remarks at the Collier County Fairgrounds."

7. In 1993, the bodies of several male American soldiers were stripped, mutilated, and dragged through the streets of Mogadishu, Somalia. Photographs of the corpses instantly appeared in newspapers across the United States, with captions consistently referring to the horror depicted as a "humiliation," not of the specific men, but of the American nation. Dauber, "Shots Seen 'Round the World,'" 666. A number of news articles on the legacy of the incident for American foreign policy similarly depict it as a grievous humiliation of the United States. These events were the subject of a Hollywood movie based on a book by Mark Bowden, both titled *Black Hawk Down*.

8. The reference here is to an incident on January 12, 2016, when Iran's Islamic Revolutionary Guard Corps seized two US naval vessels that had trespassed into Iranian waters and took the American sailors on board captive. The full quotation from these remarks is: "You see the way they captured our ten sailors 'cause they were a little bit in the wrong waters. And instead of saying nicely, 'Hey, listen. You gotta be over there a little bit,' they humiliated the sailors, humiliated their families, and humiliated our country, right." Trump, "Remarks at the Southeastern Livestock Pavilion." He invoked it again in a tweet from January 14, 2016: "Iran humiliated the United States with the capture of our 10 sailors. Horrible pictures & images. We are weak. I will NOT forget!"

ridicule from anyone else.[9] In a famous *Playboy* interview more than twenty-five years before his first run for president, Trump insists repeatedly that the entire world is laughing at the United States.[10] His conviction that the crisis of greatest moment is ridicule of those who most deserve reverence—America abroad, real Americans at home, and Trump himself—would become a central theme of his 2016 campaign to Make America Great Again. As candidate and then US President, Trump evinced equal gusto and even pleasure in humiliating his Republican competitors, the Democratic presidential candidate, Hillary Clinton, the disabled, survivors of sexual assault, and even supporters—usually cheered on by fans at his rallies.[11] Donald Trump wasn't the first to deploy humiliation politically, of course, but there's no other modern politician who has so effectively normalized it.

By the same token, humiliation is a conspicuous trope throughout Bin Laden's writings, interviews, and speeches, but in the "Declaration of War," it's an insistent

9. Insiders have speculated that Trump's very entry into politics as a presidential candidate originated at the 2011 White House Correspondents' Dinner, where he took Obama's jokes at his expense—a ritual of the roast—as an intolerable public humiliation by the first Black president. Bodenner, "'Obama Taunted Trump and Look Where It Got Us.'" Michael D'Antonio, a veteran journalist and biographer of Trump, told *Frontline*, "Donald dreads humiliation and he dreads shame, and this is why he often attempts to humiliate and shame other people. This is a burning, personal need that he has to redeem himself from being humiliated by the first black president." Taddonio, "Watch: Inside the Night President Obama Took on Donald Trump."

10. He makes the same point no less than four times in the course of a single interview. Glen Plaskin, "The *Playboy* Interview with Donald Trump."

11. For example, an article in *The New Republic* instructs future candidates to see the lesson from Trump's behavior in the 2016 presidential election: humiliate or be humiliated (Shephard and Reston, "Trump's Political Lesson"). Another describes Trump as a professional dominatrix, capable of bringing former rivals and sometime critics Chris Christie, Ted Cruz, Marco Rubio, Rudy Giuliani, and Mitt Romney to heel like lapdogs in a carnival of humiliation to which both parties have implicitly assented. Ryan, "Donald Trump Is a Professional Dominatrix." In a recent study of how humiliation figures discursively in populist narratives of national security, Trump and his rhetoric supply virtually every example. Homolar and Löfflmann, "Populism and the Affective Politics of Humiliation Narratives," 1–11. Members of his (ever-changing) inner circle exhibited similar propensities. Trump's chief White House strategist, Stephen K. Bannon (Grynbaum, "Trump Strategist Stephen Bannon Says Media Should 'Keep Its Mouth Shut'") for example, launched a verbal attack on "elite" media he characterized as utterly humiliated by an election outcome they failed miserably to predict or understand. "That's why you have no power," Bannon explained to a reporter with relish. "You were humiliated. . . . The media should be embarrassed and humiliated and keep its mouth shut and just listen for a while." See also Cillizza, "Donald Trump Humiliated J. D. Vance for Fun."

rhetorical cadence. Invoked over a dozen times in a document of only twenty-five Arabic pages, the text even closes with a prayer to God to exalt (*yu'azz*) His obedient followers and humiliate (*yudhall*) the disobedient. In this preoccupation, Bin Laden is example and lodestar. From Libya to Pakistan, Somalia to Indonesia, Islamist discourse in multiple languages is saturated with invocations of "the humiliation of Islam," accompanied by repeated exhortations to make the enemies of Islam "taste the humiliation" that has been inflicted on Muslims.[12]

This unorthodox pairing spotlights a hallmark of contemporary politics that animates this study: the pervasiveness of humiliation rhetoric and the imperative to recognize and decode it. For evidence, one need look no further than the war in Gaza, ongoing as of this writing. As very little about this complex, brutal, and destructive war is taken as settled fact by all sides, it's remarkable that all sides see humiliation at stake. In an op-ed from October 7, 2023, for example, Al Jazeera political analyst Marwan Bishara describes the Hamas attack as a "scandalous humiliation" of Israel. Humiliation is a wage of hubris, Bishara writes, the culmination of decades of degrading occupation combined with a misguided sense of invincibility and the consistent tendency of Israeli leaders to underestimate their enemies. "The Palestinians have made it clear today that they would rather fight on their feet for justice and freedom than die on their knees in humiliation," he concludes. "It is high time the Israelis heed the lessons of history."[13]

For those such as far-right Israeli Finance Minister Bezalel Smotrich, the national humiliation of October 7 is precisely why Israel's response must be ruthless and unyielding. Any cease-fire agreement hands Hamas a victory, Smotrich contends, so Israel must not yield to international pressure or hesitate to attack Rafah, the last refuge of Palestinians in Gaza: "enter Rafah immediately," he instructs Prime Minister Benjamin Netanyahu, "do not wave the white flag, do not allow Sinwar [then the top Hamas leader in Gaza] to humiliate us again."[14] In several quarters (and as of this writing), outrage at images of gaunt and haunted Israeli hostages released by Hamas has focused not just on the condition of the captives but on the humiliation of Israel their suffering is said to represent.

In December 2023, videos and photographs of unarmed, half-naked, and bound Palestinian men detained in Gaza by the Israeli army circulated widely

12. See note in chapter 2 for a brief clarification of my use "discourse" in relation to "rhetoric."

13. Bishara, "From Hubris to Humiliation."

14. Azulai, "Smotrick to Netanyahu." Yahya Sinwar was killed by the IDF on October 17, 2024.

across social media. In one of many such images, heavily armed Israeli soldiers guard kneeling, barefoot men stripped to their underwear, hands bound and heads bowed. They're arranged single-file at one edge of a street lined by bombed-out buildings with blasted windows like empty eyes. Dozens of shoes and flip-flops are strewn along the rubble-filled road in the foreground. News outlets from New York to Jerusalem captioned the images as Hamas terrorists surrendering to the IDF (Israeli Defense Forces), but subsequent reports and interviews identified the images as indiscriminate mass round-ups of all Palestinian males of "military age" in areas the army had ordered evacuated.

A spokesman for the Israeli government at the time defended the practice as a necessity given that Hamas members do not wear uniforms.[15] But in a *Haaretz* op-ed, Gideon Levy contends that the real purpose of such practices and the circulation of such images is to demonstrate the imperium of Israel by publicly forcing Palestinians literally and figuratively to their knees, a spectacle not just of surrender but utter powerlessness. The victims are young and old, some well-fed and others gaunt, he writes; "some have pale skin and others are scorched by the hardships of the war." All are men and, if their wives and children are watching, all the better. The entire tableau is, he concludes, a "Hanukkah gift of humiliated Palestinians" that shows how low Israel is willing to go.[16]

These often-brutal examples dramatize a more basic fact: humiliation rhetoric is not unique to a particular people, region, or language, and it's just as easily voiced in a nationalist as a religious idiom, by the powerful as well as the powerless, and across the political spectrum. Like a proverbial Zelig, it pops up in virtually every frame and phenomenon, perpetually protean. Humiliation is said to be a major driver of international conflict and political violence, characterized as the "single most underappreciated force in international relations" by Thomas Friedman.[17] The 2011 Arab uprisings were sparked by the humiliation of

15. Brianna Keilar interview with Eylon Levy, CNN News Central, December 8, 2023. See also Shalaby and Youssef, "Palestinian Recounts Being Stripped and Driven Away by Israeli Army."

16. Levy, "By Trying to Humiliate Gaza to Its Core, Israel Is the One Being Humiliated." Palestinian women and children are not just bystanders to the humiliation of men. At the start of the Israeli attack on Rafah, for example, Sahar Abu Nahel, a grandmother who had fled with her family to the city in search of safety, said, "I have no money or anything. I am seriously tired, as are the children. Maybe it's more honorable for us to die. We are being humiliated," (Mednick, Federman, and Mroue, "Hamas Accepts Gaza Cease-Fire Proposal").

17. Friedman, "Humiliation Factor." The argument that humiliation is a driver of international conflict and political violence has been made by journalists, policymakers, and scholars

a Tunisian fruit seller.[18] The humiliations of Iranian women propelled the 2022 protests following Mahsa Amini's death.[19] The US withdrawal from Vietnam is the humiliating failure that has haunted American foreign ventures since the fall of Saigon.[20] The partnership of racism and humiliation is integral to White supremacy in the United States.[21] Gender-based violence intensifies when men are humiliated.[22] The rise of the Third Reich is routinely explained in terms of it.[23] China even named an entire century after it. The "Century of Humiliation," one scholar contends, is the "master narrative of modern Chinese history."[24]

Depending on where you look and what you read, then, humiliation is an act and an experience, a cause and a consequence, a trope and an event, an emotion and an epoch. Given such an array of guises, it's little wonder that what humiliation actually means is difficult to pin down. This elusiveness marks a political and theoretical puzzle largely hidden in plain view: humiliation is rhetorically pervasive and politically potent, but conceptually elusive.

In the vast majority of contemporary scholarship, journalism, public policy, and even vernacular speech, humiliation is taken as self-explanatory or a

---

of international relations, psychology, and terrorism, and it became increasingly popular following the attacks on 9/11. See, for example, Bergen and Lind, "Matter of Pride," 8–16; Fontan, "Polarization between Occupier and Occupied in Post-Saddam Iraq," 217–38; Marton, "Terrorism and Humiliation"; and Lindner and Deutsch, *Making Enemies*. These are directly or indirectly indebted to earlier inquiries into the dynamics of humiliation, such as William Ian Miller's excellent *Humiliation*; Steinberg's "Psychoanalytic Concepts in International Politics," 65–84; Susan B. Miller's "Humiliation and Shame," 40–51; Gilligan's *Violence*; Klein's "Humiliation Dynamic," 87–92; and Wengst and Bowden's *Humility*.

18. The precipitating incident is more complex and contested than this suggests; see discussion in chapter 4.

19. See Moaveni, "Protests in Iran." Moaveni characterizes the protests as an expression of women's feeling of humiliation and depicts Amini's death as akin to the Bouazizi "spark."

20. There are innumerable references to US humiliation in Vietnam and its legacies by scholars, journalists, policymakers, and commentators alike. In "Post-Vietnam Syndrome," Myra Mendible argues that the "psychodrama of humiliation" around the US withdrawal from Vietnam has a gendered register particularly evident when the aversion to war becomes a "sign that America had been feminized by defeat, turned into a nation of wimps and pacifists."

21. Griffin, "Racism and Humiliation in the African-American Community," 149–67.

22. See, e.g., Fleming et al., "Competition and Humiliation," 197–215; and Heilman and Barker, *Masculine Norms and Violence*.

23. There's a vast literature in which the "humiliation of Germany" by the Treaty of Versailles following World War I is identified as critical to the rise of the Nazi Party.

24. Callahan, "National Insecurities," 204. No footnote could ever do justice to the immense literature on China's "Century of Humiliation."

"reduplicative intensifier" of more primary emotions such as vengeance or rage.[25] In striking contrast to other emotions such as shame, fear, or hate, there are few systematic efforts to define it.[26] Even political theory, a field known for such conceptual work, an increasing interest in the emotions, and a particularly rich vein of scholarship on shame,[27] has surprisingly little to say about it.[28] In more than a few instances, good work meant to address humiliation winds up circling around it, rerouted into phenomena such as shame, vengeance, scapegoating, or right-wing populism.[29]

This raises a number of political, theoretical, and methodological questions that haven't yet been posed, let alone answered. Take the two passages that opened this chapter: What do such invocations of collective humiliation say, and how do they work discursively, rhetorically, affectively, and politically? Do figures like Trump and Bin Laden even mean the same thing by humiliation? What and where are the blockages that have prevented these kinds of politically pressing questions from arising in the first place? What approach might make it possible to grasp something so pervasive yet seemingly elusive, and even identify unexpected patterns in what it says and does?

As the puzzle begins with the way humiliation is used in language, in this book, I look to language to take up the interlocking questions it raises. By this, I don't mean the impossible effort to survey invocations of humiliation in every language. Instead, I turn to one language in particular, Arabic, and focus specifically on exemplary moments in Arabic humiliation rhetoric—verbal, visual, and

25. Miller, *Humiliation*, 133.

26. This must be distinguished from the absurd claim that nothing has been written about humiliation or the presumptuous argument that there is nothing to learn from what has been written. Of particular note is Klein's "Humiliation Dynamic" (discussed below), one of the earliest and best studies of humiliation in social psychology. See also Saurette's work, particularly on Kant (see below), Frevert's informative history of public humiliation in Europe, *Politics of Humiliation*, Koestenbaum's *Humiliation*, and *Humiliation*, edited by Guru, a collection of essays both old and new about humiliation in India, and notes 20, 40, 53, 68, and 83.

27. See, e.g., Williams, *Shame and Necessity*; Locke, "Shame and the Future of Feminism"; Tarnopolsky, "Prudes, Perverts, and Tyrants"; Manion, "Moral Relevance of Shame" and "Girls Blush, Sometimes," 21–41; Saxonhouse, *Free Speech and Democracy in Ancient Athens*; and Agamben's account of shame in several of his works, especially *Remnants of Auschwitz*. Rom Harré also provides a useful analysis of shame in contrast to embarrassment in "Embarrassment."

28. The few that do so treat it very briefly. See, e.g., the references to Richard Rorty and Judith Shklar in note 86.

29. See note 71.

embodied. To analyze verbal humiliation discourse in chapter 2, for example, I draw on such influential texts as Sayyid Qutb's multivolume Qur'ānic interpretation, *Fī Ẓilāl al-Qur'ān* (In the shade of the Qur'ān). In chapter 3, I provide a reading of visual humiliation rhetoric in two particularly infamous ISIS execution videos. Chapters 4 and 5 draw on verbal, visual, and embodied expressions of humiliation from the 2011 Egyptian revolution, an archive comprised of blogs, vlogs, professional and amateur videos, poetry, tweets, songs, chants, and slogans by prominent and unnamed Egyptians alike.

These illustrations are clearly clustered around two major moments and phenomena, Islamism and the Arab uprisings, although my focus is more on texts, genres, and modes of expression than on the contested categories to which they are usually assigned. Still, these particular moments take center stage because they so sharply articulate the puzzle and its political stakes. Islamists have advanced the most visible account of humiliation in Arabic and one of the most conspicuous in the contemporary world, but it is largely overlooked and understudied. By the same token, invocations of humiliation suffused the Egyptian Revolution, yet it remains one of the most neglected and undertheorized features not just of the Egyptian Uprising, but of uprisings from Tunisia to Yemen, Syria to Bahrain. Such inattention to the ubiquity of humiliation in the mountainous commentary on the uprisings is precisely the kind of omission this book aims to identify and rectify.

Most of these Arabic invocations of humiliation are drawn from sources, sites, and genres usually situated outside the conventional jurisdiction of political theory, but I take them as texts that need to be read, analyzed, and interpreted as much as books. This is in the spirit of work in an array of fields that understands "texts" capaciously to include the practices, experiences, and articulations of "regular" people who are themselves understood as authors rather than simply objects of political knowledge.[30] I read these archives specifically for what humiliation says and how it works in these texts and the worlds in which they are embedded; I don't presume that the meaning of any single invocation is exhausted by this focus or the reading it yields. To borrow from Sara Ahmed, texts can be an invaluable entrée to how experiences are made into meaning provided we

30. From ethnographic work, to literary, cultural, and postcolonial theory, to recent scholarship on the "security vernacular" in critical security studies (e.g., Bubandt, "Vernacular Security"; Jarvis, "Toward a Vernacular Security Studies"; and Jarvis and Lister, "Vernacular Securities and Their Study"), this capacious view of texts and focus on "regular people" is hardly new. Yet longstanding disciplinary divisions of labor have meant that there are entire areas of political inquiry that do not engage in it or have only very recently incorporated it.

make certain not to assume an "equivalence between texts and the histories they keep alive."[31]

As these Arabic expressions of humiliation are vastly understudied, I take them as significant areas of inquiry in their own right and intend these close readings to contribute to ongoing efforts to understand the particular phenomena of which they are a part. At the same time, I thematize tropes, idioms, strategies, and structures that emerge within and across these archives, tracking patterns and discontinuities in the way these articulations of humiliation contest or refigure it, reproduce or shore it up. As I'll argue in greater detail below, these readings show how and why such expressions are untapped resources for theorizing humiliation not in terms of what it's said to be but in terms of the way it's articulated, produced, and contested in and through language.

Such resources come into focus only by asking different questions than those usually posed when it comes to concepts such as humiliation. The crucial questions are not: Does this qualify as humiliation? Or: Are such claims of humiliation legitimate? Instead, the questions are: Who is invoking collective humiliation and how? To whom are such invocations addressed, what collective solidarities do they presuppose, what purposes do they make explicit, and what meanings do they encode? How do these rhetorical deployments define the stakes of repair, the form such repair must take, and those tasked with it? Are there significant patterns in the way humiliation works politically, affectively, and rhetorically? How might such patterns address the puzzling conceptual vacuity that currently prevails so that we can grasp what humiliation says and does in contemporary politics?

A Busy Intersection

Given the ubiquity of humiliation, it's possible to begin this inquiry elsewhere, but Arabic rhetoric is a particularly instructive way to pursue and answer these questions. This isn't because there's a unique affinity between humiliation and Arabic-speaking peoples but precisely because such an affinity, commonly presumed and reiterated axiomatically, has made the intersection of Arabs and Muslims (rendered interchangeable) and humiliation a very busy one in recent decades.[32] All sorts of explanations for behavior, accounts of motivation, and assumptions about culture converge and entangle in its features. Crucial blockages

31. Ahmed, *Cultural Politics of Emotion*, 216.

32. Needless to say, not all Arabs are Muslim and not all Muslims speak Arabic, but the conflation of Arabs and Muslims is a critical feature of the accounts that follow.

to theorizing humiliation are readable in these features, as are the political logics such blockages both express and conceal.

Claims of national humiliation tend to appear whenever American preeminence abroad seems diminished, for example, but Arabs and Muslims have increasingly taken center stage as a major, at times primary, threat. This is particularly true after 9/11, but well before then, the "Green Peril" (green is often associated with Islam) had become a viable replacement for the communist "Red Menace."[33] Trump's insistence that devious Muslim states and savage Islamist terrorists are responsible for the "string" of international humiliations that have made America an object of ridicule is just one of the more recent variations on this theme.

What has been described as George W. Bush's strutting "cowboy masculinity," in combination with the hypermasculinist dynamics of his inner circle, helped constitute the 9/11 attacks as a national humiliation requiring public retribution to restore American potency and pride.[34] Similar masculinist logic emerged in rhetoric depicting President Barack Obama's apology for the burning of Qur'ān pages by American military personnel in Afghanistan as a national humiliation. The accusation that Obama had embarked on an "apology tour of the Middle East" returned repeatedly during the 2012 presidential election, often in language suggesting that Obama had essentially "bent over" for Muslims and Arabs.[35]

Arabs and Muslims represent the threat of national humiliation here, but at other moments are constituted as collectively humiliated. In a *Foreign Affairs* article, for example, French political scientist Dominique Moïsi argues that the

33. Sciolino, "Seeing Green."

34. Ferguson, "Cowboy Masculinity, Globalization and the U.S. War on Terror," and Saurette, "You Dissin Me?," 512, 514, 518. This particular dynamic is neither unique to the Bush administration nor American foreign policy toward Muslim-majority countries. In *Faking It*, Cynthia Weber shows, for example, that similar anxieties about symbolic castration and demonstrations of hypermasculinity characterized US foreign policy toward the Caribbean from 1959 to 1994.

35. Presidential candidate Mitt Romney invoked this characterization on many different occasions during the campaign. Sterling, "CNN Fact Check: Obama Went on an Apology Tour." The commentary on Obama in this instance—and in so many others—exemplifies the often unspoken matter of race deeply and toxically intertwined with humiliation, gender, and sexuality in American life, past and present. It also seems that such depictions are especially common when the administration is Democratic. President Jimmy Carter's handling of the Iranian hostage crisis in 1979–80, for example, contributed to depictions of him as a "wimp." And there was an outcry about President Joe Biden humiliating America when he withdrew troops from Afghanistan in 2021. In connection with the latter see, for example, Galston, "Anger, Betrayal, and Humiliation."

"Arab and Muslim worlds are trapped in a culture of humiliation" that has devolved into a "culture of hatred." Or consider a *New York Times* column on the escalation of hostilities in Southern Lebanon in which journalist John Tierney depicts Hizbollah as fighting "to humiliate the enemy, not for any particular objective."[36] In the former, humiliation is stripped of historical context and lived experience to become an ontologically grounded culture of hatred. In the latter, the act of humiliation figures as the very antithesis of an objective, by implication both self-evident and purposeless.

Humiliation has also become a fixture of explanations of why young Muslim men are motivated to heed the call of armed jihad.[37] Jessica Stern's *Terror in the Name of God*, for example, contains an entire chapter titled "Humiliation" that focuses on interviews with Palestinians about the "real or perceived national humiliation of the Palestinian people by Israeli policies."[38] Stern doesn't supply a definition of humiliation, but rather clusters it throughout the book with various other terms such as alienation, deprivation, rage, desperation, fear, hopelessness, embarrassment, and envy. How these are related to one another, in what they consist, and whether they're intended as synonyms, elaborations, triggers, or consequences of humiliation remains unclear. Stern concludes that what really explains Islamic terrorism "are perceived humiliation, relative deprivation and fear—whether personal, cultural, or both . . . holy wars take off only when there is a large supply of young men who feel humiliated and deprived."[39] Yet this begs rather than answers the central question of what counts as the experience of humiliation to these young men and why it would necessarily drive them into the arms of radical Islamists.[40]

Then there are depictions of "the Muslim world" as hypersensitive to humiliations of their own making and convulsed by what Nietzsche called *ressentiment*,

36. Moïsi, "Clash of Emotions," 8–12; Tierney, "Another Man's Honor."

37. Many of the following examples also contain excellent research unrelated to humiliation. See, e.g., Hafez, "Martyrdom Mythology in Iraq," 95–115; Khosrokhavar, *Suicide Bombers*; Khouri, "Terrorists Are Also Spawned by Humiliation"; Pape, *Dying to Win*; Danchev, "'Like a Dog!'"; Luban, "Human Dignity, Humiliation, and Torture"; Fattah and Fierke, "Clash of Emotions"; Saurette, "Humiliation and the Global War on Terror" and "You Dissin Me?"

38. Stern, *Terror in the Name of God*, 32.

39. Stern, *Terror in the Name of God*, 235–36.

40. Very few accounts in this area of inquiry supply even a brief definition of humiliation. Saurette's excellent article, "You Dissin Me?," and Fattah and Fierke's "Clash of Emotions" are exceptions, but they also exemplify the dominant philosophical formulation (see above). Saurette defines humiliation as a "process of disrespecting" (507), a violation of one's dignity and self-respect; Fattah and Fierke say much the same thing (77, 84).

the vindictive rancor that festers among those powerless against the greatness of spirit and talent animating the triumphs of the powerful.[41] Perhaps the best-known proponent of this view is historian Bernard Lewis. Well before the events of 9/11, Lewis assiduously traced contemporary "Muslim rage" to resentment at the humiliation of Islamic civilization by the accumulation of Western military, political, cultural, and economic "victories."[42] Far from alone in making such arguments, Lewis's scholarly standing nevertheless infused them with an authority and legitimacy that gave them a new lease on life among the neoconservative architects of American foreign policy in the wake of 9/11.

In the American-led "war on terror," Arabs and Muslims would be reconstituted, figured as objects as much as agents of humiliation. Many of the interrogation techniques used on detainees at Abu Ghraib as well as in Bagram and Guantánamo prisons were developed specifically to exploit the anxieties and taboos supposedly constitutive of Arab/Muslim culture. As Seymour Hersh's exposé on abuse of Iraqi prisoners by the US Army revealed, Raphael Patai's 1973 book depicting a timeless and unchanging Arab masculinity obsessed with sex and animated by avoidance of humiliation and shame was essential training for American interrogation tactics used on male detainees. According to one of Hersh's sources, Patai's book—revealingly titled *The Arab Mind*—became "the bible of the neocons on Arab behavior."[43]

The cruelty on display in the photographs from Abu Ghraib is just one part of the picture.[44] One of the most notorious photographs that began circulating in 2004 depicts Private Lynndie England holding the leash of a man cowering naked like a whipped dog on a dirty floor. To follow the leash up from the neck of the detainee is to behold the face of fun: a soldier smiling for the camera as

41. Nietzsche, *Genealogy of Morals*, I, 10.

42. See, for example, Lewis, "Roots of Muslim Rage" and *Crisis of Islam*, esp. 21–22. Lewis makes this argument in different ways in several of his other publications, and the martial metaphor is central to how he makes it.

43. Hersh, "Gray Zone"; Patai, *Arab Mind*.

44. As will become clear, the impact of these photographs on radical Islamists, and its connection to the language of humiliation, should not be underestimated. In one very early response, a video was posted depicting the beheading of American Nicholas Berg. The execution was reportedly carried out by Abu Mus'ab al-Zarqawi himself, the leader of al-Qa'ida in Iraq, as well as progenitor and inspiration for ISIS. In the video, the narrator asks: "How does the Muslim sleep, his eyelids at rest, while he sees Islam slaughtered and sees the hemorrhaging of honor [*karāma*] and the pictures of shame [*al-ʿār*] and the reports of satanic humiliation [*al-imtihān al-shayṭānī*] of the people of Islam, men and women, in Abu Ghraib prison?"

if on holiday. The picture captures what might be called the pleasure of humiliation, an unmentionable feature that simultaneously implicates spectators in a prurient voyeurism and calls on them to avert their gaze. Such satisfactions are irreducible to the sadistic pleasures of inflicting physical pain, although they commonly appear together and often work in tandem. Quickly buried by a landslide of language about the unprecedented and aberrant that eventually settled on low-level (and notably female) military personnel such as England, the pictures showed Americans as "cheerful decimators," exhibiting what Wayne Koestenbaum dubs the specifically "sportive nature of U.S. style humiliation."[45]

Preeminent threat and arrested culture. Rage and ressentiment. Agents and objects. The cumulative effect of all this traffic is to securely tether humiliation to Arabs and Muslims who inhabit an alien world of developmentally arrested honor cultures in which hypermasculine men seethe under the weight of their own humiliating failures. It does so not by way of explicit argument or persuasive speech but by a process of affective attachment that can be usefully understood in terms of what Sara Ahmed has called "sticky signs." Both metaphor and argument, "sticky signs" foregrounds the way repetition and circulation attaches words to meanings, things, and even bodies while concealing the operations that bind them.

> The 'binding' effect of the word is also a 'blockage': it stops the word moving or acquiring new value. The sign is a 'sticky sign' as an effect of a history of articulation, which allows the sign to accumulate value. . . . [But] the association between words that generates meanings is concealed: *it is this concealment of such associations that allows such signs to accumulate value.* I am describing this accumulation of affective value as a form of stickiness, or as 'sticky signs.'[46]

Given these processes, theorizing what humiliation says and does isn't simply a matter of collecting and analyzing the ways that people speak and invoke it. It's also about adhesion and blockage. It's about the way affectively laden meanings are produced by attachments sedimented through repetition and circulation. And it's about how what's stuck together also disjoins—or blocks—through concealment, producing a sense of essential cultural difference.

The present inquiry by no means exhausts the "stickiness" of humiliation. On the contrary, it showcases the need to examine its inflections by other affective attachments—for starters, the historically specific racialization of humiliation that has constituted American Black bodies as always already humiliated. At the

45. Koestenbaum, *Humiliation*, 6.

46. Ahmed, *Cultural Politics of Emotion*, 92, emphasis in the original.

same time, this point of departure throws a particularly powerful spotlight on the way humiliation has been culturalized, in this instance pegged to culturally distinctive pathologies and resentments to become just one more marker of Muslim or Arab Otherness. Close examination of Arabic invocations of humiliation, the stakes of the action they enjoin, and the dynamics of political power they refract are rendered superfluous. Parallels or overlaps in what humiliation rhetoric says and how it works viscerally and politically across time and context remain unthought. In this light, the ubiquity and opacity of humiliation is less a puzzle than what philosopher Cheshire Calhoun calls a nonlogical implication of repeated emphases and silences.[47] Such emphases and silences demonstrate the need to theorize humiliation; decoding them uncovers unanticipated resources for doing so.

From Concept to Relation

Close reading of humiliation rhetorics requires attending to the specificity of meanings written into the word that are brought out, mobilized, or remade in use. There are several different Arabic terms that, depending on context, can sensibly be translated as humiliation, and the etymological roots invest each with an array of latent valences. The most common are terms derived from the root ذلل/*dhāl-lām-lām* (low, base, vile, abased, subjected, ignominious, contemptible, humiliated) and هون/*hā'-wāw-nūn* (to despise, humble, humiliate, degrade, insult, scorn, or disdain). There are at least three other trilateral roots—صغر/*ṣād-ghayn-rā'* (to be small, to debase, make lowly or inferior), خزي/*khā'-zayn-yā'* (degradation, dishonor, humiliation, shame), and فضح/*fā'-ḍād-ḥā'* (to publicize information or expose faults that shame, disgrace, or dishonor someone else)—derivations of which can and have been translated as humiliation.

The terms derived from one final root, رغم/*rā'-ghayn-mīm*, have the widest range of meanings that connect metaphorically. This root provides Arabic words for dirt and earth; to be dirt/dust covered; to be coerced, compelled against one's will, humiliated, and abased. It is also integral to a premodern idiomatic phrase, variations of which appear in ḥadīths[48] on humiliation: *arghama anfahu*,

47. Calhoun, "Justice, Care, Gender Bias," 452–53.

48. Ḥadīth is a report concerning the words and deeds of the Prophet Muhammad, collected and recorded in the centuries following Muhammad's death. Both the major Sunni and Shi'i Ḥadīth collections are replete with references to humiliation. Unsurprisingly, humiliation figures very differently in the two corpora.

literally "make his nose cleave to the earth," which essentially referred to humiliation.[49] This link between humiliation and earth/dirt/ground is echoed in one of the derivations of *dhāl-lām-lām*, which means "to walk or ride upon [the earth or ground]."

It's instructive that the etymology of these Arabic terms signifies a push or orientation downward, a debasement or degradation. The emphasis on Arabic etymology is often viewed with suspicion, the legacy of a tendency in twentieth-century Orientalist scholarship to conflate the root of a word with the way Arabic speakers invoke, understand, and enact it. This etymology is instructive not because there's a straight line between root and action but because it directs attention to how continuities in what humiliation says and does across languages mobilizes and reworks overlaps written into the word. It's particularly significant, then, that this downward orientation is equally true of the etymology of the English *humiliation*, traceable to the Latin *humus*, "earth" or "ground," and something similar can be found both in German and biblical Hebrew.[50] Such an etymological entanglement of humiliation with earth/dirt/dust suggests the experience of being shoved into the ground, of being forced, literally, to "eat dirt."

There's a connotation of imposed powerlessness threading throughout these linked etymologies, as the passive voice at once installs and conceals the presence of two figures, one forced into the dust and another with the power to have forcibly made another eat dirt. In this sense, hierarchy is already written into the Arabic words for humiliation, much as it is in other languages such as English, German, and biblical Hebrew. This hierarchy is a relation of both stature and

49. Lane, *Arabic–English Lexicon*, 3:1113.

50. Consider the various German nouns for humiliation: *Erniedrigung* (humiliating, abasing, debasing, bring low); *Demütigung* (to be humbled, to be humiliated, to be brought low, reduction of spirit and courage); *Beschämung* (embarrassment, shame, humiliation); *Schmach* (disgrace, humiliation); and the twinned terms *Kanossa*/*Kanossagang* (to be humbled, humiliated). The closest parallel to the Arabic is evinced by biblical Hebrew, which fully expresses the links among humiliation, powerlessness, and dirt/dust/earth. A case in point are some well-known lines in the liturgy: "God makes poor and makes rich, humiliates [*mashpil*] and also exalts. He raises the nobody out of the dirt [*ʿafar*], out of the refuse heap he lifts up the poor" (1 Samuel 2:7–8). Another case in point is Isaiah 25:12, referring to how God will punish pride by razing even the most fortified walls, laying them "low and humble . . . razed to the ground, to the very dust." Humiliation and one who is brought low into the dust share the root *shin- pay- lamed*. Georgakopoulos et al., "Meaning of Ancient Words for 'Earth,'" 428. I am indebted to Jens Kruse for the German and Rachel Isaacs for the biblical Hebrew.

power expressed spatially and metaphorically as elevation and lowliness. Such "lowliness" is not a matter of relative powerlessness but absolute impotence: to be forcibly shoved into the ground, face in the dust, is to have one's body, will, status, and appearance in the world seized by another. All that you once were is eclipsed by what the humiliator has made you to be.

The distinction between humiliation and shame comes into focus here. As I indicated earlier, these terms are often used interchangeably, a tendency that likely reflects the etymological overlap between shame and humiliation in languages ranging from Arabic to Mandarin. The word most commonly used in China for national humiliation when referring to "China's Century of Humiliation," for example, is *guóchǐ*, a compound of the Chinese characters *guó* (國), meaning country, nation, state, or kingdom, and *chǐ* (恥), meaning humiliation, shame, or disgrace.[51]

There is no doubt that shame may slide into humiliation or the other way around. But both analytically and experientially, there's a significant difference between what Christina Tarnopolsky aptly refers to as the "cognition of inadequacy" characteristic of shame and what I identified earlier as the imposition of impotence by those who undeservedly have the power to do so.[52] This is why Trump, ever eager to humiliate others, is very often referred to in passing as "shameless." In these instances, common English usage captures precisely the phenomenon named: an incapacity to feel shame anchored in an inability or unwillingness to recognize any failures or failings as his own.

The distinction between shame and humiliation also elucidates what could be called the public character of humiliation written into these terms, one of the many features the opening two passages share. Donald Klein captures this character by positing a triangulation of three roles—humiliator, humiliated, and witness—constitutive of its particular structure.[53] The presence of a witness is an

51. There are several terms used in China that refer to losing face or to being disgraced, shamed, or humiliated in international relations, but *guóchǐ* is most commonly invoked in "China's Century of Humiliation." I am grateful to Paul Cohen and William Joseph for email conversations about the multiplicity of terms used for humiliation in China and the inflections of each. See also Cohen, "Remembering and Forgetting National Humiliation in Twentieth-Century China." There are many more languages in which the etymologies of terms that can mean humiliation also suggest shame.

52. Tarnopolsky, "Prudes, Perverts, and Tyrants," 477.

53. Klein, "Humiliation Dynamic." Some of the most interesting conceptual work on humiliation was done by empirical and social psychologists, some over thirty years ago. While not immune from some of the problems analyzed here, at its best, such research sought to

explicit or implicit feature of humiliation rhetoric across these chapters, where both "presence" and "witness" are broadly construed. From an omniscient God who sees everything to a crowd that has physically gathered, the sine qua non of humiliation in these expressions is visibility, even spectacle.[54]

It is precisely this public character that can make boasting of the event after the fact an extension of humiliation rather than a simple recounting of it. If humiliation lives in the rupture between unjustly imposed impotence and rightful status, repeated rehearsal of it can constitute a reenactment of the rupture, one capable of revivifying the experience itself. As the following chapters show, the same is true of retaliatory humiliation, but in this instance, what's enacted, reenacted, and potentially revivified is the repair of such rupture. Herein lies the "healing" of Bin Laden's Declaration: the imposition of humiliation upon one's humiliator offers the gratification, even pleasure, of reclaiming one's power and vindicating one's sense of significance in the social order.

Verbal, Visual, and Embodied Rhetorics

An inquiry focused on language as use must be clear about the language it uses. I take up such complex and contested terms as Islamism and dignity as they arise in subsequent chapters, but even "rhetoric" is far from straightforward. Laden with an intellectual history that usually begins with the ancient Greeks, rhetoric has fallen in and (mostly) out of favor as it has traveled through a series of debates in Euro-American thought that have continuously reconfigured its meaning, purposes, and relationship to power.[55] As I use it, "rhetoric" is not about this history or those debates, but it comes into sharp focus against this backdrop in three ways. First, I deliberately bracket the distinction, deeply rooted the intellectual history

distinguish humiliation from phenomena such as shame, guilt, and embarrassment, and to conceptualize it as an act and experience dependent upon publicly available yet contextually determined standards. See, e.g., Lazare, "Shame and Humiliation in the Medical Encounter"; Miller, "Humiliation and Shame"; and Evelin Gerda Lindner's work, one of the few who has conducted research in so-called non-Western societies. See, e.g., *Making Enemies*; "Women and Terrorism," 10–12; "Humiliation as the Source of Terrorism"; *Concept of Humiliation*; and *Anatomy of Humiliation and Its Relational Character*.

54. This brackets the question of whether entirely private humiliation exists, a subject beyond the scope of this inquiry. See Silver et al., "Humiliation," 270, 278.

55. I am indebted to conversations with Keith Topper about rhetoric in general and in connection with his current research project, provisionally titled "The Return of the Repressed: On the Rediscovery of Rhetoric in Political Theory."

of rhetoric, between emotional rhetoric designed to mobilize irrational passions on the one hand and, on the other, rational speech in which logic is leveraged to persuade equals in democratic deliberations. Such an opposition has certainly flourished over the centuries in a variety of forms, but it is nevertheless implausible and distracts from the politically pressing task of examining what invocations of humiliation say and do.

Second, inasmuch as rhetoric was once considered, in Terry Eagleton's words, a "textual training of the ruling class in the techniques of political hegemony," the expressions of humiliation that are the stuff of these chapters can be understood as antihegemonic.[56] By this, I don't mean that these figures and groups have no power, are emancipatory by definition, consistently opposed to the state, or are themselves incapable of domination. Many branches of the Muslim Brotherhood, for example, have conformed to an array of state arrangements and participated in formal political processes. It's also the case that, as Ariel Ahram argues, ISIS in many ways mimicked the patterns of violent state-building and control in the region.[57] They are antihegemonic in the sense that they have largely positioned themselves outside of and/or in opposition to both the state and the international order.[58]

Third, I adopt a capacious conception of rhetoric along the lines suggested by Keith Topper. Rhetoric encompasses diverse modes of expression that work less through formal or explicit argument than through the visceral power of address, invective, juxtaposition, metonymy, and the like.

> [T]he term "rhetoric" often signifies the persuasive sphere of language and denotes those elements of a text that are designed to persuade through means other than conventional forms of linear or transparent reasoning . . . the use of figural language, specific tropes, and other literary and framing devices, as well as stylistic choices, matters of formal organization, exploration of different literary genres, and the constitution of the ethos and pathos of the author or speaker. . . . [I]t frequently refers to the deployment of these elements not just to persuade, but also to inspire action that aims to bring about or resist political change.[59]

Defined in this way, rhetoric straddles three primary modes of expression in these materials: verbal, visual, and embodied. They work through a variety of genres and techniques, disseminated by way of disparate mechanisms of

56. Eagleton, "A Short History of Rhetoric," 86.
57. Ahram, "Sexual and Ethnic Violence."
58. Eagleton, "Short History of Rhetoric," 86.
59. Topper, "Introduction."

production and circulation that also overlap. Humiliation rhetoric is articulated visually in genres that range from photographs to screen grabs to videos, expressed through composition, symbolic and dramaturgical features, religious and pop-cultural references, narrative structure, pacing, choices of casting, clothing, props, and so on. Verbal rhetoric most obviously includes words spoken and written for particular purposes and effect, but the genres of verbal expression here range widely from vlogs to spoken poetry to published volumes of Qur'ānic interpretation.

Each of these rhetorical modes is foregrounded in the three substantive chapters of this book. These are only loose correspondences, however, as these modes are analytically distinguishable but almost impossible to fully disentangle in use. A number of poems in chapter 4, for example, were initially performed live before ever appearing in print or were never formally published at all, circulating instead as recordings uploaded to the poet's website or unauthorized videos on social media. The ISIS videos in chapter 3 are moving images that communicate by way of the words spoken along with the "casting" of those who speak, how the captives are clothed, the postures of each body, and the positioning of the executioner who looms over each in succession.[60]

The third rhetorical mode of expression is what I call an embodied idiom of humiliation, quite likely the most widely recognizable even if it sounds unfamiliar at first. Throughout these chapters, this mode is expressed in several metaphors, images, and idiomatic phrases that center the body to convey humiliation in the absence of the word itself. The most common have already made an appearance: forced to kneel, driven into dirt, bent over. These are terms in an embodied vocabulary that includes *tiksar 'aynī* ["break my eye"], which connotes being forced to cast one's eyes down, and *arghama anfahu* [literally "make his nose cleave to the earth"] or *rughimat unūf* ["noses were dirtied"]. As such examples indicate, this embodied idiom refers to both the way humiliation can operate on and through the flesh and the consistently somatic register in which it is articulated.

The final terminological clarification concerns my use of the word "discourse." A thoroughgoing account of the debates about discourse, or how the various understandings of discourse and rhetoric intersect is far beyond my focus. I use "discourse" in two interrelated senses here. The first is relatively straightforward,

60. Complicating matters, the multiple modes of humiliation rhetoric in these videos circulated widely as screen grabs that, according to Friis ("'Beyond Anything We Have Ever Seen'"), significantly reshaped American and British responses to Da'ish. For discussion, see chapter 3.

and refers to the collection of statements, assumptions, categories, terms, and so on pertaining to a particular subject. The second sense of "discourse," associated with a range of approaches including poststructuralism, refers not only to such a body of statements but also to the conditions and constraints that constitute the field of knowledge itself and make certain claims intelligible within it. In this sense, "discourses" both include and exclude, are repressive and productive, and so on. If discourse foregrounds the historically contingent imbrication of power and knowledge, following Topper, I take rhetoric to mean, first, the strategies and structures deployed to persuade others and second, the interpretive practice of making those very strategies and structures, along with their attendant assumptions and stakes, explicit and understandable.[61]

A Scaffolding of Humiliation

As is now evident, this emphasis not just on what humiliation says but also on how it works doesn't refer to effect in a positivist causal sense. Instead, it refers to the approach of this book, that is, the way the meaning and significance of humiliation are established by how they are used in language. This approach is grounded in Wittgenstein's work on language as a social practice, particularly his emphasis on meaning as use, in tandem with Charles Taylor's case for context-dependent epistemology in social science. As is well known, Wittgenstein sought to challenge philosophers who assume that the meaning of a statement exists prior to and independent of how it is employed, arguing that what a statement and the words that comprise it say are determined by how they work in concrete contexts.[62]

61. In some scholarly circles, this kind of work is referred to as Critical Discourse Theory (CDA), but I find greater clarity and precision in the rhetorical approach as defined here. It can be difficult to pin down precisely what CDA entails given how differently it's defined and practiced in various fields of scholarship that are themselves variously constituted depending upon geographic location (e.g. the United States versus the United Kingdom). Even among those political theorists who explicitly claim allegiance to CDA, there is wide variance in what they each mean and to whom they are indebted (for example, some draw on Althusser, others on Gramsci, and still others on Foucault, Bourdieu, etc.).

62. Wittgenstein most obviously intends "use" to refer to language in speech, whereas the examination of meaning in use in the chapters that follow includes speech *and* writing. This is, I think, consistent with Wittgenstein's intent, as he makes clear that "language game" is meant to emphasize the way that language is an activity (*Philosophical Investigations* I, §23). So while there are clear differences between speaking and writing, both are ultimately different kinds of resources for indicating the meaning of a statement or a word.

Taylor, for his part, argues that the effort to capture and understand human conduct must at once begin with the participants' self-understandings and recognize that such subjective understandings are not the "property of one or some individuals, but rather intersubjective meanings, which are constitutive of the social matrix in which individuals find themselves and act."[63] In other words, intelligibility depends on participants' views but isn't reducible to them. Taylor turns to the communicative capacities of the body to illustrate, pointing to the way one's public comportment—or "style of movement"—may convey a dignity or power that remains unrecognized, unknowledged, or unarticulated.[64] As Topper puts it, while accounts that "abstract from the meaning structures that house that activity obscure the very reality to be disclosed," intelligibility, descriptive accuracy, and moral reflection alike require attention to how intersubjective meanings constitute the horizon of "intelligible possibilities" for such self-understandings.[65]

An approach to humiliation informed by Wittgenstein and Taylor may be clarified in contrast to the way empiricism, causality, and generalizability is understood in positivist social science. To begin with, this shift from effect to significance is not a turn from the domain of the empirical to the purely abstract or imaginative. Quite the contrary. Analysis of what such invocations do and say is necessary precisely because of the abundance of empirical evidence attesting to the rhetorical prevalence and little understood political purchase of humiliation across both language and history. And as Taylor's argument makes clear, the deep dive into how humiliation is articulated, produced, and contested at specific moments does not represent a retreat into particularism. Instead, it demonstrates how an inductive approach rooted in language can remedy the conceptual murkiness of humiliation.

Much as this approach is greatly clarified in contrast to positivist assumptions, the account of humiliation it makes possible is best clarified through a quite different contrast, namely, with the account of humiliation as a violation of dignity or respect derived from the leading strand of moral philosophy.[66] The default

63. See, for example, Taylor, "Interpretation and the Sciences of Man," in *Philosophy and the Human Sciences*, vol. 2.

64. Taylor, *Sources of the Self*, 15.

65. Topper, *Disorder of Political Inquiry*, 72.

66. Dignity and respect are not interchangeable, but they tend to be used as philosophical and subjective-psychological ways of saying something very similar about humiliation. Still, there are disagreements about the relative merits of grounding humiliation in dignity versus self-respect. Statman argues, for example, that it's the conception of self-respect, not dignity, that is capable of explaining the "moral wrongness of humiliation" ("Humiliation, Dignity and

formulation when humiliation is given any substance at all, this account grounds such dignity or respect in the inherent and equal worth of every human being. Such worth is, in turn, said to be at once secured and expressed by the moral autonomy of a (generic) individual.

This formulation abbreviates a far more complex and contested philosophical account usually attributed to Immanuel Kant that has been taken up, refined, and elaborated in a voluminous secondary literature.[67] I leave to others the matter of whether it is or isn't Kantian and in what ways.[68] For my purposes, its import lies not in its lineage but the extent to which it has become akin to common sense. It is almost habitually asserted rather than argued or elaborated in scholarship across a remarkably wide range of fields and professions with slightly different emphases, from health care to public policy, philosophy to political science, journalism to education, human rights to law.[69]

Avishai Margalit's *The Decent Society* is one of the more sustained efforts to bring this definition of humiliation to bear upon collective life, inspired by John Rawls's idea of a just society.[70] Margalit focuses less on relationships among

---

Self-Respect," 535). *Humiliation, Degradation, Dehumanization*, edited by Kaufmann et al., contains a range of arguments and approaches in favor of the moral relevance of human dignity both in general and in relation to humiliation in particular.

67. This literature is far too extensive to catalogue.

68. While primarily associated with Kant, this formulation is historically and philosophically indebted to thinkers such as Augustine (d. 430) and Hegel (d. 1831). For an analysis of humiliation in Kant, see Saurette, *Kantian Imperative* and "Kant's Culture of Humiliation." For a discussion of Kantian humiliation, dignity and respect, see Kuch, "Rituality of Humiliation."

69. For just a few among innumerable examples, see Webster, "Degradation"; Peičius et al., "Dignity Violations and Barriers to Dignity Assurance"; Henry, "Jurisprudence of Dignity"; Lindner, "Concept of Humiliation"; Luban, "Human Dignity, Humiliation, and Torture"; Statman, "Humiliation, Dignity and Self-Respect"; Roy, *Failure of Political Islam*; and Dworkin, *Is Democracy Possible Here?*

70. Rawls himself says very little about humiliation, although assembling the few references he does make in *A Theory of Justice* is revealing. In his discussion of the original position, Rawls characterizes envy and humiliation—repeatedly coupled with shame, although not defined—as feelings and complications that inevitably "afflict men," but which must be supposed not to exist when formulating the first part of his principles of justice (124). Then there are the "outbreaks of envy" that can be managed or prevented by the "well-ordered society." This includes the feeling of humiliation that erupts when those of "subordinate ranking in public life" are "forcibly reminded" of their condition (477, 469, 471). He also refers to humiliation when distinguishing among the evil, unjust, and bad man his full theory of justice makes possible. The evil man seeks to rule in order to "manifest his superiority" by violating the

individuals than on "the setup of the society as a whole," developing an account of humiliation as part of a normative standard of decency by which to judge institutional practices. In a decent society, Margalit contends, institutions do not humiliate people. An institution qualifies as humiliating when it engages in "any sort of behavior or condition that constitutes a sound reason for a person to consider his or her self-respect injured," whether it takes the form of domination, dehumanization, or exclusion from the group to which one has belonged.[71] As self-respect and dignity are interrelated, humiliation entails "injury to human dignity." In fact, Margalit writes, "if there is no concept of human dignity, then there is no concept of humiliation either."[72]

The Decent Society is a profoundly decent book and there's more to it than a definition of humiliation.[73] Yet this formulation reprises rather than resolves the notable vacuity of most conceptual and explanatory work on humiliation by bringing the central problems with this common formulation into sharp relief. Dignity is notoriously contested; not even philosophers agree on either its content or worth.[74] But whether phrased in terms of injury or violation, dignity or respect, in this account, humiliation is entirely derivative, predicated on what it is said to violate.

---

principle of equality and offending the self-respect of others, Rawls writes. "[H]e delights in the impotence and humiliation of those subject to him and he relishes being recognized by them as the willful author of their degradation" (385–86).

71. The claim that humiliation is dehumanization that targets and expels is repeated elsewhere and in work located in very different theoretical traditions. The most notable example is Guenther's "Resisting Agamben." This convergence may have something to do with the shared emphasis on the Nazi persecution and extermination of the Jews. This is the paradigmatic example for Guenther, just as it is for those aspects of Agamben's thought she addresses. It also figures centrally in Margalit's work, implicitly in *The Decent Society* but more explicitly in his other work. This also suggests why Guenther's account of humiliation (61) is a far more apt characterization of scapegoating, which humiliation may serve but is not identical to it.

72. Margalit, *Decent Society*, 9, 262, 52, 149.

73. For a thoroughgoing analysis of Margalit's claims about what constitutes a decent society, see Honneth, "Society without Humiliation?," 306–24.

74. Among the best-known skeptics of human dignity are Pinker ("Stupidity of Dignity") and Macklin ("Dignity Is a Useless Concept," 1419–20). Many chapters in *Humiliation, Degradation, Dehumanization* emphasize the moral relevance of human dignity, yet the introductory chapter by the editors points out that the range of "dignity violations" explored in their volume demonstrate how little accord there is about the proper approach to defining human dignity (i.e., "negative" or "positive"), let alone its precise content, even among a fairly select group of "Western" philosophers.

Then there's the knotty problem that this definition presents as established fact a highly debatable conclusion, "proof" of which is already guaranteed by its starting premises. The logical result is a tautology whereby humiliation entails a violation of human dignity and respect for dignity entails not humiliating people. In his review of *The Decent Society*, Steven Lukes zeroes in on precisely this logic to identify the critical questions this account of humiliation begs: what counts as a sound reason; whether or not there is a single definition of self-respect that applies to all cultures; what constitutes a reasonable standard of injury; which individuals, communities, and audiences are relevant to determining such reasons, standards, and definitions; and whether the categories of "dignity" and "self-respect" are even appropriate to capture the content and significance of humiliation across and within cultures.[75]

For my purposes, what's critical is the default philosophical formulation of humiliation rather than the lapses of any one book or philosopher. Admirable in intent and humane in principle, this formulation says a great deal about the importance many moral philosophers attach to "dignity" and "respect," but it provides little traction on what humiliation says and does in the world. More significantly, this formulation reflects and reinforces a depoliticization that impedes such understanding. As scholars such as Chantal Mouffe, Mahmood Mamdani, Slavoj Žižek, and Wendy Brown argue, depoliticization abstracts and reroutes, either by channeling political categories into moral terms that personalize and individualize, or by culturalizing and essentializing historically contingent phenomena conditioned by power:

> Depoliticization involves removing a political phenomenon from comprehension of its *historical* emergence and from a recognition of the *powers* that produce and contour it. No matter its particular form and mechanics, depoliticization always eschews power and history in the representation of its subject. When these two constitutive sources of social relations and political conflict are elided, an ontological naturalness or essentialism almost inevitably takes up residence in our understandings and explanations.[76]

In the previous section, I argued that the conceptual opacity of humiliation is tied to a theoretical blockage hidden by the way humiliation has been consistently pegged to cultural pathologies supposedly distinctive to Arabs and Muslims.

75. Lukes, "Humiliation and the Politics of Identity."

76. Brown, *Regulating Aversion*, 15, emphasis in the original. See also Mouffe, *On the Political*, 5, Žižek, *Violence*; and Mamdani, *Good Muslim, Bad Muslim*.

Humiliation becomes a matter of essential cultural features that are unchangeable, abstracted from the conditions of history and power that produce and pattern its rhetorical expressions. The analysis here points to an additional but equally invisible blockage: a default philosophical account that shunts humiliation into matters of individual dignity defined in terms of an axiomatic moral principle. Inasmuch as these blockages effect and hide the depoliticization of humiliation, pinpointing them is essential to grasping what it means and how it works.

In the spirit of Wittgenstein's warning to resist the philosopher's "craving for generality," this inquiry takes seriously the imperative to presume less and inquire more.[77] Heeding this imperative entails reversing the order of argument and inquiry. Instead of an account that *begins* by positing a normative principle in order to adjudicate between what does and doesn't qualify as humiliation, it proceeds the other way around, building a conception of humiliation up from the meanings it acquires in use. As theory is anchored in practice rather than opposed to it, such an approach to conceptualizing humiliation is also conducive to theorizing humiliation, in the sense of discerning patterns in what might otherwise appear to be unrelated historical events or political phenomena. Rather than residing in an invariant conceptual structure prior to use in language, humiliation here emerges from patterned variation in the way people express and enact it, recurrent features that may not be equally present in every expression of humiliation nor configured in exactly the same way in identical combinations.

In the chapters that follow, I turn to the metaphor of "scaffolding" to capture what it means to theorize humiliation along these lines. Architectural metaphors can imply a certain rigidity, but I use scaffolding in an allusive rather than technical sense to evoke the skeleton of a structure, and the interplay of fixity and flexibility, materiality and multiplicity it suggests. The skeleton of a building is comprised of elements that can be configured along different lines but not in infinite variations, possibilities that at some point run up against constraints such as environment, function, and gravity. These anchor a variety of architectural styles, compositions of spaces, designs of function and flow, and expressive details of material and décor. This constrained flexibility is, in turn, conducive to thinking spatially about humiliation and to conceptualizing how different understandings capture one or many dimensions. Its visual immediacy lends a particular clarity to the relationship among its elements sometimes difficult to grasp or convey in more abstract language. It also clarifies by translating theory

77. Wittgenstein, *Nachlass*, TS 309, §27.

itself into visual terms. Theory anchored in human expression—expression that is situated in history and contoured by power—is akin to building on foundations firmly planted on the ground.

Finally, a particular scaffolding may be tethered to a single structure in one place, but scaffoldings underpin structures everywhere. In a similar vein, while this theory is anchored in patterns evident in Arabic expressions of humiliation, this is not an Arabic theory of humiliation let alone a theory of "Arab humiliation." The striking resemblances in the pair of passages that opened this chapter are discernable in a variety of combinations with different emphases across an array of languages. This suggests that while humiliation is constituted *in* language and distinctively inflected by disparate histories and experiences of power, these recurrent features also constitute a vocabulary intelligible *across* languages. If this is the case, aspects of humiliation can, like an affective Esperanto, "speak" viscerally and emphatically across context, requiring fluency in no particular language to grasp. While speculative, this point derives from examples too numerous to ignore; I return to it in the final chapter.

Given this approach, it's crucial to be explicit about what this book does not claim or aim to do. This inquiry does not provide a causal explanation about why humiliation rhetoric is currently ubiquitous, nor does the argument rest on the claim that humiliation is demonstrably *more* pervasive than in any previous era. The import of this study does not depend upon large-scale data measuring reception and uptake. As resonances usually circulate below the surface of observable behavior, a precise accounting of the extent to which such invocations resonate, how, and among which constituencies is, in any case, elusive at best.[78] The fact that such meanings and mechanisms elude quantification, Saurette observes, doesn't make humiliation any less politically significant or influential.[79] This only makes it more urgent, as Topper rightly argues, to detect and decode the communicative features and often unrecognized, hidden, or unspoken stakes such rhetoric reflects and constructs, and then trace the connection between words and deeds it renders legible.[80]

78. Resonance here signals both the literal meaning of the word as "evoking a response" and an approach indebted to Connolly's account of it as "energized complexities of mutual imbrication and interinvolvement, in which heretofore unconnected or loosely associated elements *fold, bend, blend, emulsify and dissolve into each other,* forging a qualitative assemblage resistant to classical models of explanation." Connolly, "Evangelical-Capitalist Resonance Machine," 870 and 875, emphasis in the original. See also Connolly, "Method, Problem, Faith," 342–44.

79. Saurette, "You Dissin Me?," 503.

80. From Topper, "Introduction."

The result of such work will not satisfy that deep craving for the universal and objective normative principles that enable us to judge what does and doesn't count as a legitimate claim to humiliation. Given that it's the "cognitive content of the belief underlying the emotion, and not its truth, falsity, or exaggeration that makes the emotion 'humiliation,'" it's unclear how one would go about proving or disproving whether someone is "really" humiliated.[81] Perhaps more to the point, it's unclear what would be achieved by doing so. As philosopher Bernard Williams, author of a pioneering analysis of shame, once put it, "[w]hat people's ethical emotions are depends significantly on what they take them to be," and what they take them to be emerges in the realm of thought and experience forged with others.[82]

The Arc of the Argument: An Inquiry in Four Parts

The arguments of this book proceed along four tracks that, in the absence of more inspired terminology, can be characterized as empirical, theoretical, methodological, and political. The previous section specified the approach of this inquiry and the definition of theory central to its import. The empirical entails a deep dive into how humiliation is expressed, constituted, and contested in exemplary Arabic texts illustrating different rhetorical modes and genres articulated at specific moments and sites. Such analysis detects and decrypts meanings both unspoken and explicit, as well as experiences and solidarities such invocations reflect and construct. In the process, they show how humiliation rhetoric simultaneously encodes a gendered political project and constitutes the practices to bring it about. As will become evident, humiliation isn't just an idea, argument, or evocation of powerlessness but is itself a powerful political rhetoric that summons, translates, defines, transposes, and even transforms relations of power.

These four tracks are simultaneous rather than sequential and unfold over the course of four chapters. In chapter 2, "A Theodicy for Powerlessness: Islamist Discourses and Retaliatory Humiliation," I track humiliation across a selection of some of the best-known, most influential, or most conspicuous twentieth- and twenty-first-century Islamist expressions of humiliation, all gathered under the rubric of verbal rhetoric. These texts and sources vary by genre, time period, and context, and are far from homogenous in politics, perspective, and sensibility.

81. Silver et al., "Humiliation," 278.

82. Williams, *Shame and Necessity*, 76–77, 84, 91,102.

But in all of them, humiliation is defined in terms of what it does rather than a formal proposition in need of systematic argument or evidence. What emerges is a shared understanding of humiliation as the imposition of impotence by those with undeserved power, a condition that urgently demands immediate redress. This expository definition can be rephrased experientially: humiliation lives in the rupture between one's own sense of significance and place in the social order, and acute awareness of who one has been made to be by those with more and undeserved power. It is, in a sense, to be made unrecognizable to oneself. Like two sides of a single coin, these formulations capture the same understanding of humiliation from different angles: the first centers the act of humiliating another, while the second captures the experience of humiliation produced by the act. In other words, the act and experience of humiliation here refer not to two different definitions but to this interrelationship between dual dimensions of one understanding.

Throughout these chapters, the gendered connotation of the word "impotence" is intentional and signals an essential feature of this scaffolding of humiliation. Gender norms anchored in a sexual division of labor have been reworked, challenged, and reproduced in complex and variable ways. But as these archives attest, conventional gender roles still enjoy widespread recognition, and the expectations associated with them exercise significant influence across an array of societies. Inasmuch as such norms implicitly bind gender to order and a gendered order to power, powerlessness is routinely construed as emasculation and/or feminization, its antidote translated into manliness or virility. This is precisely why humiliation rhetoric doesn't evoke a simple relation of power to powerlessness or posit a generic distinction between who deserves one or the other. As this gendering of power constitutes humiliation, humiliation rhetoric encodes powerlessness, its premises and stakes, in the viscerally charged terms of masculinity and its many metaphors. This is also why, in the opening passages and in the pages that follow, humiliation rhetoric so often becomes a goad, a taunt, an incitement or indictment.

In the Islamist texts in chapter 2, for example, impotence is taken to reflect and reinforce a deeply malformed set of social relations in which disbelievers dominate Muslims, women are lured into a betrayal of their domestic vocation, and the capacity of men to be breadwinners, defenders, and protectors is sabotaged. These features posit a gendered, heteronormative ontology as an imperative of nature and Islam to shore up a particular family structure. They also supply the grammar of a stylized script in which vulnerable or violated female bodies "speak" to, first, impeach Muslim manhood; second, conjure a cadre of male *mujāhidīn* dedicated to vindicating it; and third, goad such men into the kind of restorative acts against enormous odds Machiavelli called *virtù*—courageous deeds specifically designed to recuperate and enact masculine prowess.[83] So understood, this account of humiliation encodes an urgent demand for retaliatory humiliation, depicted as an imposition of impotence upon the humiliator. It simultaneously serves as the rhetorical mechanism to bring it about.

Islamists conjure an Islamic imprimatur for this account of humiliation in a way that addresses a central dilemma: the power God has conferred on the enemies of Islam to humiliate Muslims. Sayyid Qutb's Qur'ānic interpretation is the critical text here. It renders legible a crucial pivot from humiliation as a divine dispensation to an expression of what human beings do to one another, from a prerogative of God to an exigency of human domination. It shows how the current humiliation of Muslims at the hands of powerful unbelievers is transformed from a source of despair or a justification for imitation into a spur to restorative action. And it shows how the Qur'ān is deployed to recast the humiliation of Muslims' humiliators not only as an expression of God's will on earth, but as a premier act of devotion that realigns a world severely out of joint. The radical Islamist invocations of humiliation I also analyze in this chapter take precisely this imperative as a given.

Chapter 3, "Spectacles of Sovereignty," focuses specifically on visual rhetorics of humiliation. It advances a reading of two notorious productions ISIS put in the service of building its Islamic state—the videos staging the beheadings of two American journalists, James Foley and Steven Sotloff—along with lesser-known productions such as "Kasr al-ḥudūd" (Breaking the Borders) and "Although the Disbelievers May Dislike It/Wa-Law Kariha al-Kāfirūn." Analysis of these widely circulated, watched, and reposted videos renders legible a visual rhetoric of humiliation largely eclipsed by the security logic about "Islamic terrorism" into which these videos snugly fit.

Drawing on recent scholarship on visuality, performative violence, digital media, and affect, I analyze an overlooked disunity in what visual and verbal rhetorics say and do in these videos. While the words are about threat and retaliation, the visual and embodied rhetorics enact retaliatory humiliation. The meaning,

83. Machiavelli, *The Prince*. This understanding of *virtù* is grounded in scholarship emphasizing the gendered aspects of the term. See Pitkin, *Fortune Is a Woman*, 122–37; Brown, *Manhood and Politics*, 117; and Elshtain, *Women and War*, 56–59. Also helpful in this connection is the description of *virtù* as a "quality of action" revealing "the creative energy (or 'vitality') that one needs to respond to opportunities and dangers" (Morgado, "Threat of Danger: Decadence and Virtù," 237).

significance, and affective power of this enactment works not through explicit argument, but through the public inscription of impotence on American male bodies, symbolically converted into the American nation.[84] This enactment also constitutes the masked executioner, along with the sovereign power he represents and serves, as fearless, potent, and dominant, their march toward primacy inevitable. The videos then work in a variety of ways to effect a symbolic transposition, positioning the United States as mass terrorist, failed sovereign, and rogue state, and ISIS as legitimate, invincible, and righteous sovereign.

This chapter not only shows that the power implicated in humiliation is gendered male, but that humiliation genders and engenders sovereignty. Inasmuch as the claim to sovereignty can be understood as an assertion of self-determination, the declaration of an Islamic state in the videos is an enactment of agency that remedies impotence. At the same time, the videos transform American men's bodies into the territory on which sovereignty can be primarily and endlessly performed long after the formal destruction of ISIS's state in Syria-Iraq. In both instances, performances of sovereignty and the power they enact exceed and outlast the literal capture of territory constitutive of the conventional definition. And in both instances, the symbolic and literal violence of such an enactment is carried out by men and inscribed on male bodies. If women's bodies are thought to be the terrain over which moral and cultural battles are waged, this chapter suggests that male bodies are the terrain on which sovereignty is symbolically and literally performed.[85]

Once inserted into digital networks that have accelerated the speed of transmission and repetition, these videos work forward and outward in other ways that extend and intensify their affective power. Circulation over time attenuates the connection to precipitating events; as these fade into the background, the intensity and immediacy of witnessing violence as it unfolds take center stage, as if part of an ongoing present rather than a completed past. Given the particular content of these videos, moreover, digital repetition works to revivify the retaliatory humiliation they depict. This invites more than a sense of vicarious

84. This does not presume, as do some affect theorists, that affects are nonsignifying, nonconscious, embodied responses such that "cognition or thinking comes 'too late' for reasons, beliefs, intentions, and meanings to play the role in action and behavior usually accorded to them" (Leys, "Turn to Affect," 443). As Ahmed and others argue, affect and cognition are entangled, and the precise form of such entanglement cannot be mapped abstractly.

85. In Benhabib's phrasing, "[W]omen and their bodies are the symbolic-cultural site upon which human societies inscript their moral order." Benhabib, *The Claims of Culture*, 84.

participation; it actually eases the way for watchers to interpolate themselves into the enactment, either as humiliator or humiliated. Such an enmeshment of spectator and performance can entail taking on the humiliation and suffering of the victim—or alternatively, relishing a profoundly restorative experience.

While this analysis shows how short-cuts to grasping the past misapprehend the present, chapter 4, "'Our Dignity Is Humiliated': A Phenomenology of Humiliation in the Egyptian Revolution," shows how verdicts about the present constrain or enable future possibilities. This chapter provides a close reading of an assembled archive of expressions of humiliation from the 2011 Egyptian revolution. As these materials range from rhetorical invocations of humiliation to expressions that convey the texture of how it is lived during the critical years of 2010–14, they can be counted as among the many primary texts of the uprising. The aim here is to center the words and meanings of Egyptians by thematizing how humiliation is constituted by those who endure, witness, identify, and refuse it at a specific historical and political moment.

As humiliation is instantiated at multiple sites, the analysis distills these articulations into a number of themes, beginning with national humiliation, both in the international and domestic sense. The "rule of humiliation" is a logic animating the Egyptian regime from Hosni Mubarak to the current president, General Abdel Fattah el-Sisi. Domestically expressed in a brutal paternalism, it presupposes and enacts an ontology of ruler to ruled in which the president, conceived as an all-powerful father-figure, is required to discipline an Egyptian subject rendered as a perpetually dull and unruly child.

By contrast, international humiliation is anchored in a notion of Egyptian exceptionalism. It lives in the disjuncture between a glorious Egypt destined to lead all Arabs and the actual degradation of both nation and people by rulers who betray the august patrimony they were tasked with guarding. Humiliation is elaborated differently in these two arenas, but they are imbricated in a way that intensifies both; they constitute a single continuous chain of humiliation mapped by these materials, one that extends out and down.

Another section maps several different ways these articulations of humiliation are profoundly gendered, many of which are in tension even as others overlap or are mutually reinforcing. In an echo of the Islamist discourses of the previous chapters, for example, a number of texts here identify the "humiliation of men" as an engine of the uprising, or point to a kind of hypermasculine overcompensation in the tenor and scale of violent vengeance by the regime. Yet this co-creation of power as virility and powerlessness as emasculation is consistently disrupted by, for example, women who redeploy the assumption that masculine honor demands the protection of vulnerable females, invoking it to rhetorically goad men to join them in courageous action.

What one source refers to as "psychic violations" (*intihākāt nafsiyya*) captures both the normalization of cruelty in the realm of the quotidian as well as the routinization of extreme brutality by the regime. Common vulnerability constitutes an equality of insignificance that, in turn, becomes a thread connecting the always potentially humiliated individual to a collective "peoplehood" constituted as humiliated. The sexual modality of such psychic violations brings into particularly sharp focus the common experience not just of powerlessness but of being forcibly made into someone or something you no longer recognize.[86]

At the same time, they illustrate how the social construction of gender organizes both sexual violence and its objects: there are men who are "unmanned" and women who are made into "filthy whores" whose impurity represents not an unmaking of womanhood but the realization of an ever-present possibility entailed by it. The point isn't that such stereotypical norms of masculinity and femininity by definition describe how such brutality is experienced, but rather that these individuals are enmeshed in a set of social relations that genders sexual violence in the terms of humiliation.

In the final chapter, "Conclusion: Humiliation, Dignity, and Embodiment," I focus on the exhortations to restorative action encoded in humiliation rhetoric. These are brought into particularly sharp relief by the third rhetorical mode, what I've called an embodied idiom. A language not just of words but bodies, this idiom renders legible the visceral power and transformative character of such restoration; brings a theoretical clarity to the often-misunderstood interrelation of humiliation and dignity; and decodes the conceptual confusion entailed by the conflation of the Arabic "*karāma*" and the English "dignity."

86. This formulation in some ways dovetails with Rorty's brief if evocative characterization of humiliation as an extension—or a particular variant—of physical torture. Borrowing from Scarry's *Body in Pain*, Rorty depicts this as an "unmaking," such that a person can "no longer rationalize—no longer justify herself to herself." Rorty, *Contingency, Irony and Solidarity*, 178. Yet one who humiliates another may well be unaware of how it is experienced by the individual or group who feel themselves humiliated, or does not intend it as such. And just as physical pain need not humiliate by definition, these chapters demonstrate that direct humiliation involves far more than the mistreatment of bodies. It also operates symbolically and can be experienced vicariously. In contrast to Rorty, Shklar refers in passing to "persistent and deliberate" humiliation as a phenomenon at the heart of "moral cruelty," by which she means nonphysical pain. Shklar, *Ordinary Vices*, 37.

While "*karāma*" is usually rendered into English as "dignity" and defined in terms of an abstract principle of moral autonomy, I show how these materials constitute it as a performative practice of "restorative standing" that corresponds to Melian, rather than Kantian, dignity. Named for the islanders who defied the Athenian Empire in Thucydides's *History of the Peloponnesian War*, Melian dignity denotes neither a moral rectitude already achieved nor a normative principle of adjudication. It is kinetic, performative, and aspirational, more process than principle, as much practice as concept, and it begins in a refusal. The individual or collectivity that you recognize as yours is conjured by refusing the imposed impotence constitutive of humiliation. This refusal is itself an enactment of the power to shape the script of one's own life.

Such "restorative standing" dovetails with Ernst Bloch's evocation of the "upright gait" to refer to a dignity not of being but becoming, of materially, politically, and historically situated struggle.[87] This centers a politics produced by and performed through ongoing effort that eludes assessments of revolutionary failure so common to assessments of the 2011 Egyptian Uprising. It also draws attention to the way humiliation and *karāma*/dignity fashion one another in an inverse relation. Humiliation takes shape not in opposition to, but in terms of a posited integrity or stature, and it's the humiliation that conjures the integrity or stature that must then be restored. This suggests that moral philosophers are right to link humiliation to dignity, but for the wrong reasons. Humiliation isn't the opposite of dignity; they are mutually constitutive.

There's a significant if inconspicuous political implication that follows from these arguments. As the details of restorative action depend upon the particular account of humiliation that constitutes it, such rhetoric doesn't dictate a single kind of action that is inevitable or inescapable. Humiliation signals a powerlessness that must be urgently remedied, but the difference between retaliation and refusal is, politically speaking, a significant one. If the former promises a potentially endless cycle of humiliation and retaliatory humiliation, the latter already expresses a break from it, an opening essential to imagining alternative possibilities.

87. Bloch, *Natural Law and Human Dignity*, 155, 174, 12.

2

A Theodicy for Powerlessness

ISLAMIST DISCOURSE AND RETALIATORY HUMILIATION

> [D]o you not see that he (the Prophet, may God bless him and grant him peace) made clear that the cause of the weakness [*ḍuʿf*] of nations and the humiliation [*dhilla*] of peoples [is] the feebleness [*wahn*] of their spirits, the emptiness of their hearts of noble morals and the qualities of true manliness [*al-rujūla*], even though their numbers were great and their advantages and benefits were numerous?[1]

ISLAMISM WAS BORN in humiliation. Or at least that's the story told by Hasan al-Banna, founder of the Egyptian Muslim Brotherhood [*al-Ikhwān al-Muslimūn*]. According to Banna, the critical moment came in 1928 in Ismaʿiliyya, a city in the Suez Canal Zone. The Zone was one of many places where native Egyptians labored for the profit of foreign companies, in this case, the British-owned Suez Canal Company headquartered there. Despite the formal declaration of Egyptian independence in 1922, Britain continued to control the lucrative canal company, along with other significant aspects of Egypt's economy and politics, for another three decades. In his memoirs, Banna recounts being approached by several Egyptian laborers who had heard his sermons on Islam. The men beseeched him to deliver them from the life of humiliation [*ḥayāt al-dhilla*] and servitude to foreigners, he writes, begging for guidance on how to restore the

1. al-Banna, "Ilā ayy shayʾ nadʿū al-nās?" *Majmūʿat Rasāʾil Ḥasan al-Bannā* (Dār al-Qalam, n.d), 144.

karāma ("dignity," but see chapter 5) of Egypt, the Islamic community (*umma*), and Islam.[2]

The Egyptian Muslim Brotherhood is the organization that has spawned a number of branches across and beyond the region, and is usually considered the beginning of Islamism. Whether factual or fictional, this genesis story makes humiliation pivotal to the founding of the *Ikhwān*, and it carries an undeniable authority given that Banna is the one telling it. It's a fitting start to this chapter, not because it represents the true origins of contemporary Islamism but because the story draws attention to Islamists who have appealed to or conjured humiliation from the beginning. It also typifies the fashion in which such appeals have articulated its substance and significance. In just a few lines, the narrative establishes the meaning of humiliation not by explicit argument about what it is but by what it does, that is, how it works rhetorically *in* the story and *on* the men Banna depicts. Humiliation here is an experience and status bound up with powerlessness, yet not reducible to it; this isn't just an absence of power but an intolerable dispossession of agency, like the twist of a knife in a body already wounded to the quick. It's embodied by men laboring on their own land to enrich foreign companies whose plunder more deeply entrenches colonial power. In a metonymic slide, domination and deliverance figure as humiliation and its extirpation, and at stake is the *karāma* not just of Egyptians, but the country, the *umma*, and Islam itself.

The introductory chapter sketched the ubiquity of humiliation rhetoric in general and drew attention to the way humiliation is currently pegged to culturally distinctive pathologies and resentments, becoming just one more marker of Muslim or Arab Otherness. One consequence of this culturalization, I argued, is to preempt the need to identify and decode the rhetorical structures that show what Arabic expressions of humiliation say and do—the very sort of hermeneutic care often extended automatically to what seems familiar. In this instance, that need is particularly conspicuous, as the constitution of Muslims as the primary objects or agents of humiliation is very much a coproduction among radically different figures, including, most notably, Islamists. The very origin story of the *Ikhwān* places humiliation front and center, and it has thoroughly saturated a great deal of Islamist rhetoric ever since. Yet it remains the most overlooked and least understood element of this coproduction.

There are, of course, real differences among Islamist thinkers and activists past and present, as well as diversity in the politics they embrace, the strategies they

2. Banna, *Mudhakkirāt al-da'wā wa-l-dā'iya*, 74.

deploy, the contexts in which they operate, and the audiences they address.[3] But it's precisely the variation, complexity, and flux characterizing Islamism that makes this rhetorical pattern so striking. Given how conspicuous this pattern is, it's equally striking that there's been so little analysis of humiliation in Islamist rhetoric and writing, and correspondingly minimal effort to anatomize the ways in which it is constructed to propogate particular kinds of retaliatory action.

In an effort to address these intersecting absences, in this chapter, I draw on an array of primary sources, written and spoken, to analyze the content and significance of humiliation in Islamist discourse. These range from Sayyid Qutb's multivolume Qur'ānic commentary [*tafsīr*] *Fī Ẓilāl al-Qur'ān* [In the shade of the Qur'ān], to Bin Laden's polemical "Declaration of Jihad against the Americans Occupying the Land of the Two Holy Sites," to various missives, articles, letters, and speeches issued online or in print by radical Islamists. Such sources vary significantly by genre, style, tenor, and focus. Unlike the over four thousand-page exercise in interpretive endurance that is Qutb's *tafsīr*, for example, radical Islamist missives are often brief, fragmentary, and ad hoc.

Yet as these materials all deploy the rhetoric of humiliation, I read them together as a single archive. This requires attending to symbols, images, anecdotes, and invective, scrutinizing implicit connections as well as explicit juxtapositions, analyzing occasionally blurry logics as well as clearly articulated critiques. As in Banna's story, moreover, these sources articulate what humiliation means in terms of how it works rather than advancing it as a formal proposition in need of systematic argument or evidence. In the introduction, I contended that "how it works" doesn't refer to reception or uptake, although it's connected to both. It refers instead to the way the meaning of humiliation emerges out of multiple rhetorical operations that are analytically distinguishable but articulate together in ways that are usually impossible to disentangle. What humiliation says and does here is a matter of who invokes it and in which contexts; the authority it claims, the addressees it hails, and the solidarities it conjures; the form of repair it demands and the stakes it encodes; the victory it defines and guarantees; and the rewards and pleasures of restorative action it promises.

The texts central to each of the following sections showcase different combinations of these rhetorical operations. The first section foregrounds the interpretive work required to claim Islamic sanction for retaliatory humiliation. The second

3. For a discussion of this diversity and a definition of Islamism in terms of broad tendencies and "family resemblances," see Euben and Zaman, *Princeton Readings in Islamist Thought*, esp. chapter 1.

centers the rhetorical structures and strategies meant to bring into existence a solidarity among "Sunni Muslim men" tasked with performing such restorative action against great odds.[4] The third section shifts away from specific texts by well-known Islamist men to the scattered sites of the largely ad hoc or fragmentary expressions of the often-nameless men—and occasionally women—who heed this call to action. These strategies and structures merge in use, but this sequencing of sections focused on exemplary texts makes it easier to trace the common account of humiliation that emerges out of different rhetorical operations.

To this end, I thematize key moments, interpretive turns, and rhetorical strategies in these texts to render legible a pattern amid variation, and draw attention to some of its silences, disavowals, and lacunae along the way. In the interest of accessibility, I aim to provide the specifics necessary to do these texts justice without swamping the discussion in so much detail that only a narrow range of scholars can or want to follow the through-line of the argument. For the same reason, I focus not on overlooked or "obscure" Islamist figures but draw on an assemblage of better-known names, groups, and texts to spotlight what has largely been hidden in plain view. Foregrounding what has been there all along may, of course, make the familiar seem much less so.

Drawing on these sources, I make four arguments in this chapter. First, these texts center humiliation both as a problem of the contemporary age and illustrative of a timeless challenge to the preeminence of Islam dating back to the first community that coalesced around the Prophet Muhammad. Second, they articulate humiliation in terms now familiar from the previous chapter, as the imposition of impotence on Muslims by those with greater and undeserved power. The gendered inflection of impotence is essential to the reckoning Banna spells out in the epigraph above: the humiliation of peoples and nations indexes the depleted manliness, vigor, and virtue entailed by foreign domination. Such impotence reflects and reinforces a deeply malformed set of social relations in which disbelievers have the power to subjugate Muslims, women are lured into a betrayal of their domestic vocation, and the capacity of men to be breadwinners, defenders, and protectors is sabotaged. Herein lies my third argument: it's precisely this wedding of gender to order and a gendered order to power that

4. While solidarity is invoked in a wide variety of contexts and literatures, it is often ill-defined. The descriptive often slides into the normative, and social and political solidarities are routinely conflated. As will become clear, the solidarity I have in mind is not predicated upon an already existing social group or a set of moral commitments that speak to clearly defined members; it's performed rather than recovered, conjured by way of the practices that claim it. See Scholz, *Political Solidarity*.

translates domination into an urgent demand for restoration and constitutes restoration as retaliatory humiliation. Imposing impotence on those who have humiliated Islam is a literal and symbolic reversal of power relations that restores order and sense to a world badly out of joint.

Fourth and relatedly, humiliation discourse encodes a gendered, heteronormative ontology as an imperative of nature and Islam. So understood, the properly ordered family structure becomes both anchor and emblem of collective power. Techniques such as allusion, juxtaposition, symbolism, metonymy, and ventriloquism constitute women as wives and mothers, responsible for the integrity of the Muslim family. As the family is not only the site of literal reproduction but the primary school of moral education upon which the *umma* is built, the sexual vulnerability, availability, or disobedience of females are figured as the conduit of foreign corruption. Men are correspondingly rendered providers and guardians of women and children, culpable for any material and martial vulnerability that exposes the Muslim community to incursions and interlopers of all kinds.

A similar gender scheme has flourished in an array of times, places, and configurations, from the idealized family evinced by strains of Christian fundamentalism and Orthodox Judaism to the "cult of true womanhood" in nineteenth-century America to the paradoxical position of women in the social imagination of the ancient Athenian polis.[5] So, too, has "the status of women" very often figured as the crux of civilizational, national, or cultural destiny. In *Taḥrīr al-mar'a* (The liberation of women), for example, Qāsim Amīn famously argued that

> the status of women is inseparably tied to the status of a nation. When the status of a nation is low, reflecting an uncivilized condition for that nation, the status of women is also low, and when the status of a nation is elevated, reflecting the progress and civilization of that nation, the status of women in that country is also elevated.[6]

What Amīn depicts as the key to collective progress in the nineteenth-century, Qutb identifies in as the linchpin of communal degeneracy in the twentieth. In his best-known book, *Signposts along the Road* [*Ma'ālim fī al-ṭarīq*], much of

5. For example, see Welter, "Cult of True Womanhood, 1820–1860"; Bloch, "American Feminine Ideals in Transition: The Rise of the Moral Mother, 1785–1815"; Just, *Women in Athenian Law and Life*, esp. 152, 192; Cohen, *Law, Sexuality and Society*; Tauber, *To Become One*, 171, 173; Suchard, *Make Your Marriage Work*, 57; Ghatan, *Invaluable Pearl*, 67, 70, 73–74 (I am grateful to Batya Swift Yasgur for the latter three sources).

6. Amīn, *Taḥrīr al-mar'a* [*Liberation of Women*], translated and edited by Samiha Sidhom Peterson, 6.

which is taken from the *tafsīr*, Qutb insists that the sexual division of labor is critical to the family and the family, in turn, determines whether and to what degree a society is civilized or backward, moral or corrupt.[7] Qutb is far from alone.[8] As Humeira Iqtidar and Muhammad Qasim Zaman point out, gender is frequently the notable exception to the egalitarianism Islamists' espouse in matters of race and nation.[9] Women may have "spiritual equality" to men in the eyes of God, but the sexual division of labor remains the "fundamental condition for a well-ordered society."[10] This familiar gender scheme supplies the grammar of a stylized script that simultaneously tasks men with the work of retaliatory humiliation and renders it the sine qua non of manhood itself. Females function primarily to hail Muslim men into such work, but rarely in words. They are the vulnerable or violated female bodies that "speak" to both impeach Muslim manhood and conjure a cadre of male *mujāhidīn* dedicated to vindicating it. Such vindication requires the kind of courageous and bold action against great odds that Niccolò Machiavelli famously referred to as *virtù*, derived from the Latin *vir*, which means "manliness," the basis of the English word "virility."

Violence against actual women and girls is obscured by the spectral bodies and ventriloquized voices that goad men to scorn the formidable military and political powers arrayed against them, memorialize the glorious deaths of husbands, brothers, and sons, and entice them with the promise of unchecked sexual

7. Qutb, *Ma'ālim fī al-ṭarīq*, 112.

8. Abdessalam Yassine, founder of Morocco's Jamā'at al-'Adl wa'l-Iḥsān (Justice and spirituality association), for example, depicts females as either "blonde tourist whores" imported along with AIDS, or virtuous Muslim women characterized by "delicate sensitivities and mother love." In Yassine's rendering, a woman corrupted by the false promise of emancipation represents the breach through which foreign depravity enters the *umma* and corrodes it from within. Yassine, *Winning the Modern World for Islam*, 76. See also 'Azzam, *'Ushshāq al-Ḥūr*, 18, 49.

9. There is a broader historical and political context for this phenomenon. While impossible to do it justice here, scholars such as Wael Hallaq and Iza Hussin have argued that the administration of colonial states narrowed the jurisdiction of Islamic law to family law in a way that decimated an Islamic ecosystem of law and education and made family arrangements the focal point. Hussin, *Politics of Islamic Law*; and Wallaq, *Sharī'a: Theory, Practice, Transformations*.

10. Iqtidar, "Conservative Anti-Colonialism," 296, 301; Zaman, "Divine Sovereignty—Some Reflections," 379. In her superb analysis, Iqtidar argues that Mawdudi's particular emphasis on a "rigid biological framework" to justify such gender inequality was relatively new in Islamic thought (307–8). See also Zaman's excellent "Sovereignty of God in Modern Islamic Thought." Iqtidar and Zaman make this argument in relation to Sayyid Abu'l-A'la Maududi's thought, but many of the texts in the discussion that follows exhibit similar tendencies.

pleasure in paradise. Unlike the thousands of Muslims whose pointless deaths are noted only, if at all, in statistics about state violence, civil war, or drone strikes, these martyrs of God have names that are commemorated. This is a promise of immortality both in the paradise they have earned and in the life of the *umma* they have so selflessly served.[11]

Islamists conjure an Islamic imprimatur for this account of humiliation to resolve a pressing problem of theodicy: the power God has conferred on the enemies of Islam to humiliate Muslims.[12] In theodicies across a remarkable array of orientations to the sacred both past and present, those who take divine omnipotence as axiomatic have depicted the persistence of evil, injustice, and suffering in the world as a trial or test from God.[13] The articulation of humiliation here similarly begins with such a conventional move but culminates in a radical one: it remakes Qur'ānic humiliation from a divine dispensation into an exhortation for believers to take on themselves the work of humiliating those who have humiliated Islam. Cast in these terms, powerlessness is transformed from a signal of impotence or source of despair into a spur to action. Retaliatory humiliation becomes a preeminent proof of dedication to the divinely-ordained social order. And, paradoxically, humility in relation to God entails arrogating the divine power to humiliate.

In her genealogy of humility, Julie Cooper argues that the conflation of the secular and sovereign subject in modern Euro-American political theory has framed the religious affirmation of divine sovereignty not just as a constraint on

11. The Internet has made the commemoration of death easier and broader in scope; see, e.g., Karolak, "Online Aesthetics of Martyrdom."

12. Theodicy, of course, means justifying god, from the Greek *theos*—god—and *dikē*—justice. While Gottfried Wilhelm Leibniz is usually credited with coining the term in the early eighteenth century, it arguably captures a phenomenon that long predates him. This is so despite the contention of some scholars that the term signals a distinctively modern way of apprehending evil. For a well-made case in favor of such wide applicability, see Sarot, "Theodicy and Modernity."

13. "Orientations to the sacred," while awkward, avoids the baggage baked into the term *religion*. Scholars such as Talal Asad, Saba Mahmood, Charles Taylor, and William Connolly among others have detailed how what is taken as "religion" is based on an opposition to secularism, both of which emerged from the developments that accompanied European "modernity." They have sought something like a paradigm shift in which secularism, constituted by liberal logic as a basic precondition of modern civilized coexistence, is foregrounded as an historically contingent set of norms, arrangements and subjectivities produced and regulated by the modern state. Asad, *Genealogies of Religion*; Mahmood, *Religious Difference in a Secular Age*; Taylor, *Secular Age*; Connolly, *Why I Am Not a Secularist*. See also the work of Hussein Ali Agrama.

human agency but as a challenge to the "value and legitimacy of politics as such."[14] In this sense, the rule of God entails what Michael Walzer refers to as antipolitics that calls both the necessity and possibility of human agency into question.[15] From the vantage of this theodicy of humiliation, such a framing is not only wrong but an obstacle to recognizing the real problem and its source. The fetters on action lie not in divine sovereignty but human domination. To believe otherwise is to embrace a distortion that only exacerbates the very impotence God inspires and authorizes believers to overcome.[16]

The account of humiliation here is neither a philosophical argument nor a symptom of a culturally distinctive pathology. It defines a political project and is itself an essential mechanism to bring it about. This is an account of collective powerlessness that encodes the stakes of repair, specifies the form of reparative action, designates those who must perform it, and claims God as guarantor of victory. As will become evident in this chapter and the next, these Islamist texts constitute restoration in different ways and in terms reflective of the specific contexts in which they were forged. Qutb's understanding of restoration, for example, requires the abolition of human sovereignty along with recognition that God is the sole source of guidance and legislation for human behavior. For ISIS, restoration means building a caliphate in the historic heartlands of Islam. For Bin Laden, the route to restoration is neither sovereignty nor state-building but deterritorialized *jihad*.[17] In the Egyptian expressions of humiliation I turn to in later chapters, the restorative project takes a still different form.

These restorative projects are variously calibrated, then, but they are all encoded in a common conception of humiliation that does the double work of provocation and reassurance. As in Banna's origin story, this rhetoric sutures together multiple domains of life, scales of experience, and instances of felt powerlessness across time and space to dissolve the distinction between Muslims whose suffering is at stake and a collective "humiliation of Islam" at stake in Muslim suffering. This rhetoric binds the "I" to the "We," but the idiom of this binding constitutes humiliation and its redress as a performance of masculinity coextensive with the restoration of the *umma* and the preeminence of Islam.

14. Cooper, *Secular Powers*, 7, 4–11.

15. Cooper, *Secular Powers*, 14; Walzer, *In God's Shadow*, xii–xiii.

16. Interestingly, this bears a certain resemblance to the strand of modern political thought Cooper recovers in her genealogy, one that "views acknowledgement of human finitude as a source for collective human empowerment." Cooper, *Secular Powers*, 4.

17. See also Andrea Mura's discussion of his "transterritorial trajectory." *Symbolic Scenarios of Islamism*, 167.

And it's an exhortation designed to bring about the radical inversion of power it portrays as both imperative and guaranteed.

This does not purport to be an exhaustive analysis of every Islamist invocation of humiliation. Nor does reading these materials together as a single archive presume unanimity or even agreement of perspective among Islamists who contribute to it.[18] Moreover, the meaning of any single source or text is not exhausted by this focus or the reading it yields. In other words, I don't claim to advance *the* single meaning of an audiotape or pamphlet or declare humiliation the major or only concern of every single Islamist. On the contrary, treating the humiliation that emerges here as sui generis through and through obscures what I have referred to as the scaffolding that patterns a wide array of distinct articulations.

Given the recurrence of "Islam" and "Islamism" throughout this discussion, two final points about terminology are in order. Tacking back and forth between Islamist arguments and the sacred texts they invoke or refigure risks corroborating—or being read as corroborating—the popular maneuver whereby what Islamists do becomes an expression of what Islam says, and what Islam says is constituted by what Islamists do. Such a maneuver is premised on the dubious possibility of determining authoritatively what Islam really is and what Islam really says. Any such claim is necessarily contingent, contested, and begs as many questions as it answers, but these claims proliferate nevertheless. Scholarly and popular analyses of such claims, including the matter of who speaks for Islam, have also multiplied, and it's not my purpose to rehearse them here. Suffice it to say that, just as the Torah and Bible lend themselves to at times radically divergent interpretations of what it means to be Jewish or Christian, the Qur'ān and *ḥadīth* are complex and susceptible to many different, and at times contradictory, enactments. So understood, Islam captures what is imagined as continuous and unitary in dialectical relationship to those concrete articulations and practices by which it is transformed and adapted in different contexts for plural purposes.[19]

This is the understanding of Islam that informs my approach to Islamist discourse in the current and following chapter. These Islamists routinely claim to be

18. There are, for example, Islamists who invoke the "humiliation of Islam" yet eschew the exhortations to retaliatory humiliation evinced here. Just one case in point is the Egyptian Muslim Brotherhood's response to what they characterized as the "humiliation and abuse" of the "Innocence of Muslims" video. See Ikhwan Web, "Muslim Brotherhood Statement on Anti-Islam Film."

19. This formulation is indebted to Talal Asad's well-known account of Islam as a "discursive tradition." Asad, "Idea of an Anthropology of Islam," 14.

in possession of the authentic Islam cleansed of the corruption wrought by the ignorant, the saboteurs, and the tyrants, but their very formulation of the "humiliation of Islam" exemplifies what scholars have shown is a distinctively modern reification of Islam.[20] So understood, this remaking of Qur'ānic humiliation indicates neither the realization nor the betrayal of "the authentic Islam." Instead, it demonstrates the extent to which any political project aiming to represent or enact the "real Islam" entails (re)deployments of scriptural sources that simultaneously mobilize and erase different interpretive possibilities, charting pathways of meaning that refract historically specific conditions and imperatives.

In this discussion and throughout this book, I use "Islamism," the imperfect but still widely used term among scholars of Muslim societies, and "radical Islamism" to designate its most combative and intransigent forms.[21] This terminology resists the proliferation of polemical nomenclature in regard to all things Islamic on the one hand and, on the other, ever more refined scholarly distinctions and classifications—some more helpful than others—designed to recognize the complexity of the subject and keep pace with ever-shifting terrain.[22] Islamism may well be the worst term except for all others, but the advantage of any designation in many ways depends upon how it is defined and used.

Drawing from my work with Muhammad Qasim Zaman, I take Islamism to refer to contemporary movements that attempt to return to the scriptural foundations of the Muslim community, excavating and reinterpreting them for application to the contemporary social and political world. Such foundations consist of the Qur'ān and the normative example of the Prophet Muhammad (*sunna*;

20. Cemil Aydin, for example, argues that the idea of the "Muslim world" only developed in the nineteenth century and must be understood in terms of a genealogy that has little to do with the dictates of the Islamic tradition. Instead, it has a great deal to do with empire—specifically the emergence of European discourses about Muslims as racially distinct, unified, and inferior in tandem with "the particular intellectual and political strategies of Muslim resistance to this racialized identity." Aydin, *Idea of the Muslim World*, 5–6, also 73–75. See also Massad, *Islam in Liberalism*, 3–6.

21. "Islamism" is not universally accepted and is frequently invoked with caution and caveats. As an Algerian writer has argued, for example, Islamism wrongly implies that those who claim the name have captured the essence of Islam, and thus is no more appropriate than calling David Koresh a Christianist. Bennoune, "Algerian Women Confront Fundamentalism," 37, n. 1.

22. These classifications and distinctions are far too numerous to rehearse, and an evaluation of the relative merits of each would require a chapter all by itself. For an analysis of some of these matters of terminology, see Euben and Zaman, *Princeton Readings in Islamist Thought*, chapter 1.

ḥadīth), which constitute the sources of God's guidance in matters pertaining to both worship and human relations. In general, Islamists aim at restoring the primacy of the norms derived from these foundational texts in collective life, regarding them not only as an expression of God's will but an antidote to the moral bankruptcy inaugurated by "Western" cultural dominance from abroad, aided and abetted by corrupt Muslim rulers from within the *umma* (Islamic community).[23]

Humiliation and the Problem of Theodicy

> Say: "O God, Lord of all dominion!
> You grant dominion unto whom You will,
> And take away dominion from whom You will;
> And You exalt [*tu'izzu*] whom You will
> And humiliate [*tudhill*] whom You will." (Qur'ān 3:26)

How can God preside over a world He created in which the enemies of Islam not only flourish but dispossess, divide, and humiliate Muslims? This problem is at the heart of theodicy, and it's precisely what drives Sayyid Qutb's reckoning with humiliation in his Qur'ānic commentary, *In the Shade of the Qur'ān*.[24] To put it more precisely: Qutb's conspicuous preoccupation with humiliation in the commentary turns it into an idiom of theodicy, a way to articulate and resolve the painful paradox of divine omnipotence and Muslim powerlessness in the world.

Sayyid Qutb (d. 1966) was one of the most prominent Sunni Islamist thinkers of the twentieth century, and the *tafsīr* is usually considered his most influential work. The significance of his engagement with humiliation for this inquiry, however, isn't reducible to matters of reputation and impact. Qutb's account is a critical moment in the humiliation discourse I trace here because it is simultaneously distinctive and illustrative, both in terms of what it reveals and the authority it claims. Adumbrated in countless passages of varying length and intricacy over the course of more than four thousand pages, Qutb's reckoning represents by far the most sustained engagement with humiliation of any single Islamist thinker or activist, Sunni or Shi'i.[25] Distinct in its detail, it is unusually

23. Euben and Zaman, *Princeton Readings in Islamist Thought*, 4.

24. Qutb, *Fī Ẓilāl al-Qur'ān*.

25. Several features of this account find expression in the work of other significant Islamist thinkers of the twentieth century, such as Sayyid Abu al-A'la Maududi (1903–79) and Ayatollah Ruhollah Khomeini (1902–89), albeit in fairly brief, piecemeal form. Maududi also wrote a

instructive not because it inaugurates a direct chain of influence but because it makes explicit the premises and components of the understanding of humiliation many Islamists take as a given regardless of whether they have read Qutb's *tafsīr*—or even, for that matter, the Qur'ān.

The *tafsīr* genre itself is integral to the aura of Islamic sanction Qutb claims for *In the Shade of the Qur'ān*, and crucial to the central premise of this shared account of humiliation, namely, that it expresses the true, unadulterated Islam. Qur'ānic commentaries have typically been the work of *'ulamā'* deeply informed by and engaged with the primary sacred sources and the complexities of scriptural hermeneutics evinced by the many different elaborations, interpretations, and codifications built upon them. As is characteristic of much of Qutb's later work, however, his take on the genre frequently reads less like an interpretive offering than a definitive account of what Islam really is. His conviction that the ultimate purpose behind Divine commandments is beyond human comprehension is as uncompromising as is his confidence that he possesses the unadulterated truth.[26]

Still, it is the very length and style of the commentary genre that makes visible what is, after all, less an argument than an understanding in the making. It specifically renders legible a crucial pivot from humiliation as a divine dispensation to an expression of what human beings do to one another, from a prerogative of God to an exigency of human domination. It shows how the current humiliation of Muslims at the hands of powerful unbelievers is transformed from a source of despair or a justification for imitation into a spur to restorative action. And it shows how the Qur'ān is deployed to recast the humiliation of

---

multivolume *tafsīr*, *Tafhīm al-Qur'ān*, originally published in Urdu in six volumes, and translated into English as *The Meaning of the Qur'ān*, by Chaudhry Muhammad Akbar. In contrast to *In the Shade of the Qur'ān*, humiliation appears only in passing in Maududi's *tafsīr*. But in a particularly noteworthy comment on Qur'ān 89:15, Maududi, like Qutb, glosses humiliation as part of a trial devised by God to reveal the true character of men. In contrast to *Tafhīm al-Qur'ān*, Maududi devotes an entire section to humiliation in *Let Us Be Muslims* titled "Why Are Muslims Humiliated Today?" There humiliation is similarly framed as an idiom of theodicy, an index of Muslims' failure to follow the true message of God. Maududi, *Let Us Be Muslims*, esp. 56–59 and 99–101. Humiliation figures frequently but fleetingly in several of Khomeini's speeches and texts, including *Forty Ḥadīth*, written in 1939; "Declaration on the Occasion of 'Id al-Fitr (Sept. 6, 1978)"; "Message to Pilgrims (Sept. 12, 1980)"; "In Commemoration of the Martyrs of Qum (Apr. 5, 1963)"; "Message to the Muslim Students in North America (Jan. 10, 1972)"; and "Muharram: The Triumph of Blood over the Sword (Nov. 23, 1978)," in *Islam and Revolution*.

26. Qutb, *Fī Ẓilāl al-Qur'ān* 2:722–23.

Muslims' humiliators not only as an expression of God's will in the world, but as a premier act of devotion that realigns a world severely out of joint.[27]

The prominence of humiliation in the *tafsīr* is not simply a function of Qutb's preoccupations, as the Qur'ān itself is replete with terms that connote humiliation/debasement/degradation/lowliness. Primarily derived from Arabic roots such as *dhāl-lām-lām, hā'-wāw-nūn, ṣād-ghayn-rā', khā'-zayn-yā'*, and *fā'-ḍād-ḥā'*, these words recur almost forty times in different forms in the sacred text.[28] While often concealed by the passive voice—e.g., "they were humiliated"—these roots point to what I've argued is a relation rather than a concept. Written into the etymologies of an array of terms for humiliation across several languages, this relation is comprised of two figures positioned hierarchically: the humiliator with the power to act with efficacy in the world and the humiliated who is rendered abject, close to or in the dirt, unable to be anything other than what the humiliator has made them to be.

Arguments about who occupies each position and what must be done about it recur throughout these chapters, but in the Qur'ān, the hierarchy constitutive of humiliation is between God and His creatures. In this guise, the relation signals not domination, in the sense of unjust oppression, but dominion, the rightful preeminence of a supreme authority. This premise anchors three interrelated connotations of humiliation that emerge by piecing together the many appearances it makes in the text. First and foremost, humiliation/degradation/lowliness is a *consequence* of acts that disobey the will of God, as in Qur'ān 10:27:

> Those who have amassed evil deeds—the recompense of an evil deed will be the like of it. Humiliation [*dhillatun*] will come over them, and they will have no protector from God. It is as though their faces were covered with pieces of night, bringing darkness [to them]. They are the companions of the Fire, in which they will remain forever.[29]

Second, it is a *punishment* meted out by God to sinners, to unbelievers, to those who oppose the Prophet or overstep the limits He has set down. Qur'ān 33:57 is

27. This brief analysis is tightly focused on how humiliation figures in a *tafsīr* that is over four thousand pages long. As a result, it does not purport to be an account of all passages in it that bear on the question of theodicy. For a discussion of the complicated writing, revision, and publication process of the *tafsīr*, see Khatab, *Political Thought of Sayyid Qutb*, 160–61.

28. See the discussion of these Arabic roots in the introductory chapter.

29. Qur'ānic translations are from M. A. S. Abdel Haleem (*The Qur'an*), supplemented by Alan Jones's less elegant but slightly more direct translation in *Qur'ān*.

one such evocation: "Those who abuse God and His messenger, God cursed them in this world and the hereafter. He has prepared for them a humiliating [*muhīnan*] punishment." These two connotations inform an implicit third, in which humiliation figures much like a fate that follows transgressors wherever they go. This is exemplified in 3:112, in a locution repeated in slightly different forms throughout: "Humiliation [*al-dhilla*] was stamped upon them wherever they were found."

The Qur'ān repeatedly instructs Muslims to patiently await divine judgment, but on occasion they serve as the instruments of His will. In 9:14, for example, believers are instructed to fight the polytheists [*mushrikīn*] who have broken a treaty, told that "God will punish them at your hands, He will disgrace them." Still, the prerogative to bring low those deserving of humiliation belongs exclusively to God and is, with few exceptions, dispensed by Him.[30] Even when humiliation is expressed, as it often is, in the passive voice, it is always clear from whence the punishment originates and who administers it. Such unilateralism is dictated by the ontological inequality between humans and the divine, and it is precisely this relation that makes the forcible abasement of the disobedient both an act and requirement of justice. In this context, humiliation is at once an expression of this relation, a mode of demonstrating it, and a means of enforcing it. Moreover, as "God observes everything" (33:55), He is not only the dispenser of humiliation but an ever-present witness to it.[31] It is impossible to hide one's humiliation in this sense, rendering the aspiration to somehow keep one's humiliation "private" nonsensical.

Yet aside from these features, the Qur'ān actually supplies very little detail clarifying in what, precisely, humiliation consists. This silence is largely echoed by medieval commentators and lexicographers, perhaps because humiliation is rarely if ever the crux on which any single Qur'ānic verse hinges.[32] Humiliation

30. Qur'ān 27:34 contains what appears to be the only instance where humans humiliate one another for reasons other than God's will. In it, the Queen of Sheba says, "Kings, when they enter a settlement, wreak havoc on it, and make [*ja'alū*] the mighty of its people [into] lowly ones [*a'izzat ahlihā adhillatan*]." ("Humiliate" is the sense of *ja'alū*, combined with its object *adhillatan*.) Here as in a few other references in the Qur'ān, *adhilla* has the meaning of "abject," as contrasted with *a'izza* "mighty," and appears to be connected to the Queen's fear of losing sovereignty and being subjected to others. This is, of course, exactly what happens.

31. This divine double-duty, so to speak, cannot help but recall the triangulation of humiliated, humiliator, and witness Klein posited as the psychological structure of humiliation in "Humiliation Dynamic"; see discussion in the introductory chapter.

32. See, for example, Ibn Kathīr, *Tafsīr al-Qur'ān al-'Aẓīm*, Jalāl al-Dīn al-Maḥallī and Jalāl al-Dīn al-Suyūṭī, *Tafsīr al-Imāmayn al-Jalīlayn*; and Mụhammad b. Jarīr al-Ṭabarī, *Tafsīr al-Ṭabarī = Jāmi' al-Bayān 'an ta'wīl āy al-Qur'ān.*

tends to be elucidated more by what lies around it, rather than what is in it—in other words, how it figures in the larger web of meaning in which it is enmeshed. It is in relation to two particular oppositions, hubris and humility, uplift and debasement, that humiliation takes on greater definition.

As these terms are part of the complex elaborations, interpretations, and codifications of the Qur'ān, humiliation by no means exhausts the significance of these pairs. But specifically in relation to humiliation, humility and hubris figure as opposed human dispositions in relation to God. An expression of our insolent refusal to stay within the bounds of what He has decreed, hubris will always draw down the divine punishment that brings transgressors low both in this life and beyond, as if swallowed by dust. The degradation that arrogance earns from God is in sharp contrast to the blessings and glory He confers upon obedient, humble believers in this life and the next. The elevation arising from God's favor or the descent due to His displeasure are divine dispensations. They are attributes of the one God with many names, He who not only sustains and rewards, but punishes and destroys, the Exalter [*al-Rāfiʿ*] and the Giver of Glory [*al-Muʿizz*], but also *al-Mudhill*, the Humiliator, He who brings men low.[33]

These interrelated connotations and oppositions are all integral to the understanding of humiliation that unfolds in the course of *In the Shade of the Qur'ān.* At the same time, Qutb makes good use of the absence of detail in Qur'ānic humiliation to solve the problem that greatly preoccupied him: the power the enemies of Islam have to humiliate believers across the globe on the one hand and, on the other, the inability or unwillingness of Muslims to recognize the imperative to act and the form of action such degradation demands. To meet the challenge, Qutb reframes both sides of the problem by way of a distinction between apparent power and real preeminence. This distinction anchors his depiction of faith as the fount of true strength, in contrast to the actual weakness or baseness endemic to disbelief. All else is mere appearance.

For Qutb, the paradigmatic case in point is the Jewish community. Initially favored by God, the Jewish people lost His support and the blessings it entails

33. Believers are repeatedly instructed in the Qur'ān to call on God by one of His "Beautiful Names" [*al-asmāʾ al-ḥusnā*]. Perhaps the two best known of His names are *al-Raḥmān* [the Merciful] and *al-Raḥīm* [the Compassionate], which are central to the benediction that begins the text, *Bismillāh al-raḥmān al-raḥīm* [In the Name of Allah, the Merciful and Compassionate]. His terrible aspects carry much darker names, and these are not generally understood to be part of this instruction. Anwar, "al-Asmāʾ al-ḥusnā."

when they violated their covenant, falling to the lowest depths, condemned by God to endure "humiliation and poverty."[34] The fate of the Jews not only illustrates what happens when a community rejects His message; it evinces the intrinsic character of the Jews, stamped [*damaghahum*] by the Qur'ān as forever abased and intrinsically villainous.[35] Qutb here depicts the "fate of the Jews" as not simply a consequence of how they act but an expression of who they are. Or more precisely, what they do aligns how they act with who they are, not accidentally but essentially. By extension, the humiliation that their ingratitude, disobedience, and insolence draw down on them from God simply brings their social and moral standing into accord with their base and basic nature.

Here as elsewhere, Qutb's discussion of the Jewish community devolves into a screed that collapses the Jews of the Bible, the Qur'ān, eighth-century Arabia, and the twentieth-century world into one race of wicked, cunning, and contemptible schemers, always angling to destroy Muslims, always enemies of Islam.[36] It is tempting to dismiss this as just part and parcel of the antisemitic invective that pervades the *tafsīr*. At the same time, it raises a critical conundrum: how can humiliation simultaneously be a consequence of what one does and a destiny expressive of who one is? This becomes less perplexing if humiliation is understood as both a state of being and a process of becoming, a *telos* (end or goal) toward which a person or a thing tends by nature given the right conditions. In Qutb's account, humiliation by God becomes the *telos* of the Jews, a becoming of what they were destined to be. And just as the seed of a dwarf spruce cannot become a mighty oak regardless of the conditions of its growth, neither the economic power of Medinan Jews nor the military power of twentieth-century Israelis changes who Qutb says they have been revealed to be by nature: weak and lowly.

For my purposes, what's crucial here is that the teleology of humiliation he attributes to the Jews is not exclusive to them: all enemies of Islam are constituted by a humiliating punishment that is a state of being rather than a transitory state.[37] In fact, there are many places where crucial distinctions among Jews, pagans,

34. Qutb, *Fī Ẓilāl al-Qur'ān*, 1:69.

35. Qutb, *Fī Ẓilāl al-Qur'ān*, 1:32–33, prologue to sūra 2.

36. Qutb, *Fī Ẓilāl al-Qur'ān*, 1:566–67, prologue to sūra 4. Qutb's hostility toward Jews throughout the commentary is incongruous with what scholars characterize as the special status accorded to Jews and Christians as *ahl al-kitāb* (literally, "People of the Book") by the Qur'ān, Islamic legal doctrine, and Muslim historical practice. See, for example, Emon, *Religious Pluralism and Islamic Law*, 73. But questions of veracity or accuracy—of the fidelity of the *tafsīr* to the Qur'ān, for example, or Qutb's departure from established Islamic scholarship on it—are not my focus here.

37. Qutb, *Fī Ẓilāl al-Qur'ān*, 1:449.

apostates, and hypocrites [*munāfiqūn*] begin to collapse under the weight of this primary opposition between Muslims animated by true faith and a phalanx of enemies whose power masks the lowly condition that is at once their essence and fate. As terrible as physical punishment is, Qutb contends, it is lighter than the bone-deep and unshakable anguish of the humiliation that accompanies it.[38] Describing the hypocrites, then, he writes that humiliation "pulls them to the earth, binds them to the dirt; they are entirely unable to release or elevate themselves."[39]

Such vivid depictions of humiliation express, not Qutb's empathy for those bound to the dirt, but concern that Muslims take the correct lesson from their fate about how to understand their own powerlessness and what to do about it. First and foremost, if all enemies of Islam are intrinsically base, the worldly ascendance they currently enjoy is ephemeral and superficial rather than a measure of genuine strength. And as their future is already sealed, the victories they achieve are by definition pyrrhic. Such people can cause no true damage, Qutb writes, paraphrasing Qur'ān 3:111: "they will not do you much harm: even if they come out to fight you, they will soon turn tail; they will get no help." The injury unbelievers or false Muslims inflict is but a superficial wound that heals and leaves no trace; it has no bearing on the triumph guaranteed to believers committed to restoring the integrity and power of the *umma*.[40] True Muslims need not despair at the current state of affairs as if it is unchangeable or inevitable, Qutb insists, and there's no excuse for resigning themselves to it.

Yet the question remains: why has God granted such worldly power to unbelievers, even or especially if they, along with the undeserved power they unjustly wield, are destined to fail? Herein lies the second lesson: the power of unbelievers to humiliate believers reflects the failure of Muslims to live up to the piety exemplified by the earliest generations. God has permitted Muslims to be divided and degraded as punishment for succumbing to arrogance or apathy. Not all humiliation is the same. The humiliation of unbelievers is a fate and a state of being, but for dedicated believers, it needn't be more than a transitory trial, a momentary chastisement devised by God to both test their mettle and recall them to what His message requires. For real Muslims, the test is not a judgment but an opportunity to prove themselves.[41] In this way, the power of the undeserving to humiliate Muslims becomes a spur to "combine faith with action," a staging ground for believers to demonstrate the devotion necessary to recognize the

38. Qutb, *Fī Ẓilāl al-Qur'ān*, 4:2481.
39. Qutb, *Fī Ẓilāl al-Qur'ān*, 2:785.
40. Qutb, *Fī Ẓilāl al-Qur'ān*, 1:449.
41. Qutb, *Fī Ẓilāl al-Qur'ān*, 1:480–82.

terms of God's trial and the fortitude of character required to remake the world in accordance with His will.[42]

> However delayed victory, power, and security may be . . . when the *umma* has been strengthened by the trials and tribulations decreed by God; when they have lived in fear while striving for safety; when they have grappled with humiliation while struggling for glory . . . [then] God's promise will be realized, without fail, and no force on earth can stand in its way.[43]

It's a different matter entirely for those Muslims too ignorant to recognize that their suffering is a trial God has devised for them, who are cowed by the challenges of "standing up" [*al-ḥamīya*] for Islam,[44] seduced by the pleasures of the moment, or driven to craven imitation of those with power and status. Qutb evinces little sympathy for such hapless believers who are, he says, Muslims in name only. Domination by the powerful, he makes clear, is no excuse for silence or inaction.[45] The latitude God has given His creatures means that whatever humiliation they endure, along with the fate that defines who they are, is of their own making. This makes the test not only a spur to action but a mechanism to purge the *umma* of those unworthy of membership, a way to sift those Muslims deserving of the trust He has given them from those who, given the power to do what they really wish, reveal who they really are. The trial strips away appearances, providing no quarter or cover for those who are venal and weak.

It's notable that, in Qutb's account, the latitude God grants is highly circumscribed even for the devout. The only meaningful decision is whether to stand up in defense of His message or refuse it. While those who reject it are enemies condemned by their own hand, once accepted, Qutb avers, there is no discretion about whether to obey this or that command and to what degree. As divine supremacy is absolute, the way of life He has revealed is not like a menu from which one may pick and choose; it's all or nothing. Indeed, such complete commitment is the very essence of humility, a recognition of divine supremacy along with an enactment of the deference it requires. This yielding in will and body is the only proper posture of human beings in relation to God, and it's precisely why the righteous are released from humiliation only when they "bow down" in worship and prayer as the Qur'ān instructs (i.e., 3:43, 22:26, 22:77, 77:48). As

42. Qutb, *Fī Ẓilāl al-Qur'ān*, 1:481.
43. Qutb, *Fī Ẓilāl al-Qur'ān*, 4:2530.
44. E.g., Qutb, *Fī Ẓilāl al-Qur'ān*, 2:780–81, *al-ḥamīya*.
45. Qutb, *Fī Ẓilāl al-Qur'ān*, 2:744.

God alone is owed perfect obedience, voluntarily humbling oneself to Him is no degradation. On the contrary, Qutb insists throughout the commentary, it is obedience to anyone other than God that is humiliating.

Qutb is unusually fond of body language in the *tafsīr*, and such evocative imagery constitutes a crucial elaboration of what he means by humiliation. The bent head of humiliation [*dhull*] presages his call to raise one's head [*rafa'a*], which, in turn, constitutes a movement toward glory [*'izza*] or an enactment of *karāma*. He repeatedly exhorts Muslims to "stand up" [*ḥamīya*] in defense of Islam, a posture of refusal when believers have been forced to "bow down." Bowing down works as both a position and condition in the *tafsīr*, a double valence crucial to Qutb's-deliberate conflation of worship and obedience. He deploys several distinct Arabic terms for "bowing down," each invested with different meanings that range from the literal to the metaphorical. Unsurprisingly, he uses several Arabic words in which bowing down denotes the literal act of bending in Muslim ritual prayer (*raka'a, yarka', al-rukū*). Then there are the various terms for "bowing down" (for example, *ḥaniya, yaḥnī, al-ḥany*, to bend or bow, and *nakasa, yankus, al-naks*, to tilt, bow) he deploys metaphorically to invoke the image of Muslims forced to "bow down" to worldly authority. This posture of enforced abjection evokes the punitive imagery of the Qur'ān invoked throughout the *tafsīr*: the humiliated are pressed down into the dirt, swallowed by dust, or covered with "pieces of night."

These words all denote "bowing down," then, but that physical act or posture refers to different affects, movements, acts of devotion, and positions in relation to power. Qutb makes use of what they literally have in common to collapse the distinction between "bowing down" as a physical posture of ritual prayer and "bowing down" as metaphorical obedience to human authority. In this way, the bowing down that works as somatic symbol and synonym for the humiliation entailed by obedience to other human beings is rendered equivalent to ritual prayer. As worship entails obedience to the divine will in all matters of life, bowing to human authority—to *any* authority save God—is revealed to be an outrageously misplaced act of worship. It delivers obeisance to those who least deserve it rather than to God, the only legitimate authority to whom we should bow, the sole source of human freedom, glory, and *karāma*.[46]

46. He writes that those who reject serving God are humiliated by being forced to bow their foreheads [*jibāh*] down to human authority, offering an obedience owed only to God [*wa-yadhillūn li-'ubūdīyat al-bashar min amthālihim, wa-yaḥnūn lahum al-jibāh*]. Qutb, *Fī Ẓilāl al-Qur'ān*, 2:821; see also 5:3036, 6:3965.

What complicates these rhetorical moves, however, is that "bowing down" as a metaphor for obedience can evoke either coerced compliance or voluntary deference. Precisely because the same posture can signal the capacity to act or its absence, it can just as easily evoke the humility of yielding willingly as the humiliation of imposed powerlessness. This particular indeterminacy reprises the striking proximity of humiliation to humility in English as well as in Arabic. In the *tafsīr*, this indeterminacy works to drive home a critical point: the distinction between coerced and voluntary obedience in the *tafsīr*, along with the difference between humiliation and humility, depends not just on the character of the compliance but to whom. It is the willing embrace of divine supremacy that makes such obedience humility—a meaningful expression of will distinguishable from enforced submission. The real humiliation [*dhilla*] is submitting to those who have seized the power to dominate, Qutb writes, because "no true believer bows his head [*al-mu'min al-ḥaqq lā yaḥnī ra'sahu*] to anyone but the one, almighty God."[47]

In these terms, there's no mistaking an ennobling obedience to divine will for the abjection of yielding to anyone or anything else, just as there is no mistaking a back bent in prayer from one bowed under the weight of tyranny. The recurrence of these somatic terms and meanings in the *tafsīr* offers a kind of introduction to what I referred to earlier as the embodied idiom of humiliation. While humiliation is associated with lowliness, being forced to bow down, head bent toward the earth, and being dragged into the dust, restorative action is fashioned as a somatic inversion, to literally and figuratively stand up, head lifted. As this is the central focus of the final chapter, here I want only to point out that this embodied idiom reflects how consistently humiliation is experienced, expressed, and contested somatically across all of these materials, woven into the visual and verbal modes of expression rather than standing beside them.

The equation of obedience with worship means that restorative action has but one proper direction for Qutb, and herein lies perhaps the best-known element of his work. It must begin with the abolition of human sovereignty in its many guises, communist, liberal, democratic, socialist, nationalist, and more. Such sovereignty presumes that human beings have the right to legislate rules for collective behavior and the authority to define how life is to be lived.[48] As legislative authority belongs only to God, bowing down to any authority save Him not only usurps divine sovereignty but constitutes a form of enslavement, enchaining some human

47. Qutb, *Fī Ẓilāl al-Qur'ān*, 4:2527.

48. These arguments are elaborated in many of Qutb's writings, including *Ma'ālim fi-l ṭarīq*, the text perhaps most widely read in English and that takes a great deal from his *tafsīr*. See, for example, chapter 5 in Euben and Zaman, *Princeton Readings in Islamist Thought*.

beings to the rule of others. Liberation lies in the recognition that God's sovereignty is supreme and ubiquitous, the path forward clear: *Sharī'a* (the sacred law of Islam and the totality of Islamic legal and ethical norms) must be established as the sole source of legislation over all domains of human life. As Qutb writes, it's "through submission to God alone that our heads are raised high, and through fearing Him that we can stand up against whatever He disapproves."[49]

At one juncture, Qutb argues that release from humiliation and domination becomes possible only when God rules everywhere; only then "mankind will achieve the dignity [*karāma*] God bestowed upon it [and] humans on the earth will truly be liberated."[50] Yet the theodicy of humiliation at work in the *tafsīr* necessitates the struggle to invert relations of domination rather than to eliminate them. His effort to assure believers that the forces arrayed against them only *appear* to be insurmountable depends upon a teleology in which the ascent of true believers to the preeminence that is their destiny is fulfilled only when they are able to reduce the enemies of Islam to the lowliness that is their fate.[51] This means upending humiliation in the Qur'ān, where it primarily figures as a divine dispensation reflecting the relationship between God and His creatures, even if His creatures are very occasionally His instruments.[52] By centering humiliation in the relations of domination among human beings, Qutb's account flips this agentic primacy, effecting a subtle shift in purpose. Humiliation is still a punishment from God, and He remains the sole originator, yet He decreasingly figures as its primary executor. The sense in which humiliation mediates the relation between humans and God begins to fade as it increasingly comes to articulate what human beings do to one another and to refigure the remedy primarily in terms of human action.

Declarations of Humiliation

This book opened with a passage from Bin Laden's "Declaration of Jihad Against the Americans Occupying the Land of the Two Holy Sites," and I return to it here. As the "Declaration" presaged a series of high-profile attacks on military and civilian targets from Africa to Europe, Asia to North America, it would

49. Qutb, *Fī Ẓilāl al-Qur'ān*, 5:2931 As in Banna's origin story, Qutb frequently uses *karāma* to characterize such restoration and emancipation. I return to this in chapter 5.

50. Qutb, *Fī Ẓilāl al-Qur'ān*, 3:1509.

51. Qutb, *Fī Ẓilāl al-Qur'ān*, 1:516–34.

52. See, for example, Qutb, *Fī Ẓilāl al-Qur'ān*, 1:471, 3:1665, and 3:1611, where he writes that "God will make you the means of executing His will, and bring about the punishment of the arrogant who flaunt their power by your hands, humiliating and defeating them."

become the most (in)famous of Bin Laden's many writings, interviews, and speeches. Less widely recognized is how saturated the "Declaration" is with references to humiliation. Explicitly invoked over a dozen times—fourteen to be exact—in a document of only twenty-five Arabic pages, humiliation is not just a trope but a rhetorical technique essential to decoding the way the text works affectively, discursively, and politically. As the "Declaration" is also one of Bin Laden's longest messages, it represents the most sustained articulation of a preoccupation with humiliation evident in a number of his shorter missives.

Written thirty years after Qutb was executed, the "Declaration" is an apposite pivot from *In the Shade of the Qur'an* to the radical Islamist rhetoric featured in the following section. As in Banna's story, what humiliation means in both the commentary and "Declaration" is established by how it's used, what it does within the text, and the specific audiences the text interpellates.[53] These meanings and purposes are articulated in terms of the problem that also vexed Qutb in the *tafsīr*: the extensive power the enemies of Islam have to humiliate Muslims and the failure of believers to recognize that the survival of the *umma*, along with the preeminence of Islam it represents and serves, demand a struggle to invert the hierarchy of power humiliation entails. Like Qutb, Bin Laden insists that the very extent of the degradation must be a spur to action rather than a justification for despair or acquiescence, and he likewise assures the *mujāhidīn* who take on this urgent task that victory is certain.

This shared problematic posits humiliation as the imposition of impotence on Muslims and Islam by those with undeserved power, a condition that demands immediate redress. But unlike Qutb's reckoning with Qur'ānic humiliation, Bin Laden's focus and aims have little to do with the interpretive complexities required to recast humiliation from a divine dispensation to a problem of human domination. The "Declaration" takes it as a given that righteous Muslims are tasked with answering such humiliation in kind. The text is illuminating not because it marks the appearance of a new way of articulating humiliation but precisely because it does not.[54] A document of significant rhetorical complexity, it shows

53. Following Louis Althusser, interpellation refers to the way a text constitutes its audience by hailing or naming them as members of a group, bringing them into being by the very power of its address. See Althusser, *Lenin and Philosophy and Other Essays.*

54. It is well established that most of Bin Laden's substantive arguments in the "Declaration"—about deterritorialized warfare, armed jihad as necessary resistance to existing violence against Muslims, and the epic battle between believers and infidels—are either derived from the work of previous Muslim thinkers or recapitulate the logic of anti-imperialist writers who preceded him. These range from Ibn Taymiyya to Ibn 'Abd al-Wahhab, Sayyid Qutb to 'Abd

how a shared understanding of humiliation is constituted through distinct frames of reference, calibrated to local grammars of concern. This understanding is elaborated through patterns in the way it works politically and rhetorically across these materials, constituting the collective character not just of the humiliated but also of the humiliator, gendering this relation to render its stakes and redress an urgent matter of masculinity.

Bin Laden styles the "Declaration" as a *fatwā*, the kind of religious or juridical opinion typically issued by experts in the Islamic tradition, and especially those trained in Islamic jurisprudence. A *fatwā* is radically different from a Qur'ānic commentary, of course, but it's not accidental that Qutb and Bin Laden both adopt the conventions of two explicitly Islamic genres.[55] As they both were, like Banna,[56] autodidacts in the Islamic tradition, such fashioning is a way to infuse each text with an Islamic imprimatur neither could claim by way of formal training and expertise.[57] The *fatwā* genre both shapes the "Declaration" and serves it. Its trappings work rhetorically to assert an Islamic imprimatur for Bin Laden's diagnoses, and they impart a sense of inevitability to his directives without explicit argument or demonstrated expertise.

As in many of his messages, Bin Laden's ambitions in this text are global in scope and scale. Yet the sense of egregious humiliation that pervades the "Declaration" begins locally, in the Saudi response to Saddam Hussein's 1990 invasion of neighboring Kuwait. The circumstances are by now well known. Emboldened by the recent withdrawal of the Soviet Union from Afghanistan, Bin Laden offered to put himself and the Arabs who had fought in Afghanistan at the disposal of the Saudi regime in order to push Iraq out of Kuwait and secure the kingdom

---

Allah 'Azzam (see below), Abu Mus'ab al-Suri to dissident *'ulama'* and shaykhs who have been at the forefront of opposition politics in the Kingdom. See for example Lia, *Architect of Global Jihad*, 6, 8, and the chapter on Bin Laden in Euben and Zaman, *Princeton Readings in Islamist Thought.*

55. It's not my purpose to compare these genres or the political thought of Qutb and Bin Laden generally. Nor do I take the *tafsīr* or the "Declaration" to stand in for either *oeuvre.*

56. Both Qutb and Banna were educated at the Dār al-'Ulūm, an Egyptian school founded in the nineteenth century that was eventually incorporated into Cairo University. Reid, *Cairo University and the Making of Modern Egypt*, 139–49.

57. While none of the Islamists here are *'ulamā'*, there are prominent Islamist figures who have been formally trained in the Islamic tradition, such as Khomeini, Muhammad Baqir al-Sadr, Yusuf al-Qaradawi, 'Umar 'Abd al-Rahman, Murtaza Mutahhari, and Muhammad Husayn Fadl Allah. For a discussion of the relation between Islamists and *'ulamā'*, see Euben and Zaman, *Princeton Readings in Islamist Thought*, introduction.

against further aggression. The Saudis rejected the offer, instead permitting thousands of US troops into the Kingdom to launch Operation Desert Storm.

Stung by the rejection and infuriated by the decision, Bin Laden accused the Saudi regime of violating Islamic law by entering a pact with non-Muslims to fight other Muslims.[58] As he puts it in the Declaration, the presence of those who are essentially murderers of Muslims in the very house of Islam, the site of the Revelations, is a "defilement of her [Islam's] holy places, occupation of her land, and violation and plundering of her sanctuaries."[59] These vaunted custodians of the land of Mecca and Medina and sacred sites such as the Ka'ba (the direction Muslims face for prayer), Bin Laden writes, have relinquished the duty to defend it to infidels at the first opportunity. Such desecration, and the abdication of the duty to defend Islam that made it possible, reveal once and for all just how thoroughly the Saudis have betrayed their trust.

The violations of God's law mount, as do the multitudinous ways the monarchy "humiliated the umma" [*adhalla al-umma*].[60] The regime has not only permitted the presence of American troops on the soil of Muhammad, for example, but has tasked the army and security forces with protecting the "invaders" rather than repelling them. The humiliation of the army illustrates just how thoroughly the royal family has degraded every segment of society, from the most ordinary citizen up to the most pious *'ulamā'*. Everyone is subject to arbitrary imprisonment, the violation of basic rights, and policies of economic injustice. All respectful attempts to convey to the king the seriousness of the problems—the petitions, pleas, reports, and reminders from Muslim scholars and leaders to rule in accordance with *Sharī'a*—have gone unheeded.

The magnitude of the betrayal informs Bin Laden's refusal to grant the Saud family the legitimacy implied by even using the name Saudi Arabia, referring to

58. The most powerful accusations Bin Laden levels against the Saudi Arabian regime are indebted to more original or learned and formally trained Muslim thinkers. He borrowed arguments from dissident Saudi *'ulamā'* such as Shaykh Salman al-'Awda and Safar al-Hawali to argue that this policy was one among many indications of the replacement of *Sharī'a* with man-made law in the Kingdom, "one of the ten voiders that strip a person [of] his Islamic status." Bin Laden, "I'lan al-jihād 'alā al-Amrīkiyyīn al-Muḥtallīn li-bilād al-Ḥaram"; Gwynne, "Usama Bin Laden, the Qur'an and Jihad." Al-'Awda and al-Hawali were prominent members of a vocal group of dissident *'ulamā'* critical of Saudi foreign and domestic policy. Both were imprisoned from 1994 to 1999 as part of a Saudi crackdown on domestic dissent. See Fandy, *Saudi Arabia and the Politics of Dissent*, 22, 48–113; Lawrence, *Messages to the World*.

59. Bin Laden, "I'lān al-jihād 'alā al-Amrīkiyyīn al-Muḥtallīn li-bilād al-Ḥaramayn."

60. Bin Laden, "I'lān al-jihād 'alā al-Amrīkiyyīn al-Muḥtallīn li-bilād al-Ḥaramayn."

the Kingdom either as the "Land of the Two Holy Sites" (i.e., the land of Mecca and Medina) or simply "the country" throughout the "Declaration." But for Bin Laden, the rot that is the Saudi regime is also symptomatic of a world entirely out of joint. A once unified and mighty *umma* has been fragmented into small, weak countries preoccupied with petty local feuds and meaningless partisanship. Such division has been carefully engineered and maintained by the "Zionist-Crusader alliance," he insists, obscuring the fact that all Muslims are part of a single community of faith that transcends national boundaries. As the so-called Muslim rulers who preside over these fragments depend for support upon this hostile alliance, they have become slaves to its aims.

This is nowhere more evident than in the willingness of the Saudi royal family to serve the interests of foreign unbelievers at the expense of the people and sanctities the regime so loudly claims to protect. The Saudi regime is only the domestic face of global domination for Bin Laden, one among too many. Every single Muslim, he declares, has suffered directly or vicariously from the "aggression, iniquity and injustice" imposed on them by the Zionist-Crusader alliance and their lackeys. The "blood of Muslims has become valueless, their money and resources plundered by enemies" not just in the Middle East but in Central Asia, the Balkans, the Caucasus, Southeast Asia, and Africa.

Such a state of affairs cannot be permitted to continue. The "Declaration" promises that the wages of humiliation [*dhull*] and oppression [*ẓulm*] will be paid not just by the regime but by its enablers, collaborators, and masters. In a passage that reads like a taunt, Bin Laden writes that the bombings of the Saudi Arabian National Guard Headquarters in downtown Riyadh on November 13, 1995, and the US Air Force housing complex in Khobar on June 25, 1996, are but a small taste of what is to come. The degradation that has reached into every corner of the *umma* demands a jihad in kind that is equally global in scope.

The scope and scale of the provocations may be distinctively modern, but the jihad it necessitates is timeless, just the newest expression of what Bin Laden elsewhere characterizes as an epic war between "global unbelief, with the apostates today under the leadership of America, on one side, and the Islamic *umma* and its brigades of *mujāhidīn* on the other."[61] In Bin Laden's telling, these deeply etched fault lines not only connect the *mujāhidīn* of the present to the great battles fought by the nascent Muslim community in the past, but also knit together each seemingly discrete instance of violence across space. From Palestine to Aden, it is *Muslim* lives that are dispensable, *Muslim* resources that are plundered,

61. Bin Laden, "Depose the Tyrants," in Lawrence, *Messages to the World*, 250.

Muslim sensibilities that are trampled, and *Islamic* sanctities that are violated. Experiences forged under specific conditions prevalent at different historical moments on disparate continents are assembled into a pattern of powerlessness that expresses the collective humiliation of the *umma* and, by extension, the Islam it embodies. Details of circumstance are, paradoxically, rendered incidental to the pattern even as they serve as evidence of the scope, intensity, and timelessness of the attack on Muslim lives and sensibilities.

In Bin Laden's vision, such bloodshed, rapaciousness, and humiliation do not so much produce Muslim solidarity as recall Muslims to a long-forgotten unity that has been obscured by the amplification of small differences cultivated by those who benefit from division. For those who see clearly, the inequities wrought by this unholy alliance of enemies serve as a reminder that the "children of Iraq are our children," just as an attack on a Muslim anywhere becomes an attack on Muslims everywhere. This is the moment true Muslims must awake from the apathy and blindness fostered by the fiction of national borders and identities. At long last, Muslims can recognize that Islam itself is at stake in the Afghan jihad, that the fight for Palestinian liberation is as much the responsibility of Muslims in Jeddah as those in Hebron, and that everyone is tasked with ejecting American troops from the Land of the Two Holy Sites.

Bin Laden depicts such unifying and emancipatory purposes as acts of recognition, but he deploys specific rhetorical techniques to bring into being what the text depicts as a given. Take the matter of address. Several scholars have emphasized Bin Laden's dexterity in calibrating the "polemical register" of his messages to address diverse audiences.[62] He shifts gears repeatedly, alternately speaking to specific sectors of Saudi society, Arabs in the Peninsula, Muslims across the globe, US citizens and leaders—most in collective terms, but some by name, such as US Secretary of Defense William Perry (1994–97). At one point in the "Declaration," he evokes the everyday struggles created by inflation and debt for those with limited income, economic hardships from which his family wealth entirely insulated him.

Most of these calibrations work either explicitly or implicitly to hail "the youths of Islam, men of the brilliant future of the *umma* of Muhammad" throughout the world and in the Arabian Peninsula in particular.[63] These "youths of Islam" are

62. See, for example, Lawrence's introduction to *Messages to the World*; and McAuley, "Ideology of Osama Bin Laden," 269–87.

63. In his analysis of overlapping tribal, national, and transnational group identities in Bin Laden's discourse, McAuley draws attention to his invocations of a kind of pan-peninsular identity. "Ideology of Osama Bin Laden."

his primary addressees, the fierce champions tasked with the work of restoration that is simultaneously territorial, political, existential, and spiritual. As there is no preexisting global audience of (Sunni) Muslim men just waiting for the call to dedicate themselves to the defense of the *umma*, the "Declaration" itself launches this restorative feat by rhetorical practices designed to call precisely such men into existence. It is Bin Laden who conjures his cadre of champions by reaching rhetorically across class, tribe, nation, and continent. He weaves together images, anecdotes, indictments, Qur'ānic verses, hadith, poetry, and prayer to render Islamically urgent, viscerally immediate, and intensely personal a jihad in Saudi Arabia to Muslim men living in diverse circumstances thousands of miles away.[64]

As in Qutb's *tafsīr*, the humiliation that awakens Muslim solidarity also posits a unified humiliator, a global hegemon straddling continents, peoples, and histories. Such an enemy, murderous and relentless, ravaging the *umma*, its sanctities, and its women, is essential to the summons the "Declaration" issues. It brings into existence all those who would see themselves as dedicated, courageous, and manly enough to join the ranks of the *mujāhidīn* destined to drive this colossus to its knees and into the dirt.

Bin Laden intends the specter of this ravening enemy as a call to battle, yet the very power, reach, and relentlessness he attributes to it could just as easily quell as incite anyone's ardor for action. To this, he offers a familiar assurance. Much as Qutb had cast the worldly power of Islam's enemies as a mask for the baseness that is both their essence and fate, Bin Laden depicts the powerful "Zionist-Crusader alliance" as a paper tiger, destined for humiliating defeat when faced with true warriors. Here the opening passage bears repeating:

> [A]fter some minor skirmishes, in which dozens of your soldiers were killed and an American pilot was dragged through the streets of Mogadishu, you left defeated, repelled back, taking your dead, dragging the tails of failure,

64. Analysis of Bin Laden's use—and misuse—of the Islamic tradition is beyond the scope of this discussion, but Gwynne's account of how he deploys the Qur'ān is highly instructive. Gwynne points out that the "Declaration" does not begin with the traditional invocation of divine mercy. It invokes Qur'ān 3:110 but omits the latter part of the verse that refers to those Jews and Christians who may be considered believers. It ignores the special status granted to the People of the Book in the Qur'ān, instead promising double rewards in paradise for killing Jews and Christians. It refers to the Qur'ānic instructions to "smite the necks" of the unbelievers (47:4) but dispenses with the remainder of the verse that specifies how to treat prisoners. Gwynne, "Usama Bin Laden, the Qur'an and Jihad," 66, 68, 71, 74, 79–80.

> disappointment, defeat and humiliation [*al-hawān*]. Clinton appeared in front of the world threatening to take revenge, but this threat was only a preliminary for retreat. God has humiliated you [*akhzākum*] and you withdrew. The extent of your impotence and weakness has become clear. The spectacle of you being defeated in three Islamic cities—Beirut, Aden and Mogadishu—has "healed the breasts of a believing people."[65]

What the present proves, the past teaches. As the enemies of Islam are destined by God and their own nature to be driven into the dirt, there is no reason for *mujāhidīn* to find their vast numbers and greater firepower the least bit daunting. Muslims must be reminded that the humiliation of Americans by al-Qaʿida is only the most recent instance of outnumbered groups of dedicated believers demonstrating the impotence of much larger military forces. Herein lies a long history stretching back through time from the 1936 Palestinian revolt against British immigration policy in Mandate Palestine to the nascent Muslim community led by the Prophet Muhammad.

History, nature, and God all guarantee that the *umma* will inevitably emerge united and triumphant in a world where Islam is again ascendant, all are freed from the domination of the "Zionist-Crusader alliance," and America has been reduced to a shadow of its former self. Such a promised victory has little to do with conventional military metrics; it lies in any attack that shows the world the sight of a superpower that had long humiliated Muslims on its knees. This is not just a means to an end, not just a tactic in a protracted war. Such an inversion of the hierarchy of humiliator and humiliated performs and produces a sense of restored potency the moment it publicly demonstrates the impotence of the enemy. In these terms, victory is not only guaranteed but instantaneous, its pleasures and rewards immediate rather than deferred.

Victory here can be understood as performative in the sense that it's articulated and accomplished in its very enactment.[66] Borrowed from speech act theory, this conception of "performative" is central to the following chapter on ISIS videos, as I argue that performative violence decodes how the visual rhetoric works as an enactment of retaliatory humiliation. Such a performative sense of victory captures the logic at work in Hizbollah's declarations of victory over Israel, for example, or al-Qaʿida in Iraq's claim to have defeated the United States. Often dismissed as instances of deceit, braggadocio, or delusion, these claims make victory

65. Bin Laden, "Iʿlān al-jihād ʿalā al-Amrīkiyyīn al-Muḥtallīn li-bilād al-Ḥaramayn."

66. As Judith Butler explains in *Bodies That Matter*, "Within speech act theory, a performative is that discursive practice that enacts or produces that which it names" (13).

a matter not of tanks, troops, or tactics but the capacity to publicly humiliate the humiliator in spite of obvious asymmetries in martial might. Yet it turns out that such an understanding of performative victory is also evinced by the Egyptian archive that largely eschews the retaliatory humiliation articulated here. In this sense, it names a kind of refusal to yield either politics or power to instrumentalist logics of success or security. I return to this in the final chapter.

Deploying a now familiar somatic metaphor, Bin Laden makes the triumph of the *umma* and the humiliation of its enemies simultaneous and instantaneous: those responsible for the attack on Riyadh, he contends in the "Declaration," are "youths who raised the head of the *umma* high and humiliated its enemies, the American occupiers" [*al-shabāb alladhīn rafaʿū raʾs al-umma shāmikhan, wa-adhallū aʿdāʾaha min al-Amrīkīyīn al-muḥtallīn*]. This is why an exultant Bin Laden seems so eager to rehearse all the details to those most likely familiar with them. If these victories lie less in violence per se than in demonstrations of US impotence, such boasting after the fact is itself a component of such retaliation, a public rehearsal of an enemy's humiliation designed to ensure that all are acutely aware of who has forcibly degraded whom.

As the hierarchy of humiliation is primarily a relation among men, for Bin Laden, men must serve as agents of the retaliatory humiliation essential to victory. Defense of the community and responsibility for collective restoration alike fall upon the shoulders of the young Muslim men who are his primary addressees. The "sons of the people" [*abnāʾ al-shaʿb*], "our brothers" [*ikhwānī*] who manifest the inheritance of the righteous *mujāhidīn* of early Islam, are tasked with "raising the head of the *umma*." In a description that sounds more like a summons, Bin Laden contends that these Muslim youths are so eager to stand up [*waqafū*] in defense of Islam that they must be restrained from initiating attacks out of turn.

It is men who must not only fight the enemy but publicly drive him to his knees. The moments when females briefly materialize in the "Declaration" underscore how thoroughly the exhortation to action humiliation encodes and the pleasures it promises are gendered. First, they briefly appear in the guise of the Muslim women of early Islam, the selfless helpmeets who, Bin Laden writes, sold their jewelry to finance the Muslim army. These exemplify the virtues all Muslim women must seek to emulate today by performing the tasks appropriate to their role, such as boycotting American products. Second, women appear as virginal rewards for the martyred *mujāhidīn* in the afterlife, the *ḥūr al-ʿayn* [black-eyed ones] waiting to wed each one in paradise.

Third and finally, women serve as the cheerleaders, motivators, and mirrors of male action, ready and happy to sacrifice "their sons, brothers and husbands to fight in the cause of God." Yet women themselves do not speak in the

"Declaration". When women's voices are needed, Bin Laden ventriloquizes them, convening a chorus of wives, mothers, daughters, and sisters who goad Muslim men to jihad with images of females and *umma* alike unprotected and defiled:

> The matter is bigger than insulting words; prepare yourself like a fighter
> The wolves of *kufr* [unbelief] are eating our wings; will you abandon us to them?
> The wolves of *kufr* are drawing together evil persons scattered everywhere
> Where are the noble men defending noble women by force of arms?
> Some shames can never otherwise be blotted out; death is better than life in humiliation [*al-dhull*]![67]

Taken together, these various components and moments render powerlessness as emasculation and the imposition of impotence upon the humiliator as the preeminent mechanism of instantaneous restoration. The point is not just that men are made into the vehicles of such restoration but that restoration itself is encoded as a performance of Muslim manhood, one that requires glorious acts of courage against enormous obstacles. Just as Bin Laden's humiliation rhetoric knits together diverse sites of struggle and scales of experience, so too does the victory of this inversion render the performance of masculinity, the unity of the *umma*, and the preeminence of Islam mutually constitutive. These elements serve to outline what will become a pattern in the political and exhortatory work humiliation rhetoric does. The following section helps bring into focus a few of the disparate audiences addressed in its terms.

"Making Men"

> We shall not accept humiliation,
> We shall not accept humiliation,
> We shall not accept humiliation or subjugation,
> We will not bow our heads,
> We will not bow our heads,
> We will not bow our heads to the depraved.[68]

67. He repeats this phrase—"death is better than a life in humiliation"—in a verse with very similar content in his December 1998 interview with *al-Jazeera*, transcript available in *Messages to the World*, 94.

68. Al-Qa'ida in Iraq, "Ḥayya al-'Adl Martyrdom Operation." This is how the title is cited in Hafez, "Martyrdom Mythology in Iraq," 103. Humiliation is not a recent preoccupation

So goes a hymn in a 2005 video issued by al-Qaʿida in Iraq in the wake of the US-led invasion, just one of the assemblage of Arabic texts and sources issued by radical Islamists I analyze in what follows.[69] There are undeniable continuities of content and expression across these sections. These materials are saturated with invocations of a humiliation articulated as the imposition of impotence on Islam and Muslims by those with greater and undeserved power. The refusal to "bow our heads," moreover, is part of a shared vocabulary in which particular postures work as both metaphor and exemplary incarnation of humiliation and its repudiation.

At the same time, these materials represent a volte-face in genre from the previous discussion. As I've argued, the *tafsīr* and fatwa respectively are integral to the Islamic imprimatur that Qutb and Bin Laden produce and claim through and in the texts. In this sense, genre is not just the form of the argument but a mode of authorization. The narrative about the collective humiliation of Islam borrows certainty from the aura of divine sanction invested in the form. And it is the form that confers an aura of authority to a teleology that guarantees preeminence to believers despite the daunting power they face.

By contrast, these materials vary from one another as well as from those in the previous sections by genre, tenor, length, purpose, and complexity. They include terse communiqués, rambling interviews, grainy amateur videos, high-production mini-movies, magazine articles, radio broadcasts, press releases, elaborate speeches—circulated by way of a multiplicity of technologies, from the tape cassette to the internet. While some materials are longer than others, most tend to be brief and ad hoc, articulated by an array of organizations forged in sometimes radically different contexts, calibrated to address disparate exigencies and agendas.

---

among radical Islamists. Just consider a 2014 video titled "Downing in deep humiliation" [*al-Ghāriqīn fī al-dhull al-saḥīq*] issued by al-Sumūd for Media Production, courtesy of the Institute for Strategic Dialogue Database, hereafter ISD, and a 2005 recording "The address of the Emir of the Salafist Group for Preaching and Combat to the summit of Arab humiliation" ["Khiṭāb amīr al-jamāʿa al-salafīya lil-daʿwa wa'l-qitāl li-qimmat al-dhull al-ʿarabīya"]; see below. The original web address for materials provided by ISD are usually unavailable, removed either by those who originally posted it to avoid detection or by administrators at YouTube, Twitter, and Facebook, among others, who would remove it once alerted. On such removal and Internet archiving, see Atwan, *Islamic State*, 18.

69. As Mohammed M. Hafez shows so well, humiliation is a dominant trope in materials about martyrdom operations that circulated among Sunni fighters—or "insurgents"—in the years immediately following the US-led invasion of Iraq. Hafez, *Suicide Bombers in Iraq*, 142–45.

These materials are more often identified by organizational affiliation than by author, and the organization in question is usually classified as terrorist (e.g., ISIS and its affiliates, al-Qaʿida and its franchises, Hamas, Hizbollah, al-Shabab, Lashkar-e-Taiba). As a result, they are quite frequently grouped together in scholarship, journalism, and policy documents as propaganda. Propaganda has come to denote the kind of deliberately manipulative, false, misleading, and demagogic communication that is more properly the domain of counterterrorism experts than political theorists.[70] Such pejorative connotations presuppose a sharp distinction between persuasive and misleading discourse, despite the fact that a fair amount of communication labeled "propaganda" simultaneously expresses a deeply held view of the world as well as an effort to convert audiences to it using an array of rhetorical techniques.

It is in this spirit that I read these materials together as a single archive of—often very blunt—rhetorical expressions of humiliation rather than as simply or only misleading "propaganda." Of course, none of these materials evince Qutb's Qurʾānic fluency, pinched though it may be. Nor does any source here exhibit Bin Laden's rhetorical talents or his "literary lyricism," skills that are, unlike his arguments, very much his own.[71] Yet like the *tafsīr* and "Declaration," this archive articulates what humiliation means in terms of what it does rather than advancing it as a formal proposition in need of systematic argument or evidence. Still, if this exhausted the import of this archive for the inquiry at hand, these materials could be dismissed as just a collection of coarse, abridged echoes of far more complex and interesting texts.

What makes this archive particularly instructive for my purposes is the orientation to action rather than explication these materials exhibit. If Qutb's *tafsīr* reworks a divine dispensation to supply an Islamic imprimatur for retaliatory humiliation and the "Declaration" renders legible the political project and exhortatory strategies encoded in it, this archive brings together those who heed the urgent call they issue. These materials, in turn, starkly and sometimes brutally articulate the way humiliation constitutes powerlessness as emasculation, gendering the demand for expiation, the form of restoration, along with the agents and terrain of retaliation.

70. Thomas Huckin analyzes multiple definitions and usages in English to show that "propaganda," first deployed by the Catholic Church in the sixteenth century to describe oral and written work explicating church doctrine to counter Protestantism, is inevitably pejorative in these ways; see "Propaganda Defined," 119–31.

71. Lawrence, *Messages to the World*, xvi–xviii.

This imbrication is elaborated through several overlapping tropes that recur across a striking array of sources. First and foremost, humiliation denotes an assault on the capacity of Muslim men to defend the *umma* militarily as well as culturally, provide for their progeny, and protect their women. Just one case in point is *al-Difāʿ ʿan arāḍī al-Muslimīn: ahamm furūḍ al-aʿyān* (The defense of Muslim lands: the most important of individual obligations) by Abdullah Yusuf ʿAzzam (1941–89), a Palestinian teacher and activist often considered the architect of Arab participation in the "Afghan jihād" and one-time mentor to Bin Laden. In this text, ʿAzzam writes of the agonizing humiliation of young men unable to act when the Afghan woman is "crying out for help, her children are being slaughtered, her women are being raped, the innocent are killed and their corpses scattered."[72]

This is closely related to a second trope in which Muslim men in particular are goaded to humiliate those who have humiliated Islam. Consider an interview with the online magazine *Ṣawt al-Jihād* [Voice of jihad], where Saleh al-Oufi, a leader of the *Mujāhidīn* of Saudi Arabia, insists that only the violent humiliation of those who humiliate Muslims can recover men's honor, dignity, and courage.[73] The examples abound: a trainer of Palestinian martyrs insists that the motivation for martyrdom operations is the recuperation of men's "honor and dignity . . . when we are humiliated, we respond with wrath."[74] In an audiotape titled "Ayna ahl al-murūʾa?!" [Where are the possessors of manhood?!] and attributed to Zarqawi, the speaker claims that the *mujāhidīn* [those who struggle] have "made the international coalition taste cups of humiliation [*dhull*] . . . lessons from which they are still burning."[75] And in ʿAzzam's collection of reports and letters from slain Arab *mujāhidīn* in Afghanistan, villagers who lost one of their compatriots to jihad write:

72. ʿAzzam, *al-Difāʿ ʿan arāḍī al-Muslimīn ahamm furūḍ al-aʿyān*, 43. The focus of this investigation is Arabic, but this imbrication of humiliation and gender isn't confined to any single language. For example, in interviews, members of the Somali *al-Shabab* talked about the respect and power they receive as men dedicated to defending Islam, and some have even explained their membership in terms of a desire exact revenge on soldiers they describe as "animals" who "touch our women inappropriately at the checkpoints. Imagine when you see this being done to your mother or your sister . . . it is humiliating and infuriating." From fieldwork conducted by Muhsin Hassan in Kenya January 2011–December 2012 for an undergraduate thesis, "Lost Boys of Eastleigh." Cited here with the permission of Muhsin Hassan.

73. al-Oufi, "Interview with Saleh al-Oufi," 23–28.

74. Quoted by Hassan, "Arsenal of Believers," 41.

75. Zarqawi, "Ayna ahl al-murūʾa?!" [Where are the possessors of manhood?!].

> May God grant his blessings to you men who have restored to this *umma* its stature and power, eliminated its humiliation and suffering, and wiped from its brow the disgrace that had befallen it. You have whitened our faces after they had been blackened . . . [the USSR] was vanquished by emaciated hands, empty stomachs, minimal arms and a faith in their hearts that is firmer and steadier than the mountains. Thus God rendered you victorious over them.[76]

All these materials were forged under very specific conditions. Some are signed by individuals, while others claim collective authorship. All reflect specific geographic, temporal, and institutional locations, and respond to any number of provocations, from the materially immediate to the abstract and conceptual. A number decry the US-led invasion of Iraq or the photographs from Abu Ghraib. There are denunciations of the Arab League as a lackey of foreign power and the IMF as an institution of domination. There are condemnations of specific *'ulamā'* as too conciliatory and indictments of martial maneuvers such as Sisi's deployment of the military in Sinai. Some vilify democracy, and others are exorcised by nationalism. Still others abhor the "rule of the cross" or grieve for Palestinians. There is rage against the Asad regime, the PKK, the Saudi monarchy, the Shi'i rise to power in post-invasion Iraq, Israel, Zionism, European colonialism, or American imperialism—and in seemingly endless combinations.

Yet these invocations invariably constitute the stakes of such humiliation in collective terms to render the treatment of specific Muslims, the integrity of the *umma*, and the stature of Islam mutually constitutive. Take the 2012 response of Hassan Nasrallah of Hizbollah to the now infamous *Innocence of Muslims*, a low-budget, American-made video depicting the Prophet Muhammad as a pedophilic, philandering fraud. In a televised speech, Nasrallah called for a full week of organized outrage, declaring that the "whole world must know that this great Prophet has followers who will not be silent in the fact of insult [*ihāna*] or humiliation [*madhalla*], no matter how steep [the price] of sacrifice."[77] In June 2014,

76. 'Azzam, *'Ushshāq al-Ḥūr*, 359, my translation. The reference to whitening blackened faces has eschatological roots in the Qur'ān, which refers to the blackened faces of those in hell (3:106, 39:60), and (10:27) says of those so humiliated that it is "as though their faces were covered with pieces of night, bringing darkness [to them]." Blackening the face of the condemned was often central to "ignominious parading" [*tashhīr*], or public shaming/humiliation, a punitive practice prevalent in the later history of Islamic societies. Lange, "Legal and Cultural Aspects of Ignominious Parading (*Tashhīr*) in Islam."

77. Nasrallah, Speech on the "Innocence of Muslims."

ISIS announced the new name of "The Islamic State" (now shorn of the qualifier of "'Irāq wa'l-Shām"), claiming that this small territory in the corner of Iraq and Syria is both foundation and instantiation of what Muslims of the *umma* have always been and are destined to be:

> O Muḥammad's nation, you are still the best nation, glory is still yours, and rulership will come back to you. The God of this nation yesterday is its God today, and He who made it victorious yesterday will make it victorious today. The time approaches. It is time for generations drowned in seas of humiliation [*biḥār al-dhull*] and suckled with the milk of degradation [*laban al-hawān*], ruled over by the vilest people after its slumber in the darkness of heedlessness. It is time for it to rise up! It is time for Muḥammad's nation to wake up from its slumber, and strip off the garment of shame and shake off the dust of humiliation and disgrace [*ghubār al-dhull wa'l-shanār*]. The time of striking [one's head in anguish] and lamentation has passed, and the dawn of glory, with God's permission, has appeared anew.... Triumph looms on the horizon, and the banners of victory are emerging.... Under it the [city] walls of tyrants have crumbled, their flags have fallen, their borders have been dispelled, and their soldiers among the killed and captured are defeated, have been scattered. The Muslims are ennobled [*a'izza*], and the infidels are humiliated [*adhilla*].... Up, O Muslims, rally around your caliph so that you may return as you had been forever, kings of the earth, knights of war. Up, so that you may live ennobled [*a'izza*] [and] distinguished, honored leaders [*halummū li-ta'īshū a'izzatan kuramā', sādatan shurafā'*].[78]

In the course of the announcement, ISIS's public relations official, Abū Muḥammad al-'Adnānī al-Shāmī, extols those

> Lions in battle, thirsty
> they drank the blood of disbelief....
> The hearts of the believers have been healed.

Al-'Adnānī here illustrates one of the most pervasive features of this archive. Fierce fighters are endlessly referred to as lions [*usūd*]—one short missive mentions lions

78. The speaker is ISIS's then public relations official, Abū Muḥammad al-'Adnānī al-Shāmī. ISIS, "Hādhā wa'd Allāh" [This is the promise of God]. The title evokes a Qur'ānic theme exemplified by 30:6: God is in command of the fortunes of all, and He will step in to help the believers; "this is God's promise; God never breaks his promise" (Haleem, *Qur'an*, 30:6).

no less than six times—always vigilant and already victorious in the Herculean struggle to destroy the oppressors and bring the mighty low.[79] Such evocations explicitly valorize the staggering courage of men who have joined the fight, but the visceral power and exhortatory force of the metaphor is less obvious. These "lions of Islam" who face bullets with "open chests" are both a model and a rebuke to Muslim men who do *not* act—men content to live in subjection, to live under the thumb of corrupt lackeys of foreign interests, or to reside in non-Muslim lands ruled by unbelievers or apostates.

A 2016 video warns of what will become of such a man, content to sit passively in a living death, unable to protect his family or women: look "how he drowns among the darkness of the sea, then thrown upon the shores of the lands of unbelief, a lifeless corpse, unmoving. Others fall into the hands of criminal gangs, prostitution networks, and others. Thus through them his family and his women are turned into debauched whores in Western countries."[80] As the emir of the Algerian Salafi Group for Preaching and Combat puts it in a recording titled, "The Arab Apogee of Humiliation," a Muslim who expects any glory [*'izza*] or leadership from Arab despots who labor for cross-worshippers "is just like one who intends to harvest grapes from thorns" [*al-'inab min al-shawk*].[81] When understanding has been so beclouded by unbelief or stupidity, says 'Adnānī, "you must herd the people into Paradise in chains."[82]

Here, it's not just that Muslim men are the addressees, tasked with retaliatory humiliation; retaliatory humiliation makes Muslim men. Zarqawi leaves no doubt about what's at stake. In a video responding to the Egyptian army's offensive in Sinai issued by the Media Front for the Support of the Islamic State,

79. "Jaḥīm al-kuffār fī arḍ al-Anbār" [Hell of the infidels in the land of Anbar] is where lions are referred to six times. There are too any others to cite, but they include "Dhull wa-Mahāna fī Arḍ al-Kināna" [Humiliation and degradation in the land of Kinana] and "This is the promise of Allah."

80. "Message to the Refugees in the Land of Disbelief."

81. The complete title given to the recording is "Khiṭāb amīr al-jamā'a al-salafīya lil-da'wa wa'l-qitāl li-qimmat al-dhull al-'arabīya" [The address of the Emir of the Salafist Group for Preaching and Combat to the summit of Arab humiliation]. In the first segment, the speech is delivered by Abu Mus'ad 'Abd al-Wadūd, Emir of al-Jamā'at al-Salafiyya lil-Da'wa wa'l-Qitāl in Algeria. In more than a few videos, audio recordings, and written texts, humiliation actually figures in the title; ISIS and its affiliates had a particular penchant for such things. Consider a 2014 video issued by ISIS's Al-Sumūd for Media Production titled "al-Ghāriqīn fī al-dhull al-saḥīq" [Downing in Deep Humiliation], and another issued by Wilāyat Sinai, "al-Dhull wa'l-Mahāna fī arḍ al-Kināna" [Humiliation and degradation in the land of Kinana].

82. "Yā ahl Miṣr hādhā huwa al-ṭarīq" [O people of Egypt, this is the Way].

Zarqawi's voiceover addresses Egyptians several times as the "people of manliness" [*ahl al-murū'a*] dragged through the dirt of humiliation [*al-dhull*], evicted from their home by a tyrant—Sisi—while girls weep for a great people enchained, in servitude.[83] "Flatten, O mountains, we have scaled the summits," chant male voices in a *nashīd* included in a compilation of videos out of Anbar. "Make men [*iṣna'ī al-rijāl*], awaken ambitions."[84] A video revealingly titled "Ṣinā'at al-Rijāl" [Making men] addresses "sons of the Sunna," demanding that they choose between elections and all the trappings that exact a "tax of humiliation" [*ḍarībat al-dhull*] and the path of jihad that pays the "tax of glory and dignity [*ḍarībat al-'izza wa'l-karāma*]." These are not real alternatives, as "one side walks thrown down on its face, while the other walks upright on the Straight Path."[85]

The production of men is very often tied to females who serve as the stage on which the drama of humiliation between men plays out. Women figure either as nameless archetypes—like 'Azzam's "Afghan woman"—or bodies, but they are always violated or perpetually vulnerable to violation by the rapacious enemies of Islam.[86] They are not themselves humiliated; their violation is the instrument of male humiliation, the symbolic or literal terrain of emasculation. Here as elsewhere, the bodily integrity of women implicitly serves as a measure or mirror of Muslim masculinity. As female purity reflects the ability of men to guard and protect, a woman's violation demonstrates male impotence in need of immediate redress. While the woman doesn't have an individual voice, then, her body is made to speak volumes. But what it conveys is less the horrors of sexual violence routinely inflicted on actual women and girls than the desecration of the social order the virtuous Muslim woman represents and anchors.

For the same reason, these bodies are the paradigmatic provocation for retaliatory humiliation. They speak to implicitly impeach Muslim manhood and summon "real men" dedicated to vindicating it by stepping up as protectors and defenders. This is evinced by a number of Islamist "letters home," including one in which an aspiring martyr instructs his mother to "[r]emember me with

83. "Yā ahl Miṣr hādhā huwa al-ṭarīq"

84. "Jaḥīm al-kuffār fī arḍ al-Anbār."

85. "Ṣinā'at al-Rijāl" [Making men], title identified at 1:02.

86. Such Islamist exhortations to protect Muslim women from the rapaciousness of "Western men" parallel rhetoric about the need to save Muslim women from Muslim male violence that has accompanied recent US military ventures in Afghanistan and Iraq. Indeed, as Shirin Deylami shows, in the course of the American-led "war on terror," a pathologized Muslim masculinity helped sustain depictions of Muslim-women-as-victims in need of rescue from a beneficent Western masculinity. Deylami, "Saving the Enemy."

every resounding scream uttered by a pure Muslim woman in the land of Jerusalem, or Chechnya."[87] Or consider "The Story of a *Mujāhid*" published in *al-Hussam*, about a young man who had come to the United States to study:

> In America, his eyes were opened to the wounds of the umma. . . . Sleep was driven out of his eyes by the reports of Muslim women's chastity being violated at the hands of the Crusader criminals . . . the screams of the Muslim women were louder to his ears than the words of all seeking to hold him back.[88]

Yet another illustration is in the opening lines of the al-Qaʿida training manual, which pledges to retaliate for every "sister believer . . . whose clothes the criminals have stripped off . . . whose hair the oppressors have shaved . . . whose body has been abused by the human dogs."[89]

As a 2015 ISIS radio broadcast explains, the sword is far more than a mere tool for fighting. It's "the instrument of knowledge and resistance, the weapon of preeminence and power . . . the ballast of a man [*sanad al-rajul*], remedy for those wronged . . . defender of honor, protector of the home [*ḥarīm*] . . . destroyer of powerful enemies and the arrogant." The sword of jihad is the only antidote to the defeat, injustice, degradation, and humiliation that has settled upon all the land. This and only this is the way out of the "disgrace [*khasf*] which has settled on our men."[90]

In contrast to female bodies, made to say so much, from their mouths issue only wordless screams that conjure the unspeakable. In a five-minute audio recording, an unidentified man speaks in urgent cadences, his message framed by men singing a *nashīd*: "The country is stripped of its inhabitants and the borders are violated as if there were none," he says. "[O]ur free women are seized and raped [in prison, so] why is our response weeping and wailing like women?" Then comes the voice, most likely that of Zarqawi, a fragment from one of his speeches:

> O people of manliness [*yā ahl al-murūʾāt*] when will you rise up as one? The chastity of Muslim women [is violated] in your sight, spreading and mocking [you], while the dogs of disbelief bite at your honor, then

87. "Letter to My Mother," *al-Hussam*. *Al-Hussam* was a newsletter published by Care International in Boston, which was a new name for the Al Kifah Center in Boston, a satellite of the Afghan jihad recruiting nexus in Brooklyn. The Center renamed itself after the World Trade Center bombing. I am indebted to John Berger for access to these newsletters.

88. *Al-Hussam*, July 28, 1995.

89. Post, *Military Studies in the Jihad against the Tyrants*, 15.

90. "Shaḥdh al-himam li-dafʿ ʿādiyat al-umam" [Honing Ambitions to Repel the Aggression of the Nations].

disappear? [Look at] the prison of Abu Ghraib . . . O Muslims, don't you have any dignity? [*yā muslimūn a-mā ladaykum nakhwa?*] Don't you have a heart that aches for her?[91]

In the rare moments when female figures utter actual words in this archive, they tend to speak like a Greek chorus that mirrors the main events from the sidelines. In some cases, as in the passage from the "Declaration" above, it's clear that the chorus of women is written by men. But some Islamist publications have showcased messages they attribute specifically to women, usually relatives of men martyred in battle. *Ṣawt al-Jihād*, for example, often featured "women's voices" in the form of symbolic role models named, for example, "Umm al-Shahīd" (Mother of the Martyr), although it is far from clear that women actually write them.[92] These voices invariably express pride, and even pleasure, that husbands or sons have died in a righteous jihad, praise men who undertake retaliatory humiliation, and scorn the formidable powers the men confront.

"Women of the Islamic State," by contrast, is an instructive example of a text most likely written by Islamist women to spell out the proper role of Muslim women, the foundation of the just state. Issued by the Kata'ib al-Khansa', the name attributed to ISIS's women's brigade, the authors refer to the handbook as a "manifesto" attesting to life for women in Iraqi and Syrian cities under Da'ish control. It spells out the divinely-appointed role of women in raising virtuous men ready for battle, maintaining the harmony of the family by supporting their husbands, and staying within the home in order to be the virtuous woman best suited to perform the role of wife and mother. Women who fail to fulfill roles consistent with their "deepest nature" destroy the equilibrium necessary for "emasculated men" to again take up the responsibility as defenders of the *umma*, breadwinners for their family, and models for their sons to emulate. Women are made to be settled, the manifesto reads, to embody stillness and provide stability. The "base of society is shaken, its foundations crumble and its walls collapse" when men are made into women and women aspire to be men.

Women's voices do occasionally issue threats, as in one message attributed to the spouse of a "martyr in the Arab peninsula" and addressed to the widow of Paul Johnson, an employee of Lockheed Martin who had been beheaded by Saudi Islamists. The spouse writes,

91. "Asīrāt al-muslimīn ṣabran" [(Female) captives of the Muslims, patience].

92. "Umm al-Shahīd" [Mother of the Martyr], *Ṣawt al-Jihād* 11 (February 2004); *Ṣawt al-Jihād* 9 (January 2004); Usher, "Jihad Magazine for Women on Web."

> You must know that Muslims will by no means let the shedding of my husband's blood be in vain. We will make sure your husband's corpse will be followed by mountains of his fellow countrymen until they leave the land of the prophet—God's blessings and peace be upon him—utterly humiliated [*adhilla*].[93]

On rare occasions, less ritualized expressions concerning humiliation are voiced by sources that are most likely women. In one brief blog post, for example, a woman named Fatayat al-Tawhid chafes against the limits placed on her ability to fight for the *umma* that has been so egregiously abandoned by Muslims: "You've made me cry, O my nation . . . the only strategy left for me is crying. If I were a man, I would carry a sword or a knife, but I am a woman among men [who] are not of sound religion. They are satisfied with humiliation and degradation [*wa-raḍaw bi'l-dhull wa'l-hawān*]."[94]

On occasion, men claim to be messengers for women unable to speak for themselves. Take, for example, one segment of a video released in 2004 by a group calling themselves Majlis Shūrā al-Mujāhidīn fī al-'Irāq, which features a letter said to be from a woman named Fātima held in the Abu Ghraib prison. She writes,

> We, your sisters, are in Abu Ghraib prison, what can we say to you? The sons of monkeys and pigs violate us, they tear apart our Qur'āns, and they disfigure our bodies and humiliate us [*adhallūnā*]. An American dog raped her, then badly tortured her. So she started smashing her head against the wall until she died. I am your sister in God, Fāṭima, I say to you . . . come to us here in Abu Ghraib prison, kill us along with them, destroy us along with them . . . do not leave us to them . . . kill us along with them so that we might find peace.[95]

Unsurprisingly, there is no Fatima in the video, no woman's voice at all. Instead, a man referred to as Abu Mu'awiya al-Shomali, standing next to a Qur'ān perched atop an automatic weapon, smiles impishly at the camera. He momentarily holds up the paper that presumably contains Fatima's message but never once consults it while relaying the message supposedly written on it. It subsequently becomes clear that "Fatima"—if there ever was such a person—is dead. She has shifted into symbolic significance, no longer a violated woman crying out for vengeance but one of the *ḥūr al-'ayn* [black-eyed ones] waiting to wed the valiant martyr in Paradise. It now becomes clear why the video segment that

93. "Message to the Wife of the Slain Infidel, Paul Johnson," 43.
94. Fatayāt al-Tawḥīd blogpost, 2013.
95. "Khaṭīb Fāṭima" [Fatima's fiancé].

opens with Abu Muʿawiya is dubbed "Fatima's Fiancé." In the final scene, Shomali is shown getting into a car with a smile and a wave, asking God to accept him as a martyr so that he may avenge Fatima's violation and death and wed her in Paradise. Commentary scrolling up the screen to the sound of male voices united in a collective, wordless chant, reads,

> Abu Muʿawiya could not sleep or get any rest; he wholeheartedly resolved to avenge her and every free Muslim woman. He could not think of anything more valuable than his soul to offer to God, presenting it as [if it were] a pittance in the path of God, ransom for the honor of his sisters . . . hoping [that] God would accept him as a martyr and let him marry that girl.[96]

This video points to the last and best-known female figures central to this account of humiliation, evident earlier in Bin Laden's "Declaration," the virginal rewards for martyrs in the afterlife. These are the brides who infamously appear in the final instructions for the 9/11 hijackers, where Muslim "brothers" are urged to purify their carnal impulses, sharpen their knives for the slaughter [*dhabīḥa*], and heed the call of the *ḥūr al-ʿayn* awaiting them in paradise.[97] A "young man's death in glory" is far better than a glorious night of passion, just as it's far better to taste only a cup of humiliation than drown in it one's entire life. ʿAzzam even entitled his collection of reports and letters from slain Arab *mujāhidīn* in Afghanistan *ʿUshshāq al-Ḥūr* [Lovers of the paradise maidens], a reflection of how frequently men who expect martyrdom write about their expectations of meeting the beautiful dark-eyed maidens upon their death.[98] The subject pervades online conversations among Islamists. In one such exchange, Emerson Begolly, an American Islamist subsequently arrested, and his interlocutor excitedly discuss the dreams they have of sexually available "paradise maidens" they will bed after they are martyred.[99]

Inasmuch as these images variously figure women—or women's bodies, to be more precise—as the terrain on which relentless enemies enact the humiliation of Islam and the Muslim community, they're meant to serve as goad to retaliatory action, much as their sexual availability after death is promised as reward. Both exhortation and prize in an unquestionably heterosexual universe, these

96. "Khaṭīb Fāṭima."

97. Makiya and Mneimneh, "Manual for a 'Raid,'" 18–21.

98. ʿAzzam, *ʿUshshāq al-Ḥūr*, 7, 287.

99. Conversation on October 20, 2010, between Begolly (abunancy@almanhajribat.net) and khalidabdalhakim@almanhajribat.net. Begolly was arrested by the FBI on January 4, 2011.

bodies are addressed specifically to Muslim men; those who heed the call are, in turn, made into Muslim men, agents not just of the destruction but of the utter abjection of the enemy. The men "driving the nation of unbelievers like flocks," forcing their leaders to bow down in the "most humiliating way possible," are no less than "lions leading cubs."[100] "We don't bow our heads to any other but God, nor will we ever submit to any but God," says Abu Muʿawiya. "Bush, you lowlife, we won't stop until you bow your head."[101]

Conclusion

In the preceding pages, I have analyzed some of the most significant Islamist invocations of humiliation in Arabic, mapping both continuities and discontinuities of expression across different historical moments, contexts, and genres, foregrounding how they are articulated through an array of techniques, from repetition to juxtaposition, metaphor to image. What emerges is a consistent rather than homogeneous understanding of humiliation as the imposition of impotence on Muslims and Islam by those with greater and undeserved power that urgently demands redress. These texts not only evince a common understanding of humiliation but establish it in a similar fashion: what it means isn't argued explicitly or systematically but is constituted by what it does, that is, how it works rhetorically, affectively, and politically.

Among other things, these invocations bind individual experiences to collective powerlessness in a way that dissolves the distinction between violence against Muslims and violations of Islam. The connective tissue is the *umma*, the worldly instantiation of a timeless, divinely ordained social order that has been under attack from multiple directions. The community has been assailed from the outside by rapacious European colonialism that divvied up the *umma* into artificial nation-states. It has endured the invasions, meddling, and endless greed of American empire. It is eroded from within by brutal authoritarian regimes headed by so-called Muslim presidents or kings shored up by the flow of foreign money and subservient to alien interests. Rampant corruption, unemployment,

100. "Jaḥīm al-kuffār fī arḍ al-Anbār." The date of this video collection is unknown, but Abu Musʿab al-Zarqawi is the speaker, and the black flag logo that would become the hallmark of ISIS publications suggests it is most likely within the first few years after the United States-led coalition invaded Iraq. Courtesy ISD.

101. More literally: "O Bush, [you] lowlife, [we will never cease] until you bow [your head] [*wāṭī yā Būsh illā tuṭaʾṭi*]." "Khaṭīb Fāṭima" [Fatima's fiancé].

and poverty have compromised the capacity of men to be providers and protectors of family and *umma* alike, while secularism, materialism, and fictive gender equality have lured women into betraying their domestic vocation. A weakened *umma* leaves Muslims from Palestine to Paris defenseless against all kinds of violence and degradation, beamed into every corner of the world by satellite and social media. "[H]umiliation is frequently absorbed through images," Assef Moghadam notes, experienced "viscerally, rather than directly."[102]

This is a narrative of domination, dismemberment, dispossession, violence, and violation, not just of people and territory, but of the very norms constitutive of the Muslim family that anchors the community. The collective vulnerability to such destruction and humiliation is both symptom and symbol of how the capacities of men to defend, protect, and provide have been sabotaged. These terms translate powerlessness into the idiom of impotence, install humiliation as both cause and consequence, and render the restoration of masculine capabilities, family integrity, communal strength, and Islamic preeminence mutually constitutive.

This account is articulated in collected texts that are almost exclusively by men, but not all Islamists—however defined—are men. Women have been a significant presence in the multiplicity of organizations and initiatives that constitute the Islamist movement from the very beginning. As the founder of the Ikhwan, Banna opened this chapter, but it's notable that his contemporary Zaynab al-Ghazali founded Jamā'at al-Sayyidāt al-Muslimāt [the Egyptian Muslim Women's Association] in the 1930s, sometimes considered the sister organization of Banna's Muslim Brotherhood. More than that, al-Ghazali was crucial to sustaining and shaping the Ikhwan itself, stepping in to help lead the organization after Gamal 'Abd al-Nasser incarcerated or executed virtually all its organizational and ideological leadership.[103] More recently, online magazines, testimonials, handbooks, social media sites, and the like hosted or written (apparently) by Islamist women for women have proliferated. When ISIS embarked on a focused campaign to draw more women to the caliphate, women who had already migrated played a significant role in recruitment across an array of online platforms.[104] And scholars in an

102. Moghadam, "Suicide Terrorism, Occupation and the Globalization of Martyrdom," 722.

103. In contrast to the voluminous literature on Banna and Qutb, there are few biographies of al-Ghazali in Arabic and no complete history of her organization in English, French, or Arabic (Mahmood, *Politics of Piety*). With the exception of al-Ghazali's memoirs, moreover, much of her writing is still only available in Arabic, while Qutb's *tafsīr*, for example, has been translated into multiple languages.

104. See Atwan, *Islamic State*, 182–87.

array of disciplines have documented women's significant participation in the Islamization of Muslim-majority societies more broadly.[105]

So why the scarcity of Islamist women's voices in this account of humiliation rhetoric? An illustrative rather than exhaustive analysis always risks unintended omissions. So said, when assembling this archive I found that the much fewer texts reliably attributed to Islamist women simply do not exhibit this conspicuous focus on humiliation. In fact, the rare references link it to male action or experience. This doesn't mean that women can't be humiliated; too many women know better. Instead these arguments suggest that such gendered variation in Islamist humiliation rhetoric is less about *who* experiences powerlessness or a difference in *how* humiliation is defined than about how the gendering of power turns humiliation and its expiation into a matter among men. In texts attributed to Islamist men and women alike, men are tasked with retaliatory humiliation and goaded to act against great odds in the language of virility and its metaphors.

The crucial elements in this account—the ideal order, the violated integrity, the restorative action—hinge on the visceral resonances that such evocations of impotence and emasculation are meant to elicit and on the particular conception of masculinity entailed by them. As scholars of gender in an array of fields remind us, masculinity is not singular but multiple, fluid rather than fixed, and articulates with other aspects of identity in a variety of contexts in ways that are neither simple nor predictable.[106] By contrast, Islamist humiliation rhetoric constitutes masculinity as fixed and clear, anchored in divinely ordained gender roles that are both a given yet require effort to shore up. So understood, this account of humiliation serves not just to express a gendered order but replicate it in terms constituted by the very instability it disavows.

Restorative action is most obviously expressed as a retaliatory humiliation that symbolically and literally reverses the hierarchy in which the enemies of Islam have the power to humiliate Muslims. But given how this rhetoric binds multiple domains of collective life together with different scales of experience, the imperative of restoration implicitly extends all the way down. Inasmuch as women are constituted as the hallowed vessels of literal, cultural, and moral reproduction, sexual disobedience and sexual violation alike transform them into the despoiled bodies through which the collectivity is laid open, penetrated, and corrupted.

105. See, for example, Mahmood, *Politics of Piety*; and Cooke, *Women Claim Islam*.

106. Kimmel, "Masculinities"; Connell, *Gender and Power*; Gilmore, *Manhood in the Making*; O'Donnell and Sharpe, *Uncertain Masculinities*; and Cornwall and Lindisfarne, *Dislocating Masculinity*.

As deviation and violation alike impeach manhood, men are tasked with securing both the inviolability of female bodies and women's fidelity to their domestic vocation. This vigilant protection secures the right order of things not only within the *umma* but in relation to its enemies, as these are mutually dependent. Here is where manhood is produced or undone, performed or deformed. ISIS's characterization of men who fail to act as not just hypocritical spectators but "effeminate males" is a reminder that unacceptable desires, unmanly templates, and threatening disruptions must also be rigorously policed.[107]

Taken together, these interlocking tasks constitute a project that would normally be insurmountable, particularly given the very strength of the enemy Islamists identify as the humiliator. But humiliation rhetoric encodes reassurance as well as provocation by defining victory in terms that guarantee success. Victory doesn't require military might, martial acumen, or political power either domestically or in relation to external powers with vastly superior means of domination. Victory is performative, achieved the moment one's humiliator is publicly driven to his knees, symbolically or literally. In this sense, the gendered terms of humiliation rhetoric work less as a blueprint of a patriarchal order than as a rhetorical apparatus comprised of techniques and strategies that aim to bring into existence the very politics it presumes.

I have argued that theorizing humiliation requires attending to what it says and does when invoked by particular people in specific settings and to patterns that emerge from analyses of them. This chapter has traced the outlines of what I've called the scaffolding of humiliation through Islamist verbal discourse, foregrounding the specificity of expressions and experiences that give it form and flesh. The chapters that follow track how this scaffolding is patterned by distinct articulations *within* Islamist discourse and *across* Arabic rhetorics of humiliation. The Islamist visual rhetoric in the following chapter draws attention to the conceptual continuities articulated through the "humiliation of Islam" here, but also shows how context, genre, medium, and circulation distinctively populate its features. It is to this that I now turn.

107. "Evil: Of Division and Taqlīd," *Dabiq*, issue 11, 14. Kimmel, "Masculinities," 504. See, for example, Afsaruddin, "Early Women Exemplars and the Construction of Gendered Space," 42; and Rubin, "Thinking Sex," 267–319.

3

Spectacles of Sovereignty

ISIS EXECUTIONS, VISUAL RHETORIC, AND SOVEREIGN POWER

Ask Mosul [city] of Islam about the brave lions
How fiercely they fought, and then came liberation
The land of glory [*al-ʿizz*] strutted in the garb of exaltation
And sloughed off the garb of humiliation [*dhull*] that had been conquered

AḤLĀM AL-NAṢR, POETESS OF ISIS[1]

Introduction: Setting the Stage

On August 19, 2014, the group of radical Islamists calling themselves *al-Dawla al-Islamiyya* (the Islamic State, hereafter ISIS or Daʿish) posted a video demanding the cessation of United States air strikes against them in Sinjar, Iraq.[2]

1. al-Naṣr, "Dhī Dawlat al-Islām jā'at taz'aru," 18.

2. ISIS stands for *al-Dawla al-Islamiyya fī l-ʿIrāq wa'l-Shām* [the Islamic State in Iraq and al-Sham]. Al-Shām is an Arabic term that, depending upon speaker and context, is usually taken to refer either to Syria or "Greater Syria." At various times according to different sources, "Greater Syria" has been said to include the modern states of Syria, Lebanon, Jordan, and Israel, as well as the West Bank. After ISIS declared its caliphate (see below), it shortened its name to "al-Dawla al-Islamiyya" (the Islamic State). Many resisted the shortened name, arguing that it's neither Islamic nor a state, preferring to use Daʿish (داعش/*dal-alif-ʿayn-shin*), the Arabic acronym for *al-Dawla al-Islamiyya fī l-ʿIrāq wa'l-Shām*. Use of the acronym signals a certain irreverence, and is just one letter away from the Arabic word داعس/*dāʿis*, referring to someone or something that tramples down or crushes. I eschew "Islamic State" here, alternating instead between my preferred term, Daʿish, and ISIS. My preference for Daʿish is a small

President Barack Obama had authorized the attacks earlier that month in an attempt to save what remained of Iraq's Yazidis from massacre and sexual enslavement by ISIS.[3] The video culminated in a dramatically staged beheading of American journalist James Wright Foley, who had gone missing in 2012 while covering the emergent civil war in Syria. Despite the instant infamy of the video, the air strikes continued unabated. On September 2, Da'ish then posted a video featuring captive American journalist Steven Sotloff, repeating the demand, and reenacting the grisly drama of a "live," though edited, beheading. So began a macabre dance of demand and refusal that, by November, included a threat to British Prime Minister David Cameron about his country's "evil alliance with America," accompanied by videos with carefully choreographed decapitations of British aid workers David Haines and Alan Henning.[4]

ISIS had been years in the making, its progenitors and architects deeply implicated in the waves of sectarian violence that had nearly ripped Iraq apart several times over in the years since the American-led invasion of 2003. And it was two months prior to these videos, in June 2014, that Da'ish had declared a caliphate in territory carved from Iraq and Syria. Shortening its name from *al-Dawla al-Islamiyya fi'l-'Irāq wa'l-Shām* [the Islamic State in Iraq and Syria] to *al-Dawla al-Islamiyya*, ISIS demanded that devout Muslims around the world swear an oath of allegiance [*bay'a*] to it and its ruler, Abu Bakr al-Baghdadi.[5] But

---

gesture of solidarity with those Muslims who intentionally refuse to repeat and legitimize their claim to the name "the Islamic State." The alternation between Da'ish and ISIS is more pragmatic, in the interest of accessibility and avoidance of repetitive tedium. There are, however, direct quotations in the following pages that refer to the group as either the Islamic State or ISIL, where the "L" renders *al-Shām* as the Levant, the French term for the region.

3. Packer, "Friend Flees the Horror of ISIS." ISIS targeted the ethno-religious group as "devil worshipers." Al Jazeera identifies Yazidis as adherents of an ancient Mesopotamian faith, but its origins are uncertain. Salih and van Wilgenburg, "Iraqi Yazidis." Records of their persecution date back to at least 637 CE. The link between such persecution and recurrent characterizations of Yazidis by Muslims as "devil-worshipers" also has a long history. Naby, "Yazidis."

4. The particular group of British and US hostages killed around this time included American aid worker Peter Kassig. Kassig is much less well-known than the others in the group, and the exact circumstances of his execution remain unknown. It seems likely that Da'ish had intended to stage his execution in the same way as the others, but something seems to have gone very wrong. I will return to Kassig later.

5. Defined historically, the caliphate [*khilāfa*] is the institution of legitimate Muslim political rule that began in 632 CE when, upon the death of the Prophet Muhammad, Abu Bakr became the new head of the Islamic community. It continued in one form or another until

it was these slickly produced beheading videos, circulated instantly, endlessly, and everywhere by way of digital technologies, that made ISIS a household name globally.

The immediate meaning and purpose of these videos seemed to require neither translation nor interpretation: the executions were acts of retribution for American attacks on Daʿish, each hostage used as leverage to make it stop. Given official US rhetoric eschewing all dealings with terrorists, there seemed little chance that these videos and threats, individually or collectively, would secure an end to the air strikes.[6] For many, this served as reassuring evidence that ISIS leaders were detached from reality, humanity, or both, in thrall to self-destructive delusions of grandeur, addicted to the pornographic "pleasures of killing" that destined them for defeat or, like demons from the netherworld, driven to an unprecedented savagery by an "insatiable bloodlust."[7]

Yet this leadership, comprised primarily of well-trained former Iraqi military men and experienced radical Islamist fighters, proved fairly savvy, a point made repeatedly in strategic assessments and news reports characterizing Daʿish as remarkably resilient and highly adaptable.[8] Moreover, interviews with released European hostages who had shared Foley's internment reveal how quickly their captors learned of US (and UK) refusal to "play ball" in ISIS's profitable hostage-for-ransom ventures.[9] As Daʿish leadership included former Baʿathist officers

1924, when it was formally abolished by the architect of the Turkish state, Mustafa Kemal. But the caliphate is an ideal and aspiration as well as an historical institution; see below.

6. At the same time, scholars have noted a significant gap between the actual practices of US presidents and official American refusal to negotiate with terrorists or pay ransom. Buhite contends that no US president in the twentieth century has faithfully carried out such policy or delivered effectively on pledges of swift retribution. Buhite, *Lives at Risk*, 199.

7. Filkins, "Death of Steven Sotloff"; Reardon, "ISIL and the Management of Savagery." ISIS has been consistently described as distinctively and uniquely savage, yet the extreme forms of violence for which it became widely known are far from novel or unprecedented. See Ahram, "Sexual and Ethnic Violence"; "Sexual Violence and the Making of ISIS," 59–60; Allen et al., *Without Sanctuary*; Campbell, "Horrific Blindness"; and Fujii, "Puzzle of Extra-Lethal Violence."

8. McFate, "ISIS Defense in Iraq and Syria"; Kilcullen, *Blood Year*, esp. 122–25. See also the conclusion of this chapter.

9. Callimachi, "Horror Before the Beheadings." The August 2014 issue of ISIS's English-language *Dabiq* contains what it calls "The Complete Message from James Foley," *Dabiq* 3, 38–40. There are slight but revealing differences between the printed and the spoken script. The *Dabiq* text, for example, accuses the United States of rejecting multiple opportunities to secure Foley's release. In this version, Foley's script refers to other countries with similar

who had once been trained by Washington and were well-acquainted with its strategies and habits, it's probable that ISIS already suspected that American officials would not comply, even at the time that the videos were made.[10]

So understood, what may have once seemed a straightforward question with an easy answer is neither. In the close reading that follows, I show that the visual rhetoric of these videos expresses a retaliatory humiliation unrecognized by the usual terms, paradigms, and explanatory frameworks. If this reading is persuasive, questions about the meaning and purpose of these meticulously staged and filmed executions also become questions about the visual mode of humiliation rhetoric they contain, what it says, and how it works politically, affectively, and digitally.

To even ask such questions is, of course, to presume that there *is* some meaning and purpose that may be identified and analyzed. These are also the questions guiding the previous chapter, but the infamy of ISIS and the shock of visual violence these videos depict tend to render them morally suspect. For some, taking these videos as rhetorics in need of analysis demonstrates an indifference to evil at best and at worst, constitutes an *apologia* for savagery both antithetical to human existence and inimical to rational analysis.[11]

As Murad Idris has argued, distinctions between permissible and "savage" violence are power-laden, implicated in hierarchies with histories that establish

---

policies against negotiating with terrorists acceding to the demands necessary for the release of their compatriots, "while I and the other Americans hopelessly waited for selfish politicians who are void of any compassion to decide our fate."

10. Cronin, "ISIS Is Not a Terrorist Group." Still others—e.g., Filkins, "Death of Steven Sotloff"—contend that, because the execution videos were so obviously ill-suited to obtain the purposes ascribed to them, they *must* have been actively courting additional US attacks, perhaps to drive home to local populations the need for state order—even ISIS's bloody version of it. Yet it seems unlikely that veteran Da'ish strategists would risk so much to demonstrate the benefits of order to populations who had already lost so much to chaotic violence.

11. See, for example, Anonymous, "Mystery of ISIS." Such predetermined conclusions must be situated within a longstanding discourse exemplified by Timothy Furnish's claim that Islam is a "religion of the sword with the blade forever at the throat of the unbeliever." Furnish's article has been cited and recited as the main source on the Islamic tradition in regard to beheadings since the videos began circulating. Furnish, "Beheading in the Name of Islam," 51–57. For example, this discourse posits instances of violence by Muslims as evidence that Islamic doctrine demands violence. By contrast, instances of Christian violence are depicted as isolated acts of deranged individuals. It also presumes that, as guarantor of world peace, any US violence may be regrettable but necessary. Christian conservatives such as Phyllis Schlafly have even argued that the Christian Crusades were legitimate and defensive wars aimed at reclaiming lands Muslim had stolen. Schafly, "Christians Are Better, Regardless of the Facts."

whose violence is considered legitimate and against whom, and then underwrite aggression against such savages as necessary for peace.[12] Among other things, this means that banishing such questions as morally dangerous or offensive does not banish the violence to which they refer; it simply permits distinctions overstuffed with ready-made answers to fill the void left by the absence of actual inquiry and cedes explanatory work to security, military, and terrorism experts. Yet these questions aren't critical simply because they're unavoidable. They matter because such shortcuts to grasping the past misapprehend the present.

As the "raison d'être of terrorism studies remains tied to raison d'état," expertise in "jihadi"[13] tactics, propaganda, doctrine, and membership tends to be determined by the logic of strategic utility in the service of national security, even when experts' grasp of the subjects far exceeds such discursive constraints.[14] Such invariant logic had already established a consensus about what "jihadist beheadings" mean and do long before ISIS emerged: all videos of this sort are deliberately manipulative and demagogic propaganda designed to achieve strategic objectives—in this instance, to deter US air strikes, recruit new fighters, and "sow terror" among enemies.[15] Already overdetermined, this conclusion has been stated

12. Idris, *War for Peace.*

13. While the term "jihadism" is now ubiquitous, it obscures more than clarifies the subject it aims to name by reducing the Arabic word *jihād*, which can denote all kinds of struggle and striving, to violence.

14. Li, "Jihadism Anti-Primer." One case in point is Lentini and Bakashmar's "Jihadist Beheading." Submitted for publication in April 2006, the article draws on the emergence of beheadings during the Chechen Wars, and the resurgence of the practice during the Iraq war, (1) to recognize the historically contingent and politically specific objectives that occasion a particular beheading, but also (2) to identify a range of strategic objectives common to jihadist beheadings, prime among them recruiting supporters, psychologically terrorizing enemies, obtaining ransom payments, hampering foreign investment, and discrediting transitional states. Military and strategic analyses of the ISIS beheading videos have a narrower sense of the objectives at play, emphasizing the twin goals of recruitment and intimidation of enemies near and far. This is true despite the new emphasis on analyzing the dynamics of cyberwarfare in which ISIS seems to be unusually adept. See Siboni, Cohen, and Koren, "Islamic State's Strategy in Cyberspace," 129.

15. See for example O'Shaughnessy, "Selling Terror"; Campbell, "Use of Beheadings by Fundamentalist Islam"; Lentini and Bakashmar, "Jihadist Beheadings"; Mosendz, "Beheadings as Terror Marketing"; Siboni, Cohen, and Koren, "Islamic State's Strategy in Cyberspace"; Stern and Berger, *Isis.* Even those who emphasize the distinction between, for example, the visual violence in such ISIS acts of communication and other kinds of radical Islamist violence focus on the "strategic media functions" of propaganda. See Tinnes, "Although the (Dis-) Believers Dislike It," 76. On the current connotations of "propaganda," see chapter 2, the section "Making Men."

so frequently and with such certainty as to make further examination of the particular features of the videos seem not only unnecessary but perverse.

But perhaps perversity is underrated. After all, this conclusion provides no account of *how* precisely these videos work, to *whom* they are addressed, and *what* about them hails audiences out of disparate peoples from which they can draw new recruits, or among whom they can "sow terror." There's little effort to analyze the visual mode of this violence or the operations that constitute its visceral power—among them a rhetoric of humiliation that works to conjure, exhort, and provoke specific audiences. Questions about why the executions in these videos are so very carefully scripted, staged, and edited, while the actual beheadings are off-screen and unfilmed remain unexplored, the purposes they disclose unrecognized. In short, such a conclusion moves immediately from cause to consequence, rendering invisible or irrelevant avenues of inquiry not susceptible to the logic of instrumental rationality, and its primary focus on the most efficient means to reach a desired end. That includes inquiry into the specific politics and purposes scrubbed from this account by its very operating assumptions.

In keeping with the purposes of this inquiry, I take the videos of Foley and Sotloff as rhetorical expressions in need of interpretation rather than as tactics solely legible in terms of an instrumental rationality framed by a calculus of national security. I say *solely* because, as will become clear, there are reasons to see these videos as instruments of deterrence, retaliation, and recruitment. The problem with such accounts is less that they're wholly wrong, but rather that they are structured by a logic that at once renders them incomplete and conceals the absences they contain. In other words, deterrence, retaliation, and recruitment do not exhaust all possible or even plausible purposes, but by homology they render the videos weapons in which all parts are assumed to contribute toward a single purpose. What it says and does is constituted as a relation between means and ends; inquiry requires filling in the blanks and assessing the fit between the tactic deployed and the outcome it achieves or fails to reach. In these terms, the question never arises about whether and to what extent the verbal rhetoric and the visual rhetoric—that is, matters of composition, production techniques, symbolic and dramaturgical features, religious and pop culture references, narrative structure, pacing, choices of casting, clothing, siting, props, and the like—may actually be different.

This means that close reading of these videos implicates several additional questions. Given the dominance of this conclusion and its structuring logic, what analytic tools can make both the verbal and visual rhetoric of these videos legible? What does such legibility disclose not only about what these videos say but also about how they work? Questions about how they work require taking account of the unprecedented networks of interconnectivity, simultaneity, ubiquity, interactivity, recursivity, and user-generated content into which these videos were inserted by way of digital technology.[16] This, in turn, raises the crucial question: how does the networked delivery of these particular enactments of retaliatory humiliation constitute the relation between the images repetitively circulated and the audiences addressed?

In the introduction, I referred to three primary modes of expression—verbal, visual, and embodied—that these expressions of humiliation straddle, and suggested that they roughly correspond to the three substantive chapters of this book. The "texts" in this chapter exemplify and disrupt both sets of classifications. The videos are most obviously instances of visual rhetoric, but, as the following analysis shows, all three modes of expression entangle in them. Marwan Kraidy has pointed out that video in particular "has affordances that help it circulate widely: the ability not only to post, re-tweet, share, and comment but also to play, stop, continue, rewind, fast forward, complete, replay, and repeat."[17] As videos, these texts might be distinguished from all the others in this book but for the obvious fact that digital media is central to the Egyptian archive in chapters 4 and 5, and the perhaps less obvious fact that the books initially published in print and the songs performed live now also circulate digitally.

These messy overlaps and disruptions are a help rather than a hindrance, as they draw attention to how humiliation rhetoric is currently circulated. While there will always be important differences between reading a book and watching moving images on a smartphone, these rhetorics show just how much the gap between these genres, modes, forms of publication, and modes of circulation has narrowed. This observation may seem self-evident, but making it explicit points to the way questions about digital circulation and repetition posed most clearly by these videos are also raised by all the other archives in this book.

Answers to these questions do not depend upon matters of reception among different constituencies, the intentions of those who wrote and directed the videos, or the motivations of the tech experts who maximized the speed and reach of circulation. These are all important areas of inquiry; many are unknowable, others may still emerge in time. But much as inquiry into what humiliation says and does more generally does not depend upon measuring resonances that resist quantification, neither the coherence nor the persuasiveness of the following analysis depends upon such data.

16. Kaempf, "Mediatisation of War in a Transforming Global Media Landscape," 599.
17. Kraidy, "Projectilic Image," 1200.

In referring to what the videos do here, I mean to inquire into what such visual rhetoric performs in two senses that may be distinguished temporally and spatially. The first entails examining what the violence performed in the videos enacts, which includes not only what is seen but also what is outside the frame and unfilmed. The videos refer backward in time to what was done earlier to make them, as well as to what is usually envisioned as the main event—the beheadings—that are marked not by presence but by absence, by the temporal ellipses *in* the narratives. The second entails moving forward and out temporally and spatially, to investigate the way this particular combination of retaliatory humiliation and digital delivery makes possible a specific, personal, and viscerally immediate modality of experience out of the foreshortening of space between audience and event already characteristic of our "heteropolar media landscape."[18] It is to speculate about how such a modality of experience can transfigure watchers into witnesses that are vicariously complicit in the enactment of humiliation onscreen.

These questions collectively bring into focus areas of inquiry largely foreclosed by the dominant account, including the very aspects of visuality and violence expressive of retaliatory humiliation and relatively undertheorized in scholarship on politics.[19] They articulate the terms in which this analysis of the meaning and purpose of these videos will proceed, and specify where, how, and why these terms must depart from most that have come before. As I argued in the introduction, theorizing what humiliation says and does requires attention to the blockages that enable particular meanings and associations to prevail. Just so, these questions trace the conceptual and methodological blockages at work in the logic structuring the dominant account of these videos, enabling its substantive absences to appear in sharp relief, much like a latent photographic image suddenly made visible.

Drawing upon these terms, I bring into sharp relief a disjuncture between the verbal and visual rhetoric of these videos. While the verbal rhetoric largely hews

18. Kaempf, "Mediatisation of War," 587. As Kaempf describes it, the emergence of digital new media technology has transformed a previously multipolar media landscape into a heteropolar one characterized by the "multiplication and simultaneous diversification of structurally different media actors."

19. This is in sharp contrast to scholarship on visuality in communication studies and critical security studies. For examples of the former, see Kraidy, "Projectilic Image" and "Terror, Territoriality, Temporality." For examples of the latter (in addition to those already cited), see Hansen, "How Images Make World Politics"; "Theorizing the Image for Security Studies," 51–74; Williams, "Words, Images, Enemies," 511–31; and Campbell, "Geopolitics and Visuality"; "Cultural Governance and Pictorial Resistance."

to the logic of instrumental rationality, I argue that the visual rhetoric is an instance of performative violence.[20] Performative violence refers to the visual, symbolic, and communicative dimensions of political violence; it foregrounds the ways violence can be both an act of "communication and dramatization" as well as an instrument that aims at injury and death.[21] Performative violence signals not that such violence is somehow unreal or simulated, but rather that its meaning and purpose are simultaneously articulated and accomplished in its very enactment.

In the previous chapter, this understanding of the performative was part of the discussion of "performative victory" in radical Islamist humiliation rhetoric. In the context where the enemies are many and the obstacles daunting, I argued that such humiliation rhetoric weds exhortation to the reassuring guarantee of success. Despite enormous odds, victory is achieved the moment the hierarchy of humiliation is inverted: publicly driving one's humiliator into the dirt, whether literally or symbolically, instantly dissipates the specter of impotence. Primarily expressed in terms of retaliatory humiliation in the previous chapter, such performative victory also turns out to be critical to the emancipatory conception of dignity/*karāma* I develop in the final chapter. There the refusal to be what those with power decide is also performative reclamation of the power to shape the script of one's own life.[22]

In this chapter, performative violence works as both a lens and a concept. As a lens, it brings into focus the different message and specific repertoire of meanings at work in this visual rhetoric. As a concept, performative violence *is* what this different message does—and, as Kraidy's excellent work demonstrates, it does more than one thing.[23] In the following analysis, I show how such visual

20. The conception of performative violence I draw upon here and elaborate below is from Juris, "Violence Performed and Imagined." See also Riches, *Anthropology of Violence*; Juergensmeyer, *Terror in the Mind of God*, 125–27; and Butler, *Gender Trouble*, on the performativity of gender.

21. Juris, "Violence Performed and Imagined," 415.

22. To some extent, retaliatory humiliation links the discussion of performative victory in the previous chapter to the performative violence in this one. But while such "victory" and "violence" may converge in specific instances, they're not interchangeable, conceptually or empirically.

23. Kraidy analyzes different ISIS execution videos to bring into focus what he calls the "global networked affect of terror" in such ultraviolent videos whereby the "spectacle of death" triggers fears and intensities in the body even before it can be expressed in words. Kraidy, "Projectilic Image," 1207. See also Kraidy, "Terror, Territoriality, Temporality," 6.

violence enacts the retaliatory humiliation integral to the emergent scaffolding in the preceding chapter. Articulated visually through the particular repertoire on which ISIS draws, humiliation here is the imposition of impotence on Islam and Muslims by those with greater and undeserved power; retaliatory humiliation is the redress this condition demands; and redress is restorative action that both performs and produces an inversion of this relation.

As in the previous chapter, the meaning, significance, and power of retaliatory humiliation in these videos is not elaborated in the form of an explicit argument. It is articulated here by way of the visual inscription of impotence upon male bodies whose public subjugation is symbolically converted into that of the American nation publicly driven to its knees. This performance simultaneously constitutes the ISIS executioner, and the sovereign power he represents and serves, as virile, fearless, and dominant, its march toward primacy inevitable.

From the very outset of this book, the power at work in the relation between humiliator and humiliated has been gendered male. Men have symbolically or literally been the primary occupants of this relation, and humiliation has been continually articulated on and through male bodies. These videos draw out and amplify an interrelation largely implicit in the preceding analyses, the way humiliation genders and engenders sovereignty. If, as is often said, female bodies are the terrain over which cultural battles are waged, this reading points to male bodies as the territory on which sovereignty is symbolically and literally performed. Inasmuch as the retaliatory humiliation inscribed on American male bodies renders the fluid ground of sovereignty legible, it shows how the visceral power of these videos works independently of the state territory ISIS no longer controls.

These arguments unfold through a close reading of the videos at the heart of this chapter. But in the following section, I first situate this reading in relation to scholarship on visuality, political violence, and sovereignty on which it draws and to which it directly speaks. I specify the conception of sovereignty entailed in these arguments to differentiate it from a range of competing and/or complementary definitions that populate distinct disciplinary debates and even differentiate political science subfields from one another. For the purposes of this analysis, sovereignty primarily refers to the power over life and death that has consistently been a central prerogative of sovereign authority past and present. This is so despite the ways in which modern liberal states in particular have increasingly concealed it, whether behind thick prison walls, euphemistic rhetoric, or sanitized images of war.

The final section turns to the question of how these enactments of retaliatory humiliation work once circulated instantly and everywhere by way of digital networks. This question sharply poses another, this one about relevance, that lurks throughout the opening pages of this chapter. Given that the caliphate ISIS had claimed in territory straddling Iraq and Syria has been completely dismantled, why focus on ISIS, let alone these videos? As I turn to the significance of these particular videos in the next section, here I posit two answers to the more general question about the relevance of ISIS at this moment.

The immediate policy answer is that the dismantling of Daʿish's caliphate has failed to defeat ISIS itself. Well before the fall of its final stronghold, Daʿish had already pivoted in anticipation of shrinking territory and diminished revenues, refocusing its energies and resources elsewhere. As Atwan points out, moreover, ISIS fighters "long ago developed the technique of melting away from battles they cannot win only to reappear elsewhere where they can prevail."[24] Various threat assessments have noted that the complex conditions contributing to its rise and appeal in the first place have hardly disappeared; they also stress the strength of regional branches, particularly in places where a weak central government is unable to prevent the rise of multiple claimants to authority.[25] So it is that the very moment Trump claimed credit for ISIS's destruction, *The Washington Post* reported escalating attacks by groups declaring affiliation with the Islamic State in Mozambique and Niger.[26]

But while this is an important answer, it's not the entire answer. The matter of how these videos work doesn't necessarily depend upon the existence of a territorial caliphate. As the heyday of legitimate Muslim rule modeled a timeless ideal of an Islamic state, ISIS has always invoked "the caliphate" to recall a history that also works aspirationally. As "celluloid heroes never really die,"[27] the figures and

24. Atwan, *Islamic State*, 218.

25. See, for example, Office of the Director of National Intelligence, Annual Threat Assessment of the U.S. Intelligence Community, 2024; Wilson Center, "ISIS: Resilient on Sixth Anniversary"; Sherko, "How Islamic State Ideology Contributes to Its Resilience." A 2022 report issued by the Carnegie Endowment for International Peace contends that the US withdrawal from Syria ordered by Trump in 2019 has been a boon to the group, and notes that the "series of multi-pronged attacks in Syria and its neighboring Iraq, highlights ISIS's resolve to model its post-caliphate strategy for insurgencies that are not necessarily contingent on territorial control." Al-Hajj, "Insurgency of ISIS in Syria."

26. Paquette, Mekhennet, and Warrick, "ISIS Attacks Surge in Africa."

27. Davies, "Celluloid Heroes."

performances within the videos are forever preserved as they circulate continuously over time, even as changed conditions and differently situated audiences constitute their significance and purpose in altered terms. Symbolic enactments meant to exhort spectators to join the epic project of building ISIS's Islamic State on earth now easily serve as repositories for aspirations to establish the next caliphate somewhere, somehow. By the same token, ISIS videos that once summoned and directed *mujāhidīn* from all over the world to travel to Syria to fight for the Islamic State now inspire would-be soldiers for Daʿish to fight the *kuffār* [unbelievers] right where they are, by whatever means available.

More to the point, the arguments here suggest how circulation and repetition work to revivify the affective power of the retaliatory humiliation these videos depict, and do so as time itself attenuates the connection between the videos and the specific events that precipitated them. As I'll argue, this eases the way for millions of "users" to interpolate themselves into the enactment, either as humiliator or humiliated. This reading also dramatizes how the retaliatory humiliation articulated on and through male bodies can constitute such bodies as the terrain on which sovereignty is performed. The shift from the "terrain" of land to movable bodies points to the way in which these videos can continually perform ISIS's sovereignty and diminish the importance of a territorial state that no longer exists. At a historical moment in which the establishment of new sovereign states has become rare, a great deal of politics has become virtual, and the rhetoric of humiliation pervades public discourse like a lingua franca, the implications of this shift extend well beyond ISIS's caliphate.

Visuality, Violence, and Sovereignty

The arguments advanced here draw upon and participate in several broader, overlapping streams of inquiry. The first is scholarship theorizing the ways in which new media technologies have not only redefined the scale and speed by which visual images are circulated, but also reshaped the conditions and intensities of human engagement with them.[28] Second, this reading can be understood as part of longstanding efforts by scholars and writers located in diverse fields to articulate meanings and modalities of violence that the logic of instrumental rationality occludes, as well as to develop terminology and tools to capture

28. Benski and Fisher, *Internet and Emotions*; Hillis, Paasonen, and Petit, *Networked Affect*; Karatzogianni and Kuntsman, *Digital Cultures and the Politics of Emotion.*

them.[29] As Lee Ann Fujii rightly points out in her analysis of what she terms "extra-lethal violence," political science research into violence has become increasingly sophisticated and nuanced in recent years, yet much of it remains wedded to rationalist assumptions that render matters of *how* violence is performed, displayed, and circulated beside the point.[30]

The third is the growing literature on visuality among scholars of politics, a somewhat belated corrective to the striking fact that, as Mark Reinhardt puts it, while the "saturation of politics by visual technologies, media, and images has reached unprecedented levels, this development scarcely registers in American political science."[31] Jacques Rancière has pointed out that, while images "do not supply weapons for battles . . . [they do] help sketch new configurations of what can be seen, what can be said and what can be thought and, consequently a new landscape of the possible."[32] In this vein, a growing body of scholarship in Critical Security Studies focuses on how images can and do refigure the politics of war.[33] Such work does so, not by establishing direct causal links, but by documenting how visual images can reshape interpretive frameworks that, in turn, reconstitute the realm of what is politically thinkable and doable.[34]

Simone Molin Friis uses this approach to show how these particular videos played an outsized role in refiguring the terms through which Americans and Britons constituted Da'ish. Friis argues that the sequence of videos from Foley to Henning functioned as "visual facts" within the transformation of British and American state responses to ISIS.[35] The study specifically tracks the way the videos operated as pivots from Obama's January 2014 likening of the group to a junior varsity version of al-Qa'ida, to depictions of it in September of that year as a "cancer" and "growing threat" to the region requiring containment, and finally to American and British representations of it as "savage, inexplicable,

29. Just three examples are Arendt, *On Violence*; Blok, "Enigma of Senseless Violence"; and Fanon, *Wretched of the Earth*.

30. Fujii, "Puzzle of Extra-Lethal Violence," 411.

31. Reinhardt, "Theorizing the Event of Photography." Reinhardt argues that "political theory is at best a partial exception" to this "professional deformation."

32. Rancière, *Emancipated Spectator*, 103.

33. See Friis, "'Beyond Anything We Have Ever Seen'"; Hansen, "Theorizing the Image for Security Studies"; "How Images Make World Politics"; Campbell, "Cultural Governance and Pictorial Resistance"; "Horrific Blindness"; "Geopolitics and Visuality"; Kaempf, "Mediatisation of War"; and Williams, "Words, Images, Enemies."

34. Bleiker, "Visual Assemblages," 76; Friis, "'Beyond Anything We Have Ever Seen,'" 731.

35. Friis, "'Beyond Anything We Have Ever Seen,'" 734–36.

nihilistic," the "embodiment of evil" that is "beyond anything we have ever seen," requiring no less than complete destruction.[36]

Friis points out that an NBC News/*Wall Street Journal* poll conducted when the still images from these videos began circulating widely in the media indicated a sharp increase in the number of Americans who saw the United States as less safe in the wake of the videos than at any other period since 9/11.[37] Even more striking is the contrast between the results of this September 2014 survey and a POLITICO poll of battleground voters conducted in July 2014—before the videos circulated—in regard to views about foreign military intervention.[38] The July poll found Americans from both left and right skeptical of military engagements overseas and opposed to further US entanglements in both Eastern Europe and the Middle East by large margins. The September survey, by contrast, reported that two-thirds of Americans were convinced that aggressive military action against ISIS was necessary for US security.[39] A contrast between PEW Research surveys in 2002 and 2014 is similarly instructive: while 25 percent of Americans viewed Islam as more encouraging of violence than other religions in the wake of 9/11, that figure rose to 50 percent following the circulation of the ISIS videos.[40]

Many of the publications in this growing area of scholarship focus on still photographs or, in the case of Hansen, cartoons, rather than on moving images.[41] This is also the case in Friis's superb study, where the videos similarly register as primarily iconic—and still—images rather than as staged and unfolding performances.[42] Focusing on how these videos work as visual icons—circulating

36. Obama, "Statement by the President on ISIL"; Kerry, "Murder of James Foley"; Cameron, "David Cameron Issues Statement on the Execution of David Haines"; Hagel, "Department of Defense Press Briefing."

37. NBC News/*Wall Street Journal* Survey Study #14901.

38. Politico Poll, July 3–13, 2014.

39. A UK poll taken in the wake of the videos reported similar results: previous opposition to airstrikes in Iraq was swamped by a groundswell of support for destroying ISIS. Graham-Harrison, "UK Attacks on Isis Met with Public Support."

40. The PEW findings for 2002–14 are included in their report "U.S. Muslims Concerned About Their Place in Society."

41. Hansen, "How Images Make World Politics."

42. It is no accident that several of these studies invoke the language of the "performative" to shift the analytic frame from the instrumental to the communicative and visual. Fujii, "Puzzle of Extra-Lethal Violence," 413–14; Friis, "'Beyond Anything We Have Ever Seen,'" 731; Hansen, "Theorizing the Image for Security Studies," 60. This is so despite the fact that they understand the lineage, presuppositions, and operations of "the performative" quite differently from one another. Friis, for example, appears to use what she calls the "performative approach"

as screen grabs, for example—in the reframing of American and British responses to Daʿish, the matter of what's performed *within* them is relevant only to the extent that it bears on the analysis of which "facts" of war they help enable or occlude, and the range of responses that will subsequently appear rational and legitimate.

Taking the measure of these videos requires recognizing critical differences among visual genres and how they work, even when, as in the case at hand, the subject matter defies easy categorization. It is helpful here to consider Hansen's theorization of how various visual genres—from art to photojournalism, cartoons to documentaries—are constituted very differently in relation to "reality," the political, audience response, and temporal engagement.[43]

Clearly, these videos have an uneasy relationship to the "real." The scenes are obviously staged, the shots edited, the speeches apparently scripted. Yet the clips can't be exclusively classified as fiction or even agitprop strictly defined. Entrapped within the camera frame are unwilling performers who are not actors; their capture, degradation, and decapitation are all too real, although they are also staged. In this ambivalent relation to the real, they mimic the photographs from Abu Ghraib they were intended to echo (more on this below). At the same time, the temporal requirements of watching the videos are unlike viewing even the most horrifying still image or offensive cartoon: at least part of the ordeal of the hostages appears to unfold before our eyes in real time, and no shortcut through that progression can grasp it. This is critical to recognizing their visual power—particularly, as will become clear, when they travel forward and outward by way of digital technologies.

While the execution segments contain a visual unfolding, the entire arc of the videos trace a wholesale transposition of power and status. As I suggested earlier, the retaliatory humiliation enacted on the bodies of the condemned men in these videos performs and produces an inversion of power in two different registers. First, as the visual components convert the symbolic, psychic, and physical humiliation of Foley and Sotloff into that of the American nation, it performs ISIS's dominance through the symbolic emasculation of the United

---

to visual imagery as a synonym for a poststructuralist approach, a recognition of the lineage of "performativity" from J. L. Austin (the philosopher of language who developed the conception of the "performative utterance"), through Jacques Derrida and Judith Butler, among others. By contrast, Fujii refers to "performative analysis" in a fairly narrow way, largely stripped of this lineage and epistemological freight, as a framework that "focuses on the *process* of putting on a show," 414 (emphasis in the original).

43. Hansen, "Theorizing the Image for Security Studies," 60–62.

States. In this way, their bodies become the tableau upon which American humiliation and guilt are literally and publicly inscribed. Importantly, the *mode* of dominance is not random brutality; it is scripted to ritually mimic the signs and practices of sovereignty, that is, the power over life and death central to the conception of sovereignty in the work of Thomas Hobbes and Michel Foucault, among others. Herein lies the second register: the videos as a whole stage a familiar confrontation between sovereign state and violent outlaw only to invert the symbolic relation between them, a transposition that places the United States in the structural position of mass murderer, regicide, rogue state, and terrorist.

Given the extensive scholarship on sovereignty, as well as on Foucault and Hobbes, it's necessary to be clear about what this analysis does *not* aim to do. This is not intended to address the extensive debates among political theorists about the nature of sovereignty in general, the virtue or demerits of liberal or democratic variants, or conceptions associated with specific theorists such as Schmitt or Hobbes. Nor is it an evaluation of ISIS's brief exercise in state building in light of such theories. What's crucial to my argument is this familiar, if now less frequently invoked, conception of sovereignty, particularly as famously thematized in Foucault's *Discipline and Punish*. Here sovereignty as the power over life and death is rooted literally and symbolically in the body of the king, whose will throughout a given territory may be imposed and punished with the kind of public, ritualized, and excessive violence by which "injured sovereignty is reconstituted."[44]

My analysis draws upon a specific aspect of Foucault's argument for clearly circumscribed purposes. This largely entails setting aside the evolution of sovereign power—monarchical, panoptic/disciplinary, and biopower—delineated in his work as a whole, with one crucial exception. Precisely because of this evolutionary account, to even invoke Foucault's anatomization of monarchical sovereignty here positions ISIS as a kind of premodern revenant before the argument has even begun. Yet in his lecture of March 17, 1976, Foucault depicts what elsewhere appears as sequential stages in a historical evolution of sovereign power as complementary and coexisting modalities of power. In Foucault's phrasing, new techniques do not replace, erase, or exclude those that currently exist, but rather penetrate, permeate, infiltrate, and dovetail into them.[45]

Without overstating the case, I want to suggest that the excessiveness of reprisal Foucault associates with monarchical sovereignty is similarly at work in these videos, albeit for different reasons and elaborated under radically

44. Foucault, *Discipline & Punish*, 47–48.

45. Foucault, *Society Must Be Defended*, 241–42. See also Bargu, *Starve and Immolate*.

different circumstances. The executions are ostensibly justified in the name of a caliphate whose leaders sought to drape both its founding and policies in Islamic legal cover.[46] There's a large body of *fiqh* [Islamic jurisprudence] devoted to deriving from the sacred texts different categories of crimes, offenses, and penalties that mediate between God's will and the shifting needs and circumstances of His community. But as with the executions Foucault analyzes in such graphic detail, the "theater of hell" in these videos ultimately has little to do with the Islamic juridical tradition or with the restoration of balance.

Instead, the executions are ritualized displays of disproportionate force over the condemned who, by the very logic of the ritual, are meticulously, relentlessly, reduced to impotence. Once circulated across social media platforms increasingly functioning as a virtual public square, they come to constitute the kind of public, ceremonial violence by which the domination and invincibility of ISIS is performed and produced for the horror and satisfaction not only of a general spectatorship, but of two differently situated audiences in particular: American men meant to be humiliated by the public emasculation of their male compatriots, and "Sunni Muslim men" meant to be summoned into existence as a community by vicariously sharing in the reclamation of power the ISIS executioner partly performs in their name.

This is precisely why the affective power of these symbolic enactments and inversions of sovereignty do not require the continuing existence of the particular territorial state they were initially designed to serve. This is also why Foucault's focus on the body as a site of sovereignty is particularly instructive in this context. These enactments and inversions decouple ISIS's sovereignty from the territory they no longer control, shifting the primary ground on which it's enacted from terrain associated with a specific location to the bodies of men already dead but whose humiliation can serve endlessly as the site of ISIS's circulating sovereignty.[47]

There are overlapping narratives and logics that help constitute the executions in these terms. Foremost among them is Da'ish's determination to restore in the

46. Al-Baghdadi claimed his legitimacy was grounded in (among other things) the principle of *bay'a*, the oath of allegiance Muslims pledged to him, just as the first generations of Muslims pledged their loyalty to the first four caliphs (632–61) who led the *umma* following the death of the Prophet.

47. What I'm here describing as a shift might be rendered (inadequately) into Ahmed's metaphor of "stickiness": humiliation is "unstuck" from the Arab and Muslim bodies in the Abu Ghraib photographs that form the critical background to these enactments and attached to American men.

contemporary world what it regards as the Islamically just order of things. Any claim to restore in the present a paradigm or practice of the past is a remaking, and this one entails an appropriation of an especially partisan narrative about the distant past. In this account, the legacy of Sunni preeminence in Islamic history has been eclipsed by the rise and now global dominance of Christian, Zionist, and godless forces. These have colluded to deprive Sunnis of their political power, lives, jobs, security, and a sense of place in the historic heartlands of Islam, now entirely under the thumb of the depraved Shiʿi.

Restoring the right order of things requires the unflinching courage to do whatever it takes to unmake what is in accordance with what should be, namely, a united and powerful Islamic state headquartered in lands that represent the historic pinnacle of Muslim rule; governed by Sunni leaders whose moral guidance, political acumen, and military might render the entire *umma* invulnerable to predations from the outside and corruption from within; and in which righteous Sunnis are again ascendant and all others know their place.

These enactments of retaliatory humiliation are critical steps in this restoration, as they both demonstrate and symbolically produce the inversion of domination that will soon prevail not just on camera but throughout the world. At the same time, these displays suture ISIS's version of a just order of things to a masculinist logic of sovereignty, one in which the assertion of state power domestically—in both senses of the word "domestic"—and against foreign enemies is constituted in terms of collective virility and impotence.[48]

This narrative and logic foreground the specific repertoires these enactments of humiliation express. The point here is not that humiliation is the only lens through which to read these images but rather that, in these particular videos, humiliation is an essential visual grammar through which a number of these other subtexts are expressed. Reading them closely as texts of visual rhetoric simultaneously draws attention to features of humiliation that recur across these chapters and show why each act of violence must be read carefully in context to unpack the rhetorics deployed, the audiences addressed, and the purposes in play.

48. Scholarship theorizing the gendered dimensions of the modern state has pointed to multiple masculinist logics that derive from different models of masculinity (from dominative to protectionist) that do different kinds of work. See, for example, Young, "Logic of Masculinist Protection"; Hooper, *Manly States*; Tickner, *Gender in International Relations*; Faludi, *Terror Dream*; Ferguson, "Cowboy Masculinity, Globalization, and the U.S. War on Terror"; Mann, *Sovereign Masculinity*.

As a group with multiple aspirations, diverse affiliates, far-flung loyalists, and last-minute martyrs, there's no single meaning, purpose, or explanation to all violent acts associated with the name ISIS. What follows, then, cannot stand in for an account of every Da'ish beheading nor even of all its productions with staged executions, although it can illuminate other instances by parallel or contrast. Just as these videos are carefully cast and scripted to work in particular ways for specific reasons, as will become clear, such elements are differently constituted in other ISIS execution propaganda, whether it's a hi-tech production meant to establish Da'ish as the only remaining Sunni bulwark against Shi'i power, or a low-fi video message demanding ransom for Japanese hostages.[49]

The focus on these particular videos requires one final and essential caveat. The greater attention given to, for example, the November 2015 attacks in Paris relative to those in Beirut obscures the extent to which those who have suffered most extensively from ISIS violence have been other Muslims as well as non-Muslim Arabs and Africans whose deaths have gone almost unnoticed by the same audiences understandably outraged by the Foley and Sotloff executions. In this context, analysis of these two particular videos risks reinforcing the conviction that White Euro-American male lives are valued more than others, that ISIS's violence is enacted most significantly upon Western bodies whose deaths are again marked, in Judith Butler's words, as publicly grievable, while the untold others who have died at the behest of Da'ish are unremarked, unnamed, and unmourned.[50]

As will become clear in the following pages, the focus here is a reflection not of the greater significance of American lives, but of the power the United States both exercises and symbolizes in the region. The current geopolitical power of the United States and its violent and blundering entanglements in the Middle East made it a specific source of grievance for Da'ish. At the same time, US self-positioning as guarantor of global order and peace is precisely why ISIS depicted it as just the most recent standard-bearer of a nation-state system whose legacy in the region is an unbroken chain of domination. Given this context, I'll argue

49. In January 2015, ISIS held for ransom and then executed freelance journalist Kenji Goto and private security consultant Haruna Yukawa. The messages issued in connection to these threats, demands, and killings are very different than the videos from Foley to Henning. There's no live video, no high-tech production, no drawn-out humiliation; one contains a still image and a recorded voice, the other an apparently manipulated image in which the victim is silent and both messages are shot against a white background, seemingly indoors.

50. Butler, *Frames of War*, 75. There are still others whose very absence is invisible, who are not only literally lost but *affectively* missing. Caspar and Moore, *Missing Bodies*, 3.

that it is *precisely* the fact that these victims were Americans and, moreover, men, that constitutes a central element of what the videos say and do.

ISIS's Visual Rhetoric of Humiliation

The first video opens in silence. Arabic script gracefully unfolds against a black background: *Bismillāh al-raḥmān al-raḥīm* (In the Name of Allah, the Merciful and Compassionate), the phrase that begins the Qur'ān, suggesting an Islamic imprimatur for what follows. Then, in Arabic and English, the sentence: "Obama authorizes military operations against the Islamic State, effectively placing America upon a slippery slope towards a new war front against Muslims."[51] The sharp sound of an electric surge abruptly shatters the silence and the screen flares from darkness to a brightly lit press conference. There stands President Barack Obama, announcing two US operations in Iraq, "targeted airstrikes to protect our American personnel," and air strikes against ISIS in a humanitarian operation to prevent the takeover of Irbil. Arabic subtitles run along the bottom, the production roughed up to look rudimentary or the transmission compromised.

A quick cut back to the black screen and the sound of the electric surge—what a channel switch might sound like from inside an analog television—and the screen opens up on a blurry black, white, and gray aerial view of explosions rippling out over unidentified territory. The hum of an airplane engine almost drowns out the sounds of a muffled American military transmission, but "air strikes standing by" can just barely be heard. Arabic and English writing in the left bottom of the screen explain: "American Aggression against the Islamic State." Then a gentle fade to black returns the screen to silence and "A Message to America" slowly appears, with the Arabic underneath.

At two minutes, the screen opens out to a crystal clear, high-resolution shot of James Foley, shaved face and head, barefoot, wrists cuffed behind his back, dressed in orange, kneeling to the side of his executioner who stands, clothed all in black, a leather gun holster under his left arm. They are outside, on an almost painfully bright day, somewhere dry and arid that could almost anywhere in Iraq or Syria. Foley has a microphone around his neck and he speaks scripted words either memorized or delivered by hidden teleprompter:

51. "A Message to America/*Risāla ilā Amrīkā*." The following sections include close readings of this video—commonly referred to as the Foley video—the Sotloff video ("A Second Message to America/*Risāla thāniya ilā Amrīkā*"), and the digital circulation of both. The citations here can be taken as authoritative for all subsequent references to these videos unless otherwise indicated.

> I call on my friends, family, and loved ones to rise up against my real killers: the US government. For what will happen to me is only a result of their complacency and criminality. My message to my beloved parents: save me some dignity and don't accept any meager compensation for my death from the same people who effectively hit the last nail in my coffin with their recent aerial campaign in Iraq. I call on my brother John, who is a member of the US Air Force: think about what you are doing. Think about the lives you destroy, including those of your own family. I call on you, John, think about who made the decision to bomb Iraq recently and kill those people, whoever they may have been. Think, John, who did they really kill? Did they think about me, you, or our family when they made that decision? I died that day, John. When your colleagues dropped that bomb on those people, they signed my death certificate. I wish I had more time. I wish I could have the hope of freedom and seeing my family once again. But that ship has sailed. I guess, all in all, I wish I wasn't American.

The screen fades to black. In the next shot, only the executioner speaks, and with a British accent. He brandishes a small knife as Foley grits his teeth. He addresses Obama directly:

> This is James Wright Foley, an American citizen of your country. As a government, you have been at the forefront of aggression towards the Islamic State. You have plotted against us and gone far out of your way to find reasons to interfere in our affairs. Today, your military air force is attacking us daily in Iraq. Your strikes have caused casualties amongst Muslims. You are no longer fighting an insurgency; we are an Islamic Army and a state that has been accepted by a large number of Muslims worldwide, so effectively, any aggression towards the Islamic State is an aggression towards Muslims from all walks of life who have accepted the Islamic caliphate as their leadership. So any attempt by you, Obama, to deny the Muslims their right of living in safety under the Islamic Caliphate, will result in the bloodshed of your people.

When done, the shot shifts and the executioner moves swiftly, slicing at the front of Foley's neck with a sawing motion. The screen fades quickly to black before the knife draws blood, fading up again on a shot of Foley's prone body, stomach down, severed head resting on his back. The camera slowly pans down the length of his body, steady, then fades into a shot of the executioner holding the collar of Steven Sotloff. Then the man the press would dub "Jihadi John"—subsequently identified as Briton Mohammed Emwazi—instructs the President: "The life of this American citizen, Obama, depends on your next decision."[52]

The rapid cuts, the clips of Obama promising vigilance, the aerial view of a bombing, crackling radio contact in which only the words "air strikes" are clear, shots with flickering light, rough transmission, and drained color will look oddly familiar—but only to some viewers, most likely a demographic that skews younger. These components deliberately evoke the opening credits to the Showtime series about terrorism, *Homeland*, an echo that shades into mimicry in the opening to the Sotloff video.

The Sotloff video opens with a grim and graying Obama at a press conference announcing that "the United States of America will continue to do what we must do to protect our people; we will be vigilant and we will be relentless. When people harm Americans anywhere, we do what's necessary to see that justice is done, and we act against ISIL, standing alongside others." The sharp sound of the electric surge, a quick cut to black and in silence: *Bismillāh al-raḥmān al-raḥīm*, followed by "A Second Message to America" in English and Arabic. Another quick cut and then the screen blazes open on Steven Sotloff, most of the ritualized elements of the Foley execution faithfully reassembled, with some critical variations: his head and face are stubbled with recent growth, and at first he's visible only from the chest up, almost dwarfed by a wall of black that looms to his right—the torso of the executioner, his hand in the bottom-right corner tightly gripping a serrated knife gleaming brightly in the sun. Sotloff speaks the script of his killers:

> I am Steven Joel Sotloff. I am sure you know exactly who I am by now, and why I am appearing before you. And now, it is time for my message. Obama, your foreign policy of intervention in Iraq was supposed to be for the preservation of American lives and interests. So why is it that I'm having to pay the price of your interference with my life? Am I not an American citizen? You've spent billions of US taxpayers' dollars and we've lost thousands of our troops in our previous fighting against the Islamic State. So where is

52. Emwazi was born in Kuwait in 1988, moved to the United Kingdom in 1994, grew up in London as a British citizen, and graduated from the University of Westminster with a degree in computer science. He reportedly experienced years of harassment by British security and intelligence agencies, as well as by comparable national agencies cooperating with the United Kingdom. Emwazi was to become the "star" of multiple Da'ish productions, featured in the beheading videos of Foley, Sotloff, Haines, and Henning, "Although the Disbelievers May Dislike It/*Law kariha al-kāfirūn*," and the like. He was killed on November 12, 2015, by a US airstrike in Raqqa, Syria.

> the American people's interest in reigniting this war? From what little I know about foreign policy, I remember a time when you cannot win an election without promising to bring our troops back home from Iraq and from Afghanistan, and to close down Guantánamo. Here you are now, Obama, nearing the end of your term and having achieved none of the above, and seemingly marching us, the American people, into a blazing fire.

As he speaks, a second camera is deployed for a wider shot, although Sotloff continues to speak to the first. The ritualistic echoes of the Foley spectacle are all now simultaneously visible: he's dressed in orange, hands cuffed behind him, kneeling at the feet of his executioner, as he speaks the words of his killers to accuse the president of his own country not only of his own death, but of all American deaths to follow. Sotloff's message is shorter than Foley's, and his killer's is also terse:

> I'm back, Obama, and I'm back because of your arrogant foreign policy toward the Islamic State, because of your insistence in continuing your bombings in [unclear] and the Mosul Dam despite our serious warnings. You, Obama, have yet to gain for your actions [unclear] another American citizen, so just as your missiles continue to strike our people, our knife will continue to strike the necks of your people.

With no fanfare, Emwazi moves to slice at Sotloff's neck, but his victim begins to struggle before the fade to black. The fade up reveals a familiar tableau, and the camera takes a swifter tour down Sotloff's blood-spattered body, head resting on his stomach. This is quickly followed by a shot of the next hostage, Briton David Hawthorne Haines, along with the warning: "We take this opportunity to warn those governments that have entered this evil alliance of America against the Islamic State to back off and leave our people alone."

The last words Foley and Sotloff are forced to speak in these stilted, macabre dramas are all about means and ends, and lest we miss the point, the executioner spells it out repeatedly: the United States must cease its attacks on Daʿish, or its citizens and those of its allies will be butchered, one by one. But there's also a visual rhetoric at work here, one that conveys meaning sometimes in tandem with, sometimes independently of the words spoken. As I argued earlier, this rhetoric is brought into sharp relief through the lens of the performative, and so it is through careful reading of the components of this performance that its meaning and significance are fully and completely elaborated. This reading is necessarily recursive, to now bring into sharp relief what had previously been subsumed into a sequential narrative in which words had primacy over images.

Crucial to the elaboration of this violence are the central players carefully cast in both videos, along with the enunciation of the deeper stakes of the unfolding drama. In the first video, the executioner spells these out in no uncertain terms: addressing Obama directly—and gesticulating at oddly timed moments with his knife—Emwazi instructs the president that the United States is no longer fighting an insurgency, but a legitimate Islamic state, a caliphate that has been accepted by Muslims around the globe. The fact that the vast majority of Muslims globally have not, in fact, done so has little bearing on the semiotic parameters this declaration establishes for the visual spectacle to follow. For this claim of statehood functions as a declaration of equivalence between the United States and ISIS, serving as the ground on which the video then enacts an inversion of previous asymmetrical relations between a superpower that sees itself as a force of justice, order, and freedom against the savagery, nihilism, and chaos of ISIS.

On the basis of this claim, ISIS's retaliation can be recast from a spasm of vengeance launched by a ragtag remnant of al-Qaʿida in Iraq into a sovereign act of war authorized in principle by not one but two different traditions. First, the Islamic tradition not only justifies defense of a legitimate Islamic state, but there's a strong consensus among legal scholars that *jihād* is an individual duty (*farḍ ʿayn*) that must be fulfilled by every single Muslim in such a situation. That this tradition also strictly prohibits the mistreatment of civilians and prisoners is, again, hardly of concern to an organization whose assiduous efforts to drape every policy in Islamic legitimacy is matched only by their contempt for both the normative principles governing the Islamic juridical tradition and its "parameters of operation."[53]

Second, it's authorized by an understanding of state self-defense grounded in a Westphalian conception of sovereignty. As is well known, the claims central to this conception made the "sovereign state the legitimate political unit . . . [and] implied that basic attributes of statehood such as the existence of a government with control of its territory were now . . . the criteria for becoming a state" and, essentially, made the state's authority over its own territory complete.[54] This conception of statehood is implicit in ISIS's presumption that retaliation is the

53. Siddiqui, "Beyond Authenticity."

54. Philpott, "Sovereignty," 364.

prerogative of a sovereign state whose territorial integrity has been violated by another. Such a presumption is a central premise of the very global order the United States claims to represent, and that Daʿish here implicitly turns against it, depicting America as aggressor, transgressor, and outlaw. The parallelism underlying this inversion not only recasts ISIS as legitimate sovereign and shield, but constitutes the extent of its territory in the image of the "criminal" global order it displaces. In this sense, ISIS heralds the restoration of the territorial integrity violently sundered by empire, that unbroken chain of domination masquerading as an alliance of good-will and peace.

Yet ISIS also follows Islamist thinkers such as Qutb in rejecting nationalism, democracy, socialism, liberalism, and the like, as expressions of "man-made sovereignty" that claim the authority to promulgate laws and rules for human behavior that have already been provided by God.[55] For Daʿish, the nation in particular is multiply invidious, not just a transgression of God's authority but the site of domination. Colonialism and imperialism routinely register as the distant past to its beneficiaries, but for those whose everyday landscape has been carved in the image of imperial powers, the colonial is a constant and living presence.[56] As the borders that mark a number of nation-states in the region were drawn by colonial fiat, the nation is not an emblem of independence but of impotence in the face of illegitimate power, first colonial and now authoritarian.

For ISIS, there's perhaps no more powerful site of such humiliation, and therefore of restoration, than the border between Iraq and Syria produced by the Sykes-Picot agreement, the notorious pact whereby Britain and France divvied up the territories of the former Ottoman Empire according to self-interest rather than local affiliations. They released not just one but two videos in different languages to celebrate the destruction of the border between Syria and Iraq in ISIS territory, "Kasr al-ḥudūd" [Breaking the Borders] and "The end of Sykes-Picot." In both videos, the border works to simultaneously vivify the humiliation of the colonial present and its authoritarian afterlives and demonstrate the sovereign power performed by its erasure. The recurrent image in "Kasr al-ḥudūd" is of a jagged red line down the center of the screen exploding into shattered glass, a recurrent segue from one segment to the next. As ISIS spokesman ʿAdnānī

55. Baghdadi, "Qul innī ʿalā bayyina min rabbī"; Qutb, *Maʿālim fī al-ṭarīq*.

56. For example, European names mark many streets and quarters, Europeans imposed the borders that called into being many contemporary Middle Eastern and Central Asian states, Europeans left the imprint of a particular model of development, and stripped colonial territories of countless archeological treasures and natural resources.

explains, the path to the future is made by the destruction of these artifacts of domination, these "borders of humiliation [*ḥudūd al-dhull*]."[57] In "The end of Sykes-Picot," the speaker (subsequently identified as a Chilean fighter named Abu Safiyya) becomes a tour guide through the detritus of the razed barrier, at one point standing triumphantly atop a discarded sign with "Commander's Battalion Border" written on it in English and Arabic. "As you can see," he says with pride, "it's under our feet right now."

The rubble at the border doesn't just symbolize an inversion of preeminence in the global order but is the ground on which it is literally inaugurated. So too the human victims in these execution videos aren't just props to pantomime retaliatory humiliation but the material on which it is literally enacted. The last words Foley was forced to speak, "I guess, all in all, I wish I wasn't American," say much about the role these particular hostages play in the way this inversion is enunciated and performed. There is a profound sadness in these words, spoken in a video that opens with one of the most powerful leaders in the world, the president of the United States, announcing the unleashing of US military might against ISIS to protect American personnel and Yazidis in Iraq—then promising, in the beginning of the Sotloff video, to protect all American citizens wherever they are. As Foley and Sotloff quickly die in the ensuing scenes, these register not only as empty pledges, but as almost a mockery of the vaunted power of pledges and promises in "civilized societies."

Then there is the person delivering them: are these opening clips meant to demonstrate the impotence of President Obama specifically?[58] Inasmuch as Obama repeatedly figures as the personification of US preeminence, it appears so; elsewhere, Da'ish spells it out, characterizing the US military as "neutered" by Obama's "effeminizing" domestic financial policies.[59] Yet what's ultimately exposed for all to see is not simply the inadequacy of an individual or an administration but of a state: a basic failure to protect that Hobbes among others regarded as central to sovereignty.[60]

57. "Kasr al-ḥudūd."

58. Given that Obama is America's first Black president, such an implication can't help but evoke the racialization of Black masculinity and its toxic partnership with humiliation long implicated in US slavery, the international slave trade, colonialism, and imperialism, along with their contemporary legacies and counterparts.

59. *Dabiq* 11, 57.

60. For Carl Schmitt, there is perhaps no greater failure, for it is precisely the ability to protect subjects/citizens in exchange for obedience that constitutes the sine qua non of both political order and legitimate sovereignty. See, for example, Schmitt, *Political Theology*.

Foley's words also work on another register, as they draw attention to how each role in these dramas is carefully cast, and the particular significance of Americanness in the performances that ensue. Sotloff and Foley are much more than expendable hostages leveraged for a threat that, once delivered, makes them detritus of a failed gambit in need of swift disposal; the visual rhetoric of the staged executions transforms their symbolic, psychic, and physical humiliation into that of the United States. Put slightly differently, these two men become the American body politic upon which retaliatory humiliation is literally reinscribed. At the same time, their degraded and exposed bodies serve as public evidence and confirmation not only of the impotence of the enemy but of its guilt and failures.

Consider the shorn heads of the captured men, wearing bright orange clothing designed to evoke the jumpsuits worn by inmates at Guantánamo Bay prison. They kneel in apparent submission at the feet of their executioner, who stands over them, legs apart, masked, clothed in black from head to toe. Positioned as if prepared for the rite of confession, the hostages are forced to use their last breath on earth to speak the words of their murderers: the deeds of their families, their nation, their president, are the "real" authors of their destruction—*they* are the criminals whose "rogue" violence has placed them at war with Muslims, has signed the death warrant of all Americans ISIS chooses to kill. The intense strain in their faces only hints at what had been done earlier, outside the frame and unfilmed, to get each man to follow this script, to play the designated role in the spectacle of his own murder, to lend his own voice to this grotesque performance of "consent."

There is still much that remains unknown about Foley's and Sotloff's specific experiences in captivity. While it's not necessary to know every gruesome detail to see a connection between the suffering endured off-camera and what they could be induced to do in front of it, some of the details that have emerged in the aftermath are instructive. Pieced together from a variety of sources, including interviews with freed European hostages whose governments met Da'ish's ransom demands, the picture that unfolds is of a long captivity in which control of the hostages changed hands several times. Treatment of the prisoners fluctuated dramatically as the Syrian civil war turned increasingly violent, various radical Islamist groups splintered, shifted allegiances, and jockeyed for primacy.[61]

61. Callimachi, "Horror Before the Beheadings."

The ascendance of Daʿish signaled the end of inconsistency—gone were the intervals of deprivation and torture interspersed with periods of relative leniency—and announced the arrival of a bureaucratized brutality with an American inflection. ISIS introduced a system of cataloguing hostages similar to that used by US forces at Camp Bucca, Iraq, where Baghdadi had been held.[62] The beatings, starvation, light deprivation, mock executions, threats, and waterboarding carefully reproduced the interrogation techniques of Muslim detainees pursued during the Bush Administration. But there was one critical difference: it appears the torture was dispensed primarily to inflict suffering rather than extract information.

The composition, blocking, sequencing, and editing of the scenes in and around the decapitations combine with these other elements to transform these American journalists into immobile victims who—along with the viewer watching a sequence of events that have already transpired—are entirely powerless to influence or stop what is happening around and to them. There is a certain chilling mockery at work in the fact these two reporters, "tasked to gaze upon atrocities elsewhere, providing some form of witness to the horrors of the human condition," have here "become the objects of our forced witnessing."[63] Aside from the scripted speech, the camera largely renders them akin to animals in a sacrificial ceremony, momentarily unmoving as the executioner abruptly makes the move to the kill. The *form* of execution further reinforces this symbolic entanglement of powerlessness and dehumanization. As scholars have pointed out, beheadings target the part of the human body responsible for thought, personality, and expressiveness, while the face is the "site of figural unity of the human being and the locus of the individual personality: the face stands for the uniqueness and the vulnerable humanness of a person."[64]

But just when death is imminent, the screen goes dark, a brief ellipse in the narrative. Does Foley turn and attempt to strike at Emwazi, knowing he has nothing left to lose? Does Sotloff use his last words to plead for mercy, or curse his killers? Daʿish dominion here is total, and the questions must remain unanswered; the deaths are constituted as ISIS wants them seen, an old-fashioned enactment of "sovereignty by exercising a traditional prerogative of the sovereign," the cutting off and display of the heads of those it designates enemies of the state.[65]

62. Callimachi, "Horror Before the Beheadings."

63. Evans and Giroux, "Intolerable Violence," 208.

64. Pollock, "From Horrorism to Compassion," 173; Cavarero, *Horrorism*; Evans and Giroux, "Intolerable Violence," 208.

65. Janes, "Beheadings," 24.

Channeling the gaze of subjects at a public execution, the camera cuts back to contemplate the prone body, severed head resting upon it, slowly panning down its length, steady, to take in the cuffed wrists, the bare feet, the painful vulnerability. In the next shot, the killer grips the collar of the next kneeling victim, as if holding an unclean animal; the threat and promise of an encore performance whose ritualized elements we already know.

The hostages are forcibly and multiply exposed: their names, faces, fear, abjection, and dead bodies are there for all to see. By contrast, virtually all specific aspects of the executioner's identity are hidden by the black garb of Da'ish. Like ISIS's black flag, such attire follows the practice of other radical Islamist groups, but it also plays upon at least three different moments in Islamic mythology and history. The first is the widely repeated claim that the Prophet Muhammad flew black banners when fighting infidels. The second is a series of unreliable but widely circulated hadith (report of the words and deeds of the Prophet) in which Muhammad reportedly foresaw the suffering of his family following his death, and predicted their liberation from tyranny and the restoration of justice by an uprising from the East, heralded by black banners.[66] The third is the adoption of black as the color of the 'Abbasid Caliphate (750–1258 CE) based in Baghdad—often considered the high-water mark in the history of Muslim rule—accompanied by efforts of 'Abbasid propagandists to retroactively project as much Prophetic significance onto the color as possible.[67]

Questions of provenance and authenticity notwithstanding, the black garb now widely evokes Muhammad and righteous battle, entangling poetic prophesy and the heyday of Islamic sovereignty even as the overall aspect is far more ninja by way of Hollywood.[68] What the clothing doesn't cover, of course, is the executioner's British accent, which denies English-speaking listeners any of the usual

66. 'Athamina, "Black Banners and the Socio-Political Significance of Flags and Slogans in Medieval Islam," 307–8.

67. As 'Athamina points out, it's quite likely that the prophetic hadith about "black banners from the East" was produced long after the Prophet's death by these propagandists, and even hadith about what color flag Muhammad had flown may be of such origin. As ISIS has shown little concern for the consensus of historians or of Muslim scholars, however, it's far less important to determine the authenticity of such hadith than to recognize the imaginative hold they likely had on ISIS members and potential recruits—as well as on other radical Islamist groups who have embraced the color as a way of following in the Prophet's footsteps. 'Athamina, "Black Banners."

68. Cori Dauber and Mark Robinson point to the various ways ISIS videos mimic the "Hollywood style" in the blogpost "ISIS and the Hollywood Visual Style."

comforting signifiers of distance. All that is left to see and know of him are his eyes, maleness, height, stance, stillness, stiff delivery, and the apparent calm—even casualness—he brings to the execution.

Then there's the intimacy of the kill he's ready to perform so efficiently, a stark contrast to what Daʿish depicts as the cowardice of US aerial attacks in a letter sent to Foley's parents.[69] It takes a particular kind of hardness to kill at close range and without a gun, where there's no escape from the pleas and screams of your victim, and far easier to kill at a distance with drones and bombs.[70] "Jihadi John" is in this way constituted as the ideal masculine Islamist militant, the organization he serves constructed as implacable, unstoppable, fearless, hard, dominant—the only Islamic force sufficiently potent to drive America, the standard-bearer of Muslim humiliation, to its knees, literally and figuratively.

I have suggested that aspects of the execution scene implicitly refer to what had been done earlier, off-screen, to stage them. There are other such moments of implied absence, some more obvious than others. Relative to several other hi-tech Daʿish productions, for example, the videos are verbally parsimonious, using images, quick cuts, composition, blocking, pacing, resolution, sound/silence, camera angles, dress and casting, to "speak" as much as words. The executioner engages in no lengthy soliloquies, no impassioned invective about justice and evil. There are no references to Islamic law, no disjointed invocations of hadith or decontextualized Qur'ānic fragments in the kind of explicit effort to justify the executions or the way they are accomplished characteristic of other ISIS as well as Qaʿida publications. And there are no *anāshīd* (hymns, pl. of *nashīd*) soaring on the soundtrack to serve as a Greek chorus reframing the events in epic and poetic terms.

Such absences seem to privilege deeds over words, a trope of much radical Sunni rhetoric and Islamist thought. Qutb, for example, wrote that jihad in the contemporary world requires action rather than words, struggle rather than contemplation, revolution at home as well as resistance abroad.[71] Such an emphasis shores up the image of ISIS fighters as hardened men of action rather than "soft" men of words. The motif of the lion in the epigraph to this chapter that also pervades the previous one reappears here: as the narrator puts it in the Daʿish

69. Atwan, *Islamic State*, 130–31.
70. Grossman, *On Killing*; Collins, *Violence*; Cottee, "ISIS and the Intimate Kill."
71. Qutb, *Maʿālim fī al-ṭarīq*, 67–68, 82.

video, "Although the Disbelievers May Dislike It/*Law kariha al-kāfirūn*," these fighters are "hungry lions whose drink is blood and play is carnage."[72]

Another absence is suggested by the orange jumpsuits, which refer not just to Muslim inmates of US prisons abroad, but specifically to the sexual humiliation, torture, and assault of Muslim and Arab prisoners by American guards in the photographs taken at Abu Ghraib prison. Unlike these notorious pictures, however, there is no explicitly sexual component to the degradation in these videos. There is no segment that involves raping the hostages, no film of them hooded, with electrical wires attached to their bodies, no staged clips of them lying naked on a dirty floor, leashed around the neck, the other end held by a (female) soldier. As is now well known, that kind of sexual torture was reserved for the women and girls captured by Daʿish who were either non-Muslim or the wrong kind of Muslim.[73]

The implication seems to be that the public sexual torture of male hostages—involving the participation of a female soldier, no less—reveals the barely concealed savagery beneath American claims to embody and defend the forces of civilization and law, an instantiation of Horkheimer and Adorno's warning about the barbarism in the violence that retains "enlightened civilization."[74] The rules broken in the Abu Ghraib photographs, Butler suggests, register precisely this kind of lawlessness.[75] The humiliation and execution Daʿish carries out on film, by

72. "Although the Disbelievers May Dislike It/*Wa-Law Kariha al-Kāfirūn*." The title is taken from Qur'ān 9:32: "They try to extinguish Allah's light with their mouths, but Allah insists on bringing His light to its fullness, even if the disbelievers may dislike it." The Qur'ānic translation is from Jones, *Quran*.

73. Daʿish has offered these women and girls, many Yazīdī, some not, as enticements and use objects to ISIS fighters, endeavoring to justify such systematic sexual brutalization as an Islamically permissible practice of sex slavery based upon historical precedents and fragments from the Qur'ān and hadith—much as the Bible had been used to justify the American slave trade. Callimachi, "ISIS Enshrines a Theology of Rape." But as Fatima Seedat argues, ISIS's sexual abuse of these captives is aberrant both in relation to historical concubinage practice, and in relation to the highly detailed norms, rules, and laws meant to govern both slavery and concubinage in Islamic law and thought. Such departures are not simply a matter of reviving an archaic practice in a contemporary context, but also of deploying modern technologies to vitiate the Islamic regulations meant to govern such practices. A case in point: Daʿish "sex slaves" were forced to ingest contraceptive pills to avoid pregnancy, thereby circumventing one of the specified routes by which a concubine must be legally granted her freedom. Seedat, "Sexual Economies of War and Sexual Technologies of the Body."

74. Horkheimer and Adorno, *Dialectic of Enlightenment*, 180.

75. Butler, *Frames of War*, 92.

contrast, exhibit a certain decorum that is, moreover, *lawful*. While *fiqh* [Islamic jurisprudence] sources do not mandate beheading for capital crimes, they do not forbid it, and it had become a fairly prevalent form of execution.[76] In this way, the reference to the Abu Ghraib photographs in the videos implicitly sets up a juxtaposition that inverts the conventional allocation of roles: while the American photographs disavow all limits, the humiliation and violence in the videos proceed with *relatively* civilized restraint, operating within what ISIS considers the proper boundaries of law and gender.

Then there is perhaps the most striking absence of all, the executions themselves. Why are the beheadings off-screen? After all, in the language of pornography so often invoked to capture the prurient aspects of such radical Islamist "snuff" material, the actual decapitation is the "money shot."[77] Speculation on this particular topic abounds on the Internet where, in the absence of any verifiable information, every conceivable—and inconceivable—conspiracy theory has rushed in to fill the void. Leaving these aside, one might ask: did these particular executions prove so gory, unmanageable, and inelegant as to ruin the aesthetics of the segment? Or were the architects of the videos themselves so steeped in violence—as perpetrators, victims, and/or as witnesses—that they assumed that what could be imagined into that unmapped darkness would be far more horrifying than the reality? One thing is certain: the footage is not omitted because this particular *mujāhid* hadn't the stomach for it. Emwazi turns up in another hi-tech ISIS production released in November of the same year, one of twenty-two executioners wielding knives who behead an equal number of captive Syrian soldiers simultaneously on film.

Given that the footage of this collective execution has been retained, the video of which it is a part, "Although the Disbelievers May Dislike It," is a particularly instructive way to pursue the question of absence in the Foley and Sotloff videos.[78] "Although the Disbelievers" has many different parts, complete

76. Decapitation is not strictly mandated as are other penalties for *ḥudūd* crimes such as apostasy, theft, and fornication—that is, crimes that are considered to be offenses against God. At the same time, there are no prohibitions on beheading when the punishment required is death, as in the case of apostasy, or when it was the penalty imposed at the discretion of a judge. Both *fiqh* and historical sources suggest that beheading was a common form of execution, to the extent that capital punishment was generally understood to mean decapitation, much as the guillotine became the default method to administer a death sentence in post-1789 France.

77. Cottee, "Pornography of Jihadism."

78. "Disbelievers" is not only instructive by contrast but in some ways represents the gruesome conclusion to the particular sequence of American and British hostage executions that

analysis of which is beyond my focus, yet the central thrust of the execution segment and what precedes it is the representation of ISIS as the sole and unwavering protector of the *ahl al-Sunna wa'l-jamā'a*, the community of Sunnis. This is accomplished, in part, through a creative genealogy of radical Islamism in which Da'ish is depicted as the heir and final telos of all previous movements and moments. Beatific images of Zarqawi, Bin Laden, Abu Hamzah al-Muhajir, and Baghdadi smoothly fade into one another as the voiceover weaves a tale of continuity and unanimity divested of all divisions between al-Qa'ida and Zarqawi over his ruthless violence against Shi'i Muslims, a campaign that Da'ish has pursued with equal fervor.

It is also accomplished by a confluence of visual and verbal rhetoric demonizing the Shi'a—although they are never referred to as such. They are primarily referred to as *rāfiḍa*, meaning renegades or repudiators, a term at times used by Sunnis to disparage Shi'a. At one point in the video—in Arabic with English subtitles—they are casually described as the "filth of the *rāfiḍa*," at another, spoken of as *rāfiḍa* who have humiliated [*dhull*] the "grandsons" of Abu Bakr and 'Umar (the first two successors of Muhammad). When the narrator describes Shi'i soldiers of Bashar al-Asad's Alawite regime, he uses the term Nuṣayrī, after the Alawite founder, Ibn Nuṣayr. Accompanying such invective is a barrage of visual images designed to inflame anxieties about the spread of Iranian and Shi'i control, and offer the fortitude of Da'ish fighters as solace and solution. This convergence of visual and verbal rhetoric appears to be geared almost exclusively toward a global Sunni audience that speaks many different languages on the one hand, and ISIS's existing membership on the other.

---

began with Foley and ended in the fall of 2014. For tacked onto its end is an incongruous segment in which Emwazi inveighs against the United States while the severed head of the final hostage, Peter Kassig, lies oddly at his feet. In just one more of the odd twists accompanying these events, Kassig is now consistently referred to in print, online, and television media as "Peter (Abdul Rahman) Kassig," to reflect his conversion to Islam while imprisoned, and the names of no other American hostages are similarly modified. Yet released hostages and even a former member of ISIS say that a majority of "Western" prisoners converted to Islam, most in the understandable hope of receiving more humane treatment from their captors. Callimachi, "Horror Before the Beheadings." Sotloff was among the few who did not convert—even attempting to secretly fast on Yom Kippur—but Foley evidently converted to Islam very soon after his capture, adopting the name Abu Hamza. In the current US political climate, singling out Kassig in this way is a kind of implicit indictment, either of his bravery or loyalty. In sharp contrast to Kassig, both Foley's conversion and his Muslim name are largely erased from the public narrative, as if this death would be less horrific, less heroic, less grievable, if the world had lost James (Abu Hamza) Foley.

The elements of self-valorization and sectarianism are carefully elaborated for both spectral audiences in the execution segment, which begins with twenty-two ISIS fighters silently marching twenty-two Syrian soldiers clothed in blue uniforms through an olive grove, accompanied only by the sound of voices chanting a *nashīd*. The camera lingers on the faces of the fighters as they each grab a knife from a bucket in passing, the pace occasionally downshifting into slow motion so that viewers may fully absorb what they see: facial features that form a veritable map of the geographical reach of Sunni Islam, from Africa to Europe to Asia. At the end of the procession, the captives kneel at the feet of the fighters; the camera lingers on each of their faces and then, more briefly, on the furtive glances of several jittery Syrians who do not speak, and are given no names.

The camera pulls back and is momentarily still, taking in the entire scene. The segment has so far proceeded without speech, but now the silence is broken. The only executioner who is masked—Emwazi—speaks, and they are the first words of English in the entire film: the words are addressed to President Obama, the "dog of Rome," and the message is brief and familiar. These "soldiers of Bashar" are the victims now, but your people will be next.

There is little in "Disbelievers" up to this point that has indicated anything other than a Sunni-sectarian theme, although Emwazi's words do prefigure a shift in focus—and reversal of Arabic and English linguistic primacy—in the segments that are to come. Here, however, they are quickly eclipsed by what follows: all twenty-two executioners proceed to calmly slit the throats of the condemned, the camera duly documenting the bloodiness of the work, along with the uniformity, efficiency, and apparent equanimity of those who perform it. Then, as the voices of a fresh *nashīd* soar on the soundtrack—"we bring corruption to light / we cushion lost families / we descend upon disbelievers delivering destruction / forget the words of those who shall inevitably die"—a series of heroic shots taken from slightly below the fighters captures them singly, then in twos and threes, hair slightly windblown, clean, and untouched by the filth and blood on the floor, gazing into the middle distance, calm and cleansed. The camera pans down the line of Syrian bodies, severed heads resting upon them, and the narrator intones in Arabic: "Know that we have armies in al-Iraq and an army in al-Sham of hungry lions whose drink is blood and play is carnage."

What do these likely aims and audiences of "Disbelievers" say about the question of absence at hand? The collective execution in "Disbelievers" is not simply raw footage; it is a production that involves framing, blocking, and editing. This suggests that it was most likely the matter of audience rather than either aesthetics or habituation to graphic violence that determined the exclusion of decapitation footage in the Foley and Sotloff videos. While "Disbelievers" is primarily geared to contemporary Sunni Muslims fluent not in Arabic but in Islamic terminology, figures, symbols, and touchstones, it's probable that the Foley and Sotloff videos were edited to suit American sensibilities, approaching but not crossing that invisible line of what is watchable to ensure the widest possible dissemination.

By "American sensibilities" here, I refer to public expectations produced by the increasing sanitization of war made possible by what Kaempf has called the "oligopolization" of the global media market over the course of the last few decades.[79] More specifically, state management of major media representations of war has produced what has been described as a "grammar of killing" in which American operations appear "precise, administrative and clean," not to mention costless and humane.[80] These representations train audiences to take such sanitized images of war as reflective of "our own civilized tactics," implicitly suturing atrocities in war—from interrogation torture to abuse of prisoners, sexual violence to indiscriminate killing of civilians—to the barbarism of the enemy. In this way, this grammar of killing not only establishes public expectations of what war does/should look like, but constitutes one of the techniques by which American atrocities in wartime are concealed.[81]

If this account of the absent executions is plausible, the fact that these specific videos played such a significant role in constituting ISIS as a singularly savage and major threat to British and American interests and citizens—while understandable—becomes multiply ironic.[82] To begin with, the excision of the most explicit parts of the execution sequences mirrors and reproduces the very sanitization of "officially sanctioned" violence critical to establishing the American sensibilities to which ISIS here yields. In fact, both are exercises in sovereign

79. Kaempf, "Mediatisation of War."

80. Kaempf, "Mediatisation of War," 597–98; Der Derian, *Virtuous War*; Campbell, "Horrific Blindness," 58–61.

81. Foucault, *Discipline and Punish*, 48, 55–57. Such atrocities may be particular incidents of, say, "collateral damage" caused by drone strikes or the sheer number of people who have died since September 11, 2001, as a direct or indirect consequence of the United States' "War on Terror." Regarding the latter, there's a wide spread in the estimates, but the *lowest* assessment of those killed in Iraq, Afghanistan, and Pakistan between 2001 and 2015 is 1.3 million people. Physicians for Social Responsibility, *Body Count*; Nafeez Ahmed, "Do the Math: Global War on Terror Has Killed 4 Million Muslims or More."

82. In the immediate wake of Sotloff's execution, for example, Obama declared that "[i]n a region that has known so much bloodshed, these terrorists are unique in their brutality." Obama, "Statement by the President on ISIL."

power over death through control of what is seen and not seen, a longstanding prerogative of sovereign authority that, as I suggested earlier, modern liberal states in particular have taken increasing pains to conceal. Moreover, these images evince an almost methodical discipline relative to the unrestrained brutality of the Abu Ghraib photographs, are far more sanitized than Daʿish execution videos in which Arabs, Africans, and other Muslims are killed, and much less graphic than the beheadings—some taking more than two minutes to complete—circulating in the shadowy corners of the digital landscape.

As Friis points out, the "internet is overflowing with videos of human beings—especially non-westerners—being decapitated."[83] While frequently glossed as evidence of non-Western barbarism, such "snuff videos," and the prevalence of live beheadings among them, are anchored in forms of violence and entertainment much closer to home. Decapitation was often the preferred form of capital punishment at one time or another in the histories of European as well as Islamic societies. It's also worth noting that "leadership decapitation" is a well-known component of US counterterrorism strategy. Euphemisms are frequently deployed to conceal the violence of US military operations, but in this instance, the language aptly describes what it means, namely "targeted killings" of those identified as leaders of terrorist organizations. Among those destroyed by such "decapitation strikes" include several leaders of al-Qaʿida and its affiliates (e.g., Bin Laden and Anwar al-Awlaki, both in 2011, and Nasir al-Wuhayshi in 2015) as well as Emwazi in 2015, ʿAdnani, ISIS's powerful spokesman in 2016, and Baghdadi himself in 2019.

Moreover, the entire genre of snuff films in which these execution sequences can be placed has its origins in a global culture and economy upon which a great deal of "Western" life and wealth is built. As writers and scholars from a range of disciplines have shown, this is a culture that normalizes extreme cruelty, cultivates the pleasures of vicarious violence, and profits from converting the graphic suffering of others into titillating spectacle. Such conversion is evinced in entertainment products ranging from torture pornography to Hollywood productions celebrating military machismo and the aesthetics of slaughter. And, of course it includes video games that hone skills in massacring fleeing, vaguely Asian figures in 3-D or, as in *Kuma/War*, entice American players to hunt down Sunni terrorist "infestations" as part of the coalition forces' 2004 ground attack on Fallujah, Iraq.[84] Such suffering may be "real" or simulated, but praise and profits accrue most to those products that come closest to replicating the horrors of real war or killing.

83. Friis, "'Beyond Anything We Have Ever Seen,'" 742.

84. Šisler, "From Kuma\War to Quraish," 114–16.

In this way, the cultivated pleasures in graphic cruelty become entangled with a fetish for realism that fuels—and perhaps reflects—the desire for videos of actual death, torture, and rape, readily offered up for purchase on the darknet market.

Aside from the question of why the footage is absent, I want to argue that its effect within the execution sequence is fairly clear. The very fixation on the question of absence attests to expectations of a narrative structure in which the moment of death is both dramatic pivot and denouement. The absence of the beheadings displaces the focus from that moment of death to the conditions surrounding it: the lead up and aftermath, along with the power that has directed, staged, and edited it. In other words, the ellipse shifts the narrative focus onto what the hostages are made to say and do and suffer, how their bodies are positioned when alive and when dead. What is at center stage, then, is not the execution, but the humiliation—what it performs, inverts, and produces.

Conclusion

Immediately after the Sotloff video was posted, President Obama vowed that "[w]hatever these murderers think they will achieve by murdering innocents like Steven, they have already failed." Yet the ways in which the bodies of the victims were positioned and treated both when alive and when dead are not reducible to a strategy, or a means to achieve some end beyond itself that can be evaluated in terms of success or failure. I've argued that each execution sequence—and its relation to the production in which it is embedded—must be understood, in part, as a performative event in which the purposes of the violence are both articulated and accomplished at the moment of enactment. This lens has brought into sharp relief a disjuncture between what these videos say and how they work. While the verbal rhetoric largely hews to the logic of instrumental rationality, the visual rhetoric enacts a retaliatory humiliation that performs and produces and inversion of power in two different registers.

I've argued that the literal inscription of humiliation on the bodies of Foley and Sotloff performs the dominance of ISIS through the symbolic emasculation of America, but have also drawn upon Foucault's arguments to bring into focus a second register of this inversion. Here my suggestion is that the ritualized, vengeful, and disproportionate violence of these staged executions is meant to enact the preeminence and invincibility of the sovereign caliphate through the utter abjection of men forced to serve as standard bearers for those who have humiliated Islam. Within the semiotic parameters of the videos, the impotence of the condemned at once demonstrates and confirms the final transposition of roles between the United States, now refigured as rogue state and failed sovereign, and Da'ish, recast as injured, righteous, and lawful sovereign power.[85] Both registers effect a symbolic shift in the site of sovereignty; male bodies supplant the territorial state as the primary ground on which it is enacted.

The understanding humiliation at work here is a visual articulation of what emerged in the previous chapter, the unjust imposition of impotence by those who have more, and undeserved, power. As I argued in the introductory chapter, humiliation can be rephrased in experiential terms as the rupture between our own sense of significance and place in the social order and acute awareness of where others with more power have forcibly placed us. Among other things, this means that even a rehearsal of our humiliation in front of others after the fact is rarely a simple recounting of events but a reenactment of this rupture, one that can revivify the experience itself. For precisely this reason, a deeply restorative experience is potentially revivified in rehearsals of retaliatory humiliation: it offers up the visceral satisfaction of publicly reinscribing humiliation upon the humiliator to reclaim one's power and vindicate one's place in the social order.

This experiential account suggests how the visual rhetoric of these videos works to address particular audiences in different ways. Perhaps most obviously, it seeks to hail American audiences generally in an effort to intimidate; yet it is also specifically designed to humiliate (self-identified) American men by the public emasculation of their male compatriots. This is to be accomplished, in part, by facilitating a visceral identification of American men with the abjection and pain of the hostages. Crucial to this move is the repetition of signs, verbal and visual, identifying Foley and Sotloff not in terms of religion (Catholic and Jewish, respectively), or profession (both journalists), but *Americanness*. The act of simply watching the videos then becomes a vehicle for the larger purpose: it potentially forces American men to experience the impotence and rage of being utterly powerless to intervene in a horrific event of the past that works viscerally in the present.

At the very same time, this performance of American emasculation aims to conjure audiences from among the millions globally who harbor deep suspicion of or hostility to US power, offering them continual satisfaction, even pleasure.[86]

85. In the variation of Foley's script published in *Dabiq*, the US government is characterized as complacent and criminal, its foreign policies illegal according to its own laws. "Complete Message from James Foley," *Dabiq* 3, 39.

86. In *Dabiq*, ISIS spells out verbally what the video aims to perform visually, stating that it "was a cooling balm for the believers' hearts to witness the execution of the American James

It also specifically seeks to hail a community of Sunni men where none currently exists, and invite them to share in the potency and invincibility performed by Emwazi. Such entrée is to be facilitated both by way of aspirational identification with him as the ideal *mujāhid*, and by the restorative experience of watching, over and over again, the reclamation of power from symbols of American domination he claims to perform, at least partly in their name.

By way of conclusion, I want to return briefly to the question about how these visual enactments of retaliatory humiliation might work once inserted into digital networks that circulate them globally and repeat them endlessly across multiple media platforms. Focusing on the shift to digital media, Kaempf contends that one of the major changes wrought by digital technology is the transformation of a structural division between sender and receiver that underpins all previous mediums, from television to radio to printing.[87] Whereas previous modes of media were primarily one-directional, "mass monologues" transmitted from producer to audience, the interactivity and fragmentation characteristic of new media technology not only reduces the distance between sender and receiver, producer and audience, but in many cases renders the distinction meaningless, as endless circuits make users simultaneously consumers, generators, and conduits of information.

The conquest of distance and the democratization of information celebrated as among the triumphs of the digital age negate—by design—the sense of safety, separation, or impersonal detachment that several influential communication scholars identify with older forms of audio-visual media witness.[88] The structural transformations Kaempf analyzes mean that the "power of the visual" delivered through digital networks also offers a form of (always mediated) witness, but one

---

Wright Foley." "Foley's Blood Is on Obama's Hands," 37. The pleasures taken in witnessing ISIS violence against enemies are hardly confined to videos in which the victims are so-called "Westerners." Just one case in point is the February 2015 video of the captured Jordanian pilot, Moaz al-Kasasbeh, burned alive in a cage. Atwan notes that the video almost immediately reached hundreds of thousands of people, some of whom reveled in the horrific brutality. One Twitter account holder responded with "Burn baby Burn! Starring 'best scream' award winner Moaz al-Kassasbeh." Atwan, *Islamic State*, 22–23.

87. Kaempf, "Mediatisation of War," 593. While Kaempf traces the collapse of previous distinctions between sender and receiver, producer and audience, to new media technologies, Rancière has argued that such a distribution of roles has long been grounded in a set of distorting oppositions between passivity and activity, viewing and acting. Rancière, *Emancipated Spectator*.

88. Ellis, *Seeing Things*, 9–11; and Frosh, "Telling Presences," 281.

where the presumed safety and distance associated with electronic media have collapsed into a far more personal and viscerally immediate modality of experience. Digital interaction, then, has the capacity to connect, involve, and implicate users, as participants, targets, sufferers, or warriors.

Given the preceding analysis, thinking about the particular kinds of involvements these videos facilitate as they move forward and outward means speculating about the interaction of genre, repetition, temporality, and the visual rhetoric of retaliatory humiliation they contain. Viewed only once, the various kinds of visceral identifications and reactions these particular videos enable might well occur in attenuated form and fade quickly. But videos demand more than momentary engagement to register. As I've suggested, there's no shortcut through the unfolding ordeal of these men that is capable of registering the performance. Moreover, digital networks accelerate and expand circulation, compress cycles of reception and reaction, and multiply the types of interactivity that constitute users as virtual or vicarious participants. As Trinh Minh-ha has put it, "each repetition is never the same as the former. In it, there is circulation, there is intensity, there is innovation."[89] This kind of remaking by repetition conduces less to a slow fade than the conversion of aftereffects into dispositions that—like virtually everything else—are reinforced, intensified, and amplified by the echo chambers of social media networks constituted by the like-minded.[90]

Repetition and circulation extend in time but, in a sense, they also reshape time. As these videos repeat through endless circuits, the immediate event that precipitated them—US airstrikes against ISIS in Sinjar—becomes increasingly incidental to the visual violence they contain. When provenance recedes, so too does the sense of temporal distance built into chronological sequencing. Paradoxically perhaps, this double dissociation extends rather than curtails their affective power. Released from conventional time, the events depicted are constituted as part of an ongoing present rather than a completed past. Released

89. Minh-ha, *When the Moon Waxes Red*, 190.

90. This argument does not negate the ways in which digital technologies and social media platforms have facilitated political organizing, constituted counterpublics, and served as sites of virtual refuge or resistance that have occasionally (if not inevitably) spilled over into material life. Hillis, Paasonen, and Petit, *Networked Affect*. In this connection, it's worth remembering that the videos that are the subject of this analysis circulate out of the same region that, only a few years earlier, had become the lodestar for joining new technologies to emancipatory hopes in authoritarian settings.

from the particulars of context, millions of people across the globe are invited to vicariously experience, and even feel implicated in, the humiliation onscreen.

The retaliatory humiliation these videos depict is in this way untethered from specific time and territory, the sovereignty it performs continually unfolding and endlessly reenacted on the bodily terrain contained within them. This is so despite the fact that ISIS's caliphate in Iraq-Syria is no more. Watching is refigured as witnessing, not in the sense of "bearing witness" to events that have already transpired, but in a simulacrum of eye-witnessing the violence onscreen as it happens. At such a level of affective engagement, it takes just a small step—or a few clicks—for a watcher-witness to interpolate himself into the enactment itself, *either* as humiliator or humiliated. Particularly crucial for the chapters that follow, such affective enmeshment of spectator and performance can entail taking on the humiliation and suffering of the victim—or alternatively, relishing a profoundly restorative experience.

4

"Our Dignity Is Humiliated"

A PHENOMENOLOGY OF HUMILIATION IN THE EGYPTIAN REVOLUTION

"Our country is ruled by humiliation."

VERSE BY ESSAM EL-SAYYED[1]

"Thirty years of humiliation is enough."

SLOGAN, 2011 EGYPTIAN REVOLUTION[2]

"[The regime has] forced us to eat dirt, then accused us of being filthy."

POEM BY AMR ISMAIL[3]

1. Essam el-Sayyed, "Sikit il-lisān," Facebook post, April 21, 2012. As this is a poem, there is some artistic license in the English translation here. The line "ḥākim baladnā Hāmān dhull wa-'ihāna kamān" literally means "the ruler of our country is Hāmān, humiliation and degradation too." In the Qur'ān, Hāmān is the nasty vizier of Pharaoh in ancient Egypt. As Walter Benjamin points out, translation is inevitably a matter of approximation rather than correspondence, about locating echoes rather than reproducing meaning. Benjamin, "Task of the Translator," 76.

2. "Thalāthīn sanat dhull, bi-kaffī!"

3. The line, "[t]he regime has "forced us to eat the dust, then accused us of being filthy [*wa-khallūnā nisiff turāb wa-'ttahamūnā bi'l-nagāsa*]," is from Ismail's poem, "Ummī malhāsh fī al-siyāsa" [My mother doesn't care for politics], originally posted on Facebook, October 3, 2010. It was subsequently performed on several Arab channels as well as in Israel but was not aired in Egypt. See Toldo, "Amr Ismail: Ummī malhāsh fī al-siyāsa." Also see Ifāda Maktūba, "Amr Ismail, Ummī malhāsh fī al-siyāsa." This line from the poem is echoed in a tribute in verse to the January 2011 protesters posted on the "We Are All Khaled Said" Facebook page by Sherif Ibrahim: "Wa-qālū dah maṣrī ḥaqīr / yinḍirib bi'l-ni'āl dah yiṣīr / mālū maqām wa-ḥagmū bīn al-'arab ḍa'īl / Qālū akl al-fūl fawāl / Maṣrī muwassakh mālū kalām wa-maqāl / yi'mal 'andinā khaddām shayyāl" [They called the Egyptian filthy / And to be beaten with our heels/He's worthless and small among the Arabs. . . . / He can only be our servant]. Ibrahim, "Wa-qālū dah maṣrī ḥaqīr."

THE 2011 Arab uprisings have so commonly been associated with dignity that some have sought to brand them "Dignity Revolutions" or even attribute them to "collective dignity deficits."[4] Far less recognized is how extensively humiliation figured in the uprisings, particularly but not exclusively among those challenging the state. There were antigovernment chants of "death rather than humiliation" [*al-mawt wa-lā 'al-madhalla*] in Syria, "we will never accept humiliation" [*hayhāt minnā al-dhilla*] in Bahrain,[5] and "the Tunisian people will not be humiliated" [*sha'b Tūnis lā yuhān*].[6] This is equally true of Egypt, which has been characterized as the "fulcrum of the 'Arab Spring.'"[7] Alongside familiar slogans demanding "Bread, Dignity, Freedom!" [*'Aish, karāma, ḥurriyya!*], signs and slogans such as

4. Filiu, "L'état de grâce islamiste sera fugace"; al-Rodhan, "Dignity Deficit Fuels Uprisings in the Middle East." There are far too many examples of scholarship and commentary that refer to the uprisings as revolutions of dignity to include here.

5. The Bahraini slogan, "hayhāt minnā al-dhilla," is taken from a message attributed to al-Husayn, grandson of the Prophet Muhammad, reportedly addressed to the people of Kūfa on 'Āshūrā, the date of al-Husayn's martyrdom at Karbala. In response to an ultimatum to surrender or fight by 'Ubayd Allāh ibn Ziyād, the Umayyad governor, Husayn declared that the usurper had trapped them between the option of drawing swords or humiliation. This is no choice at all, he says, as acceding to humiliation is an impossibility. Abū Muḥammad al-Ḥasan b. 'Alī Ibn Shu'ba al-Ḥarrānī (fl. 4th/10th century), *Tuḥaf al-'Uqūl'an Āl al-Rasūl*, 240–41; Ibn Ṭāwūs (d. 664/1266), "al-Luhūf fī qatlā al-ṭufūf," 58–90.

6. While the study of humiliation rhetoric during the Tunisian Uprising would require a chapter all its own, just a brief review of tweets by Tunisians from 2010 to 2011 points to the prevalence of invocations of humiliation [*dhull*]. A sociolinguistic analysis of four hundred slogans from the Egyptian and Tunisian revolutions also identifies humiliation as a central substantive theme. Hussein, "Slogans of the Tunisian and Egyptian Revolutions."

7. Amar, "Egypt," 24. The title of this chapter is taken from a poem by Hisham el-Gakh, *Guḥā*. It's part of a couplet that became particularly popular during the 2011 uprising: "Our dignity is humiliated [*karāmitnā mit'hāna*] / And every bite is insulting [*wa'l-luqma b-ihāna*]." *Guḥā* refers to a "wise-fool" folklore hero of a wide range of anecdotes, jests, and fables. First mentioned in the ninth century by the Arabic writer al-Jāḥiẓ, Guḥā has appeared in stories from east Africa, Italy, and Turkey as well as North Africa. While Guḥā has taken on many aspects at different times, the character that emerges from all of this variety is invariably irreverent, refuses to censor himself, consistently flouts authority even when in extreme danger, manages to extricate himself from sticky situations, and always outwits those with far more power. See Pellat, "D̲juḥā"; Al-Shamy, *Folktales of Egypt*, 219ff.; Cattan, *Anthology of Oriental Anecdotes, Fables and Proverbs*; and Schwartz, "Fantasy and Morals in the Stories of Juha." See Gakh, *Guḥā*. As will become clear in the following pages, humiliation is a dominant motif in Gakh's work. On other aspects of his poetry, see Muhammad, "Arabic Performance Poetry," 815–41; Essam, "Translation and Analysis of Diasporic Colloquial Egyptian Poems of Patriotism"; Muhammad, *Sīrat ḥayāt al-shā'ir al-Miṣrī Hisham el-Gakh*" [Biography of the Egyptian

"Our Dignity Is Humiliated" [*Karāmitnā mit'hāna*] and "Enough Humiliation!" [*Kifāya dhull!*] pervaded the rhetorical landscape from Upper to Lower Egypt, as well as virtual communities of Egyptians living at home and abroad.

Given the extensive study of virtually every aspect of the Egyptian Uprising since then, this inattention is itself notable and exemplifies the paradox framing this book: the extent to which humiliation is at once rhetorically ubiquitous and conceptually vacuous.[8] This empirical and theoretical lacuna raises several interlocking questions. What do Egyptians mean by humiliation here, and what does it do, rhetorically, politically, and affectively? How does humiliation figure in an uprising branded a "revolution of dignity"? What are its implications for what I've called the scaffolding of humiliation, which I've traced through the previous chapters? Might such an inquiry augur a different way of grasping humiliation both experientially and conceptually, along with that elusive "dignity" with which it is invariably twinned?

Guided by these questions, in the following pages, I take up this significantly understudied dimension of the revolution, and of the Arab uprisings generally, through a close reading of Egyptian expressions of humiliation from 2010 to 2014. This exemplifies the approach centering meaning-as-use that informs this entire inquiry. It also dovetails with a growing body of work by political theorists who take "regular people," from activists to migrant day laborers to prisoners serving life without parole, as potential agents of theorizing rather than simply its objects. As Paul Apostolidis argues, close reading of the languages and practices regular people use to express their concerns can render legible how individual articulations "congeal into shared practices of narrating the social world and thus help to constitute it."[9]

Rather than focus on the objectives of the state, I aim to center the lived experiences of regular Egyptians by thematizing how humiliation is constituted in language among those who endure, witness, identify, and refuse it at a specific historical and political moment. This focus does not discount the purposes of the

poet Hisham el-Gakh]; and Al Jazeera, "Hisham el-Gakh . . . shā'ir bi-uslūb masraḥī" [Hisham el-Gakh . . . a poet of theatrical style].

8. Even the few who identify humiliation as among the most important "root causes" of the revolution leave it undefined. Two cases in point are Delkhasteh, "Humiliation"; and Fahmy, "An Initial Perspective on 'The Winter of Discontent.'"

9. Apostolidis, *Breaks in the Chain*, xxxii; and *The Fight for Time*, 39. See also Pineda, *Seeing Like an Activist*; Coles, *Visionary Pragmatism*; Hauerwas and Coles, *Christianity, Democracy and the Radical Ordinary*; and Bennett, "'The State Was Patiently Waiting for Me to Die': Life without the Possibility of Parole as Punishment."

state—an impossibility in any case—but decenters them analytically. As I will argue, the Egyptian regime is dedicated to humiliation as a tactic of domination and a logic of rule. In this setting, shifting the theoretical perspective is essential to register the articulation of humiliation from another location. It additionally displaces humiliation in its most familiar public guise, as a buttress of hierarchy. It then becomes legible as a site where the meaning, features, and inhabitants of that hierarchy are constituted and contested, where the hierarchy itself is reinscribed or disavowed.

To this end, I've looked to sources, sites, and genres usually considered outside of the jurisdiction of political theory, including blogs, vlogs, professional and amateur videos, poetry, tweets, Facebook posts, songs, chants, slogans, signs, and the relatively freewheeling "oppositional talk" that flourished briefly on independently owned satellite channels. Much conventional print and broadcast media in Egypt has been subject to state control or owned outright by the regime, but this is not the sole or even primary reason I have turned to these sources. As these materials range from explicit invocations of humiliation to expressions that convey the texture of how it is lived during this critical period, they can be counted as among the many primary texts of the uprising. They collectively comprise an archive that's distinctive not only by virtue of the particular content it gathers together, but also by virtue of the plurality of voices that comprise it, the diversity of genres through which they communicate, and the polyphony of expressions it contains, from off-the-cuff tweets to grainy smartphone videos to extensively refined poems long in gestation.[10] As a result, the Egyptians who "speak" here are young and old; famous singers and the unemployed; academics and workers in Egypt's informal economy; professional journalists and amateur commentators; students and laborers; government officials and supporters of the regime as well as its opponents; those from the south and north of the country; Coptic Christians and Muslims; residents and expatriates; Islamists, Salafis, liberals, and leftists; men, women, and many more whose identities, locations, and commitments are unidentified (see this chapter's appendix on the archive).

Given the focus and composition of this archive, I argue that analysis of these materials constitutes a phenomenology of humiliation in the 2011 Egyptian revolution. By "phenomenology," I refer simply to lived experience rather than to the philosophy associated with Edmund Husserl, Martin Heidegger, Maurice Merleau-Ponty, and others. To call it a phenomenology is not to claim that this

10. Poetry played a significant communicative and performative role in the 2011 demonstrations. See Colla, "Poetry of Revolt," 77; Saad, "Egyptian Revolution"; Ghanem, "2011 Egyptian Revolution Chants"; and Sanders and Visonà, "Soul of Tahrir."

archive contains every single invocation of humiliation in these years or that these materials somehow represent all Egyptians. They are illustrative rather than exhaustive, illuminating the meanings, textures, and registers of humiliation experienced by a wide range of Egyptians in their daily lives. Reading them as texts brings into focus largely unrecognized resources for theorizing humiliation not in terms of what it's said to be, but in terms of how it's instantiated, felt, and contested in and through language.[11]

As in chapter 2, these sources are grouped together by virtue of a shared emphasis on humiliation, but this is not the same as accord or unanimity; the materials here evince disagreements of politics, perception, and purpose. Moreover, these expressions are inflected differently by vulnerabilities of varying kinds and intensity, from the women protesters subjected to state-sponsored sexual assault (so-called virginity tests), to the men driven to consider or commit suicide by the loss of jobs, income, and self-regard, to the extreme precarity of families driven to take up residence in Cairo's dangerous graveyards, preyed upon by police, disease, and despair.[12] As before, I read these for what humiliation says and does in these texts and the worlds in which they are embedded, but I do not presume that the meaning of any single expression is exhausted by this focus or the reading it yields. Again, my aim is to render legible patterns, tropes, and themes in how these voices constitute humiliation, how they seek to contest or refigure it, as well as where they reproduce or shore it up.

Inasmuch as humiliation is instantiated at multiple sites, the following analysis distills these articulations into six sections with titles taken from quotations in this archive: Our Country Is Ruled by Humiliation, We Do Not Want a Humiliated Nation, The Market of Humiliation in Egypt's Time of Degradation, Where Are the Real Men of Egypt?, We're All Equal in Humiliation and Torture, and They've Forced Us to Eat Dirt and Accused Us of Being Filthy.

11. The focus on language means that this phenomenological analysis is grounded in modes of communication in common. This doesn't bear much resemblance to what Mona el-Ghobashy, in her recent study of the Egyptian revolution, depicts as immersion in the maelstrom of lived experience characteristic of "hermeneutic study that recovers and represent subjects' inner states (emotions and dispositions)." *Bread and Freedom*, 41–42. It does, however, decenter precisely the competition over state powers and authority Ghobashy adopts as her analytical framework.

12. Ellissy, "'Amr Ellissy fī manṭiqat maqābir al-Imām al-Shāfi'ī" ['Amr Ellissy in the cemetery of Imām al-Shāfi'ī]. In 2008, Egypt's National Statistics Agency reported that 1.5 million were living in Cairo's cemeteries alone. Mahmoud, "Meet the People Living in Graveyards in Egypt." Interviews with the over 1,300 families evicted from apartments by landlords in Maspero in the wake of the revolution tell similar stories. See, for example, Shaaban, "Iḥnā mish balṭāgiyya" [We are not thugs].

Apprehending such texts and expressions thematically rather than chronologically or by person makes it easier to trace the through-line of the central arguments across these sections and the chapters of this book. My aim is to bring into focus the elements of what I've termed the scaffolding of humiliation, including the ways these elements are constituted at multiple sites by way of a particular repertoire of symbols, images, tropes, and coded terminology forged in a shared historical and political context. To this end, I fill in detail about the events of the moment as necessary to avoid swamping them in the extensive historical or biographical details required to do justice to every event and person that makes an appearance. This strategy is also dictated by the materials, as the number of sources and voices here are considerable, many are anonymous or nearly so, and the biographical information of more than a few who do identify themselves is unavailable.

There are some drawbacks to this composition. It risks temporal disorientation, anonymization of the particular individuals writing and speaking, and the confusion of a shifting cast of characters, some of whom reappear in several sections while others do not. To navigate these challenges, I explore these themes through specific figures whenever possible, treating them and the texts they generate as agentic—as architects of meaning rather than just products of power. My aim is to render these patterns legible without reproducing the very powerlessness and ventriloquism of "the people" most of these voices so vigorously contest. Even if these materials are inevitably mediated by technology, selection, translation, and interpretation, I can at the very least showcase rather than undercut their efforts to rewrite the scripts that govern their lives.

As no revolution comes out of nowhere and its reverberations can extend into the future indefinitely, there will always be a certain arbitrariness to the start and end date set by any study of it. In this case, the 2011 uprising was decades if not centuries in the making, and it must be understood in relation to a long list of antecedents and influences. Perhaps the most obvious is the Tunisian revolution of 2010–11 that brought down Zine al-Abidine Ben Ali, the president of twenty-three years. The Tunisian Uprising is referred to repeatedly in this archive as both model and foil, but there are an array of tributaries from within Egypt.[13] The revolution drew upon coalitions and organizational experience previously forged

13. Many voices in these materials take Tunisia as inspiration and exemplar, but several pundits and commentators argued for a variety of reasons that "Egypt is not Tunisia" [*Maṣr ghayr Tūnis*]. Officials of the regime and its supporters eagerly took up the slogan as a rallying cry for order. Tunisians themselves often expressed the hope that Egypt would follow their path, but that is a subject beyond the focus of this chapter.

during mass-scale labor strikes, the *Kifāya* [Enough] movement of 2005–6, and protests against virtually every aspect of Egyptian life, including low and stagnant wages, job insecurity, unemployment, corruption, nepotism, water and electricity shortages, attacks on Coptic Christians, police brutality, gender-based harassment and violence, infringements on academic freedom, and government interference in the judiciary.[14]

This study begins in 2010 not because it represents the beginning of the uprising, then, but because it marks two events that are frequently invoked as significant catalysts for the unrest that followed. The first is Egypt's parliamentary elections, described by some observers as "breathtaking" in the extent of its fraud, not to mention intimidation by security forces.[15] The second is the death of twenty-eight-year-old Khaled Mohamed Said in the custody of the Alexandrian police on June 6. Accounts of exactly what happened and why differ, but most concur that officers beat Khaled to the point of death in full view of witnesses, eventually dumping his lifeless body on the street. Demonstrations and vigils spread out from Alexandria in the weeks and months that followed, fueled in part by circulating accounts of his murder and a photograph posted online of Khaled's brutalized face taken in the morgue, disfigured beyond recognition, bearing an expression of "horror, frozen forever."[16]

For more obvious reasons, this study ends in 2014, the year that saw the "election" of General Abdel Fattah el-Sisi to the presidency of Egypt after three relatively rapid shifts in regime leadership and a great deal of violence. The sequence

14. Ali, "Precursors of the Egyptian Revolution"; Amar, "Egypt," 25; Beinen, "Workers' Protest in Egypt," 452; and "Militancy of Mahalla al-Kubra." Tahrir Square alone had been the site of protests and riots in 1972 (the march of university students), 1977 (the bread riots), 2000 (solidarity with the second Palestinian intifada), 2003 (against the Iraq War), and 2005 (Kifāya), just to mention a few. Ayata and Harders, "'Midān Moments,'" 118. And of course, the history of Egyptian revolts has hardly been confined to Tahrir Square. See el Shakry, "Egypt's Three Revolutions."

15. Dunne and Hamzawy, "From Too Much Egyptian Opposition to Too Little."

16. Ghoneim, *Revolution 2.0*, 58. Ghoneim is one of a group of young, tech-savvy middle-class activists often made into the face of the revolution. This depiction is often accompanied by a tendency to downplay the significance of other contributions, i.e., lower-income youth who identified as fighters (rather than protesters) in their direct confrontations with police, in-person networks, organizations, political savvy forged by decades of labor struggles; and revolution in the countryside. See Ryzova, "Battle of Muhammad Mahmoud Street in Cairo," 273; Abu-Lughod, "Living the 'Revolution' in an Egyptian Village"; Ould Mohamedou, "Neo-Orientalism and the e-Revolutionary"; Ali, "Saeeds of Revolution," 60–71; and Beinin, "Egyptian Workers and January 25th."

is well-known but dizzying: Mubarak had presided over the Egyptian military regime for three decades (1981–2011), but finally stepped down after mounting pressure from demonstrations finally forced him out in early 2011. He was immediately replaced by a so-called "caretaker" government, the eighteen-member Supreme Council of the Armed Forces (SCAF). Far from representing a new era of Egyptian politics, SCAF inaugurated a campaign of relentless retaliation, shooting people randomly, dousing protesters with lethal doses of tear gas, beating them to death, crushing them with tanks and other army vehicles, stripping women, and pounding them senseless.

The interim reign of SCAF officially ended in June 2012, when the Muslim Brotherhood [*al-Ikhwān al-Muslimūn*] candidate, Mohammed Morsi, was elected president in what many characterized as the freest and fairest elections in Egyptian history.[17] Yet just months after the election, in December 2012, Morsi announced a constitutional amendment to give himself unchecked power. Opposition leaders denounced the decree as a betrayal of the new democratic era the election was meant to herald, calling for both revocation and protests. As detailed and depicted in the Al Jazeera documentary, "The Night of Ittihadiya," security and police forces stood by or melted away as violence escalated between protesters and supporters self-appointed to protect their new president.[18] Resorting to familiar rhetoric, Morsi demonized the demonstrators as thugs and Mubarak supporters, a prelude to familiar strategies of repression as the Brotherhood increasingly deployed violence, torture, and detention to silence opposition.

Some have argued that, on Morsi's watch, there was actually a "normalization" of torture as it moved from police cells and military detention centers to public spaces such as mosques and street corners, carried about by Ikhwān vigilante groups assisted by Muslim Brotherhood leaders.[19] But whatever the case, violence erupted along new fissures: as pro- and anti-Brotherhood camps coalesced and the divide between them deepened, civilians increasingly found themselves fighting other civilians—family members, friends, former comrades—as well as security forces.[20]

17. Beverley Milton-Edwards is one of many who have characterized the election in these terms. Milton-Edwards, *Muslim Brotherhood*, 43.

18. Al Jazeera, "'Laylat al-ittiḥādiyya'—Tajriba fāshila li-inqilāb Yūliyū" [The night of unity—A failed experience for the July revolution].

19. Matthies-Boon and Head, "Trauma as Counter-Revolutionary Colonisation," 273. See also Revkin and Auf, "Egypt's Fallen Police State Gives Way to Vigilante Justice"; and Hussein, "Egyptian Protesters Claim They Were Tortured by Muslim Brotherhood."

20. Matthies-Boon and Head, "Trauma as Counter-Revolutionary Colonisation," 274.

In July 2013, Sisi, then chief of the Egyptian military, ousted Morsi, justifying the coup as necessary to safeguard stability and protect the constitution from the Ikhwān's unlawful efforts to grab more power. He then proceeded to suspend the constitution and to outlaw and hound the Ikhwān—the major opposition party—as part of an extensive and ruthless crackdown on dissent. By some accounts, SCAF outdid even Mubarak at his worst in viciousness, a path that Sisi has pursued with equal ruthlessness and evident pride: in a leaked recording of an off-the-record conversation with a journalist, he reportedly refers to himself in the third-person to boast, "people think I'm a soft man, [but] Sisi is torture and suffering."[21] Given that Sisi has now accomplished a "more comprehensive closure of public space than existed even under Mubarak," it has become extremely dangerous for those residing in-country to speak out publicly and in explicitly political terms against the abuses of the regime.[22]

Inasmuch as these events are grouped under the rubric of the Arab uprisings, in the following discussion, I refer to Egypt's Uprising. But I also refer to Egypt's Uprising as a revolution [*thawra*]. This is not an effort to relitigate debates about whether and to what extent this constituted a revolution, a revolt, or a coup, if it failed, was defeated, stolen, or is ongoing.[23] My aim instead is to take my cue from the language many Egyptians themselves use, particularly those in this archive.[24] Still, as such terminology is contested, such choices don't simply classify a subject already transparently at hand; they implicitly take a position on what the subject is that's being studied. In the case of the uprisings in general and the Egyptian Revolution in particular, such classifications reflect how political transformation is defined, in what forms and in which domains such transformation "counts," whose accounts count, and the temporality centered by different frames of analysis.[25]

As one implacable authoritarian Arab regime after another exacted its brutal revenge on opponents and demonstrators, many participants in the uprisings have

21. Kirkpatrick, "Egypt's New Strongman, Sisi Knows Best."

22. Barnett, "Book Review: *Dispatches from the Arab Spring*," 171.

23. As such citations are too numerous to list, the following may serve to illustrate some of these tendencies: Brownlee, Masoud, and Reynolds, *Arab Spring*; Monks, "Could Egypt's Revolution Be Stolen?"; Hessler, "Egypt's Failed Revolution"; and Khlebnikov, "Why Did the 2011 Egyptian Revolution Fail?"

24. Mostafa, "Egyptian Women, Revolution, and Protest Culture," 120.

25. In this connection, see Schwedler's excellent "Taking Time Seriously." Schwedler elaborates and demonstrates many of these arguments in *Protesting Jordan*, "Against Methodological Nationalism," and "Comparative Politics and the Arab Uprisings."

been silenced, expressed a loss of hope, or even refashioned themselves as regime supporters. A cascade of popular and scholarly publications has followed suit; with the exception of Tunisia, the "Arab spring" is usually consigned to the history of object lessons in the triumph of force and the *Realpolitik* it demands. Since the "Arab Spring" has so obviously given way to the "Arab Winter," all that remains to debate is whether the Arab uprisings failed, were defeated, or had never been revolutions in the first place.

This verdict does significant political work, eliding transformations resistant to such logics, the parameters of politics they prioritize, and the historical horizon they presuppose. As Jillian Schwedler argues, such assessments confirm the narratives of these authoritarian states. They also assume a temporality in which the uprisings appear as "failed transitions" to democracy based on the absence of "demonstrable outcomes" such as transformed institutions or even bigger movements or events. Such convergence, she writes, "silences, obscures, erases, and even denies those who continue to struggle, those who refuse to accept that the time of the uprisings is over."[26] As Youssef El Chazli points out, the narrow focus on visible, institutional rupture so common to verdicts of failure overlooks the political import of incremental shifts in subjectivities, and the "hundreds if not thousands of microscopic arenas of social change" that were opened up by experiences of "people doing things they had never done before—never even imagined doing before."[27]

Many of these matters are far afield from the focus and purposes of this inquiry. Still others are the subject of the following chapter, which concerns the performative and transformative character of repair encoded in these expressions of humiliation. There's one particular way the arguments there bear on the matter of terminology here. The current chapter shows that rewriting the revolution as a failed bid by thugs, terrorists, and agents of foreign powers to destroy the country is one way the regime has assiduously sought to nullify the political significance of Egyptian sacrifices and suffering in the lead-up to and during the uprising. The

26. Schwedler, "Taking Time Seriously." See also van de Sande, "Prefigurative Politics of Tahrir Square," 225–26. For an excellent analysis of how female activists under Sisi have refigured rather than abandoned their strategies during the "lean years of resistance," see Allam, "Activism Amid Disappointment."

27. El Chazli, "Egyptian Revolution Is Not a Failure." See also Bayat, *Revolution Without Revolutionaries*, 183; Amar, "Egypt," 30, 38–39, 25, 30; "Egypt after Mubarak"; and "Why Mubarak Is Out."

following chapter draws on these very Egyptian sources to demonstrate how "standing erect" through action or utterance loosens the grip of powerlessness just enough to make real who you recognize yourself to be rather than who you are made to be.[28] Such restorative enactments shift the parameters of what is thinkable in ways that can no more be expunged from the world than one can unring a bell.

To take my terminological cues from the Egyptian voices in this archive, then, is to refuse the narratives of the state as well as pervasive narratives of "revolutionary failure."[29] While the previous chapter showed how shortcuts to grasping the past misapprehends the present, this analysis draws attention to how verdicts about what is accomplished in the present condition the possibilities for such struggle in the future. This is precisely why declarations that the revolution has failed, is over, or never was, become one more aspect of its undoing. In the ongoing struggle between revolutionaries and the state over memory and history, this and the following chapter constitute one very small effort to bear witness to the achievements of such moments and the legacy of what they brought into the world.[30]

"Our Country Is Ruled by Humiliation": Paternal Authority and Unruly Subjects

"Our country is ruled by humiliation and degradation." So begins a poem by an Egyptian named Essam el-Sayyed.[31] Essam is not a professional poet; little is known about him aside from the verses he penned and dedicated to Eslam el-Sayyad, one of the more than seventy people who died in a massacre after a soccer match in Port Said on February 1, 2012. Witnesses describe how, when the game was over, security forces bolted the stadium doors shut, cut the floodlights, and

28. Even as they cannot but reinscribe, to a greater or lesser degree, aspects of the hierarchical conditions under which they were forged. I will return to this in the next chapter.

29. Mostafa, "Egyptian Women, Revolution, and Protest Culture," 120.

30. Çidam makes a similar argument in connection with the 2013 Gezi protests in Turkey: "Keeping a record of those practices, that is to say, recognizing, honoring, and remembering them, may be our only defense against the current trivialization and/or criminalization of these events, which play into the hands of those who seek to obliterate the memory of democratic moments and their subversive dimensions so as to ensure that the past can no longer become a citable source, an emancipatory force in the present." Çidam, *In the Street*, 6.

31. See note 1 above.

stood by as soccer fans were slashed with knives and swords amidst a stampede that crushed dozens.[32]

The poem is an expression of outrage and despair, as well as an indictment of SCAF that, just twelve months after assuming control of Egypt, was widely accused of having orchestrated the massacre at Port Said in ruthless retaliation against the Ultras, groups of die-hard soccer fans. The Ultras had already become a thorn in the side of the regime prior to 2011, challenging its tight control over public spaces, collective gatherings, and social expression, at times through direct confrontation with police and security forces. At critical moments during the uprising, they stepped in to safeguard protesters, at times battling police on the ever-shifting front lines of the revolution.[33]

Occasioned by a specific act of state violence, Essam's evocation of the "rule of humiliation" is both a recurrent trope and an organizing theme in this archive. It encompasses not only Mubarak's thirty-year rule, but also the brutal reign of SCAF, the governance of the Muslim Brotherhood during the one-year tenure (2012–13) of President Mohammed Morsi, and the Sisi regime after Morsi was overthrown.[34] It's phrased in various ways with different emphases depending upon the figure at the helm. In contrast to the full-throated indictments of SCAF viciousness, for example, Morsi's brief tenure elicits as much ridicule and embarrassment as condemnation. "What humiliation [*al-dhull*], what shame, the mother of the world is ruled by a donkey," goes one of the protesters' chants in 2013.[35] On the Egyptian news satire called *Elbernameg* [The program], host Bassem Youssef adds up all the evasions, contradictions, and inanities of Morsi's speech as "'Arabī Ikhwānī" (Brotherhood Arabic) requiring translation using a

32. Doward, "Egyptian Police Incited Massacre at Stadium, Say Angry Footballers"; Londoño and Hassieb, "At Least 74 Dead After Egypt Soccer Match."

33. Jerzak, "Ultras in Egypt." See also Ryzova, "Battle of Muhammad Mahmoud Street in Cairo," esp. n. 39; and Woltering, "Unusual Suspects."

34. Such constancy is exemplified by four Facebook posts by discrete users, each from a different year. On June 17, 2010, six months before the uprising, Egyptians are said to be "drowning in humiliation." "How long are we going to live through the humiliation [*dhull*], degradation [*hawān*], oppression and fear of emergency law?" asks another on January 15, 2011. On August 15, 2012, just two months into Morsi's brief presidency, the rule of the Ikhwān is accused of inventing "new forms of humiliation." And a March 23, 2013, post refers to the utter relentlessness of "humiliation upon humiliation" [*dhull fī dhull*].

35. Repeated in Taha Emsallam (@TahaEmsallam), "Iḥdā shiʿārāt muẓāharāt #miṣr yādī al-dhull wa-yādī al-ʿār umm il-dunyā ḥākimhā ḥimār, nazīkīn al-maṣriyya hahaha."

special *Ikhwānī* dictionary.[36] But tying them together is a mode of rule that is no joking matter; this is not a characteristic specific to a person, office, or agency, but a system of domination in which humiliation is an animating logic as well as a technique of control.[37]

Such logic is anchored in and enabled by representations of the president as an all-powerful father and Egyptian politics as a family affair. Mubarak was fond of calling himself the "father of Egypt," routinely referring not just to the youth of the country but citizens generally as his children.[38] Up to the very end, he presented himself as an unappreciated father devoted to his unruly children, telling Egyptians in his final address that he speaks as a "father to his sons and daughters" [*al-ab li-abnā'ihi wa-banātihi*].[39] But the really "strange phenomenon," activist Alaa Abd El Fattah says in a 2012 interview, are those Egyptians who co-produce such paternalism, calling themselves the "children of Mubarak" [*abnā' Mubarak*].[40] A particularly intense burst of filial fealty around the time of Mubarak's forced exit is a case in point. One emotional caller into a television program in 2011protested that "[t]his president is more than our father, he is the father of all of Egypt. He is our father—our father, our father!"[41] Many Egyptians not only

36. Elbernameg, *'Indamā ya'tī al-khiṭāb - al-ḥalqa 15 - al-juz' 2* [When the speech arrives, episode 15, part 2].

37. See, for example, Negm, "Ilā al-mutaḍarrirīn . . . ḥaqqkum ma'a Mubarak mish ma'ānā" [To those who have grievances . . . this is Mubarak's fault, not ours]; Elbernameg, *al-Nāshiṭ wa'l-mudawwin Wael Abbas* [Activist and blogger Wael Abbas]; and Al Nahar TV, "Doma . . . ya'ūd lil-ḥurriyya" [Doma . . . returned to freedom], interview with Ahmed Doma, former member of the Muslim Brotherhood and revolutionary activist.

38. Just one example (of too many to cite) is Elbalad, "Muḥākamat al-qarn: kalimat al-ra'īs al-asbaq Mubarak amāma hay'at al-quḍāh" [The trial of the century: the former president's speech in front of the Judicial Council].

39. Dhākirat Maspero, "al-Khiṭāb al-akhīr li-Mubarak" [Mubarak's last speech].

40. AlMasry AlYoum, "Alaa Abd El Fattah fī 'Studio AlMasry AlYoum'" [Alaa Abd El Fattah on Egypt Studio Today]. Fattah is a software developer, blogger, and political activist who participated in organizing opposition to the regime both prior to and during the January 2011 revolution and has been in and out of prison ever since. He and his sisters Sanaa and Mona are part of an intergenerational family of activists that includes Seif Abd El Fattah (d. 2014), a human rights lawyer, and Laila Soueif, a mathematics professor at Cairo University, an activist on behalf of women and political prisoners.

41. Elbernameg, *I'tibruh abūk yā akhī* [Consider him your father, man]. Bassem Youssef excerpted this sound bite on his show, but the person had called into a different program, Mehwar TV's *90 Minutes.* Youssef took another sound bite—"i'tibruh abūk yā akhī, i'tibruh ab yā akhī" [consider him your father, man, consider him a father]—from a protester who happened to be captured on a Nile TV program from February 3, 2011.

mourned for the "father of the country" but, on satellite TV, social media, and in daily conversations, exhorted their compatriots to "have mercy on an honorable man humiliated."[42]

Dr. Manal Omar, a specialist in child psychology, sees such behavior not as strange but as indicative of a predictable developmental pathology. According to Omar, Egyptians have been taught to regard the ruler as the father who is owed obedience, trained to see dissent as filial transgression. Continually treated as incapable of thinking for themselves, she says, they have ceased to do so. In a sense, Mubarak is the abusive parent, Egyptians the brutalized children, unable to recognize how they have been remade by violence and, as a result, unable to demand what they are due. Development and maturity, she concludes, is impossible until the offender is punished.[43]

The instant and widespread outrage that greeted the eruption of filial devotion surrounding Mubarak's exit suggests a more complicated conclusion. In the words of one emblematic tweet at the time, this so-called father and "honorable man has humiliated [*dhull*] Egypt for thirty years, stealing, betraying, imprisoning, enforcing emergency law, selling out Gaza and stealing 70 billion dollars."[44] Another tweet orders Mubarak apologists to stop talking nonsense; the real humiliation lies in the failure to bring a dictator to justice.[45]

42. See, for example, Hanaa Alalwani (@hanaa-alalwani), "Rajul khadama bilādahu ka-'askarī, wa-qādahā ka-ra'īs 30 'āman, wa-in fa'ala mā fa'ala . . . hal yakūn jazāhu sijn wa-muḥākamāt . . . am 'azl wa-iqāma jabriyya . . . irḥamū 'azīz qawmin dhull yā Miṣr." Another version of this sentiment that circulated at the time substituted "decent" for "honorable," or claimed that he was a decent/honorable man whose dignity should be restored. See, for example, Veto Gate, "Aḥad Abnā' Mubarak yuṭālib el-Sisi bi'l-'afw 'an al-ra'īs al-asbaq." "Shame on us [*'ār 'alīnā*] for not respecting this great leader," the Egyptian man continues, standing next to a headshot of Mubarak in a grainy video. The reference to Mubarak's heroic role in the 1973 War has also been widespread among his supporters, and is part of a broader discourse depicting leaders who fought in the October War as heroes who restored Egyptian dignity through victory after the humiliation of defeats. It is also evident in commentary about Ahmed Shafik's campaign for Egyptian president in 2012. See, for example, عبد الرحمن (@Abdelrahman_3), "Shafīq min abṭāl ḥarb Uktūbir, hādhā al-jīl al-rā'i' alladhī intashala Miṣr min dhull al-hazīma ilā karāmat al-naṣr wa'l-'ubūr #ḥamlat-da'm-Shafīq-ra'īsan-li-Miṣr."

43. Al-Dīb, "Dr. Manal Omar, ablagh mā qīla 'an al-thawra al-Miṣriyya" [Dr. Manal Omar, the most eloquent thing said about the Egyptian revolution].

44. محمد الاحمري (@alahmarim), February 9, 2011; it's worth noting that this tweet is from a Saudi, not an Egyptian.

45. Gamal Eid (@gamaleid), "Lā taqul irḥamū 'azīz qawm dhalla!! qul ḥākimū dīktātūr wa-illā aṣābakum al-dhull." See also Asmaa Mahfouz (@AsmaaMahfouz), "'Ahd Mubarak mish lāqīn yāklū shūfū dhull al-nās wa-intū ti'rafū līh Mubarak bi-yitdhall dilwaqtī." Also Alaa

Sisi's penchant for such familial language is less widely known than that of Mubarak but just as telling. Characterized as "disciplined and domineering" by one journalist, Sisi has depicted his leadership of Egypt as a relation of father to a wayward son.[46] He has publicly—and, to some of his compatriots, ridiculously—referred to Egyptians as the "light in our eyes" (akin to "apple of my eye" in English). Privately, he has described the military as "like the very big brother, the very big father who has a son who is a bit of a failure and does not understand the facts. . . . Does the father kill the son? Or does he always shelter him and say, 'I'll be patient until my son understands'?"[47] Supportive media have hastened to feature grateful interview subjects describing Sisi as a "second father" and the "father to all Egyptians."[48]

Recourse to paternal imagery of this sort is neither unprecedented nor unique to Egypt, and its history demonstrates the emotive power of such rhetoric, the political sensibilities it can conjure or transform, and the forms of rule it can justify. In *Egypt as a Woman: Nationalism, Gender, and Politics*, Beth Baron points out that, in an array of contexts, "kin idioms" have served to ground national unity in the idea of a single family with shared blood modeled on the bourgeois family, headed by the father who rules over his "sons" and "daughters" with a strong hand.[49] These materials likewise show that such rhetorical invocations in contemporary Egypt do significant affective and political work. They catalyze the emotional power of familial loyalties for the nation-state and fashion rule in masculinist terms. In the process, they conflate political and paternal authority

---

abd El Fattah (@alaa), "Yā rīt nib'at al-shihāda dī li-kull ḥadd ti'rafūh ma'a faḍḍ al-i'tiṣām bil-quwwa, 'ashān yi'rafū al-gīsh al-maṣrī duruh iyah, ta'dhīb wa-dhull wa-ihāna."

46. Kirkpatrick, "Egypt's New Strongman, Sisi Knows Best."

47. The quote is from a leaked recording of Sisi talking to fellow officers in a meeting, reported in *The New York Times*. Kirkpatrick, "Egypt's New Strongman, Sisi Knows Best." See also "Egypt's el-Sisi."

48. A woman named Nahid Gamal Said was featured on al-Bawabah News saying that Sisi is a "father to all Egyptians" [*ab li-kull al-maṣriyyīn*]. Al Bawabah News, "Sayyidat al-trūsīkil 'an al-ra'īs el-Sisi." Another program recently featured Loujain Ebeido, the young daughter of a military officer killed while fighting in North Sinai, saying about Sisi, "Mr. President is like a second father to me." Ṣabāḥak Miṣrī, "Ibnat al-Shahīd Muṣṭafā 'Ibīdū."

49. Such familial metaphors were in evidence prior to the rise of the nation-state, for example, in the imperial paternalism of the late Ottoman Empire, but Baron points out that kin idioms have characterized almost all nationalist discourses and are historically entangled with the rise of the modern capitalist state and consolidation of its power. Far from a revenant of the premodern past, then, paternal authority has been integral to the emergence of modern nationalism from Europe to the Middle East. In fact, Baron argues that nationalists deployed them much more extensively (and with different emphases) than ever before. Baron, *Egypt as a Woman*, 4–5.

to infantilize Egyptians as dull, child-like, and most certainly incapable of ruling themselves. Paradoxically, this reproduces the earlier tendency of colonial powers to depict the colonized not just as representing an earlier stage of development, but as embodying the infancy of Europe itself, in need of both subjugation and tutelage.[50]

A contrast with John Locke's paradigmatic formulation of paternal authority is instructive. For Locke, paternal authority is appropriately exercised over children for their own good, as they have not yet developed the capacity to reason. Like the patriarchal authority of a husband over his wife, paternal authority presumes a relation of unequals. This is precisely what distinguishes it from properly political authority anchored in a relation among equals.[51] But in the usual course of events, children—at least of the male variety—grow up and develop capacities of mind that admit them to the fraternity of equals, thereby rendering such tutelage at once unnecessary and inappropriate. This distinction between paternal and political authority is a crucial component of Locke's famous refutation of absolute and hereditary political power. It has simultaneously functioned to mark the emergence of modern liberal political authority from the subjugation of premodern monarchies and anchored liberal justifications of colonialism in the colonized-subject-as-child.

In contrast to Locke's account, the instantiation of paternal authority in the humiliation regime constitutes such tutelage as permanent rather than transitory. It is anchored in an ontology of ruler and ruled that renders Egyptians eternally immature, always unequal to the strong father with a heavy hand whose discipline must be imposed for their own good. Already routine, pervasive, and longstanding, this variation of paternal authority turns domination into a necessity of nature.

When citizens are in perpetual tutelage, the polity is evacuated of politics not just by state brutality but by a logic that figures the public sphere as an extension

50. See, for example, Massad, *Desiring Arabs*, 55. The literature on this is extensive, so it will perhaps suffice to mention just a few: Cohen, "Colonized as Child"; Marangoly George, "Homes in the Empire, Empires in the Home," 112; Clancy-Smith and Gouda, *Domesticating the Empire*; and Prakash, "Writing Post-orientalist Histories of the Third World," 386.

51. Locke, *Second Treatise on Government*. This distinction is famously central to Locke's repudiation of Robert Filmer's justification of absolute monarchy as anchored in "fatherly authority, right of fatherhood," which Filmer also refers to as "royal authority" (bk. I, ch. 2). There is extensive secondary literature on Locke delving into every facet of his thought, but my interest in him here is narrowly confined to his widely known formulation of paternal authority.

of the (conventional) domestic realm. This is one reason why several of these texts depict Egyptians as starving for politics itself.[52] Inasmuch as paternal authority in the domestic realm tends to constitute the family as a kind of property, moreover, this ontology figures the state as the possession of the ruler rather than an expression of the community or an instrument of collective power. A guest on the TV program *al-Ḥaqīqa* [The truth] suggests just this when referring to Mubarak as *ṣāḥib dawla*. In Egyptian, *ṣāḥib* often means "owner," so *ṣāḥib dawla* connotes "owner of the country."[53] The implication here is that the regime owns Egypt; Egyptians just live in it.

Schools have long been an arena for indoctrination, but this collapse of the public into the domestic has accomplished a particular kind of fusion of the politics of the regime and the education of children.[54] In a 2013 blog post, for example, novelist Shady Lewis worries that the brutalization and indoctrination of children in schools, long a feature of Egyptian education, has just become an extension of the paternal discipline "required" to restore the political order upended by unruly youth incapable of self-rule during the uprising. Flags, microphones, anthems, and broadcasts scream at children each morning to fall into line in the school yards and beyond, Lewis writes, hammering into them "the chants of the nation and rites of daily submission and humiliation [*ṭuqūs al-khuḍūʿ wa'l-mahāna al-yawmiyya*]," reinforced by the smack of batons wielded by teachers all too eager to play tyrant in the only arena they command.[55] Schools have become the newest front in the regime's counterrevolutionary offensive, turning the "playground into a performance stage for the army, where they introduce the students to their

52. See, for example, Fadl, "Man huwa al-ra'īs al-qādim?"

53. *Ṣāḥib dawla* can also mean prime minister, but "owner" is the meaning implied here given that it is used to describe Mubarak, not his prime minister. I am grateful to my intrepid research assistant for pointing this out. Dream TV, "Al-ḥaqīqa—Wael el-Ibrashy—Muwājaha maʿa alladhīna ḥāwalū al-intiḥār ḥarqan fī misr wa-maʿa ʿā'ilatihim" [The Truth—Wael el-Ibrashy—interview with those who attempted self-immolation in Egypt and their families].

54. This suggests that in education as in politics—to borrow from Ramadan's work on Egyptian secondary schools—the discipline of humiliation becomes almost "an integral and necessary part of the regime's particular neoliberal project of governance." Ramadan, "Education and the Production of Citizenship in the Late Mubarak Era," 282. Ramadan argues that "beating and humiliation" have been normalized in Egyptian secondary schools (153). It is perhaps worth noting that, despite the centrality of humiliation to the argument and the fact that the word or a variant of it appears over one hundred times, this otherwise very compelling dissertation doesn't supply a real definition of it.

55. Lewis, "Maʿrakat al-madāris wa'l-aṣābiʿ al-arbaʿa" [The Battle of Schools and the Four Fingers].

American-made automatic weapons to induce awe and amazement, [all] with the masculinity and aggression of the military."

In this archive, most of those who speak not only recognize but seek to publicly name and indict the politics of this ontology. The president has ensured that Egyptians remain locked in "ignorance, backwardness, humiliation and degradation [*dhull wa-mahāna*]," reads one Facebook post; no wonder Mubarak's intelligence chief and vice-president, Omar Suleiman, said publicly that Egyptians are not ready for democracy.[56] "They don't think us worthy of speaking the truth even if we die," go the lyrics of "This Is the Story," a ballad that would be sung widely at demonstrations. Patronized at every turn, citizens don't even register as agents capable of sacrificing for Egypt, the song continues, of breaking our own chains, or of restoring our *karāma*.[57] There are many "who say we are children—we are not children," Gakh writes in "Mikammilīn" [We'll keep going].[58]

Such lyrics are not reducible to artistic hyperbole, as an Al Jazeera documentary on the last weeks of Mubarak's presidency makes clear. It shows a man unable to conceive of Egyptians as developed and disciplined enough to organize a sustained and serious challenge to his power.[59] Believing himself the ruler not of citizens but of foolish and ungrateful children more deserving of disdain than love, he seemed entirely confident that "it could never happen here." Like many of his supporters, Mubarak was certain that "Egypt is not Tunisia" [*Miṣr ghayr Tūnis*]—almost a mantra among some—because, unlike the tyranny in Tunis, his benign, selfless rule was a boon to his people.[60]

Outpaced by events to the very end, interviewees say, Mubarak dealt with the uprising "as if it was a storm in a teacup," unable or unwilling to see the magnitude of a challenge that was, for him, literally unthinkable. Unruly children, after all, do not organize. Certainly, they may be driven by passing impulse to converge around

56. Amr Afia, "Ḥadūtha thawriyya" [A revolutionary story]. Afia is referring to Christiane Amanpour's interview with Suleiman, ABC News, "Egypt's Vice President Omar Suleiman."

57. Doooozz28, "Hiya dī kull el-ḥikāya . . . Muḥammad el-Wadi" [This is the entire story . . . Muhammad el-Wadi]. Wadi is one of the officers who joined the protests on April 8, 2011, and was subsequently imprisoned.

58. Gakh, "Mikamilīn" [We'll keep going].

59. Al Jazeera, "al-Laḥaẓāt al-akhīra fī ḥukm Mubarak" [The final moments of Mubarak's rule].

60. As Reem Saad points out, the Egypt-is-not-Tunisia argument was not unique to the regime and its dependents; at least some prominent political analysts and political scientists made the same argument, albeit for different reasons. Saad, "Egyptian Revolution," 63–64. Commentary in English and Arabic on this theme is extensive. Just as an example, see El-Shobaki, "Opinion: Egypt is not Tunisia."

the pursuit of, say, bread or a toy, or cry when in pain, but coincidence is not coordination. For Mubarak, the fact that they have converged in the streets demonstrates just how vulnerable such simpletons are to manipulation by nefarious foreign powers. But there is little political threat in the momentary concatenation of unregulated desires.

In a final twist worth noting, many of these materials turn these familial metaphors around to indict the regime for having "raised" Egyptians on humiliation and "breast-fed humiliation" to them. These double as denunciations of their fellow citizens, as is evident in a conspicuous surge in such imagery in the year after Morsi was removed from the presidency.[61] The anger, frustration, and even disgust at the complicity of so many Egyptians in the military coup that nullified a notably fair election is palpable. This doesn't seem to reflect any great love for Morsi; on the contrary, many here express a combination of contempt and alarm at the policies and power grabs that characterized the Brotherhood's brief rule. It's the role of Egyptians in restoring the humiliation regime that draws intense contempt, and in language that paradoxically evokes Dr. Omar's diagnosis: Egyptians have been nursed on humiliation since infancy, trained in it by schools, and habituated to it by endless repetition.[62] Apparently, one tweet reads, "[s]laves never have enough submission . . . they love a life of humiliation."[63] Egyptians have become "addicted" to humiliation and abjection, to the point where they even "crave" it like a drug they can no longer imagine living without says another.[64] "Forgive me, I had no idea," reads one Facebook post. "It turns out humiliation [*al-dhull*] is a habit" and a way of life.[65] Graffiti in Mustafa Mahmoud Square, Mohandessin, put it pointedly: "the free mourn their martyrs; the slaves cry for their slave drivers."[66]

61. دراسات عسكرية (@samyalhasan), August 22, 2013; تسلم الايادي (@masriaawi) July 5, 2013; محمد الهاشمي الحامدي (@MALHACHIMI), December 1, 2013. احمد الزايد (@AHM_RGL), April 2, 2010.

62. Zogby research polling indicates that Morsi's removal was supported by almost half of Egyptians (44 percent before, 51 percent after). But polls before and after the removal—in May, July, and September 2013—not only point to substantial disaffection with the rule of the Brotherhood's Freedom and Justice Party but also increasing polarization about the military's action deposing him afterward. This included sharp disagreements about whether the deposition should be called a "coup" at all. Zogby Research Services, "Egyptian Attitudes."

63. الخطاري (@Truthcaller), Twitter, June 10, 2014.

64. Mohamed Hamdy Omar (@mhamdyooo), Twitter, May 26, 2014.

65. Ayman Baghat Amar, post on Facebook, "Miṣr Dawla Madaniyya" [Egypt civilian state], February 2, 2013.

66. *Al-Judrān tahtif: jirāfītī al-thawrah al-Miṣrīyya* [Walls Talk: Graffiti of the Egyptian Revolution], 226–27.

"We Do Not Want a Humiliated Nation": Egypt in the World

In a snippet of video filmed at a protest in Tahrir Square, a young boy named Hassan points out that, as poverty makes Egyptians look like "beggars in front of the whole world," it's not just an individual humiliation but also a national one.[67] If the first domain of the rule of humiliation is domestic, Hassan puts his finger on the second: the humiliation of Egypt in front of the world.[68] These voices constitute national humiliation in relation to shifting identities and layered frames of reference, but they leave no doubt as to the culprit common to them all: a succession of autocratic rulers whose domestic despotism is matched only by their willingness to bow down and bend over to foreign powers and institutions, all but delivering Egypt into financial and political vassalage.

In a post published five days after Mubarak was forced from power, journalist and activist Nawara Negm, daughter of the well-known poet Ahmed Fouad Negm, rails against a regime expert for belittling Egyptians and trivializing their suffering. For Negm, such indifference is compounded by a hypocrisy epitomized by Mubarak's policies toward Israel[69]—foremost among them his concern for the safety of Israelis in Egypt and his cooperation in the Israeli blockade of the Gaza Strip following Hamas's electoral victory there in 2006 and in the 2009 Gaza war—with devastating consequences for the Palestinian population.[70] As Negm argues, there was no comparable concern—or indeed, evidence of any concern at all—when it came to the greatest maritime disaster in Egyptian history: the sinking of a thirty-five-year-old Egyptian ferry in the Red Sea on February 3, 2006. At least one thousand passengers died, many of whom were poor

67. "Ḥassan ṭifl shawāriʿ fī mīdān al-taḥrīr yarudd ʿalā raʾīs al-wuzaraʾ al-mukallaf Kamal al-Ganzoury" [Hassan, a street child in Tahrir Square, responds to Prime Minister-designate Kamal al-Ganzoury].

68. This is precisely the sentiment in the title of this section, "We Do Not Want a Humiliated Nation," a line from Gakh's poem, "We'll Keep Going." The phrase for humiliated—or degraded—nation here is *waṭan madhlūl muhān.*

69. Unsurprisingly, the history of Mubarak's policies toward Israel is complex and contested, and well beyond my focus. Suffice it to say that Mubarak pursued policies that shrewdly navigated among competing interests and commitments to strengthen his regime.

70. Human Rights Watch, "Deprived and Endangered." Mortality is only one metric of the toll on Palestinians from Israel's "Operation Cast Lead," but B'Tselem, the Israeli Information Center for Human Rights in the Occupied Territories, reports that over 1,300 Palestinians were killed, of whom an estimated 759 were civilians. Btselem, "Fatalities."

laborers returning home from Saudi Arabia for vacation.[71] Bristling with sarcasm, Negm writes,

> Thank you for being a servant of the United States . . . for 30 years of subservience to them while they humiliate us [*tadhillnā*]. Thank you for . . . allowing everyone to call us traitors and agents of Israel. . . . Thank you for the scandal of Gaza war. . . . Now we, with our 7000 years of history of farmers and workers, are equated with a 60-year-old country of gangs and outlaws. Thank you for forcing us to humiliate ourselves [*dhāllīn*] in exchange for peace with Israel, while you continue to send our children to die everywhere. You sent them to die in Iraq and Iran and [deploy them in wars] that have nothing to do with us. . . . You sent them again to die when Saddam attacked Kuwait. Aren't you the one who supported Saddam all these years? You sent them again to Afghanistan to be rid of them, and when they return, you sentence them to death. You sent them to Bosnia and kill them when they come back.[72]

Negm's post captures a particular thread of indignation that suffuses this archive, one that's grounded in a narrative of Egyptian exceptionalism at the very heart of the national humiliation presumed by literati and tuktuk drivers alike.[73] Egypt is not just one nation among many, but "mother of the world" [*umm al-dunyā*], the honorific for a civilization of great antiquity, source of extraordinary achievements over the millennia, epicenter of Arab lands and Islamic learning. This grand patrimony bestows upon Egyptians a singular status and confers upon Egypt a special burden and destiny to lead the Arab nation [*al-waṭan al-ʿArabī*] as a whole.[74] As evidence, one need look no further than the charismatic

71. The Associated Press reported demonstrations by the families of the missing, including one where family members who had been waiting for two days to know the fate of their relatives shouted at the police: "Where is the president, where are our sons? Where are the bodies? We want to know the fate of the children." Associated Press, "Families of Ferry Passengers Lash Out."

72. Negm, "Jumʿat al-istimrār wa'l-intiṣār fī maydān al-Taḥrīr wa'l" [Friday of perseverance and triumph in Tahrir square]. The Egyptian government has been accused of gross negligence not only in regard to the condition of the ferry but also in connection with what some characterized as a botched rescue operation. Al Jazeera, "Report Blames Egypt for Ferry Disaster."

73. Tuktuk is the name for a small three-wheel automotive rickshaw in Egypt. Relatively inexpensive, many of the vehicles are unlicensed, and are a crucial part of the Egyptian informal economy, particularly in cities like Cairo.

74. See Jankowski, *Nasser's Egypt, Arab Nationalism, and the United Arab Republic*, 32.

Egyptian president, Gamal abd al-Nasser, who popularized the very notion of a contemporary "Arab nation"—along with others such as *al-umma al-ʿarabiyya* and *al-waḥda al-ʿarabiyya*—in the first place.[75]

All national narratives cohere by way of omission, whether it's the story of Egyptian exceptionalism or of America's foundation in freedom and progressive inclusion. But for my purposes, the historical accuracy of this sense of exceptionalism is far less important than the way it infuses the experience of Egyptian humiliation, both of the nation and its people, articulated in this archive. Negm is incensed by Mubarak's utter indifference to human life, for example, but it's his degradation of Egypt's people and national stature that makes his hypocrisy especially galling to her. As president, Mubarak is meant to shepherd and embody Egypt's storied inheritance. Instead, he publicly derides and callously destroys the people most deserving of reverence and offers obeisance and protection to those most worthy of contempt. As she sourly points out, Egypt is forty-six times larger than Israel with almost thirty centuries of history to modern Israel's seven or so decades. According to Negm, the world is profoundly out of joint when the "gangs and outlaws" of a puny, upstart nation next door have devastated the "mother of the world" in a succession of military conflicts, at the cost of tens of thousands of Egyptian lives and billions of dollars.

As in the previous chapters, my interest isn't in the accuracy of such claims but in the way they construct humiliation. And like the Islamist discourses of the previous chapters, outrage at Israel here is folded into a broader narrative of humiliation in which Palestinians themselves remain strangely out of focus. Where Islamists tend to subsume the degradation of Palestinians into a narrative about the humiliation of Islam, these materials turn them into an index of Egyptian humiliation. The peace agreement with Israel brokered by Anwar al-Sadat in 1979 is, in the succinct words of one Egyptian tweet, nothing less than a "treaty of humiliation [*al-dhull*]."[76] In this account, the impunity with which Israelis continue to oppress Palestinians attests to how the Treaty has enchained Egypt, rendering it impotent

75. A charismatic champion of Arab unity and redistributive land reform who famously nationalized the European-dominated Suez Canal Company, Nasser's tenure is commonly lionized—and particularly by an older generation of Egyptians and Arabs—as the highwater mark of Arab unity, defiance of imperial power, and modern Egyptian prestige. He implicitly figures as the modern touchstone of the august legacy betrayed by his successors. See, for example, Brand, *Official Stories*, 27–68. But Nasser's legacy is also highly contested. Some for example, see his leadership and policies as ushering in the contemporary Egyptian police state.

76. بلا اقنعة (@truth4ever1), "Hal sawf tughlaq sifārat Israel fī Miṣr wa-hal sawf tulghā muʿāhadat al-dhull maʿa al-kayān al-ṣahyūnī?"

to lead the region against an interloper that has dispossessed and oppressed hundreds of thousands of Arabs. Egyptian complicity in such polices, moreover, turn it from a beacon of Arab unity into its most conspicuous saboteur. Any hope that the end of Mubarak's rule would signal the end of Egyptian impotence and complicity has long since passed. Morsi openly coordinated Egyptian security operations with Israel and the United States to control "militants" in the Sinai that bordered Gaza, and Sisi has committed Egypt to participating in the blockade as part of his campaign against "Islamist terrorism."[77]

The exceptionalism that threads throughout this archive also imbricates the fate of the Egyptian and Arab nation in a very particular way. As Egypt is simultaneously one Arab country but also a prototype and pattern for all others, what knits them together isn't simply a shared Arabism but Egyptian predominance. Just as the Arab world is elevated by the leadership and grandeur of Egypt, an Egypt powerless to lead is a harbinger of the disunity and humiliating weakness of the Arab nation, *al-waṭan al-ʿArabī.*

As Egypt's economic reliance on other Arab states turns leader into suppliant, it is the very antithesis of Arab unity rightly understood. Egyptian financial indebtedness to Gulf monarchies, for example, signifies a dependence indistinguishable from abjection.[78] "Egypt is like a decent girl who ran to the street when the earthquake hit, then was kidnapped by a pimp dressed like a shaykh who used her to beg for money," tweets one Egyptian in 2013. "I do not belong to the Egyptian republic of begging; I will not be part of this humiliation [*al-dhull*]."[79] It's not just that such debt has transformed the nation into a beggar but, as Lewis points out, that essential parts of Egyptian sovereignty are being sold off piecemeal to the highest bidder by those tasked with its protection. The military whose mandate is defense is violating the very national *karāma* [*imtihānan li-l-karāma al-waṭaniyya*] it claims to embody and protect.[80]

It's not only the condition of national indebtedness and the often-public obeisance Egyptian leaders pay to the petty potentates awash in oil money that are humiliating, but also any whiff of smug superiority from the lenders themselves.

77. Dekel and Perlov, "President Morsi and Israal-Egypt Relations"; Brumberg, "Morsi's Moment on Gaza." See also Amar, *Dispatches from the Arab Spring*, 33–34.

78. Just for example, a 2007 report listed Egypt as the second-largest recipient of aid from three major Arab donors, Saudi Arabia, Kuwait, and the United Arab Emirates. Villanger, "Arab Foreign Aid." See also Butter, "Egypt and the Gulf."

79. Abbas Abdelhassan (@Abbasyz), "Maṣr ʿāmila zay bint uṣūl tizlit al-shāriʿ fī al-zilzāl gāy khāṭifhā quwād lābis shaykh wa-sarah yishhat bīhā . . . anā lā antamī ilā gumhūriyyat Miṣr al-mutasawwila. Laysa lī fī al-dhull."

80. Lewis, "Miṣr taḥta al-wiṣāya" [Egypt under guardianship].

This is particularly evident in relation to Saudi Arabia, conspicuous among the Gulf lenders to Egypt but also a major employer of Egyptian migrant workers. Along with other foreign laborers, these Egyptians comprise a substantial segment of the workforce in the Kingdom but, lacking the protections afforded by Saudi citizenship, have been especially vulnerable to exploitation and abuse. Saudi power relative to Egypt is also driven home each year at the time of the pilgrimage [*ḥajj*] to Mecca that all Muslims are encouraged to make at least once in their lifetime. The Saudis have positioned themselves as gatekeepers of the *ḥajj*—among other things, instituting quotas in the 1990s that limit the number of pilgrims permitted per country annually—turning it into what critics call just "one more tool in Saudi Arabia's foreign policy arsenal."[81]

Under the hashtag #Sisi-kisses-the-head-of-king, a flood of tweets in 2014 exploded in outrage when King Abdullah seemed to summon Sisi to a meeting on his private plane. "What humiliation and degradation [*dhull wa-mahāna*]," goes one tweet. "Begging is an art / Petro has its part / and this is the time of Egypt's humiliation and degradation," writes another.[82] A letter the Saudi monarch sent Sisi on the occasion of his election is more of a patronizing command than an expression of support, Lewis complains in 2014.[83] In it, the King portrays Egypt as chaotic and immature, a burden to its allies, in desperate need of guardians who can help steer the country out of what the King refers to as a "tunnel of darkness." Elsewhere, Lewis indicts Sisi for his brutal paternalism; here, he seems incensed that Abdullah dare lecture Sisi as a parent would a child about how to restore economic and political order in his own house. "Tell me, is this Egypt?" asks a tuktuk driver in a 2016 television interview. "Egypt, who once ruled over Chad, Sudan, and Saudi Arabia. Now some Gulf countries laugh at us and make fun of us and brag about their roles compared to Egypt? [They say to us] 'Look what we give you and what we do for you.' . . . Is this fitting for Egypt's stature?"[84]

81. Kayaoglu, "It Is Time to Reform the Management of The Hajj."

82. محمد البلال (@mohdgnibi), "'Abd Allah bin 'Abd al-'Azīz yadhill el-Sisi wa-yastad'īh li-ṭā'iratuh al-khāṣṣa lil-ḥadīth ma'ahu thumma yughādir, hadhā huwa el-Sisi al-dhalīl alladhī ightaṣab al-ḥukm fī Miṣr ayyi mahāna wa-ayyi dhull."

83. Lewis, "Miṣr taḥta al-wiṣāya" Carolyn Barnett emphasizes that the pressure on post-revolutionary Egypt comes from multiple directions, including not only the IMF, UAE, and Saudi Arabia, but also Euro-American governments, wealthy Egyptian business leaders, and Qatar, among others. Barnett, "Review Essay *Understanding the New Middle East*," 175.

84. Al Hayah TV Network, "Sawwāq 'Tūktūk' bi-100 rājil yulakhkhiṣ ḥāl Miṣr fī daqīqa wa'l-jamī' yusaqqif lahu."

The making and dynamics of national debt are just the surface of what's characterized here as the "republic of begging."[85] Equally if not more humiliating is the haggling for "gifts" and luxuries from any potentate with money to burn, for which the Mubarak family in particular was notorious. In an interview, the president's private secretary, Shafiq al-Banna, describes the president and his son, Gamal, soliciting luxury cars and brand-name goods from oil-rich Arab rulers in private telephone calls, behaving as if Egypt is nothing more than a "beggar, a hobo."[86] Small wonder, Banna says, that Libyan President Muʿammar al-Qaddafi described Mubarak as "the beggar president [*al-raʾīs al-shaḥḥāt*]!"[87] At such moments, "I despised myself for being Egyptian [*kunt b-aḥtaqir nafsī inn anā Maṣrī*]. This is how low we've fallen."[88]

Here as elsewhere, there's an imbrication between the "domestic" and "international" articulations of humiliation that intensify both. Egyptian exceptionalism not only ties together nation and people but also binds the "I" to the "we" such that national diminishment in the world can feel intensely personal. At the same time, it makes the brutal infantilization of Egyptians by the regime not just an appalling injustice inflicted on human beings but an outrage perpetrated on a people of great stature. Lastly, Egypt's historical and political stature draws the attention of the entire world, turning the globe into a vast witness of both its triumphs and its failures. Only months after electrifying images of the uprising exploded across social media and dominated global news outlets, Lewis writes, the world watched the "chaotic spectacle" of citizens turning against one another, all to the benefit of the military, whose tactics of "intentionally destroyed opportunities" helped precipitate the very turmoil that effectively positioned the

85. The reference to begging here refers not only to the behavior of the Mubarak family and Egyptian national debt, but also to the innumerable poor driven to panhandling on the street and corruption and bribery so generalized as to have become what Galal Amin refers to as a "way of life," one that has turned most citizens into supplicants for basic services. Amin, *Egypt in the Era of Hosni Mubarak*, 8–9, 43.

86. Ellissy, "Sikritīr Mubarak wa-ḥadīth ʿan tasawwul Mubarak wa-akhlāqihi" [Mubarak's secretary and discussion of Mubarak's beggary and his manners]. Shafiq al-Banna was Mubarak's private secretary of twenty-five years.

87. What Qaddafi actually said is that "Mubarak used to beg for the benefit of the Egyptian people. He would come to me and beg for ferries on your behalf, he went to Saudi Arabia to beg for trucks. He would beg anybody who would listen, to your [the Egyptian people's] benefit." See al-Quds al-Arabi, "al-Qadhdhāfī lil-Miṣriyyīn: Mubarak rajul faqīr wa-mutawāḍiʿ wa-yuḥibbukum . . . kāna yashḥat min ajlikum," and a similar article al-Najjār and Zaydān, "al-Qadhdhāfī" in *AlMasry AlYoum*.

88. Ellissy, "Sikritīr Mubarak wa-ḥadīth ʿan tasawwul Mubarak wa-akhlāqihi."

"security state" as savior. It is not just the wreckage of Egyptian politics at stake but the national humiliation [*al-mahāna al-waṭaniyya*] it has entailed.

"The Market of Humiliation" in Egypt's Time of Degradation: Neoliberalism and the Business of Theft

A number of poems rearticulate such national humiliation in a different register by situating in relation to what I want to call a radical disjuncture in the materiality of Egypt. There are three different meanings of "materiality" that interweave in these poems to constitute the terms of the disjuncture. First, there's the literal sense of the material existence of Egypt as a tangible, physical, and bounded domain, from the land to the Nile to the built environment. The second is the way this material and physical domain is the tangible expression of what Egypt essentially is and means: Egypt is bound up with the land but also transcends it. At times, these two senses are so closely conjoined as to seem indistinguishable, but by sliding between them, these poets can figure Egypt as a land defiled but also untouchable. Third, materialism connotes the excessive and corrosive pursuit of money and the things it can buy, evinced both in the venality of Egyptian leaders and the neoliberal state that serves their greed so effectively.

All three of these registers are entangled in Farouk Guweida's (b. 1946) three poems about the Egyptian regime, "Irḥal" [Leave], "Ilā kull jallād ṭāghī" [To every tyrant executioner], and "Ka'anna al-'umr mā kāna" [As if life never was]. The regime becomes a rotted ship of state with Mubarak at the helm, seeking comfort with rats though they bit through the vessel on which he sailed.[89] "This is your miserable ship sailing aimlessly in the night / No safety, no sails / All the ship rats are escaping," Guweida writes in "Leave."[90] Reeling from a plague of its own making, the regime has rendered unnatural all in its path. Every part of Egypt is infected and undone: the land is violated, the trees are stilled, the beaches empty, the streets dark, the morning is suffocated, and the "sad cities" are crushed by loneliness. A "great people" have been brought to ruin, bled by violence, drowned in an "ocean of poverty," he writes, fed with humiliation [*dhull*] rather than food.

89. Guweida, "Ilā kull jallād ṭāghī" [To every tyrant executioner]," and Guweida, "Irḥal" [Leave]. Originally written as an indictment of US President George W. Bush and published in the *Arab Times* in January 2009, "Irḥal" was adapted to the Mubarak regime and published February 1, 2011, on Al Jazeera. "Ka'anna al-'umr mā kāna" [As if life never was], first performance on June 20, 2011.

90. Guweida, "Irḥal."

Guweida calls this moment a "bastard age" that has managed to betray both past and future. Millennia of ancestors bear witness to the lost glory of Egypt and its squandered patrimony, both now ground into the dust. But it is not just the "caravans of history" that end up dead under the sea; all "hopes of a life" are stillborn and all visions are in "the color of death."[91] In this Egypt, children scream but do not dream; "the light of the morning has died" in their eyes. "[W]hat have you left for the land of greatness?" he asks at the end of "Leave."[92] The answer, it seems, is in "To Every Tyrant Executioner": the achievements of a great nation have been replaced by "the market of humiliation and slave trading and doubts" [*fī sūq al-mahāna wa-l-nikhāsa wa-l-ẓunūn*].[93] Thieves masquerade as presidents while acts of selling, stealing, and ruling become virtually indistinguishable. "Slave traders" hold the nation hostage. Now all aspects of life are stolen, bartered, sold, or wagered: labor, land, livelihoods, honor, conscience, even history.

Guweida is not alone in depicting the regime as a corruption that infects and sickens everything it touches, nor is he the only poet who identifies the relentless pursuit of money as a pivotal source and symptom. In *al-Mīdān* [The Square], the poet ʿAbd al-Raḥmān al-Abnūdī (1939–2015) writes of rabid old men, all alike in greed, malice, and degeneracy, ravaging Egypt, stealing its blood, and growing fat on its wealth.[94] If you are the father of the country and really love her, Abnūdī asks, why do you permit her to be devoured by worms?[95] The regime *is* the parasite, Gakh contends in "Guḥā," eating deep into the very roots from which Egypt's life springs, rendering lands barren, wells dry, and oil just another "treasure stolen."

These poems derive their rhetorical power as much from the sheer devastation they evoke as from the linguistic artistry they exhibit. The foundering ship not only conjures the ship of state careening into disaster, but also the hundreds drowned in the Red Sea on the decrepit ferry. Fouled water evokes the industrial pollution of the Nile river, the "dark cities," electricity cuts.[96] The children who

91. Guweida, "Ilā kull jallādṭāghī"; "Ka'an al-ʿumr mā kāna."

92. Guweida, "Irḥal."

93. Guweida, "Ilā kull jallād ṭāghī."

94. Abnūdī, "al-Mīdān" [The square]. Abnūdī read it over the telephone on "al-Hayat al-Youm," best4egypt, "Qaṣīdat al-Mīdān—ʿAbd al-Raḥmān al-Abnūdī."

95. The reference to worms here is both figural and literal. Mekky, et al., "Human Fascioliasis."

96. See, for example, al-Ṣabbāgh, "al-Nīl ilāh lil-farāʿina . . . wa-ṣalāt lil-aqbāṭ . . . wa-nahr min al-janna ʿinda al-Muslimīn . . . ilā mustawdaʿa lil-mukhālafāt" [The Nile was a god to the pharaohs . . . a prayer to the Copts . . . a river from heaven for the Muslims . . . now a repository of violations]. In 2010, electricity cuts contributed to demonstrations and provoked the Egyptian Centre for Human Rights to demand the resignation of the Minister of Electricity for the

haunt these poems symbolize the nation's squandered future. They also summon the material, educational, and aspirational deprivation of entire generations of Egyptians, from children who labor in the informal economy to the thousands of families who literally live with the dead, having taken up residence in the tombs of city cemeteries so dangerous that children are kept indoors after sunset.[97]

In the poem "My Mother Doesn't Care for Politics," Amr Ismail spells this out in more prosaic language than that of Guweida and Abnūdī. "We have been bent for years," he writes. "Our water has yellowed, our birds infected, and the power is always out." Likewise, the streets are overcrowded, medication is scarce, and jobs and industry have been decimated by privatization.[98] The Omar Effendi Department Stores are gone, sold in 2007 to Anwal, a Saudi Arabian company, that resulted in the firing of at least three thousand workers.[99] "Poor workers accept humiliation [*madhalla*]," he concludes, while "his highness excels at selling," thick with thieves who take bribes to do their jobs, line their beds with stolen cash, and happily profit from Egyptian labor sold for mere pennies.

Such recurrent images of the market, of buying and selling, plunder and profit, most obviously evoke the massive corruption and private enrichment for which the Egyptian regime and its many accomplices are by now well known.[100] At the same time, they capture the quite specific destruction wrought by neoliberal policies in Egypt.[101] Neoliberalism here refers to, first, the privatization, consumerism, and intense concentration of wealth produced by capitalist economic policies and, second, the political rationality that accelerates capitalist transvaluations, from the elevation of entrepreneurship to a virtue to the monetization of all aspects of life to the disappearing boundary between economics and politics.[102]

---

failure to provide alternative energy solutions and for making poorer neighborhoods bear the brunt of the cuts. Al Jazeera, "Azmat kahrabā' tuhaddid Miṣr" [An electricity crisis threatens Egypt].

97. Ellissy, "'Amr Ellissy fī manṭiqat maqābir al-Imām al-Shāfi'ī."

98. See note 3 above. Toldo and also Ifāda Maktūba, "Amr Ismail: Ummī malhāsh fī al-siyāsa."

99. Carr, "Omar Effendi Workers Resume Strike Against Wage Discrimination."

100. At the time of Mubarak's departure, scholars estimated the Mubarak family wealth at $50–70 billion. Kim, "Egypt's Mubarak Likely to Retain Vast Wealth." Efforts of the family to hide its holdings has made any figure guesswork, and other estimates put it at closer to $300 million.

101. Guweida referred to the Egyptian government as a "real estate broker" in a 2010 volume collecting his newspaper columns. Guweida, *Ightiṣāb waṭan* [Raping a country].

102. Harvey, *Brief History of Neoliberalism*; Mitchell, *Rule of Experts*; Brown, "Neoliberalism and the End of Liberal Democracy."

As Walter Armbrust suggests in his analysis of the Egyptian Uprising, given how neoliberalism works, state policies and plunder must be understood not as distinct phenomena but as complementary aspects of a regime in the business of theft. To "describe blatant exploitation of the political system for personal gain as corruption" misses the fact that elites "were enriched through a conflation of politics and business under the guise of privatization. This was less a violation of the system than business as usual. Mubarak's Egypt, in a nutshell, was a quintessential neoliberal state."[103]

Casting the "market of humiliation" in terms of neoliberalism just seems to anchor a metaphor in an abstraction. Yet there is nothing abstract about the powerlessness and despair that many of these materials articulate, and that are symptomatic of the macrolevel processes and political rationality to which both metaphor and abstraction refer. Consider, for example, a TV program from January 22, 2011, in which host Wael el-Ibrashy interviews several men about a wave of suicides in Egypt, many of which are traceable to the privatization of public industries.[104] One of the guests is Moustafa Ma'shat, who survived an attempted self-immolation. Ma'shat had been a department manager at the Misr Shebin al-Kom Spinning and Weaving factory. In 2006, the factory was sold to Indorama, an Indonesian-based company, and a workforce that had once numbered 11,000 was reduced to 4,200 employees.[105] He describes feeling "crushed" when he was then transferred to a steel factory and demoted to security guard, a dramatic change in status that also entailed a sharp reduction in salary. Given the value of his pension relative to his paltry paycheck, he came to feel that he could better provide for his wife and five children dead than alive. It's clear from the interview that there was much more than money at stake. "I had no hope," he says. "Everything was closed in my face," and everywhere he turned, he was met with indifference or even contempt.

> I was humiliated [*it'hānt*]. . . . I am a department manager, and suddenly . . . I am now a security guard. . . . That's it. I have a daughter in secondary school. Her name is Reham. She said she's never going back to school. "People are calling me the 'guard's daughter,'" she said. "What did your father do wrong? What did he steal?" People are asking my children, my married daughter,

103. Armbrust, "Revolution against Neoliberalism," 114.

104. El-Ibrashy, "Al-Ḥaqīqa Wael el-Ibrashy: Muwājaha ma'a alladhīna ḥāwalū al-intiḥār ḥarqan fī Miṣr wa-ma'a 'ā'ilātihim" [The Truth (with) Wael el-Ibrashy: interview with those who attempted self-immolation in Egypt and their families].

105. Carr, "Factory Workers Strike in Menufiya, Demand Bonuses"; and Beinin and Vairel, *Social Movements, Mobilization, and Contestation in the Middle East and North Africa*, 217.

"what did your father steal? What crime did he do?" . . . I just want to make a living.

Ahmed Hashem al-Sayed was a twenty-five-year-old trained architect who committed suicide by dousing his body with petrol and lighting himself on fire. According to his brother, Ramadan, when Ahmed was unable to get a job, he felt powerless to get married or build a future, trapped in what Diane Singerman has termed "waithood," the "liminal position between childhood, adolescence, and adulthood, which is socially equated with marriage."[106] With no control over or say in his own life, his brother tells Ibrashy, the entire world was closed to him. Ahmed Meghawry Youssef, also from the Shebin Company, describes readying the match to self-immolate when workers jumped in to stop him. Ibrashy asks him how he could do such a thing given that suicide is contrary to Islam. "I'm just a worker," Youssef protests, then turns the question back on his host: why didn't the manager who ruined my life consider the Islamic imperative to be merciful?[107]

Such self-immolations have drawn a fair amount of attention for obvious reasons,[108] but they are few relative to the number of Egyptians who describe being slowly ground down by poverty, homelessness, and starvation.[109] In a video titled "Iḥnā mish balṭagiyya" [We are not thugs], residents of a makeshift camp housing over 1,300 families recall being evicted from their apartments and fruitlessly seeking help from an array of officials.[110] "Not a single official cared

106. Singerman, "Youth, Gender and Dignity in the Egyptian Uprising," 10. Singerman shows that, while waithood is experienced by both men and women, it's a particularly long limbo for men, who often have to wait a decade or more to "finish their education, begin working, seek a spouse, and finance their marriage" (12–13.)

107. "Al-Ḥaqīqa, Wael el-Ibrashy—Muwājaha ma'a alladhīna ḥāwalū al-intiḥār ḥarqan fī Miṣr wa-ma'a 'ā'ilātihim."

108. The response of the Ministry of Religious Endowments was to order all Friday sermons to concentrate on the Islamic prohibition on suicide. Al-Beheri, "Friday Sermons to Discuss Religious Prohibition of Suicide."

109. While some survivors of such spectacular attempts invoke Bouazizi as inspiration, this leaves open the question of what drives any of these men to self-immolation in particular as opposed to other modes of self-killing. Blair, "Egyptian Tries to Set Himself Alight."

110. "We are not thugs." *Balṭagiyya* [بلطجية] is a label with wide application, multiple deployments, and resignifications. It has been used against activists from Tunisia to Yemen, and the Egyptian regime has routinely described demonstrators as thugs to discredit them. Gasim, "Explaining Political Activism in Yemen," 122. On the shifting deployments of the label and analysis of the discourse of *balṭagiyya* as a technique of control see Ismail, *Political Life in Cairo's New Quarters*, 22, 122, 140–44. For the way the state resignified the term to invoke

to see what happened to us," one man says.[111] According to residents, the only government response was to cut the electricity in the camp and block the toilets to make them unusable, forcing sewage to flow out in the open. They describe being unable to afford permanent residences let alone legal fees, leaving the army free to abuse them with impunity. One soldier raped a boy openly in the camp until residents forcibly intervened. A woman in the video points out that residents are continually called beggars and thugs who don't deserve help, but none of them would have spent a single night in the camp if they had any alternative place to go. "We've been completely degraded [*itmarmaṭnā*]," she says. Everyone and everything is covered in dust and garbage, and no resident has been spared constant struggle. "We're not asking for a miracle," says another resident. "We're just asking for mercy, mercy and justice."

In a blog post written during the rule of the Muslim Brotherhood, activist and lawyer Malek Adly points out that neither justice nor mercy is possible when there's widespread outrage about a frivolous video such as "The Innocence of Muslims" because it insults the Prophet Muhammad, but the grinding degradation of citizens continues unnoticed and unabated. I do care about Muhammed's life and legacy, Adly writes, "but which Muhammad do I mean?"[112]

> [There's] Muhammad, the child who died in the incubator because of a power cut. . . . Muhammad, the child who never finished his education because his parents were so poor they had to send him to work . . . Muhammad, the student whose parents have no idea how to cover his expenses, whose school fills his head with all kinds of crap and transforms him into an illiterate stone who doesn't know how to think for himself. Muhammad, the teacher who makes 120 pounds a month, so he neither learns nor teaches. Muhammad, who never misses a chance to sexually harass our daughters, sisters and wives. Muhammad, the victim of torture. Muhammad, whose vote and acquiescence are bought with a bottle of oil and a kilo of sugar. Muhammad, who sleeps on the ground and covers himself with the sky because no one ever thought to give him shelter. Muhammad, whose boss has abused and ignored him, thrown him out onto the streets without pay, pension, or insurance, and your justice system never takes his side. Muhammad, who you silenced into

---

nineteenth-century Orientalist depictions of the "Arab street," see Amar, *Security Archipelago*, 211–12. Amar calls this the "baltagi effect."

111. Shaaban, "Iḥnā mish balṭāgiyya" [We are not thugs], June 14, 2011.

112. Adly, "Ḥayāt Muḥammad" [The life of Muhammad].

> submission and resignation with promises of a heaven that's not yours to promise, a heaven I seriously doubt you'll ever see yourself. . . . Muhammad, wounded in our revolution, but denied the basic humanity granted a ordinary person. Muhammad, the bribed employee, the corrupt, the slave to the master who never hesitates to submit to his bosses and in turn humiliate [*ihāna*] his subordinates. Muhammed who died at his own hands on the train or at the theater, or killed by the Zionist enemy at the border, or run down every day on the roads. This is the Muhammad I understand your revolution and anger to be for, the Muhammad you need to defend against degradation [*ihāna*] and struggle to improve his life.

In 2010, a blogger who goes only by the name of 5FadaFada describes swollen ranks of the homeless on the streets, populated by almost every kind of person imaginable. They form a kind of gauntlet, she writes with sorrow, gathering in the dozens around every single pedestrian to beg. No livable minimum wage, soaring prices, unemployment, rampant corruption, cuts in education and health care—but somehow, she notes, there's always enough money for tear gas to be used against protesters. She recalls a woman in her forties in the street begging, her face suffused with shame, eyes on the floor as if "asking the ground to open up and swallow her." Haunted by her image, 5FadaFada writes of being unable to stop imagining herself in the woman's place, begging. I know now, she concludes, that "none of us is safe."[113]

"Where Are the Real Men of Egypt?": The Gendering of Humiliation

The show on suicides showcases a particular gendering of humiliation that is, in many ways, a pivotal backstory to the Arab uprisings. The stories of these men show the extent to which unemployment, slashed wages, and disappeared pensions register not just as a hardship but as a failure to perform the breadwinner role they regard as essential to both the standing and responsibilities of manhood, whether as a father, husband, or son. Said Hammoudi, a sixty-eight-year-old man who tried to set himself on fire just three days before January 25, 2011, describes this anguish in an interview with Al Jazeera: "The worst day of my life was when they handed me back my daughter's folder at university and she was prevented from her education for a year because we couldn't afford the tuition." He had been

113. 5FadaFada, "Khāyifa" [I'm scared].

denied his full pension, he explained, making him unable to provide for his family. It made him, he said, a "father in name only."[114]

These accounts presuppose an archetypical masculinity experienced not as the ground of patriarchal power but as a powerful source of particularly male anguish. They articulate a painful disjuncture between the force of male gender roles predicated on fully empowered capabilities and the "vulnerabilities, dependencies and disempowerments" that constitute so many of these lived experiences.[115] This disjuncture is critical to encoding humiliation as masculine, and is essential to the scaffolding I trace throughout this book. Articulated in a particular language and setting, the features of this disjuncture are neither unique to Egypt nor to Arabs. Several studies of gender and poverty point out that, inasmuch as the breadwinner role remains central to social constructions of masculinity across the global North and South, lack of waged work and poverty register not just as privation but as a failure to meet the expectations of manhood.[116]

This disjuncture is at the heart of the story that has come to function as a kind of originary myth of the uprisings, the self-immolation of Muhammed Bouazizi, the street vendor whose death on December 17, 2010, is often referred to as the "spark" that set off the Tunisian Uprising. According to his mother, Bouazizi's suicide was precipitated both by his inability to adequately support his struggling family and the very public, humiliating slap of the woman officer enforcing a zoning law that, in effect, denied him his meager livelihood.

The power of this account, circulated widely and repeated endlessly, has effectively drowned out the protestations of the police officer, Faida Hamdi, that a traditional Arab woman such as herself could not possibly have slapped a man, and that earning a living to support her own family required that she do her job, in this case applying the law regulating where street vendors could go. In an unintentionally absurdist television interview with Hamdi, Ibrashy, the host of the Egyptian program, opens with the pledge to find out what really happened. Yet in the course of the exchange, Hamdi's denials appear to simply bounce off him: he presents her with assertions rather than questions and proceeds to repeat them regardless of her answers. "At the end of the day, a woman slapped him on

114. Al Jazeera, "Ẓāhirat muḥāwalāt al-intiḥār ḥarqan fī Miṣr qabla thawrat 11 Yanāyir 2011" [The phenomenon of attempted self-immolation in Egypt before the January 11 revolution].

115. Tadros, "Challenging Reified Masculinities," 328; Inhorn, *New Arab Man*. Ghannam's research on masculinity in urban Egypt speaks to the tension between directives to be a "real man" and the variability of contexts and conditions that shape how masculinity is and can be fashioned and embodied. Ghannam, *Live and Die Like a Man*.

116. See, for example, Fodor, "Different Type of Gender Gap," 14–39, and Strier, Eisikovits, and Buchbinder, "Masculinity, Poverty and Work," 331–49.

the face and this is a devastating humiliation," Ibrashy says to her at one point. He then concludes by telling her that "when a woman slaps a citizen, she puts him in a dress and makes him into a woman—this is the most egregious kind of humiliation [*aqṣā darajat al-ihāna*]."[117]

The Ibrashy interview illustrates just how integral this slap by a woman employed by the state is to the story of Bouazizi's suicide and the humiliation that drove him to it. Whether or not Hamdi actually slapped Bouazizi has become incidental to the way the account dramatizes, compounds, and performs a powerlessness inseparable from emasculation. Here is a regime so corrupt that it has empowered a woman to publicly slap a man struggling to provide for his family. The degree to which Hamdi also feels the burden of providing for her own family, for instance, is locked out of this story as an incongruity that might even begin to unravel it.

My aim here isn't to establish "what really happened," but to draw attention to the omissions required for this account to cohere and point to the operations of the story these specific omissions, in turn, render legible. Most notably, it construes the struggle to provide for one's family as masculine and, by metonymic slide, encodes the many dimensions of powerlessness under domination as emasculation.

This account of Bouazizi is particularly instructive for my purposes, but not only because humiliation is central to the story and the story has become central to the narrative of the Arab uprisings as well as the Tunisian revolution. The operations that gender humiliation in this story are also evinced in this archive by those who construe powerlessness as emasculation and make it pivotal to the impetus and effects of the Egyptian revolution. As Gakh writes in "We'll Keep Going," it's impossible to know why Egyptians took to the streets without understanding "the humiliation of men" [*mahānit al-rigāl*].[118] Mubarak belittled Egyptian men's manhood and made them feel worthless, Negm writes, but the uprising was restorative. The chant "Egypt still has real men" was more than just words. "When they found out that they were still men, they cried," she writes.[119]

117. Ibrashy, "Ḥiwār ma'a al-shurṭiyya ṣāḥibat ashhar ṣaf'a fī al-tārīkh wa-tasababat fī intiḥār Bouazizi al-Tūnisī" [Conversation with the policewoman who gave the most famous slap in history and caused the suicide of the Tunisian, Bouazizi]. There are multiple and competing reports of the events of that day, and while it does appear that Hamdi told Bouazizi he had to leave because he was violating a law that prohibits market venders in a public zone, the story of the "slap that started a revolution" is far more dubious. Day, "Fedia Hamdi's Slap Which Sparked a Revolution 'Didn't Happen.'"

118. Gakh, "Mikamilīn."

119. Negm, "Mādhā taf'al law kunt ḥarāmī?" [What would you do if you were a thief?].

Yet these sources articulate several different ways the experience of humiliation is gendered, many of which are in tension even as others overlap or are mutually reinforcing. On the one hand, several voices here not only recognize the significance and extensive role women played in the revolution but emphasize how their exemplary bravery set the standards for men's participation. In a March 2011 video, for example, a woman holds a sign that says, "Down with military regime, the manliest [*argal*] thing about you, Egypt, is your women."[120] The "bravery of the revolutionary Egyptian girls" doesn't just threaten the Mubarak regime, one tweet reads, but all those "cowards who accept humiliation [*al-dhull*] for the sake of security."[121] Mohamed Tarek al-Wadi, one of the military officers who risked imprisonment to join the protests on April 8, 2011, serenades Egyptian women directly in "Banāt bilādī" [Girls of my nation]: "You, we can never replace tomorrow / To every girl with the spirit of a fighter / You taught people how to struggle."[122]

On the other hand, several texts register females primarily as terrain over which male opponents struggle. Consider the 2011 verbal screed by Salafist Hazem Shoman against Mohamed al-Baradei (b. 1942), the former director of the International Atomic Energy Agency (who would very briefly serve as vice-president in 2013). As a "Muslim liberal," he writes, Baradei exemplifies a worldview by definition hostile to the worship of God and the rule of Islamic Law. According to Shoman, the fact that al-Baradei permitted his Muslim daughter to marry a Christian "infidel" is proof of his perfidy, but also symptomatic of a deeper erosion of the proper order of things in Egyptian society. The liberalism unleashed by the revolution has eradicated the very idea of men and women, Shoman complains. "You can't even talk about manhood and masculinity" anymore.[123]

Then there are expressions that figure women more as victims in need of defense or protection than agents and posit a manhood dependent upon protective

120. AlMasry AlYoum, "Samira Ibrahim tanhār ba'da ḥukm 'al-'askariyya'" [Samira Ibrahim devastated after military court verdict].

121. Alaa Aswany (@AlaaAswany), "Shujā'at banāt Maṣr al-thawriyyāt lā tuqliq niẓām Mubarak faqaṭ lākinnahā tuz'ij al-jubanā' fāqidī al-nakhwa alladhīna yaqbalūn al-dhull min ajl al-salāma wa-yarfuḍūn al-thawra li-karāmatihim."

122. Doooozz28, "Banāt Bilādī . . . Muḥammad al-Wadī."

123. Shoman, "El-Baradei wa-ḥukm Miṣr" [El-Baradei and ruling Egypt]. The video of Shoman circulated rapidly and widely and was a troubling harbinger of the attempt of the Muslim Brotherhood—along with the Salafists—to depoliticize women once Morsi was elected. Based on interviews with prominent Egyptian women, Emily Dyer argues that, despite rhetoric and even initiatives supportive of women's empowerment, Morsi and the Brotherhood sought to 'domesticate' women's political participation in multiple ways. Dyer, "Marginalising Egyptian Women," 54.

acts of valor. In one conspicuous trope, violence against women and girls during the revolution becomes evidence of the absence of "real men" to step up and perform their duty to protect vulnerable females. This is articulated both by those who take the duty to protect as an assertion of masculine preeminence and those who take it as crucial to making the public domain safe for women's activism.[124] An Egyptian cleric in Canada, Tariq Abdelhaleem, exhorts Ikhwāni and Salafi men of Egypt to challenge the false Muslims and "fake men" of SCAF who victimize women, widows, children, and orphans.[125] Egypt's girls and women are a "red line," agree several men in the short documentary "Down with the Military Regime"; those who can watch mothers beaten and girls publicly stripped and are not moved to act in their defense "don't deserve to be called men." At a December 20, 2011, march of women in downtown Cairo protesting widespread sexual violence by soldiers and police, a prominent sign suggests that men who have failed to protect females have forfeited their manhood: "Go on, shave your moustaches; Tantawi [Field Marshal Mohamad Hussein Tantawi, head of SCAF] has stripped your daughters naked."[126]

Such protection of women and defense of the nation become mutually constitutive in several texts that depict Egypt as a beautiful woman whose decades-long defilement by the regime and its collaborators cries out for restorative action.[127] Guweida's poem "To Every Tyrant Executioner," for example, refers to Egypt as a "land raped by corruption," who "sold her wedding dress, betrayed her honor / surrendered to the gang of bastards that violate her."[128] The Internet activist Wael Ghoneim deploys the same metaphor in a February interview to expose the cynicism of a cornered authoritarian regime suddenly willing to speak to its people: "Egypt has been raped for thirty years. This country was being ripped off and the honor of its children [*yinhatak a'rāḍ`hum*] violated for thirty years. [It's like a] girl who was being raped and, when she found a knife

124. Tadros, "Challenging Reified Masculinities," 335.

125. Abdelhaleem, "al-Majlis al-'askarī al-khā'in yaghtāl Miṣr Tariq Abdelhaleem" [Traitorous military council assassinates Egypt].

126. Mosireen Collective, Cabinet Clashes, Women's March, Blue Bra Girl (2011-12-10) at Downtown, Cairo.

127. In "Yā Sitt al-Kull" [My lady], Abnūdī exemplifies this personification of Egypt, speaking to his country as if to a lover, positing her eternal brightness standing between a generation and the taste of humiliation [*al-dhull*]. CBC Egypt video of Abnūdī performing "Yā Sitt al-Kull" available on YouTube, "Ḥaṣrīyan . . . qaṣīdat 'Sitt al-Kull' bi-ṣawt al-shā'ir 'Abd al-Raḥmān al-Abnūdī" [Exclusive . . . the poem "My Lady" in the voice of the poet 'Abd al-Raḥmān al-Abnūdī].

128. Guweida, "Ilā kull jallād ṭāghī."

in front of her, grabbed it. As she was turning around [to defend herself], someone behind her said 'let's calm down and talk about this!'"[129]

This complex interplay of gender, honor, humiliation, and the nation has a history bound up with the familial fashioning of modern Egypt mentioned earlier.[130] As Baron argues, the modern idea of national honor at once remade and mobilized the emotive power of family honor, even as the Egyptian family was itself being transformed by the extension of state control.[131] An honor code predicated upon female purity and an ideal of men as tasked with protecting or policing women's virtue—or cleansing the family of the stain when it was violated—proved useful to nineteenth-century Egyptian nationalists, who refashioned it in collective terms.[132] At the same time, nationalist discourse remade Egypt as a woman. Baron points out that the "depiction of political abstractions in female form goes back to antiquity" and is also a common feature of European nationalism.[133] But like the Egyptian nation-state itself, both the idea of national honor and the personification of Egypt as a woman were forged under conditions of foreign occupation. British domination made the honor of Egypt depend as much on restoration as protection, and constituted it in opposition to humiliation, shame, and insult.[134]

During the uprising, a number of women made good use of the exhortatory power of precisely these gendered associations, appealing to masculine honor and the protection of vulnerable females it entails to goad men to act courageously with them.[135] Perhaps the best-known example is the January 18, 2011, vlog by

129. Ghoneim and el-Naggar, interview with Hafez el-Marazy, "Tawthīq al-thawra al-Miṣriyya 25 January 2011—Wael Ghoneim—Mostafa el-Naggar—Bayān al-thawra" [Documenting the Egyptian revolution 25 January 2011—Wael Ghoneim—Mostafa el-Naggar—declaration of the revolution]. Mostafa el-Naggar is a well-known progressive activist, blogger, and former member of parliament. In 2017, the Egyptian government convicted him, along with a number of other activists, of insulting the judiciary. He has been missing for a number of years, and his whereabouts are unknown as of this writing. The regime characterizes him as a fugitive from justice, but many believe the government "disappeared" him. See, for example, Ahram Online, "Former MP Mostafa El-Naggar not 'forcedly disappeared,' still evading 3-year jail sentence, Egypt's SIS."

130. For a discussion of this interplay specifically with regard to sexual assault during the Egyptian revolution, see Tadros, "Understanding Politically Motivated Sexual Assault in Protest Spaces."

131. Baron, *Egypt as a Woman*, 42.

132. Baron, *Egypt as a Woman*, 40ff.

133. Baron, *Egypt as a Woman*, 6, 57ff.

134. Baron, *Egypt as a Woman*, 43–44.

135. This is just one example of the way women have negotiated a gendered script that posits women and domesticity as coextensive and constitutes their public political

Asmaa Mahfouz, one of the founders of the April 6 Youth Movement, in which she urges her fellow citizens to demonstrate in Tahrir Square on January 25.[136] In the 4:36-minute, grainy video, the camera is tightly focused on Asmaa's face, framed by her *ḥijāb*; she speaks directly to the lens, her speech becoming increasingly rapid-fire as the recording progresses. In her opening salvo, Mahfouz refers to the attempted suicides of four Egyptian men who sought to "protest the humiliation [*al-dhull*] and hunger and poverty and degradation [*al-bahdala*] they have had to live with for thirty years." But you won't find me setting myself afire, she says, and throws down the gauntlet:

> If you think you're a man, come to the streets. Everyone who says girls shouldn't go to protests, that it's *haram*, and that they're asking for it if they go needs to get some pride [*yikhallī ʿanduh nakhwa*] and be a man [*rugūla*] and join us on the twenty-fifth. To everyone who says that the turnout will be small and nothing will happen, I want to say: you're the reason why things are this way—yes, you. You're part of the problem, like the president, like every corrupt officer who assaults and degrades us [*yibahdilnā*]. You're the reason. Coming with us will make a difference, not a small difference, a big one. . . . Staying at home, watching television or the news, or following Facebook just means more degradation for us [*beibahdilnā iḥnā*]. Degradation for me [*beibahdilnī anā*]. If you have dignity [*karāma*], if you're a human being and a man in this country, then you have to come. You have to come protect me and every girl who goes. If you stay home, then you deserve everything that's happening to you—and not just to you. You'll be part of the problem, responsible and to blame for what's happening to the country and to everyone living in it.[137]

---

participation as profoundly threatening to the social order. See, for example, Mahmood, *Politics of Piety*; and Cooke, *Women Claim Islam*.

136. The April 6 Youth Movement refers to the small group of activists who launched a Facebook page in support of a planned strike on April 6, 2008, by the textile workers of Misr Spinning and Weaving Company in Mahalla al-Kubra in the Nile Delta.

137. Mahfouz, "Call to Protest on January 25, 2011." In an interview, Mahfouz makes clear that she intentionally used language meant to goad Egyptian men into action. Mahfouz, "al-Ḥaqīqa Wael el-Ibrashy 26 Yanāyyir" [The truth with Wael el-Ibrashy, January 26]. On Asmaa and her vlogs, see, for example, Wall and el Zahed, "'I'll Be Waiting for You Guys,'"; and Amy Goodman's interview on *Democracy Now*, "Asmaa Mahfouz and the YouTube Video that Helped Spark the Egyptian Uprising." Mahfouz had been blogging before the revolution and followed up this video with two additional vlogs in rapid succession, on January 24 and 26, 2011.

In previous chapters, I have argued that humiliation rhetoric operates as an exhortation to restorative action and shown how its specific terms fashion certain acts of refusal and restoration as existentially imperative. Likewise, these materials show how the different but tangled ways in which humiliation is gendered patterns the reparative action encoded within it. Despite what has been described as women's extensive public presence and "leading and influential role" in the revolution, for example, the gendering of powerlessness as male renders the challenges to domination as a staging ground for performances of masculine courage, ferocity, and strength.[138] Consider the lines from "Egyptian Karāma," a rap song by Ahmed Mekky and singer Mohamed Mohsen from February 2011, in which the uprising is depicted as both an enactment and achievement of masculinity. "Thank you to every young man who said his opinion without fear / A man from a man, he made the world look and learn . . . / Manhood and morals only appear in times of crisis."[139]

The power of the revolution, Fattah writes, is exemplified by the youth who "stood with bare chests facing bullets in front of the Zionist embassy."[140] In a similar vein, in the poem "Iktub yā tārīkh" [Write this down, O history], Sherif Ibrahim calls upon history to witness the bare, open chests, strong hands, and unbreakable hearts of young men who courageously banish humiliation and degradation.[141] Ibrahim characterizes such men as "fierce tigers" with "lion hearts," metaphors for masculine prowess and bravery that suffuse radical Islamist humiliation rhetoric and recur throughout these materials. In "To Every Tyrant Executioner," Guweida writes, "They were men when the crowds of dawn erupted / They stood their ground / In a scream of hope for the child of the Nile / They attacked like lions, roaring."[142] Notably, Guweida repeats this imagery, but

138. Women have been at the forefront of the Egyptian labor movement, pro-democracy protests, and the Islamist movement, just to name a few. See, for example, Mostafa, "Egyptian Women, Revolution, and Protest Culture," 124. Al-Mahdi, "Does Political Islam Impede Gender-Based Mobilization?"

139. eProductionHD, "A. Mekky raps for the Egyptian Revolution (Jan 25th) Karāmat al-Maṣrī."

140. Fattah, "al-Ḥilm Awwalan" [Patience first]. This is echoed in Malek Adly's July 7, 2011, blog post with the heading "The revolution is neither yours nor mine . . . it belongs to those who faced the bullets with their chests wide." Adly, "Al-Thawra lā milkak wa-lā milkī."

141. Ibrahim, "Iktub yā tārīkh" [Write this down, history].

142. See also eProductionHD, "A. Mekky raps for the Egyptian Revolution." In some cases, it is revolutionaries in general who are characterized as lions, as when the band Cairokee sings of the "roaring lions" that brought down a regime. But given the field of meanings in which

in reverse, in "As if Life Never Was," writing of lions turning into rats by the shores of the Nile. A blogger called Me and Them does much the same thing, cursing the humiliation that, almost a full year after the initial uprising, continues unabated, while those who thought themselves lions in January now hide their heads in the sand rather than confront how worthless life has become.[143]

It is striking that often-fierce opponents collude in fashioning the powerlessness and power encoded in the rhetoric of humiliation as impotence and virility. Some here wield it to disparage the passivity of their fellow-citizens, to deride them not only as members of the "party of the couch" [*ḥizb al-kanabeh*], but as a people whose leaders (e.g., Morsi) can be humiliated because, in Negm's words, "we have no real men left among us."[144] Such rhetoric is repeatedly wielded against the regime, cropping up in indictments of a succession of rulers. In keeping with Negm's tweet, one Facebook post refers to the Morsi administration as a "government of borrowed beards."[145] In a February 2011 interview, Amr Adeeb depicts the Mubarak regime as populated by those who "aren't real men" but have still silenced and "castrated an entire nation."[146] And Lewis suggests that the disproportionately vengeful and muscular reimposition of control over the public realm by SCAF and Sisi can be understood as compensatory, reflecting a sense of diminished virility.[147]

And of course, it has been repeatedly deployed by the regime. The October 6 celebration of 2013, held just two months after security forces used live ammunition to disperse anti-coup protests, is an illustration that also makes Lewis's point. Ostensibly a celebration of the fortieth anniversary of the Egyptian

---

this metaphor operates, "lions" reads as masculine even when gender isn't specified. The Glocal, "Maṭlūb za'īm li-farīq Cairokee—al-shāri' yughannī" [Leader wanted, by the band Cairokee—the street sings]."

143. Guweida, "Ka'an al-'umr mā kāna"; Me and Them, "'Ām yakād yamḍī wa-lā zilnā naṣrukh!" [Almost a year has passed, and we are still screaming!].

144. As Negm (@nawaranegm) tweets on July 31, 2012, "Mursī madhlūl dhull al-ibil wa-kullnā kidah mish 'ārifīn ni'mal lahu ḥāga 'ashān iḥnā wa-huwa khubu'āt ya'nī shwayyat al-rijāla illī ḥīlatnā mātū wa-lā ēh?" [Morsi [is] humiliated, beaten like a donkey, and we are too. We don't know how we can do anything, because we're cowering, the few [real] men that we had left have died, no?].

145. Ramy Boulos, FaceBook, August 18, 2012. Original in the tweet: Salāma (@MYousrySalama), "Ḥukūma tabda' 'ahdahā bi'l-sa'y li-iqtirāḍ 4.8 milyār dūlār min ṣandūq al-naqd al-duwalī wa-niṣf milyār min Amrīkā hiya ḥukūmat al-luḥā musta'āra!"

146. Abdul-Latif, "Tanaḥḥī Mubarak wa-ta'līq Amr Adeeb 'alā ẓulmihi" [Mubarak steps down and Amr Adeeb's response to his unfairness].

147. This is the implication of Lewis's blog post, "Bi-lā "ishsha' wa-lā 'tuktuk'" [No 'Huts,' No 'TukTuk'].

surprise attack on Israeli forces at the Suez Canal in 1973, the event was staged to convey the insurmountable potency of the military. Presided over by Sisi with interim Egyptian president Adly Mansour at his side, the live spectacle included the Saudi singer Hussein al-Jasmi performing a song, "Mr. Citizen, Son of Egypt," with the recurring refrain "you come from the country that bears real men."[148] Sisi has subsequently made sure that no one missed the point. In an October 2019 speech, for example, he says the Egypt of the revolution is like a woman who intentionally exposed and prostituted herself, and so deserves what she gets.[149]

These examples show the extent to which those with radically different commitments speak this language together, deploying and reproducing a rhetoric that does particular kinds of political work. Among other things, it rhetorically and symbolically renders the revolution as a struggle among "real men" that disavows the experiences of men as both objects and agents of domination, and renders women invisible, irrelevant, or, like Egypt herself, the terrain over which men battle.

This discussion would be incomplete without reference to the few voices here who take this gendering of power and powerlessness as literal and descriptive rather than symbolic or metaphorical, who insist that the uprisings consist of men struggling to contend with the disorder wrought by grasping women who must be put back in their place. In a January 2011 television broadcast of *Egypt Today*, for example, host Khairy Ramadan and his guest, Amr Mahmoud Abd al-Nabi, the former media consultant to the Egyptian Embassy in Tunisia, heartily agree that the current chaos in Tunisia is the direct result of women having been given far too many rights. According to Nabi, Habib Bourguiba had to be overthrown by Ben Ali lest his wife, Wassila Bourguiba—a political activist in her own right—seize even more power than she already had. The revolution overthrowing Ben Ali was necessary in turn because of another problem woman: his corrupt second wife, Leila Trabelsi. Bouazizi was driven to suicide less by the abuses of an authoritarian regime than by the fact that the officer

148. Al-Ḍamīr al-Arabī, "Ughniyat Ḥusayn al-Jasmī Siyāda muwāṭin ibn Maṣr" [Ḥusayn al-Jasmī sings Mr. citizen, son of Egypt]. It was sung by Hussein al-Jasmi in this performance, but the lyrics were written by Nader Abdallah and the music was composed by Walid Saad. It was played repeatedly during Sisi's January 2014 election campaign. See, for example, Abū al-Yazīd, "Istikhdām kalimāt ughniyat 'Siyādat al-muwāṭin' lil-Jasmī."

149. What Sisi actually said was "when the country revealed her back . . . [and] exposed her shoulder, then anything goes. If you are not careful, a lot more than this will happen to you." TeN TV, "al-Ra'īs al-Sisi: lammā al-balad kashafit ẓahrahā wa-'arrit kitfahā fī 2011 ḥaṣalit azmit sadd al-nahḍa" [President Sisi: The crisis of the renaissance dam occurred when the country exposed her back and shoulders in 2011].

whose slap publicly humiliated him was female. All the political troubles in Tunisia are due to "the woman" [*al-mar'a*], he says. The implication is that Egyptians must learn this lesson, and fast.[150]

"We're All Equal in Humiliation and Torture": Violence and Psychic Violations

> Military rule has devoured our country. . . . Do you think that your beatings don't do much? Your assaults kill us. When you strike, we die. We die and we have children to raise. I just got married, I have my wife to worry about now and I want a son. If I die, who will raise my son? Will you raise my son? Will the officer behind you raise him? Will your leaders raise him? No, they will smack him on the back of the head [*ḥa-yiḍrabūh 'alā qafāh*] and tell him his father was a thug.[151]

This excerpt is from a 13:45-minute video in which an unidentified man delivers what seems to be an extemporaneous monologue at the top of his lungs, aimed directly at a phalanx of soldiers outside the Ministry of Defense. A group of protesters is centered in the frame while the soldiers are largely draped in darkness; only the line of their shields is visible. It is sometime in the winter of 2011–12 and SCAF controls the state, but the precise date is unknown. The video is grainy and out of focus, and the speaker's face is almost constantly turned away from the camera; he moves continuously at the edge of the frame in an agitated dance. His voice cracks and breaks with what his words strain to convey. The protesters listen in relative stillness to the soliloquy, interrupting only occasionally with a smattering of applause. At the end the man, now hoarse, screams, "Yasquṭ, yasquṭ, ḥukm al-'askar!" [Down, down with military rule!]. In an instant, the crowd becomes his chorus, taking up the chant in an apparently spontaneous sequence of call and response.[152]

This brief video captures the despair and outrage accumulated over decades of living with the brutality of a police state, along with the depth and dimensions of

150. Maṣr Elnahārda EG, "Maṣr innahārda wa-ḥiwār ḥawla aḥdāth Tūnis."

151. Sayed, "Ru'b al-ḍubbāṭ min kalām aḥad al-thuwwār li-junūd ta'mīn wizārat al-difā'" [The officers' horror at the words of a revolutionary to the defense ministry's security soldiers]. This litany of violence by SCAF is repeated throughout these materials, and there is a similar rehearsal of the touchstones of violence perpetrated under Mubarak. See, just for one example, the interview with activist Ahmed Doma, Al Nahar TV, "Doma . . . ya'ūd lil-ḥurriyya."

152. Mehrez, *Translating Egypt's Revolution*, 19.

humiliation integral to it. Much as the crowd becomes this man's chorus, the voices in this archive echo his anguish and the experiences of almost surreal cruelty behind it. These contain often excruciatingly detailed accounts of the physical violence meted out by the regime; they also articulate what one activist calls "psychic violations," those often-hidden and far less-studied dimensions of humiliation routinely imbricated in it.[153] This and the following section suggest that such humiliation resides less in physical pain per se than in a particular kind of psychic damage implicated in experiences not just of powerlessness but of being forcibly made into something or someone you no longer recognize.[154]

Ahmed Doma is a former member of the Egyptian Ikhwān who was one of the founders of April 6th Movement and a prominent activist in the January revolution.[155] Incarcerated for years for his political activities, in a rare moment of freedom in 2012, Doma spoke in a television interview about the experience of imprisonment under both Mubarak and SCAF. The names may have changed, he notes, but the regime and its logic are the same. If there is any difference, it's for the worse because—as another voice in this archive puts it—"we've exchanged a dictator for tyrants."[156] Doma talks about how he was physically tortured, but stresses how techniques designed less to cause physical pain than to humiliate can shatter one's sense of self. It is Doma who refers to these as "psychic violations" [*intihākāt nafsiyya*], and he locates them in a number of particularly inventive rituals the commanding officer devised for the prisoners. The detainees were forced to defecate together and eat barely edible food like animals. But it didn't end there:

> Every morning, he [the officer] forces the new inmates to kneel to him. They are made to stand in one line, and he calls out their names one by one. This

153. The violence of the Mubarak regime has been particularly well documented, as have the almost dizzying array of political, military, and security institutions and subgroups, with at times overlapping and at times cross-cutting interests, that have meted it out. See, for example, Al Jazeera, "Egypt's Security Apparatus"; and Amar, "Why Mubarak Is Out."

154. This is not tantamount to the claim that humiliation is an experience of the mind that can or should be sharply distinguished from the body that is the locus of physical pain. Subsequent sections and chapters foreground those expressions in which particular bodily postures are themselves an embodied idiom of humiliation rather than a mere symbol or vehicle of it.

155. Al Nahar TV, "Doma . . . ya'ūd lil-ḥurriyya" [Doma . . . returns to freedom]. In 2013, Doma was convicted of violating a law banning unauthorized protests. In 2019, he was sentenced to fifteen years and ordered to pay a fine (the equivalent of $335,000) for supposed force against military officers, among other things. As of this writing, he remains in a maximum-security prison in Egypt.

156. Adel, "Al-Fīlm al-wathā'iqī: yasquṭ ḥukm al-'askar" [The short documentary film: Down with the military regime].

> can last for three hours or more, when he does nothing but sit in his chair, with one leg over the other and two guards in front of him. He calls a prisoner's name; the prisoner has to then kneel in front of him and take off all his clothes except for his underwear. If the prisoner is slow to kneel and take his clothes off, the guards facilitate the process by attacking the prisoner and beating him up. There's no difference between a political inmate or a criminal one, whether you're fifty or fifteen, everybody has to do it. We're all equal in humiliation and torture.[157]

Many of the psychic violations described in this archive are far less dramatic than the rituals of torture Doma details. In fact, many show the normalization of cruelty in the realm of the quotidian and routine. In a 2010 blog post, Fattah recounts his arrest at the Cairo airport on a false charge of check fraud for which he had been sentenced in absentia in 2009. Ordinary holding cells, he writes from experience, are usually overcrowded and violent. Police are routinely brutal and detainees are endlessly transferred from one station to another until it's nearly impossible for their families—or their lawyers—to locate them. Fattah concludes, "That's just part of daily life here in Egypt; that's what they do to cause misery and inflict indignity and completely consume the best of us in pointless battle after battle," until the energies and resolve of regime opponents are effectively depleted.[158]

Well-heeled professionals as well as individuals with minimal resources who were simply in the wrong place at the right time have regularly been trapped in a machine of both casual cruelty and spectacular brutality. The story of Sherif Gamal Seyam, a young man arrested and killed at the hands of the security forces just a month after Morsi was removed, exemplifies both.[159] On August 14, 2013, security forces killed an estimated eight hundred to one thousand civilians (counts vary

157. The line, also the title of this section, is "al-kull sawāsīya fī al-ihāna wa'l-tadhīb wa-mā ilā dhālika." Al Nahar TV, "Doma . . . ya'ūd lil-ḥurriyya." One of many citizens arrested in a December 2014 attack on a public *ḥammām* (see below) echoes Doma when describing how detainees were treated by police upon their arrival. AlMasry AlYoum, "Al-ḍaḥiyya al-thāniya fī qaḍiyyat Ḥammām al-baḥr: 'al-ḍubbāṭ amarūnā nihawhawū zay al-kilāb'" [The second victim in the Hammam al-Bahr case: "The officers ordered us to bark like dogs"]. See also i24NEWS Arabic, "Khawf wa-qalaq mutaṣā'id wasṭa al-mithliyyīn fī Miṣr" [Growing fear and anxiety among homosexuals in Egypt].

158. Fattah, "About Those Bouncy Bouncy Checks."

159. On September 4, 2013, writer and TV host Bilal Fadl turned his newspaper column over to Gamal Seyam, the father of Sherif Gamal Seyam, so that he could tell the story. Fadl, "Tafwīḍ bi'l-baṭsh!" [Authorization to assault!].

widely) in the course of dispersing anti-coup protests, making it into one of the "world's largest killings of demonstrators in a single day in recent history."[160] In the course of the operation and lockdown of the area, police also arrested thousands of Ikhwān members, Egyptians opposed to the reinstatement of military rule, and residents who had nothing to do with the protests. Sherif was among those arrested in a sweep of the East Cairo neighborhood around Rabi'a al-'Adawiyya Square, the site of the largest anti-coup demonstration and the greatest bloodshed.

CNN actually captured the arrest on video. It shows Sherif walking calmly between three men in black vests toward an armored truck. They have their hands on his back and shoulders, propelling him forward. He stops momentarily to say something to them but then continues walking forward without any resistance. Out of nowhere, a police officer leaps in to kick him in the chest, and more instantly converge around him, beating him with batons on the back and shoulders as they drag him toward the truck.[161] At one point, their assaults knock him to the ground; they help him up only to continue striking him over and over again.

Sherif's father, Gamal Seyam, a professor at Cairo University, recounts the moment when he and his family were finally able to visit Sherif at the police station, and found his son to be "very quiet in a strange way." Shortly thereafter, Sherif was stuffed with forty-five other prisoners into a transport van meant to meant to hold a maximum of twenty-four people and transferred to Abu Za'bal prison. At the end of that now infamous day in August 2013, thirty-seven of the detainees were dead, including Sherif.[162] The military blamed the deaths on rioting prisoners in the van, an account rendered suspect at best by the few surviving detainees who say that the vehicle had been left in the courtyard of the prison for six hours in almost 90-degree heat.[163] Many of the prisoners had trouble breathing from the lack of oxygen and water in combination with the overcrowding and intense heat. They pleaded for help; the policemen responded by making fun of them. "They told us we had to curse Dr. Morsi, in order to get out," one survivor said. "So the young people started to curse him. But after that [the

160. Human Rights Watch, "All According to Plan"; Fisher, "Egypt's Dictator Murdered 800 People Today in 2013."

161. The original CNN video link is unavailable, but a video of Sherif's arrest can be viewed on the Egyptian channel Shabakat Raṣd, "Ḥaflat saḥl li-aḥad mu'taṣimī rābi'a 'alā yad ḍābiṭ wa-junūdihi."

162. These events were dramatized in a 2016 film by Mohamed Diab, *Ishtibāk* [Clash].

163. This account is based on Gamal Seyem's account in Bilal Fadl's blog post, along with Motaparthy, "Unknown Man, and the Deaths at Abu Zaabal"; Kingsley, "How Did 37 Prisoners Come to Die at Cairo Prison Abu Zaabal?" and "Canadian Pair Describe 'Shared Trauma' of Ordeal in Egyptian Prison."

police] said we couldn't leave. Then they said: call yourselves girls' names. Some did." Feigning a piety likely intended as a parody of the Muslim Brotherhood, the police then told the prisoners: "we don't talk to women."[164] A spokesman for the mortuary eventually determined that the thirty-seven prisoners died from tear gas lobbed into the van in combination with a lack of oxygen.

Devastated by the death of his son, Gamal says Sherif wasn't even a supporter of the Ikhwān, let alone a participant in the anti-coup protests; in fact, he had demonstrated against both Mubarak and Morsi. But along with many others caught in the dragnet, Sherif was accused of a number of acts of violence, including rioting, vandalism, belonging to a terrorist group, and the attempt to murder a police officer. The anguish of this loss, Gamal says, is compounded by the fact that his son was so publicly degraded, that he was "arrested in this aggressive and humiliating [*muhīna*] manner witnessed by millions."[165] Then there are the persistent accusations that Sherif was a terrorist, along with the implication that he somehow deserved what he got. "All I ask is to know the truth of what happened and that those responsible would be held accountable," he says. Instead, the initial ten-year sentence for the commanding officer responsible for the transport of the prisoners was vacated the following year in appellate court, the day before Sisi's inauguration as president.

Sherif's story illustrates two interrelated phenomena evident throughout this archive. The first is the relentless effort of the regime to remake protesters and bystanders alike into filthy thugs, agents of foreign powers, and terrorists.[166] The second is the formidable power of the state to determine and disseminate accounts of both individuals and the uprising in which such violence becomes necessary and justified. Mubarak was fond of dark references to demonstrators serving the interests of foreign powers. Even in his court speech in 2014, he insisted that the events of January and February 2011 were fomented by terrorists and their allies from abroad.[167] SCAF routinely depicted demonstrators as *balṭagiyya* even as it unleashed machete-wielding thugs onto soccer fans or trained gangs to

164. This survivor's account of the exchange between the prisoners and the police is in Kingsley, "How Did 37 Prisoners Come to Die at Cairo Prison Abu Zaabal?"

165. Bilal Fadl, "Tafwīḍ bi'l-baṭsh!" [Authorization to assault!], September 4, 2013.

166. The parallels here with the language used to vilify Black Lives Matter protesters in the United States are striking.

167. Mubarak's Speech in court, Sada Elbalad, "Muḥākamat al-qarn: Kalimat al-ra'īs al-asbaq Mubarak amāma hay'at al-quḍāh" [The trial of the century: the former president's speech in front of the Judicial Council].

sexually assault protesters.[168] In this distorted reality, Sherif Ibrahim writes, the "honorable man is treated like a thief, and the thief treated like a mighty hero."[169] It's not enough for the regime and its torturers to kill at will and systematically inflict pain on citizens; it must do so in a way that denies victims and their families the chance to endow their sacrifices, suffering, and loss with political significance.[170] As Kamel puts it, "they always find a way to make your choice meaningless and worthless."[171]

Mona Seif (Fattah's sister and an activist in her own right) contends that, under such conditions, efforts to identify and punish those responsible are not just fruitless but dangerous. Victims of police brutality are routinely subjected to retribution when they try to pursue charges or seek any kind of accountability. Long before Trump's discourse of fake news and false facts, Egyptian officials routinely dismissed the authority of forensics and other incriminating evidence. In an interview on Tahrir TV in December 2011, for example, a lieutenant simply denies the authority of a forensic report, insisting against countervailing evidence that protesters could not have been killed by the military but must have been shot by "enemies of Egypt" standing next to them.[172] Moreover, Seif says, citizens accused of crimes but found innocent are "still being dragged to prison and humiliated [*dhull*] and degraded for things they did not do."[173] Journalist and author Bilal Fadl concurs: in a post addressed to Morsi in 2013, he accuses the security services and police of brutalizing citizens with impunity, just as when Mubarak ruled.[174] There's overwhelming evidence of citizens being beaten, raped, and killed all over the country, he tells Morsi, but you just discredit those who speak of it as the "magicians of Pharaoh" who seek to undermine your authority.[175]

168. Amar, "Why Mubarak Is Out," 84.

169. Ibrahim, "Iktub yā tārīkh."

170. 5FadaFada, "Huwa fīh eih?" [What's going on?].

171. Kamel, "Maqāl maktūb bi-baṭāriyyat al-laptop" [Post on a laptop battery].

172. Al-Diab, "Dina Abdel Rahman fī mawqif shujā' jiddan wa-mushādda kalāmiyya ma'a liwā' jaysh li-ithbāt ḥuqūq al-mutaẓāhirīn" [Dina Abdel Rahman takes an incredibly brave stance in a debate with a military lieutenant attesting to the rights of the protesters].

173. Reem Maged, "Kaffāra yā Abū Khālid wa-'uqbāl al-barā'a līk wa-illī zayyak" [Blessings, Abū Khalid, and all the best wishes for your innocence and all those like you].

174. Threatened by the Sisi regime, Bilal Fadl left Egypt in 2014. All of his writing cited here was written while residing in Egypt.

175. Fadl, "Qabla al-ṭūfān" [Before the flood]. Both the Bible (Exodus 7:11) and the Qur'an (7:113) refer to the "magicians of Pharaoh" summoned by the Pharoah of Egypt, ordered to use sorcery to discredit Moses's claim to prophethood and justify keeping the Israelites in bondage.

In many of these texts, there's a rhetorical slide from individual to collective humiliation that turns Doma's "equality in humiliation" into the connective thread between the two registers of experience. Take, for example, Omar Kamel's 2012 blog post. Everyone in Egypt is treated like dogs, Kamel writes; after all, "both [Egyptians and dogs] walk the same destroyed streets, breathe the same polluted air, live in the same darkness." The only difference between a dog and a citizen, he says, is that the citizen is permitted to vote.[176] 5FadaFada goes even farther: as police behave as if they are masters and the people their slaves, all citizens share a status even lower than animals; they have become things rather than beings, objects that can be casually wiped from the earth without thought or consequence.[177]

To see their point, one need look no further than the express permission Sisi gave to security forces to use live ammunition for ordinary traffic violations. Lewis argues that this simply formalizes the "unrestricted right to kill" anyone at any time that has been a consistent feature of the Egyptian regime for decades.[178] An incident in 2011 in which a police officer shot a bus driver when the bus got in his way is not all that rare, but Sisi's edict arguably goes even further than before.[179] Given traffic density, the infamous absence of working traffic signals, and the almost universal disregard of driving regulations, it essentially authorizes incremental mass murder, particularly in cities such as Cairo and Alexandria. Those who think that express loyalty to Sisi's regime protects them from such "equality" are not paying attention. In 2013, a reporter and manager for two state-owned newspapers known for pro-regime coverage were gunned down at an army checkpoint in Damanhour for violating curfew. In 2014, security forces opened fire on a microbus going in the wrong direction, killing the driver—a man,

176. Kamel, "Maqāl maktūb bi-baṭāriyyat al-laptop."

177. 5FadaFada, "Iqrā al-ḥāditha" [Listen to this].

178. Lewis, "Fawwaḍtahum lil-qatl . . . fa-qatalūka" [You authorized them to kill . . . they killed you]. The announcement itself would be humorous if it were not so deadly. In a Sada Elbalad "exclusive," the former Assistant Minister of Interior, Major General Muhammad Nour al-Din, "warned citizens not to drive in the wrong direction in the areas surrounding vital installations, security directorates, police stations. . . . The citizen in this case puts his life at risk and may be killed immediately on suspicion of being a 'terrorist' carrying explosives if he does not respond to warnings." Sada Elbalad, "Nagat Attia al-Gebaly, 'Khabīr amnī yuḥadhdhir 'al-muwāṭinīn': al-sayr 'aks al-ittijāh bi'l-qurb min al-akmina yu'arriḍ ṣāḥibuhu lil-'qatl' lil-ishtibāh fīhi" [A security expert warns "citizens": [Car] owners driving in the wrong direction near hidden security stations risk being "killed" on suspicion].

179. 5FadaFada, "Iqrā al-ḥāditha."

it turned out, who was a staunch supporter of Sisi.[180] In another incident in early 2014 in Isma'iliyya, an officer shot and killed a retired member of the military regime for refusing to show his identification card.

These voices articulate the ways in which humiliation knits Egyptians together in a shared sense of equality of insignificance. In other words, this equality again connects the "I" to the "we," in this case, the always potentially humiliated individual to a collective "peoplehood" constituted as humiliated. Such "peoplehood" doesn't by definition yield a collective solidarity. As Bilal Fadl notes in a 2012 blog post, rather than cultivating a sense of common cause anchored in a shared fate, such equality of insignificance has trained Egyptians to look out for themselves. Desensitized and fearful, Fadl writes, Egyptians duck rather than stand up for one another. During Ramadan, a citizen crossing a street without a single pedestrian crossing was run over by three cars in rapid succession. Not one of the drivers stopped, and cars that were there sped away quickly out of fear of being blamed by security forces for the hit and run.[181]

A "peoplehood" defined by equality in humiliation is further fractured by class, which constitutes such vulnerabilities and violations differently and conditions how they register, or if they register at all. As Amro Ali points out, the fact that Khaled Said was middle-class, tech savvy, and killed in the storied coastal city of Alexandria helps explain why his death in particular became a rallying cry against the regime despite the many low-income Egyptians who have endured the same brutality for decades but have disappeared into obscurity. "One wonders if Tunisians would have reacted as vehemently if Mohammed Bouazizi were labeled a *fellāḥ* [farmer] fruit vendor rather than an unemployed middle-class university graduate, as erroneously reported in initial accounts."[182]

The story of Takadum al-Khatib, a professor and member of the March 9 Movement, is a particularly apt example of how status and connections inflect the way humiliation is instantiated, experienced, and curtailed.[183] During Morsi's presidency, Khatib had been traveling with his family for an Eid vacation in Luxor,

180. Lewis, "Fawwaḍtahum lil-qatl . . . fa-qatalūka."

181. Fadl, "al-Miṣrī lil-miṣrī ka'l-bunyān . . . al-mahdūd" [The Egyptian social fabric is like an edifice . . . demolished].

182. Ali, "Saeeds of Revolution," 66, 67.

183. This refers to the organized movement of university professors that sought greater academic freedom and the end of police and intelligence interference in Egyptian higher education.

when his bus was stopped and a police officer boarded and began to check the identity cards of all the passengers. Dissatisfied with the speed with which Khatib supplied his ID, the officer started to scream at him. "You don't have the right to speak to me that way," the professor told him. "The world has changed and there is a revolution against this treatment." The officer jeered in reply: "don't imagine you're a man [*rāgil*]; just keep going this way and you'll see what'll happen to you." -Khatib was then kicked, beaten, thrown off the bus, and put into a car where there were already four impoverished looking men. He was taken to a police station where he was accused of attacking three officers and carrying drugs. All along the way, he was called a "son of a filthy bitch" whose father is a woman, and a "filthy dog" who must be taught how to behave.[184]

But Khatib had resources and connections: he was able to obtain his cell phone from the head detective, and promptly called his contacts in journalism, law, and academia. He eventually spoke to Malek Adly and the deputy minister of justice, Omar Marwan. His connections apparently pressured the minister of interior at the time, Ahmed Gamal al-Din, to concede that the professor was not, in fact, carrying drugs. Khatib recognized that the officers would likely pin the drug charges on the four men in the car who lacked his resources and connections. "If I didn't know anyone and no one knew who I was," he concludes, "I would now be dead in the [police] station and my family would be called to receive my lifeless body."[185]

In a 2010 blog post reflecting on a notorious instance of violence against Coptic Christians, Wael Abbas writes that Muslims and Christians are "Egyptians of one nation and one prison."[186] But if Khatib's story illustrates how class mitigates the sense of equality in humiliation and its entailments, many Coptic Christians—at an estimated 10 percent of the population, the largest religious minority in Egypt—in this archive attest to the way religion can intensify and distinctively inflect it. Consider Mina Danial, a twenty-year-old Copt and political activist who was among those killed in October 2011 at Maspero, the site of one of the worst massacres of Coptic Christians in recent history.[187] In a

184. Jaheen, "Kilāb al-dākhiliyya wa-kīf ta'āmlū ma'a al-nāshiṭ al-siyāsī Dr. Taqādum al-Khaṭīb" [Takadom's case: The hounds of the ministry of interior].

185. Samia Jaheen, "Kilāb al-dākhiliyya wa-kīf ta'āmlū ma'a al-nāshiṭ al-siyāsī Dr. Taqādum al-Khaṭīb" [Takadom's case: The hounds of the ministry of interior].

186. Abbas, "Bayān al-'ā'idūn min Naga' Ḥammādī" [A statement by the returnees from Naga' Hammādī].

187. Maspero refers to the destination of the protest on October 9, 2011: the Maspero building where Egypt's state-run television and radio station was housed.

documentary, Danial speaks of feeling dead in the country that he loves, not simply because of sectarian violence but because he is perpetually marked as Christian rather than Egyptian, constituted as conspicuously suspect by fellow (Muslim) Egyptians as well as by the state. The contempt, dismissal, and degradation from all sides is, in Danial's account, both totalizing and exhausting.[188]

Several Coptic Christians here point to a distinctive kind of insignificance arising from the way humiliation figures in sectarian violence. Consider a man named Emad Magdy who appears in a video standing in front of a large posterboard of pictures depicting a succession of attacks and insults endured by the Coptic community since January 11. Speaking with both anger and urgency, he catalogs one outrage after another for the camera, beginning with a church being torn down in Atfeeh, Helwan, and proceeding to the Bishop Bishoy Monastery, where security forces attacked monks who had been forced to protect themselves. Then he points to a picture of a procession where Muslim marchers carry a poster with the image of the Coptic Pope Shenouda III, scrawled with accusations of inciting sectarian violence, and recounts how people hurled shoes, insults, and profanities at it. No one speaks out or consoles Copts for their dead children, he says. There's no attempt to locate and return their stolen women. The lesson is clear, he says: Copts are "worthless [garbage] who don't deserve your effort."[189] A distraught protester at Maspero puts an even finer point on it in a BBC News Arabi broadcast:

> What makes people trivialize Christian blood? . . . Why, when the martyr Marwa al-Sherbiny [a Muslim] was murdered, everybody mobilized, even the president. But when six of our brothers are killed, nothing happens? As if they were animals or dogs? They probably would have mobilized if they had been animals or dogs. How come? Is our blood that cheap? . . . They are stepping on our necks [*dāyisīn 'alā raqabitnā*] and won't allow us to scream in pain; they want us to stay silent. They are shooting us and they don't want us to bleed. We have had enough, there is no more time for silence.[190]

188. Artists for the Revolution, "Thā'ir yaḥlam bi-waṭan . . . Mina Dānīāl" [A revolutionary dreaming of a nation . . . Mina Danial].

189. Coptic Maspero, "Aḥdāth al-aqbāṭ ba'da thawrat 25 Yanāyir" [Post-January 25th revolution Coptic events]

190. "Mā lā yuqāl - aqbāṭ fī al-shāri'" [What is not said: Copts in the streets].

"They've Forced Us to Eat Dirt and Accused Us of Being Filthy": Sexualized Violence and Psychic Unraveling

Given what one scholar refers to as the "sexualized state terror" deployed tactically by the Egyptian regime, there is a conspicuous sexual modality to the "psychic violations" articulated in this archive.[191] The vast majority of materials that articulate this entanglement of sexualized violence and humiliation are by or about women, many of whom have experienced it directly or witnessed it firsthand and who often struggle to find words for how deeply such ferocious cruelty cuts into their very being. One of the most indelible public documents of what these women endured is visual: the amateur video footage depicting a woman surrounded by soldiers in Tahrir Square, her *'abāya* pulled over her head to reveal only a blue bra on the upper half of her body, being dragged along the ground while beaten and kicked. At one point, she's being attacked by no less than nine soldiers who have converged around her prone, unmoving body, one of whom stomps his foot onto her chest with what looks like as much force as possible.[192] The woman has remained anonymous—known only (and with affection) as "sitt al-banat" [the best of all girls]—and has never spoken publicly about it, remaining silent as a screen grab of her half-naked body circulated widely across social media platforms and in newspapers from *al-Arabiyya News* to *The (London) Sunday Times* to *Haaretz*.

The footage is from December 16, 2011, the date of demonstrations that would become known as the Cabinet of Ministers [*Majlis al-wuzarā'*], which left at least seventeen dead and hundreds injured.[193] Far less well known outside of Egypt is

191. Amar, *Security Archipelago*, 201–3.

192. Footage from Cabinet of Ministers events [majlis al-wuzarā'], demonstrations, December 16, 2011, https://www.youtube.com/watch?v=mnFVYewkWEY (accessed March 20, 2021). This link no longer works but, as of this writing, is available on the Jewish News One YouTube channel; see "Police brutally attack Egyptian women, US condemns, with 'Blue Bra Girl' video on Qasr Al-Ainy." The man in the video who attempts to help her and is beaten into unconsciousness for his efforts, Hassan Shahin, discusses the incident with Yousry Fouda. See Shahin "Faḍīḥatunā taluff al-'ālam min aqṣāhu ilā aqṣāhu" [Our disgrace is spreading all over the world, from one end to the other]. For an example of the international coverage, see Kainaz Amaria, "The 'Girl in The Blue Bra.'"

193. The name refers to protests against SCAF's appointment of a Mubarak loyalist, Dr. Kamal al-Ganzoury, as prime minister. Hiba 'abd al-Sattar, "Aḥdāth majlis al-wuzarā' . . .

a grainy video, also shot on that day: as demonstrators run from soldiers, a man bends down to help up a woman in an *'abāya* who has fallen, when a soldier in riot gear leaps in and down on him, kicking him with the full force of his body.[194] No less than eight soldiers, many with batons, almost instantly surround the two unarmed figures on the ground, kicking and beating them with unflagging energy. In a subsequent interview, the woman in the video, a doctor named Farida al-Hasa, recalls the threats whispered into her ear during the assault, as her assailants detailed everything they planned to do to her. She says,

> All I could do was stay silent. I knew he was trying to humiliate me [*yidhill fiyyā*].... He was trying to provoke me to insult him back or do something. He was [sexually] harassing me and I kept pushing his hands away. I didn't try to resist because I knew if I resisted it would only get worse. He acted like he was being challenged, like he had an inexplicable grudge.... It was all about intimidation.... I tried not to look him in the eyes because they consider that a challenge. They consider everything a challenge. I kept my eyes lowered so he didn't think I was challenging him because I couldn't handle any more beating, to be honest.... All the girls were really destroyed. Another girl, her face was full of tears and blood. He told her "you're from a whorehouse" and some other really bad things and kept insulting her.... When I went outside, I started crying... not because of all of the beating, but because of what he said.[195]

In the course of the interview, Hasa recounts being thrown on the floor in a corridor next to a twenty-eight-year-old pharmacist named Ghada Kamal, an activist and member of the April 6 Movement who had a head injury from being beaten. Hasa saw a number of high-ranking officers in black masks grabbing Kamal's crotch and sexually threatening her. Speaking about the experience not long after the attacks, Kamal describes running from the soldiers that day but turning back when she saw ten of them converge around a girl of about twelve years old, beating her and pulling her hair. Trying to block the girl from the blows,

dhikrā ḥarīq wathā'iq al-majma' al-'ilmī wa-ta'riyat sitt al-banāt wa-iltizām 'al-'askarī' bi-naql al-sulṭa" [Minister of cabinet events... remembering the science complex fire, the stripping of the lady and SCAF's commitment to transfer power].

194. Adel, "Yasquṭ ḥukm al-'askar."

195. Al-Hasa, "Shahādat al-fatāh allatī saḥalahā al-jaysh yasquṭ ḥukm al-'askar" [Testimony of the girl whom the army dragged topples military rule]. The video is dated 2014, but it was most likely filmed in late December 2011.

she was beaten all over her body, especially on her chest, neck, and head, resulting in five stitches. She recalls that one of the soldiers

> looked directly at me and he started to move his clothes [to show his erection]. . . . It was a really filthy sight. So, he dragged me—there's a picture of him dragging me by the hair—then he started hysterically beating me all over my body. He said: "We want this one inside," and they started dragging me inside the building. Of course, everyone on the way took their turns beating me. . . . I had been bleeding for what felt like an hour. . . . [One of them] slapped me and kept saying "I will show you whether or not I am a man today. We'll all have our fun with you. You're not getting out of here." I was silent, what can I say? He asked me, "Where's your father?" I said "He's in Saudi Arabia." He said, "That's why you're a ***." A bad word, and more threats, like "I will do this and that to you."[196]

While uniforms clearly identify soldiers or police in such instances, it's often difficult to determine who was responsible for the many other incidents of sexual violence directed against women during the revolution. Women who were sexually harassed and assaulted at Tahrir Square, for example, provide harrowing descriptions of being surrounded, separated from their friends, and assaulted by groups of men in civilian dress. In a number of cases, the men claimed to be protecting the woman they were assaulting and, in the chaos, it was difficult for the women to discern the difference between the assailants and men who were, in fact, attempting to help.[197] In anonymous testimony gathered by El Nadeem Center for the Rehabilitation of Victims of Violence in Cairo, several women said it was clear that the assaults were orchestrated rather than spontaneous; many suspect that the regime was directly or indirectly behind them, although both the military and Islamists have been accused.[198] A few

196. Gihan Mansour interview, "Shihādat Ghada Kamal ba'd i'tidā' al-gīsh 'alīhā 16 December" [The testimony of Ghada Kamal after the army attacked her on December 16]. Images of Ghada Kamal's brutalization can be seen along with others at Woman News Agency-Cairo, "Tadāwul ṣuwar 'ṣādima' li-junūd Miṣriyyīn yasḥalūn nisā' mutaẓāhirāt fī maydān al-taḥrīr" [The circulation of "shocking" images of Egyptian forces dragging female protesters in Tahrir Square].

197. al-Zohairy, "Faḍīḥat al-taḥarrush al-jimā'ī bi-mutaẓāhirāt al-Taḥrīr bi-'aṣr al-ikhwān" [The scandal of group harassment of female protesters in Tahrir in the age of Ikhwān].

198. Tadros, "Challenging Reified Masculinities," 329. There are reports of Muslim Brotherhood supporters engaging in sexual violence as well, as evinced by an attack on two photographers for al-Shurouk newspaper by Islamists in July 2013. The female photographer, Gihan Nasr, describes a man who tried to drag her, saying, "Come, I'll take you into a tent and show

alluded to ways in which the ordeal continued in ambulances and in hospitals after the assaults. One woman described being stripped and manhandled through a gauntlet of sexual assaults in January 2013, only to be greeted by doctors and nurses who suggested that she herself was to blame.[199]

As many voices here have pointed out, the regime is adept at obscuring responsibility and refusing accountability. Setting aside the question of whether such assaults were spontaneous attacks by civilians or orchestrated by the regime, I want to focus on the way such experiences are articulated here by the women who endured and are haunted by them. One woman remembers going to Tahrir Square with some friends not to demonstrate but simply out of curiosity. Before long men surrounded her and separated her from her friends. They groped her and grabbed at her *ḥijāb*, manhandling her so that she felt "as if I was in high sea and all the waves are just tossing me all over the place."[200] Hind Nāfiʿ Badawī, a woman brutalized by soldiers during the Cabinet of Ministers events, likened the experience to being ripped apart by a "pack of human wolves."[201] Another woman recalls looking into the faces of the assailants during an extended nightmare of gang rape in Tahrir Square: "the men were like lions around a dead piece of meat . . . the looks in their eyes were really like animals. Not human at all, and the way they were throwing me around was as if I were not a human, but a piece of garbage."[202] Interviewed about a similar gang assault that occurred on January 25, 2013, the second anniversary of the revolution, a woman identified only as Zeinab recalls,

> I wasn't trying to do anything but scream. At a certain moment, I lost my ability to speak, I couldn't even scream. My voice was gone from all the pulling and pushing in every direction. My voice was gone, nobody would hear you; it's pointless. I fell silent, I stopped talking or screaming. My hands were

---

you what media is." *Al-Shurouk*, "Al-Ikhwān yaʿtadūn ʿalā muṣawwirīn min jarīdat ʿAl-Shurouk' fī Rābiʿa wa'l-Gīza" [The Brotherhood attacks Al-Shurouk photographers at Rabaʿa and al-Giza].

199. El Nadeem Center for the Rehabilitation of Victims of Violence, "Live Testimonies on Sexual Torture in Tahrir Square and Surrounding Neighborhoods." For a discussion of El Nadeem's innovative challenge to the Egyptian regime's gendered logic of repression, see Amar, *Security Archipelago*, 214ff.

200. El Nadeem, "Live Testimonies."

201. Naṣṣār, "Hind Nāfiʿ Badawī tarwī kayf ʿadhabahā rigāl al-gīsh bi-waḥshiyya ṣādima" [Hind Nāfiʿ Badawī recounts how the men of the army tortured her with shocking brutality].

202. El Nadeem, "Live Testimonies."

constrained. I wasn't being beaten, not a single slap. I was broken down without a single hit.[203]

One of the most infamous incidents during this period is also the most bizarre, the so-called "virginity tests" conducted on the twenty or so women who had been detained by the military for several days after protesters were brutally attacked in Tahrir Square on March 9, 2011.[204] Just one day after International Women's Day and one month after demonstration chants that "the people and the army are one," these women were taken to the Egyptian Museum, a building dedicated to the artifacts of Egyptian greatness, strip-searched, and repeatedly beaten. They were subsequently transferred to a military prison. There, Salwa Husseini Gouda says in an interview with *Der Spiegel*, she was told to lie naked and spread her legs for a man in a white coat who "tested her virginity" while soldiers watched.[205] Several detainees reported that there were women present, tasked with assisting systematic government-sponsored rape. Many also said that the assaults were photographed by gawking soldiers. Throughout the ordeal, the women were showered with verbal abuse, called whores, and threatened with charges of prostitution.[206]

SCAF initially denied carrying out such "tests," but months later, a senior military officer who remained anonymous told CNN that they were necessary to protect the army from allegations of rape by female detainees, a justification publicly repeated by Sisi, then a member of SCAF and head of military

203. "The Scandal of Group Harassment of Female Protesters in Tahrir in the Age of Ikhwān."

204. While it is outside of the timeframe of this chapter, an article published in 2019 shows the continuities between what the military has depicted as anomalous sexual assaults of female political protesters and the appalling treatment of women prisoners, including routinely invasive "examinations" that, as one prisoner put it, are designed not to search the prisoners but humiliate them. Ouf, "al-taftīsh al-dhātī lil-sajīnāt al-Miṣriyyāt . . . taḥarrush wa-tarkība qātila min adawāt qahr al-nisā'" [Body-searches of Egyptian female prisoners . . . harassment and a deadly combination of tools to subjugate women]. Such continuities are also evident in al-Qady, "Dimā' fī al-sijn: al-dawra' al-shahriyya adāt idhlāl al-sajīnāt fī Miṣr" [Blood in prison: monthly periods are a tool for humiliating female prisoners in Egypt].

205. Shafy, "'Horribly Humiliating.'"

206. As Samira Ibrahim attests, she and other women were then charged with breaking a number of laws, including the attempt to assault an officer on duty. Ibrahim was sentenced to a year in prison, although it was suspended. Akhbār al-Yawm al-Sābi', "Al-Shahāda al-kāmila li-fatāt al-'udhriyya Samīra Ibrāhīm" [The complete testimony of the virgin girl, Samira Ibrahim]. Amnesty International, "Egypt: Admission of Forced 'Virginity Tests' Must Lead to Justice"; "Egyptian Women Protesters Forced to Take 'Virginity Tests.'"

intelligence.[207] "The girls who were detained were not like your daughter or mine," the anonymous officer explained. "These were girls who had camped out in tents with male protesters in Tahrir Square." In any case, the general continued, none of them were virgins in the first place.[208]

The officer's comments spell out the tautological logic at work not only in the "virginity tests" but also the gang rapes at demonstrations and a great deal of commentary about them.[209] Women's presence at public protests alone serves as evidence of promiscuity and sexual availability. As Maged points out, the question is always: if these were really virtuous women, why did they leave home and go to the streets in the first place?[210] This logic constitutes such women as always already sexually soiled, releasing men from any obligation to treat them with the respect only virtuous women deserve. This renders the protesters rather than the perpetrators responsible for being sexually attacked. It also ensures that such assaults, along with the humiliation entailed both by the violence and its aftermath, do not count as such, as only proven virgins can be raped. In the final irony, proof of the virginity that would qualify a female as "really" raped and humiliated in the first place is furnished by way of the woman's sexual violation.

Many of these women stress the difficulty of putting into words the shattering effects of such sexual brutalization, but in the attempt to do so, almost all of them repeatedly use the word "humiliation." Echoing Gouda's account of it as "horribly humiliating," Rasha ʿAbd al-Rahman struggles to describe the "extremely degrading" [*bi-muntahā al-ihāna*] experience: "I don't know how to describe this feeling, no matter how much I talk and try, there are no words. I can't describe

207. Sisi told Amnesty International that such "virginity tests" were designed to "protect" the army from rape allegations. Amnesty International, "Egypt: Military Pledges to Stop Forced 'Virginity Tests.'"

208. Amin, "Egyptian General Admits 'Virginity Checks' Conducted on Protesters"; Amnesty International, "Egypt: Admission of Forced 'Virginity Tests' Must Lead to Justice." The tendency to blame victims of state violence, Fattah points out, helps explain why it took months to convince the public that the military, still thought to have ushered in a new era of Egyptian politics, had done such things. Fattah, "Alaa Abd El Fattah fi 'Studio AlMasry AlYoum'" [Alaa Abd El Fattah on Egyptian Studio Today].

209. Tadros points out that some Egyptians sought to publicly refigure such women "not as victims of disgrace but as heroes and icons of liberation." It appears that such attempts were largely drowned out by the logic of victim blaming. Tadros, "Challenging Reified Masculinities," 330.

210. Maged, "Damnā sāl wa-ʿirḍinā ithatak wa-sharafnā itmarmaṭ" [Our blood was shed, our honor was violated, and our dignity was trampled]. For a discussion of the origin and notoriety of the phrase "Why did she even go there?" see Amin, "Is God for Revolution?," 135ff.

that feeling. But I feel such anger and resentment!"[211] "We weren't beaten up; we were completely destroyed," Samira Ibrahim says in an interview. "No matter how much I describe it, I can't tell you how I felt that day. . . . They humiliated us. They humiliated us! [*Dhallūnā. Dhallūnā!*] I wanted to die that day."[212]

There are very few texts in this archive that speak to or about male experiences of such sexualized violence during the revolution, but such paucity is no reflection of how extensively men endured it or how the valorization of a heteronormative, fully empowered masculinity was weaponized against them. Lewis is alone in noting the December 2014 attack on a public *ḥammām* in central Cairo.[213] Engineered by the Ministry of Interior's General Directorate for Protecting Public Morality, the attack can be understood as part of a broader effort by the Sisi regime to out-Ikhwān the Muslim Brotherhood with an aggressive campaign to protect "tradition" and "morals."[214] Over two dozen Egyptian citizens were arrested and charged with homosexual depravity under a law that bans "debauchery" [*fujūr*], part of a 1951 law on the "Combatting of Prostitution."[215] This was only one of many such "raids"—what Asef Bayat aptly calls witch hunts—that have marked both the military and Islamist regimes, although Sisi's ascendence gave them a particular inflection: "[i]n the euphoria of exalting General Sisi as the 'lion of Egypt' and the 'real man' of the nation, the depiction of gays as 'female-like' or 'half men' certainly served the new national chauvinist narrative that the post-Morsi counterrevolutionaries championed."[216]

211. Shafy, "'Horribly Humiliating'"; Egyptian Initiative for Personal Rights, "Shahādat Rashā 'Abd al-Raḥmān 'an kushūf al-'udhriyyat fī al-sijn al-ḥarbī" [Testimony of Rasha 'Abd al- Rahman's about virginity tests in military prison].

212. Akhbār al-Yawm al-Sābi', "al-Shahāda al-kāmila li-fatāt al-'udhriyya Samīra Ibrāhīm."

213. Lewis, "'Ḥammām Ramsīs' wa'l-hawas bi'l-naqd" ['Hammam Ramses' and the obsession with criticism]. I24NEWS Arabic, "Khawf wa-qalaq mutaṣā'id wasṭa al-mithliyyīn fī Miṣr" [Growing fear and anxiety among homosexuals in Egypt]. Lewis is the only one in this archive to even acknowledge non-heteronormative citizens "whose lives and dignity have been crushed along the hallways of courts and forensic clinics . . . and on TV screens."

214. I24NEWS Arabic, "Khawf wa-qalaq mutaṣā'id wasṭa al-mithliyyīn fī Miṣr."

215. According to a 2017 report issued by the Egyptian Initiative for Personal Rights, the average number of arrests and court referrals on this charge in the less than four years from October 2013 to March 2017 skyrocketed to 232 people, from the 189 such arrests and referrals in the 13 years from 2000 to 2013. Egyptian Initiative for Personal Rights, "Trap"; Matthies-Boon, "Shattered Worlds," 640n6. There is a history to this: as Scott Long points out, *fujūr* has historically been one of the sexual categories critical to the emergence of the modern nation-state and consolidation of its disciplinary powers. Long, "When Doctors Torture," 119.

216. Bayat, *Revolution Without Revolutionaries*, 183.

Lewis aptly describes *fujūr* as a conveniently vague charge, and its elasticity has proven a particularly effective way for the regime to turn the tables on those who try to bring rape charges against police and security forces. The logic here is familiar. For those charged with *fujūr*, sexual assaults are performative: even if such sexual assaults did happen, the fact that these individuals could be raped demonstrates that they weren't real men in the first place. Like the constitution of women protesters as too sexually soiled to be dirtied by rape-that-is-not-rape, this "disappears" atrocities for which police might be held accountable. Sexualized violence is disassociated from the actions of the perpetrators, making it "stick" to the bodies of the assaulted who are in this way reconstituted through the act of violence and its afterlives.

The few men willing to speak on record about the sexualized violence they endured describe a kind of psychic shattering that several of them present as an assault on manhood, or even an unmaking of it. In their work gathering narratives of trauma in Egypt, Matthies-Boon and Head document how extensively the military and police raped men in custody during the rule of SCAF, and there's extensive evidence of such practices during the time of Mubarak, Morsi, and Sisi as well.[217] One young man they interview, describing a horrific scene of soldiers systematically raping male protesters under a Cairo bridge in September 2011, said that, despite having been electrocuted, beaten, and burned in jail before, this time "something inside of me was broken."[218]

A man identified only as Karim echoes this sense when describing what he had endured after his arrest at a Tahrir Square sit-in: "Beatings don't make much difference. Beatings, insults [*shitīma*]—fine, go ahead. But that other thing... they make you hate the whole world, hate yourself. Hate even the smell of your own body... they try to destroy man's self-respect, destroy their pride as men" [*in humma yiqallilū min rāgil aw yiqtilū haybat al-rāgil guwāh*].[219] Ayman Mehanni describes being beaten, electrocuted, and sexually assaulted by central security officers who mocked him all the while, saying, "[F]at lot of good your revolution's done you." He continues, "I couldn't even look my son in the eyes. He's supposed to be proud of his dad, but how could he be proud of a father who

217. The Mosireen Collective, "Al-Taʿdhīb al-jinsī manhajī min Mubarak lil-Majlis al-ʿaskarī wa-lil-Ikhwān" [Sexual torture under Mubarak, SCAF, and the (Muslim) Brotherhood]; Kingsley, "Egyptian Police 'Using Rape as a Weapon' Against Dissident Groups."

218. Matthies-Boon, "Shattered Worlds," 628.

219. Mosireen Collective, "Al-Taʿdhīb al-jinsī manhajī min Mubarak lil-Majlis al-ʿaskarī wa-lil-Ikhwān."

couldn't defend himself or his rights, who can't do anything? That alone is bad enough. I can't live, I can't sleep, I can't eat, I can't do anything."[220]

Taken together, these harrowing accounts allude to a shared experience of psychic rupture that is constituted differently by social constructions of gender. Police and security forces are explicit, and consistently so, that the sexual assault of men is not just about inflicting pain but specifically about stripping them of their masculinity. In one well-known incident in 2006, police officers arrested a microbus driver on the slightest of pretexts and then filmed themselves sexually assaulting him while telling him to "say you're a fag, say you're a whore, say that there isn't a single [real] man in your neighborhood."[221] As the previous discussion shows, such taunts are integral to regime violence and quite deliberately deployed during rape. Many of the men willing to speak about it depict such psychic violations as an "unmanning," and interviews with male survivors of sexual assault across an array of violent conflicts show that they are not alone.[222] The very reluctance to speak of it is among the afterlives of rape constituted as emasculation.

By contrast, there is no suggestion here that assailants constitute the sexual assault of females in terms of breaking or unmaking "womanhood," nor do the women who survive it seem to experience it as such. Targets are simultaneously presumed to be and made into whores by the act of sexual violation. Women are either pure or filthy, but "womanhood" itself is not at stake in this distinction either in intent or effect.[223] This too gives a distinctive shape to the afterlife of such violence, conferring a kind of untouchability to bodies permanently stamped by the stain of violation.

220. Mosireen Collective, "Al-Taʿdhīb al-jinsī manhajī min Mubarak lil-Majlis al-ʿaskarī wa-lil-Ikhwān."

221. Mosireen Collective, "Al-Taʿdhīb al-jinsī manhajī min Mubarak lil-Majlis al-ʿaskarī wa-lil-Ikhwān." Also, Human Rights Watch, "Egypt: Bus Driver Raped by Police Faces New Risk of Torture."

222. In an interview, an Iraqi named Dhia al-Shweiri who had been detained and sexually assaulted by the US military at Abu Ghraib says something very similar. Faramarzi, "Former Prisoner Prefers Saddam's Torture to US Abuse." See also Sivakumaran, "Sexual Violence Against Men in Armed Conflict and Adhiambo Onyango and Hampanda, "Social Constructions of Masculinity and Male Survivors of Wartime Sexual Violence."

223. Another woman describes how relentless sexual harassment had contributed to the disintegration of her sense of self: "I am very tired emotionally and feel that I am not pure. I want to be pure and feel my worth and reap the benefit of those years of hard work. I am really tired, and I hate myself." Fadl, "Fī maḥkamat al-sayyida Nafīsa" [In the court of Mrs. Nafīsa].

The implications of this contrast are that, first, the humiliation of sexualized violence is conditioned by the social construction of gender and, second, techniques of "masculine" and "feminine" humiliation forge as much as reflect this construction. As in chapter 2, violation is masculinity denied or negated, such that sexually defiled bodies are no longer male in any meaningful sense. If men are humiliated rather than violated, females are violated—or always potentially defiled—rather than humiliated. Women's bodies may be forever soiled by the stain, but such violation indexes masculine humiliation rather than their own.

At the same time, the materials in this chapter show how sexual assault turns *all* bodies into a theater for the performance of aggressive masculinity, from the soldier who tells Ghada Kamal, "I will show you whether or not I am a man today" to the security officers who inscribe the virility of the regime and the impotence of the revolution into Mehanni's flesh. Sexual humiliation may be calibrated to emasculate or defile, but centering the experiences of those who endure rather than dispense it draws attention to a common articulation: humiliation as rupture between who one is and who one has been made to be—in a sense, to be made unrecognizable to oneself.

Conclusion

In the preceding pages, I've sought to provide a close reading of the ordinary language through which many Egyptians have constituted the meaning, textures, and registers of a humiliation instantiated at multiple sites. I've aimed to thematize what humiliation says and how it works across these sites, and what emerges is by now a familiar pattern. Humiliation lives in the relation of power to powerlessness, but of a very distinctive kind. Powerlessness is instantiated as abjection and emasculation; it enacts an inversion and transvaluation in which eminence is brought low and parasites prevail; and it entails a rupture between who you are and who you're made to be.

Just as declarations of the failure of the Egyptian revolution can be one more aspect of its undoing, it would be a mistake to conclude either analysis of this particular archive or broader inquiry into humiliation rhetoric with an examination of abjection and rupture. After all, the language of rupture points to a state of integrity, belonging, status, or coherence that has been undone. There is no breach unless there is something that could be sundered, perverted, or betrayed. This suggests that, in constituting the terms in which powerlessness is experienced and understood, humiliation rhetoric also posits what must be restored and encodes the stakes and urgency of doing so. Absent an examination of such restorative action, this inquiry into what humiliation says and does would be incomplete. More than that, it would contribute to the erasures entailed by narratives of revolutionary failure. In the next and final chapter, it is precisely the character and urgency of restoration encoded in humiliation rhetoric that takes center stage. So too does the visceral power and emotional frequencies at work in such rhetoric, the mutually constitutive relationship between humiliation and dignity/*karāma*; and the performative achievements of restorative action irreducible to the matter of who controls the state.

As a prelude to the final chapter, it is especially fitting to conclude this one with a 2013 video of a young veiled Egyptian student standing on an upper floor of her school. Lips unmoving, she holds up both of her hands to flash the four-fingered sign known as R4ba'a in the presence of security officers who are gathered among others in the school yard below. Her four-finger salute is a reference to the Rabi'a al-'Adawiyya mosque (Rābi'a is the name of a Sufi saint, but the name is derived from the same root as four, arba'a), where the army had massacred hundreds in the process of clearing encampments of anti-coup protesters in August 2013. In the video, the student's teachers fret in the background, their nervous commands just audible: "someone take her inside!" and "what are you filming?!"[224]

A performance of solidarity with the protesters and an expression of anti-coup sympathies, the salute has become a powerful symbol, evincing the afterlife of an uprising that refuses to be over. The two-minute YouTube video of the student was apparently viewed half a million times on the first day, suggesting just how tenuous the outward settlements violently imposed by the military state are.[225] What Lewis refers to as the student's "four small fingers" are a reminder of the extent to which political transformations are ongoing and often incremental, residing in those struggles in between, behind, and beneath the eruptive events so often taken as the stuff of real politics. If one of the most insidious expressions of power is the conviction that what is can never be otherwise, these "four small fingers" are a reminder that, to paraphrase Sheldon Wolin, resistance to

224. Bahaa, "Arjal bint fī Miṣr bidūn niqāsh ṭāliba tarfa' shi'ār Rābi'a athnā' idhā'at Tislam al-ayādī fī ḥudūr mudīr al-amn" [The manliest girl in Egypt hands down raises the raba'a sign during the broadcast of "Tislam il-ayadī" in the presence of the head of security].

225. Lewis reports this in "Ma'rakat al-madāris wa'l-aṣābi' al-arba'a" [The battle of schools and four fingers], where he also refers to the student's "four small fingers." The R4bia salute appeared widely of social media as a bright yellow sign with four black fingers. El-Shenawi, "Four-Finger Salute."

domination is a recurrent possibility as long as memory of political challenge survives.[226]

Appendix: Constitution of the Archive

The research for this chapter was conducted on and off from February 2019 to June 2021, with an extended hiatus at the height of the Covid-19 pandemic in 2020. It focused specifically on the period from June 2010 to July 2014, occasionally supplemented by materials slightly outside of these parameters. The main materials were gathered by searching for the various Arabic terms for humiliation in multiple grammatical forms in both Egyptian colloquial and Modern Standard Arabic. The search also included expressions that conveyed humiliation or its cognates in the absence of the actual word, from metaphors to images to descriptions of acts or experiences that capture the texture of how it is lived.

The result is an archive of expressions that range widely across genre and medium and incorporate a fairly broad range of expressions—all mediated, of course, by technology, selection, translation, and interpretation. These include 45 poems/songs, 206 tweets, 31 Facebook posts (new privacy protocols reduced what could be searched), 70 blogs, 86 professional and amateur videos/vlogs, 17 signs, numerous newspaper and magazine articles, images, chants, slogans, and television programs, among them broadcasts on Mehwar TV, OnTV, AlArabia TV, Dream TV, CBC, Tahrir Channel, Today TV, Egyptian Studio, AlNahar TV, Al Jazeera, and Art America channel. Notably, the two terms for humiliation that recur most frequently throughout this archive are *dhull* (296 times) and *ihāna* (168 times). Four additional terms derived from ذلّ/dhāl-lām-lām frequently recurred: *d̲alīl*, *mad̲alla*, *id̲lāl*, *mad̲lūl*. Four additional terms derived from هون/hā'-wāw-nūn also recurred: *imtihān*, *muhān*, *mahāna*, *mitʿhān/mitʿhāna*.

In the years since I began this research, the Egyptian state has continued its vigorous and violent campaign to not only shut down dissent but erase, as much as possible, all evidence that legitimate criticism and real opposition ever existed. This bears on the current chapter in three ways.

First, this erasure has not just targeted expression but people, with serious consequences for several of the well-known figures who appear in this chapter. For obvious reasons, it is difficult to obtain information about all of them, and the information that exists is hard to confirm. In addition to those killed during the revolution, many of them no longer live in Egypt, and others remain in prison.

226. Wolin, "Fugitive Democracy," 23.

Several of them are now voluble supporters of Sisi. Most who remain in Egypt have gone quiet or have receded so completely from view that information about them is difficult to find. Those who are still visible have significantly scaled back and toned down what they say and about whom. A few—Mona Seif, Malek Adly, and some members of the Choir Project—continue to oppose the regime, speaking out about its abuses or struggling on behalf of those imprisoned or disappeared. It's unknown how the many unidentified Egyptians who speak in this archive have contended with these pressures, dangers, and targeted violence, or if they have even survived. What these materials do make clear is that vulnerability to such threats and violence are significantly conditioned by class, connections, and degree of precarity.

Second, any record of public criticism accessible to the regime remains a source of danger to those associated with it. To avoid further jeopardizing the safety of those who had the courage to speak out against a police state during the uprising, I have sought to remove the names of many of the lesser-known sources collected in this archive.

Finally, many of these websites, links, and posts have moved several times over the course of this research, only to ultimately vanish or cease to work. Some of this is a function of the way older materials on the Internet are relocated or archived and of changing protocols on platforms such as Facebook and Twitter. But some of this is due to regime efforts to scrub all traces of criticism from the Internet. In some cases, the authors themselves have expunged such evidence from the public record to safeguard themselves from regime retaliation. As a result, all citations in this chapter should be taken to refer to materials that were "live," widely available, or more safely public, on the dates initially accessed.

Chronology of Key Events Mentioned

February 3, 2006	Hundreds of passengers die when a thirty-five-year-old Egyptian ferry sinks in the Red Sea
March 23, 2008	April 6 Movement formed by a small group of activists who launch a Facebook page in support the planned textile workers' strike at Mahalla al-Kubra
April 6, 2008	Massive textile workers' strike at Mahalla al-Kubra

June 6, 2010	Khaled Mohamed Said is killed by Alexandrian police officers
November/December 2010	Egyptian Parliamentary elections
December 17, 2010	Muhammad Bouazizi sets himself on fire
January 14, 2011	Zine el-Abidine Ben Ali, Tunisian president for twenty-three years, forced to step down after massive demonstrations over months
January 25, 2011	Mass demonstrations, often referred to as the beginning of the Egyptian Revolution
February 11, 2011	Mubarak transfers power to vice-president Omar Soliman, SCAF assumes power
March 9–13, 2011	Women detained by the military following an assault on protesters at Tahrir Square are stripped, beaten, and subjected to "Virginity Tests" for several days by government officials and soldiers
October 2011	Maspero Massacre
December 16, 2011	Cabinet of Ministers sit-in; brutal dispersal by military
February 1, 2012	Massacre at Port Said
June 30, 2012	Muhammad Morsi elected president
July 3, 2013	Morsi ousted by military (imprisoned since coup, Morsi dies in June 2019)
August 14, 2013	Massacre of anti-coup protesters at Rabiʿa al-ʿAdawiyya Square
August 18, 2013	Thirty-seven detainees die in a transport van in front of Abu Zaʿbal prison from heat, tear gas, and oxygen deprivation
September 23, 2013	Egyptian Muslim Brotherhood outlawed
November 2013	Anti-protest law passed
May 2014	General Abdel Fattah el-Sisi elected president; ruthless crackdown on all opposition, protests, and dissent

5

Conclusion

HUMILIATION, DIGNITY, AND EMBODIMENT

[T]o submit is to give ourselves over to despair,
while action still preserves for us a hope that we may stand erect.

THUCYDIDES, *THE HISTORY OF THE PELOPONNESIAN WAR*[1]

Only thus did the person who was not docile, the person who held himself upright . . . become indisputably visible.

ERNST BLOCH, IN *NATURAL LAW AND HUMAN DIGNITY*[2]

IN FEBRUARY 2011, President Hosni Mubarak sat in a television studio preparing to deliver the speech announcing the transfer of power to his vice-president, Omar Soliman. Mubarak had expected to outlast the popular challenge to his rule as he had so many times in the past, but this time growing demonstrations and mounting foreign pressure among a host of other factors were rapidly narrowing his options. The speech was prerecorded, but his Minister of Information, Anas el-Fiky, nixed the first version. Mubarak should not be looking down as he read the speech, Fiky insisted. It must be recorded a second time, and edited to eliminate any angle in which the Great Man's head is bent.[3]

Fiky's insistence is of a piece with the reported concern among many military officers at the time to secure a "dignified exit" for a president who was, by his own

1. Thucydides, *History of the Peloponnesian War*, book 5, chapter 17, 102.

2. Bloch, *Natural Law and Human Dignity*, 12.

3. "Wathā'iqī: al-Laḥaẓāt al-akhīra fī ḥukm Mubarak" [The final moments of Mubarak's rule].

frequent telling, the last surviving member of the great officers who restored the *karāma* of a humiliated Egypt in the October 1973 war with Israel. As activist Fattah points out, a "dignified exit" meant orchestrating a departure free of any impression that this national hero had been humiliated by the "millions in the streets, dancing and singing, jumping around and shooting fireworks celebrating his end."[4]

The bowed head of a president who governed with an iron fist for thirty years is a viscerally powerful symbol to those who suffered at his hands as well as to those whose fortunes depended upon his continuing dominance. This indelible image, deliberately edited out of the public record, exemplifies the conspicuously somatic register of humiliation that characterizes all these archives to varying degrees. I've called this an embodied idiom to first, capture the way humiliation is articulated on and through the flesh and; second, draw attention to the specific bodily postures and gestures that are both symbolic of humiliation and an essential mode of its expression.

This idiom is the last of the three primary rhetorical modes—verbal, visual, and embodied—through which humiliation is articulated in these materials. In the earlier chapters, it is woven into the visual and verbal modes of expression rather than standing beside them. The present chapter draws on the Egyptian archive to place this embodied idiom and its distinctive vocabulary front and center. The discussion refers back to pivotal texts and moments in the previous analyses, but the collected expressions from Egypt are the obvious point of departure. More than any other archive, they graphically convey the imbrication of body and psyche in the way humiliation is enacted and articulated, at a fleeting moment when unimaginable cracks in a virtually impregnable structure of domination come into view.

On the one hand, the following analysis throws a spotlight on what has been there all along. It collates the somatic vocabulary—from forced kneeling to standing up—prevalent in the Egyptian materials and throughout these archives. Such a spotlight brings into sharp focus the visceral power and emotional frequencies at work in these expressions of humiliation, crystallizing the stakes of powerlessness and imperatives of restoration encoded within them. On the other hand, the singular communicative capacities of the body as both the literal target of humiliation and an expressive medium makes this idiom more than just another rhetorical mode. As this analysis will show, it enunciates with unique clarity the often misunderstood or obscured interrelationship between humiliation and dignity. It

4. "Alaa Abd El Fattah fī Studio AlMasry AlYoum" [Alaa Abd El Fattah on Egyptian Studio Today].

does so in part by identifying and analyzing the conceptual distortions entailed by the common conflation of the Arabic *karāma* and the English "dignity." Such a conflation is a crucial manifestation of what I referred to earlier as the blockages to theorizing what humiliation rhetoric says and does.

This is the last chapter, then, but it's not the kind of conclusion that heeds the conventional wisdom to wrap up arguments already made rather than introduce new ones. In the following discussion, these theoretical and conceptual arguments culminate in three interrelated conclusions, most likely counterintuitive, that unfold concurrently rather than sequentially. First, humiliation and *karāma* (or "dignity") are mutually constitutive rather than opposed. Second, *karāma*/dignity is integral rather than antithetical to what invocations of collective humiliation say and do. Third, as *karāma*/dignity is articulated from within the terms of humiliation rhetoric, it's an essential component of the scaffolding this book seeks to build rather than outside of it.

To frame this discussion, I want to briefly return to this scaffolding, initially sketched in the introduction, drawing together features fleshed out in the intervening chapters to rearticulate what I have argued is a theory of humiliation grounded in patterns in the way people actually use it in language. The pattern begins with the very manner in which the substance and significance of humiliation is articulated. Regardless of genre, rhetorical mode, or the specificities of context, the meaning of humiliation in these texts is established not by explicit argument about what it is but by what it does.

The result is a consistent rather than homogeneous understanding of humiliation as the imposition of impotence by those with undeserved power, a condition that demands immediate redress. As I've shown by example and argument, this understanding corresponds to the experience of rupture between one's own sense of significance and place in the social order, and acute awareness of who one has been made to be by those with more and undeserved power. These capture the act and experience of humiliation, two dimensions of a single understanding in which the imposition of impotence produces the experience of being made into someone or something you no longer recognize.

In these terms, humiliation is a relation of power to powerlessness, but of a very distinctive and viscerally charged kind. This is not a generic relation of power with interchangeable inhabitants. It reflects and reproduces the way roles anchored in familiar norms of masculinity and femininity encode power in gendered terms to constitute powerlessness as emasculation and construe the antidote in terms of manliness or virility. The hierarchy of humiliation largely becomes a matter among men, authorized, enacted, and remedied by, between, and on men. The primary roles of humiliator and humiliated are symbolically or literally occupied by men. Male bodies are simultaneously the terrain upon which humiliation is inscribed and the instruments of inscription. Men are both culpable for the initial dis-ordering of power that humiliation entails and tasked with the restoration of the right order of things.

This is not an empirical argument about where, when, or to what extent the gender roles that anchor this order of power hold sway, are institutionally privileged, or enforced. There is now a good deal of scholarship that takes up these matters; my focus lies elsewhere, in the way such commonplace conceptions of gender have thoroughly infused the language of power that humiliation rhetoric encodes and deploys. Inasmuch as humiliation becomes synonymous with a lack of power constituted as unmanning, it operates rhetorically both to both describe a general powerlessness *and* to index depleted manliness, vigor, and virtue.

I have argued that the gendered terms of humiliation rhetoric work less as a blueprint of a patriarchal order than a rhetorical apparatus comprised of techniques and strategies that aim to bring into existence the very politics it presumes. Integral to such a political project is an account of collective powerlessness that sutures together disparate historical events, multiple domains of life, and scales of experience to describe and produce the character of the humiliator as well as the solidarity of the humiliated. As this hierarchy of humiliation, its premises and stakes, are constituted in terms of emasculation and its many metaphors, men are not just tasked with the arduous work of restoration; the undertaking itself makes them "men."

Humiliation rhetoric works to reassure as well as to provoke, and the female figure is critical to each operation. Inasmuch as the integrity of the family is bound up with the sexual inviolability of the female body, women become a mirror or measure of masculinity. Female vulnerability to male predations signals a failure of manhood even as it summons and incites men to feats that simultaneously perform masculinity and recuperate collective preeminence. Success is guaranteed regardless of the mlitary might, political hegemony, or consummate deviousness of the humiliator. This is not only because restoration of the proper order of power is destined by nature and/or God. It's also because victory is performative, achieved at the very moment such intolerable impotence is banished by action.

As the previous chapters show, Islamist expressions of humiliation, both visual and verbal, clearly exhibit this pattern. More than that, they render remediation as retaliatory humiliation, the imposition of impotence on those who have humiliated Islam. Given a narrative in which masculine capabilities, family integrity, communal strength, and Islamic preeminence are mutually constitutive, such reversal instantaneously restores order all the way down. Much as the initial experience of rupture can be revivified in rehearsal of one's humiliation after the fact, both the reversal and rehearsal of retaliatory humiliation can provide a deeply restorative experience, offering up the visceral satisfaction of publicly reinscribing humiliation upon the humiliator to reclaim power and vindicate one's place in the social order.

Yet these Islamists notably define the form of restoration and its achievement in different ways. Retaliatory humiliation does not denote uniformity, then, but serves as a common frame through which these Islamists articulate disparate purposes, calibrated to different political contexts and concerns. The character and requirements of restoration exhibit even greater variegation in the Egyptian materials, and differ much more dramatically from the retaliatory humiliation of the Islamists than any of the Islamists do from one another. I will return to this point in the final pages.

"Raise Your Head High": An Embodied Idiom of Humiliation and Restoration

As this chapter opened with the image of Mubarak's bowed head, it's fitting to turn first to an interview with one of his former drivers to focus on those who served him. The driver, Alaa el-Din el-Nawawy, recounts being forbidden to look at Mubarak when he worked for the President, required literally to avert his eyes whenever in his presence. Elsewhere in the interview, Nawawy describes being humiliated [*tihīn*] by Mubarak's Chief of Staff, Zakaria Azmy, who kicked him and insulted his parentage simply because he asked for a day off to care for his sick daughter.[5] Azmy's aim, Nawawy says, was to "break my eye" [*tiksar ʿaynī*], a figurative phrase that recurs throughout these materials and conveys being forced to cast one's eyes down or bend one's head in silence.[6] The metaphor in

5. Nawawy, "Biʾl-fīdiyū sāʾiq Mubarak al-raʾīs al-makhlūʿ kāna kathīr al-sabb wa-yakrah samāʿ al-Qurʾān" [In the video, Mubarak's driver: "the removed president had a foul mouth and hated to hear the Qurʾān"].

6. In the poem "The Phone Call," Gakh uses the same figure of speech in a couplet about the punishment of a poet who insulted the president. "Drag him bit by bit through the mud / Break his eyes and his jaw [*wa-iksarū ʿaynuh wa-dāghuh*]," he writes of a poet forced to avert his gaze and stifle his voice. Gakh, "al-Mukālama" [The Phone Call]. The phrase recurs in a January 5, 2011, demonstration of Coptic Christians, who chant, "Nobody can break your eye" [*inta maḥadash kāsir ʿaynik*].

the second instance works by evoking the literal demand in the first, exemplifying the kind of cross-referencing of the physical and symbolic that animates the meaning and power of these somatic terms.

References to a bowed head are particularly prevalent and work similarly throughout these materials. Take two songs that were especially popular during the revolution. The main refrain of the first, "Ṭāṭī Ṭāṭī" [Lower, lower] at once evokes a head bowed from the weight of degradation and bent down by physical force: "when I see humiliation [*al-dhull*] in your eyes, come put your misery next to mine/lower your head, lower, you are in a 'democratic' nation."[7] The second song, "Izzay" [How], became a staple of independently owned satellite television during the uprising. It asks: "How can I keep lifting your name high and you keep pushing my head down, how? / How can I cover your back, if mine is always bent and exposed?"[8]

A bowed head is often linked to slaps on the face or neck; both similarly play across these physical and symbolic registers to center the humiliated body. The "sticks and batons fly / and in the police station / with slaps on faces," writes Mostafa Ibrahim.[9] As the previous chapter showed, the slapping of faces and heads refers to a specific form of violence favored by Egyptian police and security forces. They also function metaphorically, to evoke the systemic and systematic degradation of Egyptians collectively by the humiliation regime—or what a 2010 song refers to simply as the place of "100 slaps."[10] In a May 2011 blogpost, Adly describes SCAF and the police as a "criminalizing machine . . . that slaps us on the back of our heads every time we turn around," with a force that befits thieves caught at a checkpoint, not a nation of free citizens.[11]

The second somatic term of humiliation, a bent back, is captured by both the lyrics of "How?" and Amr Ismael's lament that "[w]e have been bent for years."[12] The posture simultaneously evokes what it's like to feel ground down and

7. "Ṭāṭī Ṭāṭī" [Lower, lower].

8. "Izzay" [How]. In much the same vein, in "Ka'an al-'umr mā kāna" [As if life never was], Guweida writes of a nation abandoned to humiliation "from the day it bent."

9. Ibrahim, "Nadart il-nadr" [I made the promise].

10. Reham Abdel Hakim, "Bi'l-waraqa wa'l-qalam" [With paper and pen].

11. Adly, "Allāh yirḥamik yā rugūla" [May manhood rest in peace]. See also Bilal Fadl's reference to "beating on the back of the neck" in "al-'Ā'ishūn fī al-dibāja!" [Living in the preamble!]. Similarly, in a poem composed during Morsi's rule, Gakh writes, "We're tired of words and the back of our necks are sore from deceit." El-Gakh, "Anā Ikhwān" [I am brotherhood].

12. Ismail, "Ummī malhāsh fī al-siyāsa" [My mother doesn't care for politics].

a body forced to the ground. Deployed to play across these two meanings, there is yet a third valence embedded in it, a posture of enforced vulnerability not just to generic attack but to a sexual violation that at once reflects and enacts feminized submission. Here the cross-referencing is to the performative aspects of sexualized violence discussed in the previous chapter, particularly the way an opposition between the vulnerable, violated, submissive female and a masculinity constituted as unconquerable has been deployed to symbolically translate enforced powerlessness into unmanning, sexual abjection, effeminacy.

Being forced to the ground is often linked to being trampled with the dirt of shoes, itself an expression of contempt. One 2013 tweet refers to the humiliation of "living under America's feet."[13] Another contends that Egyptians have been enslaved for seven thousand years by ancient and modern pharaohs who walk all over them with their shoes, but are schooled by humiliation [*al-dhull*] to worship them nevertheless.[14] In video footage from February 2011, a crowd in Tahrir Square chants its defiance using the same metaphor, rejecting Mubarak's demand that the people kiss his feet [*ʿāyiz il-shaʿb yibūs riglayh*], vowing to "walk all over" him with their shoes [*wa-iḥnā ʿalayk biʾl-gazma nidus*].[15] By 2014, Negm captures the sharp turn against the uprising by referring to the January 2011 protesters as orphans beaten with shoes, hung from the legs, and ridden like donkeys by almost everyone.[16]

13. Elyan (@saberalian), "#Li-mādhā_yuḥākimū_Mursī? Li-annahu al-raʾīs al-Miṣrī al-waḥīd alladhī arāda li-#miṣr al-ʿizza waʾl-karāma baʿdamā jaʿalahā al-sābiqūn taḥyā fī al-dhull taḥta aqdām #Amrīkā."

14. العراب (@AhmedSalah007), "Firʿawn dās ʿalīhum bi-gazmituh, qaddisūh . . . el-nabī Mūsā aʿṭā lahum ḥurriyyithum, ʿabadū el-ʿigl . . . qiṣṣit 7000 sana ʿubūdiyya . . . wa-kull man tarabbā ʿalā el-dhull fī #Maṣr yaṣbaḥūn #shaʿb-ʿabīd" [A Pharaoh walked over them with his shoes, they worshipped him . . . the prophet Moses liberated them, they worshiped a cow. A story of 7000 years of slavery . . . and all those who were raised on humiliation in #Egypt become #an enslaved people].

15. Jamasyali, "Hitāfāt Mīdān al-Taḥrīr" [Chants of Tahrir Square]. Another example is the line "We are the ones beaten with the edge of your shoes and heel," in Cairokee and Zap Tharwat, "Ethbat makānak" [Hold your ground]. This is also a collaboration with Abnūdī, who lends lyrics and his spoken voice to the song. For additional examples, see Abnūdī, "Ḍiḥkit el-masāgīn" [The prisoner's laughter]. "Tawthīq al-thawra al-Miṣriyya 25 January 2011—Wael Ghoneim—Mostafa el-Naggar—Bayān al-thawra" [Documenting the Egyptian revolution 25 January 2011—Wael Ghoneim—Mostafa El Naggar—declaration of the revolution]; and hip-hop artist ZAP Tharwat's "Nahārnā nadā" [Our morning is dew], see translation in Sanders and Visonà, "Soul of Tahrir," 233.

16. Negm, "Quwwitnā fī rukūbitnā" [Our strength is in being ridden].

As this archive makes painfully clear, these somatic terms do not by any means exhaust all the ways humiliation can be and has been inscribed upon the flesh. At the same time, these particular metaphors repeat like an insistent beat not only within these materials but across these chapters, albeit with variable emphases in different texts. For Qutb, the bent head of humiliation is echoed in the posture of believers forced to "bow down" to human authority, a form of obedience indistinguishable from enslavement. For radical Islamists, "we will not bow our heads in humiliation" is the ultimate pledge to resist domination, just as the greatest expression of recuperated power is forcing your enemy to his knees.

In every chapter, men are not just figuratively but literally driven to their knees at the feet of fully clothed captors, a recurrent tableau that doesn't just convey but enacts a relation of impotence to dominance. Being forced to kneel, naked, is essential to the ritual of torture Doma details in Egyptian prisons. Emwazi looms over Foley and Sotloff, heads shaved and hands bound, just two of many men forced to kneel at the feet of their ISIS executioners. One picture from Gaza shows Israeli soldiers milling about rows of blindfolded Palestinian men stripped to their underwear, on their knees with heads bowed and hands bound. The photos from Abu Ghraib show one detainee kneeling, apparently menaced by a dog; in another, a naked and hooded prisoner is forced to balance, bent over, on boxes; in still another variation, prisoners are lying naked in a row on the floor, on their backs, while a US soldier actually kneels on top of them.

Enforced kneeling, bending over, bowing down: these constitute a somatic vocabulary of obeisance and abjection that work by centering the body without purporting to be descriptions of *specific* bodies. These somatic terms work through the kind of slide between the literal and the figurative at work in the interview with Mubarak's driver, a cross-referencing that evokes what particular men actually endure without tethering any one posture to a single moment or experience.

But encoded within this embodied idiom of humiliation are two particularly conspicuous terms of repair that are also articulated somatically, standing up and raising one's head. These terms are by now familiar. Islamists in the previous chapters frequently call upon Muslims to show their mettle by "standing up" for Islam despite the seemingly overwhelming power of its enemies, or insist that joining the struggle to raise up the head of the *umma* also makes it possible to lift one's own.[17]

17. Invocations of this posture tend to cluster around the verb *qāma*, the Arabic root of both *maqām*, meaning standing, station, rank, and dignity, and *qawām*, which denotes,

Take, for example, the song "Egypt Is Standing Up," which opens with "Egypt is standing up and casting off her dress of humiliation [*al-dhull*]."[18] The lyrics to "Hold Your Ground," a 2011 collaboration by the Egyptian rock band Cairokee and the rapper Zap Tharwat, tie the posture of standing up to holding one's ground, both of which are figured in opposition to humiliation [*mahāna*] and submission: "Hold your ground, for the sunlight shall return / you either die standing or live in submission . . . you demand *karāma* / they respond with humiliation [*mahāna*] / you demand justice, they accuse you of betrayal . . . I'm standing my ground no matter what they say or do."[19]

Just as the regime and its opponents exhibit equal fluency in the postures of humiliation, the protesters are far from alone in claiming firm resolve by "standing up." Government officials often depicted their refusal to relinquish power in precisely these terms to convey steadfastness against treachery and "thuggery." Answering a question at a press conference at the time of Mubarak's demise, for example, Safwat el-Sherif, Secretary General of the National Democratic Party, shot back: "Escape with a plane? Who said this? We're all here, standing tall."[20]

The second bodily expression of restoration is captured by a signature slogan of the Egyptian Uprising. The exhortation to "raise your head high, you are Egyptian" [*irfaʿ raʾsak fawq inta maṣrī*] pervaded the revolution, appearing in chants, signs, songs, graffiti, and rhetoric alike.[21] The phrase became its own hashtag on Twitter and a common theme in street art. Typical graffiti in this vein is captured in a picture of a wall along Shaykh Rihan Street in downtown Cairo: an Egyptian flag is accompanied by the message "Hold your head up, you're Egyptian."[22]

---

among other things, an erect or upright posture. I'll turn to the complex gendering of this posture later.

18. "Ahī qāmit Maṣr" [Egypt is standing up]. The song was performed by Mohamed Mounir in a 2011 video that circulated widely throughout that year and those that followed, up to and through Sisi's election campaign.

19. Cairokee and Zap Tharwat, "Ethbat Makānak." Language exhorting Egyptian people to stand or hold their ground, or valorizing protesters who persist as doing so, has been a recurrent theme on Twitter as well.

20. Al Jazeera, "Wathā'iqī: al-Laḥaẓāt al-akhīra fī ḥukm Mubarak" [The final moments of Mubarak's rule].

21. The locution echoes what has been characterized as Nasser's signature call to "lift your head up, my brother, the era of colonialism is over. Al Jazeera, "Arab Unity: Nasser's Revolution."

22. *Al-Judrān tahtif: jirāfītī al-thawrah al-Miṣrīyya*, 76. On the prevalence of the slogan along with variations containing exhortations for Egyptians to raise their heads, see Anwar, "Pragmatic Analysis of the Protest Slogans of the Egyptian 2011 Revolution."

In several instances, such exhortations render the refusal of humiliation and restorative action as mutually constitutive. In a revolutionary chant directed at SCAF, for example, "raise your head" conveys resistance to all that bows or bends the body toward or into the ground: "Raise your head and never bow, those who humiliated you are [just] a lowly council."[23] The lyrics to "Ḥayāt al-Mīdān" [Life of [Tahrir] square], composed and sung in February 2011 by The Choir Project, a collaborative music workshop, say something similar: "We will not fear, we will not bow, we scorn the hushed voice. / The Egyptian people are rising from the fields and the factories. . . . Raise, raise, raise, raise [your head], Egypt will always be free."[24] In a BBC Arabic video, an unnamed Coptic man protesting the explosion at a church in Alexandria on New Year's in 2011 vowed, "We will never submit. We will remain standing, with our heads high, standing our ground and resilient."[25] Even expressions of despair at the punitive brutality of the regime deploy this vocabulary. In an interview, the grieving father of Mohamed Moustafa, a nineteen-year-old protester killed in December 2011, phrases his anguish in terms that echo across this archive: Egyptians raised their heads high during the revolution, he says, but they've since been pushed back down to the ground, bit by bit.[26]

23. The Mosireen Collective, "Sexual Torture Under Mubarak, SCAF, and the [Muslim] Brotherhood."

24. The Choir Project, "Ḥayāt al-Mīdān" [Life of [Tahrir] Square]. The workshop series that produced this song was referred to as the Utopia Choir. For more on the Choir Project, see http://www.choirproject.net/?fbclid=IwAR3qltNxohJVBzRLeyJIyCzb5k0RT7a-kEHW1-oSQ69D7X12lniAoQUb438. For additional examples, see Ahmed Mekky and Mohamed Mohsen, "Karāma al-Maṣrī" [The Karāma of the Egyptian]; and the November 2011 Khairy Ramadan interview with Egyptian actor Khaled al-Nabawi, "Khaled El Nabawy—ʿĀr ʿalīkum waṣf el-thuwwār bi'l-balṭagiyya" [Khaled El Nabawy—Shame on you for calling the revolutionaries thugs].

25. BBC News Arabic, "Bi'l-fīdiyū: muẓāharat iḥtijāj lil-aqbāṭ fī Shubrā ʿalā al-hajamāt" [Video: Copts protest in Shubra against the attacks].

26. Dina Abdel Rahman interview with Mohamed Moustafa's father, "Shāhid risāla katabahā shahīd qabla mawtihi wa'l-iʿlāmiyya Dina Abdel Rahman tuwāṣil al-bukā' al-shadīd ʿalā al-hawā' al-ān wa-tufassir" [A message written by a martyr before his death, and TV host Dina Abdel Rahman cries intensely on air and explains]. In a similar vein, an unidentified Coptic man at the Maspero protest in May 2011 said, "After we started a successful revolution and raised our heads high, we're lowering them to the ground again." Coptic Maspero, "Mā hiya al-awḍāʿ fī Miṣr al-ān liqā' fī Maspero" [What are the conditions in Egypt now? Encounters in Maspero]. See also Mekky, "Karāma al-Maṣrī." Relevant in this connection is the question that arose over and over again in testimonies of women who had survived sexual brutalization: "How can I raise my head again?" El Nadeem Center for the Rehabilitation of Victims

Both Banna and Qutb explicitly invoked the Arabic word *karāma* to characterize restoration and emancipation. This is also true of the uprising, where the nature and import of such restorative postures are most often expressed by *karāma*, sometimes explicitly, at other times linked by proximity or associative meanings.[27] The song "Hold Your Ground" is one example among many, but the song "The *Karāma* of the Egyptian [*Karāmat al-Maṣrī*]" is particularly explicit about these connections. In the lyrics, the "youth who raised Egypt's head high . . . standing like lions" are valorized as the embodiment of collective *karāma* constituted as a recovery, an enactment of who Egyptians "really are" rather than who they are made to be:

> Look how high we've become when we put our hands together
> Christian, Muslim, educated, illiterate, rich and poor
> When all their chants turned into a roar
> Even if we don't achieve all our demands, we've still won
> It's enough that the world now knows who we really are.[28]

The idea of "real Egyptians" whose *karāma* is restored draws on the sense of national exceptionalism articulated through the various sites of humiliation that emerged in the previous chapter. Such exceptionalism locates national humiliation in the sharp disjuncture between the august stature that is specifically Egyptian and a succession of brutal, greedy, and venal dictators that have dragged both country and people into the dirt. From this vantage, *karāma* entails a felt moment of recognition, a long overdue arrival of the "real Egyptians" expressive of a national character that is simultaneously a property of the golden past and an ideal outside of history.

Invocations of the "real Egyptians" recovered during the uprising have a parallel in Islamists' call to recuperate the "real Islam." Bin Laden frames his arguments as recalling Muslims to an existing solidarity in abeyance even as "The Declaration" is itself the rhetorical mechanism that brings it into being. The ISIS videos aim to constitute an audience of "Sunni Muslim men" assumed to already

---

of Violence, "Live Testimonies on Sexual Torture in Tahrir Square and Surrounding Neighborhoods."

27. The point is not, of course, that *karāma* was not the only watchword of the uprising; aspirational rhetoric included *ḥurriyya* [freedom], *'aysh* [bread that is life sustaining], *'adl* [justice, sometimes modified by *ijtimā'iyya* to mean social justice], *'amal* [work], and, of course, *irḥal* [leave].

28. eProductionHD, "A. Mekky Raps for the Egyptian Revolution (Jan 25th) Karāmat al-Maṣrī."

exist, inviting watcher-witnesses to interpolate themselves into the tableau of humiliation and coax them toward migration or retaliation. These references to an ideal solidarity in the past or outside of time is a designation that marks a process: each "authentic" solidarity is constituted at the moment of enactment. These operations are at work notwithstanding the experience of such solidarity as a restoration of what had been or always was.

Of course, the Islamists here take Egyptian solidarity as the very problem to be solved. It's not just that restoration of the "real Islam" takes primacy over the "real Egypt," but that an exclusively Sunni Muslim audience is simultaneously posited and conjured. Such solidarity must nullify other allegiances, just as restoration of the *umma* and, by extension, the preeminence of Islam, vitiates national borders and indicts those who preside over them, whether non-Muslim or so-called Muslim. Qutb is well known for his indictment of all forms of human authority—national, liberal, monarchical, communist, socialist, and democratic alike—as transgressive of the sovereignty that is God's alone. Bin Laden refuses to even call Saudi Arabia by name lest he grant legitimacy to the Saudis or the nation they rule. ISIS takes as its restorative project the eventual destruction of all national borders drawn by colonial fiat.

Such a powerful sense of recovery no doubt intensified the elation of the revolutionary moment in Egypt, but it must be similarly understood as an act of invention rather than one of recuperation. The "real Egypt" here is aspirational and performative, a goal and a process of becoming at the same time. In other words, the individual or collectivity that you recognize as yours is instantiated at the moment of enactment, an achievement in the here and now that is at least in part the creation of something new, even if it is simultaneously experienced as a recuperation of what had been. To borrow from J. Peter Euben's description of a different world, at this moment of felt recognition what actually arrives is a "people coming to understand themselves as spinners of their own webs of significance."[29] This is so even or especially when that web is woven from the stuff of humiliation. Figured by the regime as permanently immature children, Egyptians' "restorative" practices defy these terms in a gesture of refusal—one that simultaneously enacts a collective "peoplehood" as self-constituting rather than always already constituted as humiliated, impotent, undone.[30]

29. Euben, *Corrupting Youth*, 66. Euben is, in turn, reworking Clifford Geertz's reference to the "suspended webs of significance human beings have spun for themselves." Geertz, *Interpretation of Cultures*, 5.

30. This conception of "self-consitution," then, does not presuppose the modern notion of an "easy, instrumental control over the self." Hall, *Subjectivity*, 25.

This is precisely the sense of achievement articulated by those, such as Fattah, who see the uprising as victorious the moment Egyptians act to shape the script that governs their lives, claiming for themselves destinies they had always assumed was in other hands.[31] In this sense, what he characterizes as the remarkable and "legendary" accomplishment of the revolution has little to do with who rules and a great deal to do with the collective perseverance of citizens not just in Tahrir Square but far beyond it—in the alleys, streets, and factories across the country where there were no cameras. Their triumph is in conjuring in the present what they feel Egypt truly is by way of practices that defy what the humiliation regime has made of the country and its citizens for decades.

The meaning of such achievements comes alive in the words of those who had been least able to see themselves in Mubarak's Egypt. Malek Adly writes of a conversion with a sixteen-year-old named Mohsen in Tahrir Square on January 28, 2011. Bearing many of the marks of poverty, Mohsen describes how strangers had once looked at him as filth. But in a moment, he said, everything shifted, and instead of contempt for his impoverished appearance, he found only concern for a boy in Tahrir without his parents. "I'm happy because every time I meet someone they tell me they're worried about me," Mohsen says. "I don't mind dying today."[32]

Then there is Mina Danial, the young Coptic Christian activist. Once ground down by a sense of exile in his own country, Danial expresses wonder at the discovery that, during the revolution, someone he didn't know had covered him with a jacket while he slept on the street, and that strangers had taken him to the hospital when he was injured. Here at last we see the "real Egyptian who loves his brother, though he doesn't know him and they've never met," he says. What joy there is to live "among people who are just as happy to have me among them as I am to be with them." He adds, truly, the "revolution is beautiful with you at my side."[33]

Mohsen and Mina were killed during the revolution, but what they describe was not. They are echoed by the many here who insist that the Egypt they recognize is realized in those practices of self-rule wherever protesters congregate,

31. Fattah, "al-Ḥilm Awwalan."

32. Adly, "Moḥsen."

33. "A Revolutionary Dreaming of a Nation." "These are the Egyptian people," Mahfouz says in her vlog. "This is we have been dreaming of. I can now say that I am proud of being Egyptian." Mahfouz, "Ākhir kalima qabla 25 yanāyir" [Last word before January 25]; "Mīʿādnā yawm el-gumʿa baʿd el-ṣalāt fī kull mayādīn maṣr." Negm says much the same thing in "Ilā ḥabīb el-malāyīn baʿda al-bayān al-khāmis" [To the beloved by millions].

the gestures of care suddenly proffered by strangers who no longer seem so, and the shared elation of belonging to a moment of collective power in defiance of all expectations and enforced habits. In this country, citizens place their bodies between the blows of the police and other Egyptians rather than standing by as another Khaled Said is murdered in plain view. In this Egypt, men and women fight together in the streets to seize politics that is rightly theirs. Here, low-income young men battle heavily armed security forces with only Molotov cocktails and rocks in defense of protesters, many of whom are middle class, under a flag bearing the visage of Mina Danial.[34] In this Egypt, Christians and Muslims literally cover one another's backs in a solidarity that refuses the sectarianism and mutual suspicion cultivated by the regime.[35] In this country, Egyptians break the silence to publicly name the crimes of the regime and identify the perpetrators.[36] And here, citizens "tell stories upon stories to the living and dead" to keep alive the Egypt they recognize as their own.[37]

Here, clarity is critical given the many pitfalls demonstrated by successive waves of scholarship and commentary about the Arab uprisings. The point of anatomizing these particular moments is not to romanticize the uprising, overstate its achievements, sanitize what actually happened at the demonstrations, or canonize prominent participants. Nor is it meant to minimize the lethality of the regime at the time and its assiduous efforts to erase what was accomplished ever since. Finally, these arguments are not intended to valorize nonviolence as the mode of political challenge most appropriate to the already disempowered at the expense of "less conventional repertoires of revolutionary action and forms of agency" that were so critical to the uprising.[38]

In keeping with the purposes of this inquiry, my aim is to further decode the terms and texture of restoration entailed by these invocations of humiliation,

34. See Ryzova's account in "Battle of Muhammad Mahmoud Street in Cairo," 273. A number of Cairo's police stations were also attacked and burned down. See Abdul-Magd, "Occupying Tahrir Square," 566; and Ismail, "Egyptian Revolution Against the Police."

35. See, for example, Saleh, "Egyptian Revolution Brings Show of Religious Unity"; and Cole, "Christians, Muslims 'One Hand' in Egypt's Youth Revolution." Far from being unprecedented, Cole argues, such expressions of interreligious solidarity heralded a kind of return to expressions of national unity that accompanied Egyptian protests against British colonialism in 1919.

36. Paulo Friere has characterized similar practices as instances of "armed love," the duty to announce and denounce. Freire, "Fourth Letter," 74.

37. Essam al-Sayyid, "Sikit il-lisān," Kullenā al-shahīd Eslām el-Sayyād.

38. Ryzova, "Battle of Muhammad Mahmoud Street in Cairo," 276.

and bring into focus essential features of what they say and do in use. I've argued that Islamist rhetoric defines restorative action as retaliatory humiliation, the imposition of impotence on one's humiliator. By contrast, the restorative action articulated in these materials is a refusal of the sectarianism, fear, silence, greed, brutality, and mutual indifference that are the regime's rules of humiliation. This isn't to say that the Egyptian archive is devoid of all desire for vengeance, or that it should be. It is to say that the expressions of humiliation it contains work less as an exhortation to reverse the relation of humiliator and humiliated than to reject its terms.

Melian, Not Kantian Dignity

At this point, a generous skeptic might press the question: what does this depiction of *karāma* as an embodied practice of standing erect have to do with what "dignity" means in English? Or to put the same question more contentiously: as "dignity" in English simply captures what dignity is, and so needs no qualification, why should anyone who cares about it concern themselves with *karāma*, let alone how these Arabic expressions of humiliation constitute it? Moreover, this is a book on humiliation; why attempt a foolhardy venture into the overcrowded academic territory of dignity in its final pages? The answer to the latter question is an answer to the former. First, as humiliation rhetoric simultaneously encodes a political project and constitutes the mechanisms to bring it about, *karāma* is an indispensable part of what such invocations do and say, integral to the scaffolding of humiliation rather than a departure from it. Second (and this will be more controversial), the concept and practice I have derived from these expressions of *karāma* capture the meaning of dignity and much of its expressive power in use.

As in so much of this book, these arguments begin in language. *Karāma* has multiple meanings (nobility, honor, standing, dignity), but the translation of *karāma* as "dignity" in connection with the 2011 Arab uprisings is ubiquitous and references to them as "revolutions of dignity" are likewise commonplace.[39]

39. As the introductory chapter suggests, when it comes to Arabic-speaking or Muslim-majority societies, "honor" tends to activate an elaborate essentialist apparatus that divides "honor societies" captured by the past from those in the Global North who left honor behind with feudalism. But in Arabic alone, there are several terms routinely translated as "honor" that designate different phenomena that are gendered in quite complex ways. See, for example, Baron, *Egypt as a Woman*, 41. See also Stewart, *Honor*; and Bowman, *Honor*.

As the uprisings could have been dubbed "revolutions of social justice" [*thawrāt al-ʿadl al-ijtimāʿiyya*] or named for other rhetorically conspicuous terms such *ḥurriyya* [freedom], it's worth asking why they have been almost exclusively branded as "revolutions of dignity," but that's a question for another time. For my purposes, the critical point is that such branding has presumed and reinforced an automatic equivalence between *karāma* and dignity that obscures the default definition the English word "dignity" has acquired.[40]

Frequently articulated in partial or abbreviated terms, "dignity" reflexively carries what Jeremy Waldron refers to as a "specific Kantian resonance," anchored in the now familiar moral autonomy said to express and secure the "priceless worth conferred on us by our freedom to choose."[41] Waldron characterizes the influence this conflation has had on [Western] philosophy and law as "deplorable," arguing that it fails even to do justice to the complexity of Kant's arguments on the subject.[42]

As before, questions about the right or wrong way to read Kant on dignity and whether such definitions of dignity called Kantian really are so is outside the scope of this inquiry, as is the substantial philosophical scholarship devoted to debating, elaborating, or refining it. What's crucial here is that this default and abbreviated dignity, like the definition of humiliation derived from it, is taken as a given well beyond the arenas of philosophy and law. Skepticism about the meaning and utility of the concept in some corners of philosophy have done little to dampen the popularity of dignity in ordinary speech, international declarations of human rights, healthcare and business ethics, software engineering, and public relations training, among many other professions and discourses.

What this means is that references to dignity are invariably already overburdened with Kantian connotations that have become common sense precisely because they are assumed rather than argued. This isn't a question of whether or not the commitments the word "dignity" usually denotes are worthwhile, but rather of what this reflexive resonance might distort or foreclose. In its dominant register, "revolution of dignity" identifies the Egyptian Uprising as driven by a

40. This is so despite the fact, as virtually every study of dignity points out, it has a long history and a complex genealogy that contain multiple critical touchstones, including ancient Rome and Catholic theology.

41. Waldron, *Dignity, Rank and Rights*, 22–27. The latter phrase is from Moyn, "Dignity's Due?," 34. Waldron contends that dignity is routinely conflated with a particular reading of *The Groundwork of the Metaphysics of Morals*, glossed as "value beyond price . . . and worth that inheres in every human being in virtue of his or her moral capacity."

42. Waldron, *Dignity, Rank and Rights*, 22–27.

collective interest in a normative principle of moral autonomy that says very little about the meanings of *karāma* articulated in practice. As a result, it elides the way in which *karāma* is constitutively embedded at the same site as humiliation and leaves strangely out of focus how and why Egyptians are actively negotiating the terrain in which they find themselves.[43]

Again, to be clear: the argument here isn't that such a classification is wrong, that the translation of *karāma* as dignity is inaccurate, or that "revolutions of dignity" ought to be replaced with, say, "uprisings of humiliation." Rather, the point is that distortion often flourishes undetected at precisely those moments when different languages seem to most closely overlap, and the direction of distortion tends to reflect historical patterns of power. To put it into less abstract terms: in the context of European colonialism, it is unsurprising that the Kantian inflections of dignity infuse translations of Arabic *karāma* and not the other way around.

If these arguments are persuasive, the affinity between *karāma* and "restorative standing" articulated in this archive becomes intelligible only by refusing such a collapse of *karāma*, dignity, and this "specific Kantian resonance." Such a refusal doesn't presume and police a boundary between hermetically sealed worlds of meaning, as if to say some version of "Arabs care about X, but non-Arabs care about Y." Instead it holds at bay, at least momentarily, the Kantian resonance automatically injected into the English "dignity." With this conflation briefly suspended, there's room to argue that the "restorative standing" signaled by *karāma* is indeed captured by the word dignity, but a dignity that's more Melian than Kantian.[44]

"Melians" refers to the inhabitants of Melos in Thucydides's *History of the Peloponnesian War* who refused to submit to the Athenian empire, even when threatened with destruction and slavery. "[T]o submit is to give ourselves over to despair," the Melians tell the Athenian envoys deputized by an army poised for

43. This borrows from White's excellent "Subordination, Rhetorical Survival Skills and Sunday Shoes," 53.

44. There are very few efforts to theorize *karāma* in connection with the uprisings, despite an entire book on it (West, *Karama! Journeys through the Arab Spring*). A few promising engagements are limited by length, focus, and a tendency to simultaneously posit it as a site of contestation (where it can mean almost anything) on the one hand and, on the other, take it as unproblematically equivalent to dignity despite the baggage the English carries. See Ali "Kinetic Karama"; and Hermez, "On Dignity and Clientelism." In 2005, a network of Arab women founded a transnational grassroots organization dedicated to fighting violence against women in the Middle East and Africa; they named it "Karāma." See https://www.elkara.ma (accessed January 7, 2025).

conquest, "while action still preserves for us a hope that we may stand erect" (*stēnai orthōs*, meaning upright or standing).[45] Against Athenian warnings to consider only what conduces to their survival, the Melians insist that there's an imperative to resist that is irreducible to instrumental calculations, that such resistance includes standing up for a sense of themselves that's recognizable, and that doing so, particularly given the threat to their very existence as a people, is itself a kind of victory.

To characterize *karāma* as more Melian than Kantian is to depict it as a symbol and enactment of such restorative standing, where "standing" is understood both literally and figuratively. This is where the somatic vocabulary in the previous section is particularly instructive. While various archives in these chapters constitute the form and route to restoration quite differently, the embodied idiom they share renders legible the ways in which *karāma* is constituted in terms of humiliation, an interrelation that's easily overlooked and very often misunderstood. Whereas one is to be physically bent to the ground, dragged in the dust, head bowed, and back bare, the other is to literally and figuratively stand erect, head held high.

Apprehending humiliation and *karāma* as terms in a somatic idiom that fashion one another in an inverse relation suggests that conceptually as well as experientially, they are mutually constitutive: humiliation takes shape not in opposition to, but in terms of a posited integrity or stature, and it's the humiliation that conjures the integrity or stature that must then be restored. As what humiliation and dignity/*karāma* mean and do are adumbrated at and through the same site and bodies, it's impossible to grasp the ontology and politics of one without the other.[46] Rather than marking the coordinates of an abstract norm of moral autonomy or a principle by which violations may be adjudicated, this understanding of dignity is, much like humiliation, an embodied practice. Restorative standing is a performative reclamation of the power to shape the script of one's own life that loosens the grip of impotence central to humiliation.

I envision at least two immediate objections to this recasting of dignity as Melian anchored in the metaphor and posture of "restorative standing." First, as is well known, the Melians' resistance to the Athenians did not end particularly well. As Thucydides tells it, Melian defiance was met by an Athenian siege of the city. As a consequence of an unspecified treachery from within Melos, the Melians

45. Thucydides, *History of the Peloponnesian War*, book 5, chapter 17, 102. There is, of course, much more to the dialogue than this brief exchange, but it's this response by the Melians that is so evocative for my purposes. I am grateful to Jill Frank for the Greek.

46. I am indebted to Jill Frank for this insight.

eventually surrendered. The Athenians proceeded to kill the men of military age, sell all the women and children into slavery, and populate Melos as a new Athenian colony. While standard practice at the time, this horrific ending lends a funereal cast to a dignity named for a people long gone whose leaders were willing to sacrifice freedom, lives, land, and culture alike in the name of momentary resistance.

It's precisely because the Melians paid so dearly for refusing the vastly superior military might of the Athenian empire that this dialogue so frequently serves to dramatize the timeless triumph of power politics in International Relations courses. The calculus of political realism neatly wraps up the Melian dialogue in precisely the terms the Athenians dictate: think only of your prospects of winning, not of hope or of what you imagine you can achieve by fruitless resistance. Yet this calculus proceeds only in terms of what the immediate temporal frame recognizes as relevant, and in terms quite similar to the consensus about the "failure" of the 2011 Arab uprisings.

A more expansive sense of time makes that conclusion far less untenable. As we know from the rest of *The History*, the Athenians were eventually defeated, "beaten at all points and altogether" in Sicily, their empire vanquished. Many of the thousands of Athenians captured by the victorious Syracusans were not only destroyed slowly in the quarries where they were imprisoned but humiliated by the dying itself; the rest were sold into slavery. This longer view suggests that the enduring power of "The Melian Dialogue" lies as much in the resistance it memorializes as in the ruthlessness of domination it depicts. Among all those destroyed by the Athenian empire, the Melians are unforgettable precisely because they refused to capitulate, because they insisted, in contemporary parlance, on "dying with dignity."

In this sense, the "standing up" of Melian dignity begins in precisely the kind of refusal that characterizes *karāma* in the previous section, instantiated as a practice more than a principle. The somatic register of "standing up" opens this practice up to evoke either a movement or a posture. Ernst Bloch mobilizes precisely this sense of dignity as a practice in motion in *Natural Law and Human Dignity*. He exhibits little patience for moral abstractions inattentive to power, materiality, and the multiple though not infinite emancipatory possibilities latent in the concrete. For Bloch, capitalism is the major "blockage" that "obstructs and closes the path on which one is able to walk upright," reducing human beings to the posture and position of beasts of burden.[47]

47. I am indebted to Loren Goldman for his insights on Bloch, both in conversation and in chapter 2 of his excellent book, *The Principle of Political Hope*.

Release from such encumbrance is the freedom to claim the dignity of the human. But he notably fashions such release by reference to the body rather than to a principle of moral autonomy. Bloch does so, moreover, drawing on the same somatic vocabulary as Thucydides, deploying the Greek word the Melians used to denote standing erect, *orthos*: dignity is the "orthopedia of the upright carriage." This refers less to an erect posture already achieved than to what he characterizes as the pride of becoming "indisputably visible," presumably to others but also simultaneously to oneself.[48]

Bloch reiterates this emphasis when, discussing the Stoics' typically sobering variety of dignity, he even deploys the second somatic term for restorative action in the Egyptian archive, holding one's head high. In Bloch's rendering, this somatic metaphor acquires a similar valence: neither a fixed stature nor a statue in repose, it evokes an arising predicated on a willingness to struggle, to eschew docility, withdrawal, or stillness. For the Stoics, he writes,

> happiness was no longer a ticket to the dignified life. Rather, happiness should follow as a consequence of this dignified life: For the Stoics happiness was not a sensible, palpable happiness, but something stronger—the pride of being human. From the time of the Stoics dignity was detached from happiness; the difference between their paths was that on one there was a willingness to enter into a struggle. Passion continued, stoically, to flow into severity, for it was still the head held high that was, in the end, considered worthy. Only thus did the person who was not docile, the person who held himself upright, who from the outset related to natural right, become indisputably visible.[49]

If the posture of holding one's head high is predicated upon a "*willingness* to enter into a struggle" (my emphasis), the locus of dignity shifts from principle to process, kinetic in the sense of ongoing struggle. It's also worldly, both in the sense that the struggle is situated materially, politically, and historically, and that such visibility presupposes the presence of others. These together point to

48. Bloch, *Natural Law and Human Dignity*, 155, 174, 12.

49. Bloch, *Natural Law and Human Dignity*, 12. The "orthopedia of the upright gait" in German is "Orthopädie des aufrechten Gangs" (Bloch, *Natural Law and Human Dignity*, 199). "Head held high" is the translation of "erhobene Kopf" (25), literally "raised/lifted head," and what's rendered as docility here is "das Ungebeugte, Aufgerichtete," literally meaning "the unbent [person], upright[ed]/held up [person]." The original German and these translations are Loren Goldman's, from a series of personal exchanges in July 2023.

a transformation that will remain in outline form, as its course and conclusion cannot be fully fleshed out in advance. By the same token, as "standing erect" performatively loosens the grip of impotence central to humiliation, the particular terms in which it is expressed will be determined by the concrete and felt conditions of its absence. These terms cannot be specified in advance any more than meaning is constituted prior to use. This is precisely because the pattern of variable components differently assembled will remain skeletal until fleshed out in execution. As I argued earlier, this includes the precise form of restorative action carved out of the conditions of felt powerlessness.[50]

The second objection to recasting dignity as Melian rather than Kantian follows from the imbrication of masculinity and power I have posited as consistently central to the way these invocations of humiliation work and a critical component of the scaffolding I've traced. If dignity and humiliation define one another, and the "restorative standing" constitutive of dignity emerges out of the conditions of imposed impotence, what is performatively reclaimed is just as likely to be masculine potency as collective empowerment.[51]

From this angle, "Melian dignity" can be understood as just another valorization of what Adriana Cavarero refers to as the "specifically masculine mark" of the erect posture or, more bluntly, the posture of erection.[52] In Cavarero's analysis, the upright gait is not just symbolically and linguistically suggestive of a phallus but constitutes verticality as the fundamentally patriarchal paradigm of moral rightness or rectitude—literally *Homo erectus*. Such "virile verticality" and its ontological entailments are preeminent features of what she calls the "geometrical imaginary of western culture," but its apotheosis is philosophy, particularly the

50. This bears some resemblance to Vincent Lloyd's depiction of Black dignity as an activity one does in struggle rather than a status denied or conferred. Lloyd, *Black Dignity*, 8.

51. Scholars have drawn attention to the way the term "empowerment" has been coopted and depoliticized by liberal, neoliberal, neoconservative, and even leftist discourses. See Rushing, "What's Left of Empowerment After Neoliberalism?" Scholarship in critical pedagogy has raised similar concerns. See, for example, Archibald and Wilson, "Rethinking Empowerment," 22. Feminist theorists, political theorists, and progressive educators alike have sought to (re)constitute empowerment in emancipatory and transformative terms, depicting it as a pedagogical praxis, desire, process, agenda, ends, and means rolled into one. Despite important differences, these critics aim to center rather than evacuate power from "empowerment," figuring it (in Rushing's apt description) as a "distinctly relational orientation toward freedom, self-direction, and collective social transformation . . . while never ignoring the complex reality of neoliberal capitalism that necessitates vigilance in how these aspirations are given voice." This is the understanding of empowerment I intend here. See also Sardenberg, "Liberal vs. Liberating Empowerment."

52. Cavarero, *Inclinations*, 42.

Kantian self that celebrates the "autonomy of a free and rational individual who, by freeing himself from the world, proudly raises himself over himself."[53] This is a dignity in which agency is a function of the "masterlessness" that, in George Shulman's apt description, not only disavows interdependence but constitutes others as threats to a "masculine fantasy of self-sufficiency that mobilizes men's aggression against symbols of emasculation, while excluding actual women from the circle of the 'we.'"[54]

As feminist critiques of Marxist movements and Black feminist critiques of liberation movements dominated by White women or Black men attest, emancipatory movements, practices, and expressions rarely seek emancipation all the way down. They routinely reproduce the aspects of the hierarchal conditions under which they were forged, even those arrangements they explicitly disavow. It is unsurprising, then, that enactments of restorative standing within and across these materials would reinscribe to a greater or lesser degree the masculinization of power constitutive of the humiliation they reject. The explicit masculinization of power evinced in radical Islamist rhetorics of humiliation is also articulated in the Egyptian archive, if often implicitly and in tandem with vocal challenge.[55] Yet it seems to me that this observation draws attention to the strengths of the Melian conception of dignity rather than to the weaknesses revealed by such political impurities. As opposed to the conception of dignity predicated on a moral autonomy that floats outside the very relations of power that determine who can claim and live it, dignity as restorative standing centers the conditions and terms of that reinscription rather than masking, denying, or ignoring them. The word "standing" itself anchors dignity in a bodily posture and a particular location,[56] just as "restorative" evokes a potentially ongoing process rather than a rectitude already accomplished. From this vantage, Kantian dignity looks like a phantasm that masks the very motility, materiality, and location Melian dignity centers.

53. Cavarero, *Inclinations*, 11, 42, 70. Cavarero contrasts the patriarchal paradigm of *Homo erectus* with the posture of inclination: the essential feminine gesture of refusal is embodied in the mother bending over her child or, in Honig's phrasing, the "inclined posture of maternity" (Honig, *Feminist Theory of Refusal*, 47). Honig's analysis takes up Cavarero's posture of inclination, expressive of a disposition toward another, but anchors the feminist gesture of refusal not in maternalism but sorority, "the more egalitarian kin relation" (102), along with a recognition that even practices of love and care can be implicated in violence.

54. Shulman, "Chasing the Whale," 87–88.

55. See discussion in chapter 4.

56. The same point may be made about another potential objection, i.e. that this widely invoked metaphor reinscribes a kind of ableism.

I want to conclude with two potential political implications that are far from obvious. In the opening chapter, I referred to theorizing generally as an activity that renders patterns legible, and characterized this theory of humiliation in terms of patterned variation. The analysis in this chapter shows how and why the mutual imbrication of humiliation and dignity/*karāma* must be understood as integral to this patterned variation. It also shows that "restorative action" is a site where both the pattern and a significant variation come clearly into view, both within these clusters of materials and across them.

The Islamist materials may evince a shared emphasis on retaliatory humiliation, but the roles, categories, and stakes that comprise it are filled in very differently, in accordance with disparate contexts and concerns. The contrast between the character and requirements of restoration in the Islamist texts and the Egyptian archive in this chapter is much starker and politically significant. For Qutb and Alaa Abd El Fattah alike, humiliation signals a powerlessness that must be urgently remedied, but there's a significant discontinuity in the *kind* of remedy required. The difference between retaliation and refusal cuts sharply against the commonality, but more to the point, it heralds considerably different political convictions and practices.

These discontinuities indicate that, even when common elements are articulated in the same language, using the same categories and terminology, very different political commitments can emerge when the details are filled in. As the specific form of restorative action, along with the solidarities it conjures and the aims it expresses, are constituted by the account of humiliation rather than prior to it, such remedies are resistant to both modeling and prediction. Yet the contingency that makes the remedy resistant to prediction is precisely why the reproduction of humiliation is far from inevitable. Humiliation rhetoric encodes redress as urgent and imperative, but it neither dictates the form restoration must take, nor does it render an endless and escalating cycle of humiliation and retaliation unavoidable or inescapable.

The final implication of this patterned variation is speculative. I have so far stressed how this pattern is constituted *in* language, but there's good reason to regard the features of this pattern as a kind of vocabulary intelligible *across* languages. Without overstating the case, I suspect that very little knowledge of Somali or English, Arabic or Hebrew is required to grasp what humiliation generally says and does in the ISIS videos, the pictures from Mogadishu, images from Abu Ghraib and Gaza. Knowledge of Arabic isn't required to grasp the message that Mubarak's bowed head might convey, the image Fiky sought to erase from the public record. Or consider once more the passages that opened this book: one is in English, the other in Arabic, but both Trump and bin Laden "speak" the common idiom of humiliation. Once in focus, instances of such mutual intelligibility abound.[57]

The point is not that humiliation exhausts what these examples and images reflect, say, or do. Nor is it to presume that the humiliation they convey registers or resonates everywhere in the same way, or minimize how this vocabulary is distinctively inflected by disparate histories and experiences of domination. My argument is that, like an affective Esperanto, humiliation rhetoric can and does "speak" viscerally and volubly across communities fluent in very different primary languages. It does so regardless of whether others, including philosophers, consider the meaning it speaks empirically valid or morally justified. Humiliation is not just about power but is itself a powerful language, and it does far more than reflect contemporary politics. The language of humiliation remakes the world in which we live.

57. Just one notable case in point: Trump and Vladimir Putin speak this idiom of humiliation fluently and obsessively, marking another aspect of their mutual political intelligibility. As many argue, Putin's performances of masculinity and his ongoing efforts to "remasculinize" Russia are tied to a sense of national humiliation entailed by the loss of Soviet territories and correlative diminution of international importance. See, for example, Ashwin and Utrata, "Masculinity Restored?"; and Riabov and Tatiana, "Remasculinization of Russia?"

BIBLIOGRAPHY

Abbas, Wael. "Bayān al-'ā'idūn min Nag' Ḥammādī." [A statement by the returnees from Naga' Hammādī]. *Misr Digital Blog*, January 22, 2010. http://misrdigital.blogspirit.com/archive/2010/01/24/من-نجع-حمادي.html (accessed June 12, 2021).

ABC News. "Egypt's Vice President Omar Suleiman, 'The Islamic Current Has Pushed These People.'" Interview by Christiane Amanpour, February 6, 2011. YouTube video, 5:36. https://www.youtube.com/watch?v=HxXnMDngyCE&t=263s (accessed March 19, 2021).

'Abd al-Sattar, Heba. "Aḥdāth majlis al-wuzarā'... dhikrā ḥarīq wathā'iq al-majma' al-'ilmī wa-ta'riyat sitt al-banāt wa-iltizām 'al-'askarī' bi-naql al-sulṭa" [Minister of Cabinet Events... remembering the science complex fire, the stripping of the lady and SCAF's commitment to transfer power]. *Al-Ahram*, December 16, 2014. https://gate.ahram.org.eg/News/573197.aspx (accessed March 24, 2021).

Abd El Fattah, Alaa. "About Those Bouncy Bouncy Checks." April 21, 2010. Original in English. https://web.archive.org/web/20170620015618/http://manalaa.net/bouncy_checks (accessed January 5, 2025).

Abd El Fattah, Alaa. "Alaa Abd El Fattah fī Studio AlMasry AlYoum" [Alaa Abd El Fattah on Egyptian Studio Today]. January 9, 2012. https://www.youtube.com/watch?v=dw1TezgpZK4 (accessed May 4, 2021).

Abd El Fattah, Alaa. "al-Ḥilm Awwalan" [Patience first]. *Shorouk News*, June 24, 2011. https://www.shorouknews.com/columns/view.aspx?cdate=24062011&id=cd2f555b-e375-479c-a878-1d40b05af52c (accessed June 23, 2021).

Abd El Fattah, Alaa (@alaa). "Yā rīt nib'at el-shihāda dī li-kull ḥadd ti'rafūh ma'a faḍḍ al-i'tiṣām bil-quwwa, 'ashān yi'rafū el-gīsh el-maṣrī duruh iyah, ta'dhīb wa-dhull wa-ihāna." Twitter, August 9, 2011. https://twitter.com/alaa/status/100985328390770688.

Abdel Hakim, Reham. "Bi'l-waraqa wa'l-qalam" [With paper and pen]. Lyrics by Nour Abdallah. Black Honey Production Co.: Betros for Media Production, 2010. May 22, 2010. YouTube video, 3:00. https://www.youtube.com/watch?v=mZYt0S14QH0 (accessed January 7, 2025).

Abdel Haleem, M. A. S., trans. *The Qur'an*. Oxford University Press, 2005.

Abdelhaleem, Tariq. "al-Majlis al-'askarī al-khā'in yaghtāl Miṣr" [The traitorous military council assassinates Egypt]. December, 18, 2011. YouTube video, 14:42. https://www.youtube.com/watch?v=JbcGUlXHx48 (accessed April 5, 2021).

Abdelhassan, Abbas(@Abbasyz). "Maṣr 'āmila zay bint uṣūl tizlit el-shāri' fī el-zilzāl gāy khāṭifhā quwād lābis shaykh wa-saraḥ yishḥat bīhā... anā lā antamī ilā gumhūriyyat Miṣr al-mutasawwila. Laysa lī fī al-dhull." Twitter, April 5, 2013. https://twitter.com/Abbasyz/status/320090774639357952.

Abdel Rahman, Dina. "Shāhid risāla katabahā shahīd qabla mawtihi wa'l-i'lāmiyya Dina Abdel Rahman tuwāṣil al-bukā' al-shadīd 'alā al-hawā' al-ān wa-tufassir" [A message written by a martyr before his death, and TV host Dina Abdel Rahman cries intensely on air and explains]. Tahrir Channel, September 8, 2014. YouTube video, 6:58. https://www.youtube.com/watch?v=On1B0O88rr0 (accessed May 14, 2021, no longer available).

Abdul-Latif, Muhammad. "Tanaḥḥī Mubarak wa-ta'līq 'Amr Adīb 'alā ẓulmihi" [Mubarak's resignation and Amr Adeeb's comment on his injustice]. OnTV with Yousry Fouda, February 11, 2011. YouTube video, 5:39. https://www.youtube.com/watch?v=OAGlBZBfIgE (accessed February 19, 2025)

Abnūdī, 'Abd al-Raḥmān. *Aḥzān 'ādiyya* [Ordinary sorrows]. Dār al-Qibā', 1999.

Abnūdī, 'Abd al-Raḥmān. "al-Mīdān" [The square]. In *al-Mīdān: Dīwān*. al-Hay'a al-Miṣriyya al-'Āmma lil-Kitāb, 2012.

Abnūdī, 'Abd al-Raḥmān. "Ḍiḥkit el-masāgīn" [The prisoners' laughter]. In *Qaṣīdat 'ḍiḥkit el-masāgīn' lil-shā'ir 'Abd al-Raḥmān al-Abnūdī*. Egyptian General Book Authority, 2012.

Abnūdī, 'Abd al-Raḥmān. "Yā Sitt al-Kull" [My lady]. Poem performance on CBC Egypt. "Qaṣīdat 'Sitt al-Kull' bi-ṣawt al-shā'ir 'Abd al-Raḥmān al-Abnūdī#Hunā_al-'Aṣima." April 27, 2015. YouTube video, 4:41. https://www.youtube.com/watch?v=eDlkccM3NvA (accessed January 7, 2025).

Abū al-Yazīd, Aḥmad. "Istikhdām kalimāt ughniyat 'Siyādat al-muwāṭin' lil-Jasmi fī hamlat da'm el-Sīsī ra'īsan" [Using the words of the song "Mr. Citizen" by al-Jasmi in Sisi's campaign for president]. *Al-Yawm al-Sābi'*, January 30, 2014. https://www.youm7.com/story/2014/1/30/استخدام-كلمات-أغنية-سيادة-المواطن-للجسمى-فى-حملة-دعم-السيسى/1482059 (accessed June 22, 2021).

Abul-Magd, Zeinab. "Occupying Tahrir Square: The Myths and the Realities of the Egyptian Revolution." *South Atlantic Quarterly* 111, no. 3 (2012): 565–72.

Abu-Lughod, Lila. "Living the 'Revolution' in an Egyptian Village: Moral Action in a National Space." *American Ethnologist* 39, no. 1 (2012): 21–25.

Adams, Michael, Amy Lanstaff, and David Jamieson. *Fire and Ice: The United States, Canada and the Myth of Converging Values*. Penguin, 2003.

Adel, Amin. "Al-Fīlm al-wathā'iqī yasquṭ ḥukm al-'askar" [The documentary film: Down with the military regime]. January 3, 2012. YouTube video, 15:50. https://www.youtube.com/watch?v=SEkUy71P3Vo (accessed March 2, 2012).

Adhiambo Onyango, Monica, and Karen Hampanda. "Social Constructions of Masculinity and Male Survivors of Wartime Sexual Violence: An Analytical Review." *International Journal of Sexual Health* 23, no. 4 (2011): 237–47.

Adly, Malek. "Allāh yirḥamik yā rugūla." *MalekAdly Blog*, May 22, 2011. http://malekadly.blogspot.com/2011/05/blog-post_22.html (accessed May 4, 2021).

Adly, Malek. "al-Thawra lā milkak wa-lā milkī . . . milk illī yawmhā sanad ṣadruhu 'al-sūnkī." *MalekAdly Blog*, July 7, 2011. http://malekadly.blogspot.com/2011/07/blog-post_07.html (accessed June 23, 2021).

Adly, Malek. "Ḥayāt Muḥammad." *MalekAdly Blog*, September 13, 2012. http://malekadly.blogspot.com/2012/09/blog-post_13.html (accessed June 23, 2021).

Adly, Malek. "Moḥsen." *MalekAdly Blog*, May 15, 2011. http://malekadly.blogspot.com/2011/05/blog-post_15.html.

Afia, Amr. "Ḥadūtha thawriyya" [A revolutionary story]. Facebook, June 7, 2012. https://www.facebook.com/notes/10150878234938723/ (accessed March 4, 2020).

Afsaruddin, Asma. "Early Women Exemplars and the Construction of Gendered Space: (Re) Defining Feminine Moral Excellence." In *Harem Histories: Envisioning Place and Living Spaces*, edited by Marilyn Booth. Duke University Press, 2010.

Agamben, Giorgio. *Remnants of Auschwitz: The Witness and the Archive*. Translated by Daniel Heller-Roazen. Zone Books, 2005.

Ahmed, Nafeez. "Do the Math: Global War on Terror Has Killed 4 Million Muslims or More." *Mint Press News*, August 3, 2015. http://www.mintpressnews.com/do-the-math-global-war-on-terror-has-killed-4-million-muslims-or-more/208225/ (accessed February 8, 2016).

Ahmed, Sara. *The Cultural Politics of Emotion*. Edinburgh University Press, 2014.

Ahram, Ariel "Sexual Violence and the Making of ISIS." *Survival* 57, no. 3 (2015): 57–78.

Ahram, Ariel. "Sexual and Ethnic Violence and the Construction of the Islamic State." *Political Violence at a Glance*, September 18, 2014. https://politicalviolenceataglance.org/2014/09/18/sexual-and-ethnic-violence-and-the-construction-of-the-islamic-state/ (accessed July 1, 2023).

Ahram Online. "Former MP Mostafa El-Naggar Not 'Forcedly Disappeared,' Still Evading 3-Year Jail Sentence, Egypt's SIS." October 18, 2018. https://english.ahram.org.eg/NewsContent/1/64/313658/Egypt/Politics-/Former-MP-Mostafa-ElNaggar-not-forcedly-disappeared.aspx (accessed January 7, 2025).

Akhbār al-Yawm al-Sābiʿ. "Al-Shahāda al-kāmila li-fatāt al-ʿudhriyya Samīra Ibrāhīm" [The complete testimony of the virgin girl, Samira Ibrahim]. December 28, 2011. YouTube video, 22:45. https://www.youtube.com/watch?v=VTxYdDXT5bo (accessed July 1, 2021).

Alalwani, Hanaa (@hanaa_alalwani). "Rajul khadama bilādahu ka-ʿaskarī, wa-qādahā ka-raʾīs 30 ʿāman, wa-in faʿala mā faʿala . . . hal yakūn jazāhu sijn wa-muḥākamāt . . . am ʿazl wa-iqāma jabriyya . . . irḥamū ʿazīz qawm dhull yā Miṣr." Twitter, June 19, 2012. https://twitter.com/hanaa_alalwani/status/215195106746183680.

AlArabiya. "Faḍīḥat al-taḥarrush al-jimāʿī bi-mutaẓāhirāt al-Taḥrīr bi-ʿaṣr al-ikhwān" [The disgrace of sexual harassment at the Tahrir demonstrations in the age of the Brotherhood]. April 25, 2014. YouTube video, 14:08. https://www.youtube.com/watch?v=R0_FczcK1Kg (accessed June 30, 2021).

al-Banna, Hasan. "Ilā ayy shayʾ nadʿū al-nās?" In *Majmūʿat Rasāʾil Ḥasan al-Bannā*. Dār al-Qalam, n.d.

al-Banna, Hasan. *Mudhakkirāt al-daʿwā wa-l-dāʿiya*. Dār al-Kitāb al-ʿArabī, 1974.

al-Bawabah News. "Sayyidat al-trūsīkil ʿan al-raʾīs el-Sīsī: 'Ab li-kull al-Miṣriyyīn'" [Motor-tricycle owner on President Sisi: a father to all Egyptians]. *Al-Bawwāba*, March 22, 2021. https://www.albawabhnews.com/4299634 (accessed May 27, 2021).

al-Ḍamīr al-ʿArabī. "Ughniyat Ḥusayn al-Jasmī Siyādat al-muwāṭin ibn Miṣr fī iḥtifālāt 6 October 2013" [Song of Hussain al-Jasmi, "Mr. Citizen, Son of Egypt," during the October 6, 2013 celebrations]. Channel 1, October 9, 2013. YouTube video, 5:52. https://www.youtube.com/watch?v=lrPa3qtfcP4 (accessed June 22, 2021).

al-Dīb, ʿAlī Ibrāhīm. "Dr. Manal Omar, ablagh mā qīla ʿan al-thawra al-Miṣriyya" [Dr. Manal Omar, the most eloquent thing said about the Egyptian revolution]. Manal Omar, ART America, November 29, 2011. YouTube video, 14:51. https://www.youtube.com/watch?v=MCuGTlEli3k (accessed March 8, 2021).

"al-Ghāriqīn fī al-dhull al-saḥīq" [Drowning in Deep Humiliation]. Al-Sumūd for Media Production, 2014. Video courtesy ISD, 7:09.

al-Hajj, Taim. "The Insurgency of ISIS in Syria." Carnegie Endowment for International Peace, March 15, 2022. https://carnegieendowment.org/sada/86643 (accessed March 4, 2023).

al-Hasa, Farida. "Shahādat al-fatāh allatī saḥalahā al-jaysh yasquṭ ḥukm al-ʿaskar" [Testimony of the girl whom the army dragged topples military rule]. Interview by Yousry Fouda. OnTV, September 8, 2014. YouTube video, 14:16. https://www.youtube.com/watch?v=QqVx-uhPTT70 (accessed March 20, 2021; no longer available).

Al Hayah TV Network. "Sawwāq 'Tūktūk' bi-100 rājil yulakhkhiṣ ḥāl Miṣr fī daqīqa wa'l-jamīʿ yusaqqif lahu" [A tuktuk driver with 100 pedestrians sums up the state of Egypt in a minute, and everyone applauds him]. Wāḥid min al-nās, October 12, 2016. YouTube video, 3:13. https://www.youtube.com/watch?v=u6Q2bRxZKkE (accessed January 6, 2025).

Ali, Amro. "Kinetic Karama: Bargaining for Dignity in the Pursuit of a New Arab Social Contract." In *The Modern Arab State: A Decade of Uprisings in the Middle East and North Africa*, edited by Youssef Cherif. Konrad Adenauer Stiftung, 2021.

Ali, Amro. "Saeeds of Revolution: De-Mythologizing Khaled Said." In *Mediating the Arab Uprisings*, edited by Adel Iskandar and Bassam Haddad. Tadween Publishing, 2013.

Ali, Khalid. "Precursors of the Egyptian Revolution." *IDS Bulletin* 43, no. 1 (2012): 16–25.

Al Jazeera. "Arab Unity: Nasser's Revolution." June 20, 2008. https://www.aljazeera.com/news/2008/6/20/arab-unity-nassers-revolution (accessed October 26, 2022).

Al Jazeera. "Azmat kahrabā' tuhaddid Miṣr" [An electricity crisis threatens Egypt]. August 23, 2010. https://www.aljazeera.net/news/ebusiness/2010/8/23/أزمة-كهرباء-تهدد-مصر (accessed March 24, 2021).

Al Jazeera. "Egypt's Security Apparatus." January 29, 2011. https://www.aljazeera.com/news/2011/1/29/egypts-security-apparatus (accessed March 26, 2021).

Al Jazeera. "Hisham el-Gakh . . . shā'ir bi-uslūb masraḥī" [Hisham el-Gakh . . . a poet in theatrical style]. May 24, 2016. https://www.aljazeera.net/encyclopedia/icons/2016/5/24/هشام-الجخ-شاعر-بأسلوب-مسرحي- (accessed April 8, 2021).

Al Jazeera. "'Laylat al-ittiḥādiyya'—Tajriba fāshila li-inqilāb Yūliyū" [The night of unity—A failed experience for the July revolution]. April 25, 2014. https://www.aljazeera.net/programs/black-box/2014/4/25/%D9%84%D9%8A%D9%84%D8%A9-%D8%A7%D9%84%D8%A7%D8%AA%D8%AD%D8%A7%D8%AF%D9%8A%D8%A9-%D9%86%D8%B2%D9%8A%D9%81-%D8%A7%D9%84%D8%AF%D9%85-%D9%88%D8%A7%D9%84%D8%B9%D8%AF%D8%A7%D9%84%D8%A9. (accessed January 8, 2025).

Al Jazeera. "Report Blames Egypt for Ferry Disaster." April 19, 2006. https://www.aljazeera.com/news/2006/4/19/report-blames-egypt-for-ferry-disaster (accessed February 15, 2025).

Al Jazeera. "Wathā'iqī: al-Laḥaẓāt al-akhīra fī ḥukm Mubarak" [The final moments of Mubarak's rule]. January 26, 2012. YouTube video, 54:54. https://www.youtube.com/watch?v=R7voLdhr7V0 (accessed May 14, 2021).

Al Jazeera. "Ẓāhirat muḥāwalāt al-intiḥār ḥarqan fī Miṣr qabla thawrat 11 Yanāyir 2011" [The phenomenon of attempted self-immolation in Egypt before the January 11 revolution]. January 25, 2012. YouTube video, 2:20. https://www.youtube.com/watch?v=vSlD_LfLkI4 (accessed January 7, 2025).

Allam, N. "Activism amid Disappointment: Women's Groups and the Politics of Hope in Egypt." *Middle East Law and Governance* 10, no. 3 (2018): 291–316.

Allen, James, Hilton Als, John Lewis, and Leon F. Litwack. *Without Sanctuary: Lynching Photography in America*. Twin Palms Publishers, 2000.

al-Maḥallī, Jalāl al-Dīn Muḥammad, and Jalāl al-Dīn al-Suyūṭī. *Tafsīr al-Imāmayn al-Jalālayn*. Dār al-Kutub al-ʿIlmīya, 2001.

AlMasry AlYoum. "Alaa Abd El Fattah fī studio AlMasry AlYoum" [Alaa Abd El Fattah on Egyptian Studio Today]. January 9, 2012. YouTube video, 22:49. https://www.youtube.com/watch?v=dw1TezgpZK4 (accessed January 7, 2025).

AlMasry AlYoum. "Al-Ḍaḥiyya al-thāniya fī qaḍiyyat Ḥammām al-Baḥr: 'el-ḍubbāṭ amarūnā nihawhawū zay el-kilāb'" [The second victim in the Hammam al-Bahr case: the officers ordered us to bark like dogs]. January 23, 2015. YouTube video, 4:17. https://www.youtube.com/watch?v=zIn1-Ljq7T0&t=112s (accessed July 1, 2021).

AlMasry AlYoum. "Samira Ibrahim tanhār baʿda ḥukm al-ʿaskariyya" [Samira Ibrahim devastated after military court verdict]. " *AlMasry AlYoum*, March 11, 2011. YouTube video, 2:44. https://www.youtube.com/watch?v=rteSK9SWFtY (accessed June 24, 2021).

al-Mizīnī, Hazzāʿ. "Ahī qāmit Maṣr bi-tiqlaʿ tūb el-dhull @ gumʿat al-ghaḍab 28 Yanāyir" [Egypt is standing up and casting off her dress of humiliation @ the Friday of rage, January 28]. Lyrics by ʿAbd al-Raḥmān Abnūdī (1998). YouTube video, 5:42. February 2, 2011. https://www.youtube.com/watch?v=cR7qtGE0O3Y (accessed February 19, 2025).

Al Nahar TV. "Doma . . . yaʿūd lil-ḥurriyya" [Doma . . . returned to freedom]. *Ākhir al-Nahar*, April 12, 2012. YouTube video, 17:51. https://www.youtube.com/watch?v=7CyjoOjMIKg (accessed June 2, 2020).

al-Najjār, Samir, and Fāṭima Zaydān. "al-Qadhdhāfī: Mubarak faqīr wa-mutawāḍiʿ wa-kāna yashḥat min ajl shaʿbihi wa-lā yastaḥiqq al-bahdala." *AlMasry AlYoum*, July 25, 2011. https://www.almasryalyoum.com/news/details/1816155 (accessed March 3, 2020).

al-Naṣr, Aḥlām. "Dhī Dawlat al-Islām jā'at taz'aru." *Dīwān Uwār al-Ḥaqq*. ed. al-Ḥamd and al-Qaḥṭānī. Damascus: Fursān al-Balāgh lil-I'lām, 2014. https://www.calameo.com/read/0040147384df26e156cc9 (accessed June 28, 2024).

al-Oufi, Saleh. "Interview with Saleh al-Oufi." *Sawt al-Jihad*, no. 8 (2004): 23–28. http://archive.org/stream/Sawt-aljihad-magazine/Sawt-aljihad8#page/n23/mode/2up (accessed July 28, 2013).

al-Qady, Youmna. "Dimā' fī al-sijn: al-dawra' al-shahriyya adāt idhlāl al-sajīnāt fī Miṣr" [Blood in prison: monthly periods are a tool for humiliating female prisoners in Egypt]. *Daraj*, November 16, 2020. https://daraj.com/59752/ (accessed June 30, 2021).

al-Quds al-ʿArabī. "al-Qadhdhāfī lil-Miṣriyyīn: Mubarak 'rajul faqīr wa-mutawāḍiʿ wa-yuḥibbukum . . . wa-kāna yashḥat min ajlikum" [Qaddafi to the Egyptians: Mubarak is a poor and humble man and he loves you . . . he used to beg for you]. *Al-Quds*, July 25, 2011. https://www.alquds.co.uk/القذافي-للمصريين-مبارك-رجل-فقير-ومتوا/ (accessed January 8, 2025).

al-Rasheed, Madawi. *A Most Masculine State: Gender, Politics, and Religion in Saudi Arabia*. Cambridge University Press, 2013.

al-Rodhan, Nayef. "Dignity Deficit Fuels Uprisings in the Middle East." *Yale Global Online*, September 10, 2013. https://yaleglobal.yale.edu/content/dignity-deficit-fuels-uprisings-middle-east (accessed March 12, 2023).

al-Ṣabbāgh, Nafīsa. "Al-Nīl ilāh lil-farāʿina . . . wa-ṣalāt lil-aqbāṭ . . . wa-nahr min al-janna ʿinda al-Muslimīn . . . ilā mustawdaʿa lil-mukhālafāt" [The Nile was a god to the pharaohs . . . a prayer to the Copts . . . a river from heaven for the Muslims . . . now a repository of violations]. *AlMasry AlYoum*, June 7, 2010. https://www.almasryalyoum.com/news/details/1863193 (accessed March 24, 2021).

Al-Shurouk. "Al-Ikhwān yaʿtadūn ʿalā muṣawwirī 'al-Shurouk' fī 'Rābiʿa wa'l-Gīza'" [The Brotherhood attacks al-Shurouk photographers in Rabiʿa and Giza]. *Shorouk News*, July 27, 2013. https://www.shorouknews.com/news/view.aspx?cdate=27072013&id=ce47fb94-aaf4-46c0-8976-4b9d05fe189d (accessed October 20, 2020).

"Although the Disbelievers May Dislike It/Law kariha al-kāfirūn." Video, 15:23. Al-Furqān Media. Released November 14, 2014.

Althusser, Louis. *Lenin and Philosophy and Other Essays*. Translated by Ben Brewster. Monthly Review, 1971.

Alyousef, Baker. "Bil-fīdiyū sā'iq Mubarak al-ra'īs al-makhlūʿ kāna kathīr al-sabb wa-yakrah samā' al-Qur'ān" [On video: Mubarak's driver, the ousted president was very blasphemous and hated hearing the Qur'an]. January 23, 2011. YouTube video, 11:30. https://www.youtube.com/watch?v=JNB46oLRYMQ (accessed May 4, 2021).

al-Zarqawi, Abu Musʿab. "Ayna ahl al-murū'a?!" [Where are the possessors of manhood?!]. September 12, 2004. Arabic transcript at www.hanein.info/vb/showthread.php?t=168357 (accessed February 1, 2013; site now unavailable).

Amar, Ayman Baghat. "Miṣr Dawla Madaniyya" [Egypt civilian state]. Facebook post, February 2, 2013.

Amar, Paul. "Egypt." In *Dispatches from the Arab Spring: Understanding the New Middle East*, edited by Paul Amar and Vijay Rashad. University of Minnesota Press, 2013.

Amar, Paul. "Egypt after Mubarak." *The Nation*, May 23, 2011. https://www.thenation.com/article/archive/egypt-after-mubarak-2/.

Amar, Paul. *The Security Archipelago: Human-Security States, Sexuality Politics, and the End of Neoliberalism*. Duke University Press, 2013.

Amar, Paul. "Turning the Gendered Politics of the Security State Inside Out?" *International Feminist Journal of Politics* 13, no. 3 (2011): 299–328.

Amar, Paul, and Roger Owen. "Why Mubarak Is Out." In *The Dawn of the Arab Uprisings: End of an Old Order?*, edited by Bassam Haddad, Rosie Bsheer, and Ziad Abu-Rish. Pluto Press, 2012.

Amaria, Kainaz. "The 'Girl in The Blue Bra.'" NPR, December 21, 2011. https://www.npr.org/sections/pictureshow/2011/12/21/144098384/the-girl-in-the-blue-bra (accessed January 5, 2025).

Amin, Galal. *Egypt in the Era of Hosni Mubarak, 1981–2011.* American University in Cairo Press, 2012.

Amin, Nareman. "Is God for Revolution? Youth and Islam in Post-2011 Egypt." Unpublished manuscript, cited with author permission.

Amīn, Qāsim. *Taḥrīr al-mar'a* [*The Liberation of Women*]. In *The Liberation of Women/The New Woman: Two Documents in the History of Egyptian Feminism.* Translated and edited by Samiha Sidhom Peterson. American University in Cairo Press, 1992.

Amin, Shahira. "Egyptian General Admits 'Virginity Checks' Conducted on Protesters." CNN, May 31, 2011. http://edition.cnn.com/2011/WORLD/meast/05/30/egypt.virginity.tests/ (accessed March 20, 2021).

Amnesty International. "Egypt: Admission of Forced 'Virginity Tests' Must Lead to Justice." May 31, 2011. https://www.amnesty.org/en/latest/news/2011/05/egypt-admission-forced-virginity-tests-must-lead-justice/ (accessed March 20, 2021).

Amnesty International. "Egyptian Women Protesters Forced to Take 'Virginity Tests.'" March 23, 2011. https://www.amnesty.org/en/press-releases/2011/03/egyptian-women-protesters-forced-take-e28098virginity-testse28099/ (accessed March 20, 2021).

Amnesty International. "Egypt: Military Pledges to Stop Forced 'Virginity Tests.'" June 27, 2011. https://www.amnesty.org/en/press-releases/2011/06/egypt-military-pledges-stop-forced-virginity-tests/ (accessed June 30, 2021).

Anonymous. "The Mystery of ISIS." *The New York Review of Books*, August 13, 2015. http://www.nybooks.com/articles/2015/08/13/mystery-isis/ (accessed January 7, 2016).

Anwar, Ghazala. "al-Asmā' al-ḥusnā." In *The Oxford Encyclopedia of the Islamic World.* Oxford University Press, 2009. http://www.oxfordislamicstudies.com/article/opr/t236/e1131 (accessed August 5, 2017).

Anwar, Randa. "A Pragmatic Analysis of the Protest Slogans of the Egyptian 2011 Revolution." Conference paper, Cairo University, n.d. http://erepository.cu.edu.eg/index.php/ARTS-Conf/article/view/6526 (accessed December 3, 2024).

Apostolidis, Paul. *Breaks in the Chain: What Immigrant Workers Can Teach America About Democracy.* University of Minnesota Press, 2010.

Apostolidis, Paul. *The Fight for Time: Migrant Day Laborers and the Politics of Precarity.* Oxford University Press, 2019.

Arab News. "Egypt's El-Sisi: Undisputed Leader and 'Father Figure.'" March 30, 2018. https://www.arabnews.com/node/1276046/middle-east (accessed February 15, 2023).

Archibald, Thomas, and Arthur L. Wilson. "Rethinking Empowerment: Theories of Power and the Potential for Emancipatory Praxis." Adult Education Research Conference, 2011. http://newprairiepress.org/cgi/viewcontent.cgi?article=3127&context=aerc (accessed March 10. 2023).

Arendt, Hannah. *On Violence: Crises of the Republic.* Harcourt Brace & Co., 1972.

Armbrust, Walter. "The Revolution Against Neoliberalism." In *The Dawn of the Arab Uprisings: End of an Old Order?*, edited by Bassam Haddad, Rosie Bsheer, and Ziad Abu-Rish. Pluto Press, 2012.

Artists for the Revolution. "Thā'ir yaḥlam bi-waṭan . . . Mina Dānīāl" [A revolutionary dreaming of a nation . . . Mina Danial]. August 14, 2012. YouTube video, 10:26. https://www.youtube.com/watch?v=mUdBIgr3Hqg (accessed January 7, 2025).

Asad, Talal. *Genealogies of Religion: Discipline and Reasons of Power in Christianity and Islam.* Johns Hopkins University Press, 1993.

Asad, Talal. "The Idea of an Anthropology of Islam." *Qui Parle* 17, no. 2 (2009): 1–30.

Ashwin, Sarah, and Jennifer Utrata. "Masculinity Restored? Putin's Russia and Trump's America." *Contexts* 19, no. 2 (2020): 16–21.

"Asīrāt al-muslimīn ṣabran" [(Female) captives of the Muslims, patience]. Mu'assasat al-ʿādiyāt al-iʿlāmiyya. Audio courtesy ISD, 5:07.

Associated Press. "Families of Ferry Passengers Lash Out at Egyptian Government over Response to Tragedy." VailDaily.com, February 5, 2006. https://www.vaildaily.com/news/families-of-ferry-passengers-lash-out-at-egyptian-government-over-response-to-tragedy/ (accessed October 3, 2024).

Aswany Alaa (@AlaaAswany). "Shujāʿat banāt Miṣr al-thawriyyāt lā tuqliq niẓām Mubarak faqaṭ lākinnahā tuzʿij al-jubanāʾ fāqidī al-nakhwa alladhīna yaqbalūn al-dhull min ajl al-salāma wa-yarfuḍūn al-thawra li-karāmatihim." Twitter, January 19, 2012. https://twitter.com/AlaaAswany/status/159965249171234816 (accessed September 7, 2020, URL no longer available).

ʿAthamina, Khalil. "The Black Banners and the Socio-Political Significance of Flags and Slogans in Medieval Islam." *Arabica* 36 (1989): 307–26.

Atwan, Abdel Bari. *Islamic State: The Digital Caliphate.* University of California Press, 2015.

Ayata, Bilgin, and Cilja Harders. "'Midān Moments': Conceptualizing Space, Affect and Political Participation on Occupied Squares." In *Affect in Relation: Families, Places, Technologies*, edited by Birgitt Röttger-Rössler and Jan Slaby. Routledge, 2018.

Aydin, Cemil. *Idea of the Muslim World: A Global Intellectual History.* Harvard University Press, 2017.

Azulai, Moran. "Smotrick to Netanyahu: 'Enter Rafah Immediately, Don't Wave the White Flag, Don't Let Sinwar Humiliate Us Again." *Yedioth Ahronoth*, April 30, 2024. https://www.ynet.co.il/news/article/rjagldaz0 (accessed May 22, 2024).

ʿAzzam, ʿAbd Allāh. *al-Difāʿ ʿan arāḍī al-Muslimīn: ahamm furūḍ al-aʿyān.* Dar al-Mujtamaʿ, 1987.

ʿAzzām, ʿAbd Allāh. *ʿUshshāq al-Ḥūr.* Maktab Khadāmat al-Mujāhidīn, 1990.

Baghdadi, Abu ʿUmar, et al. "Qul innī ʿalā bayyina min Rabbī" [Say: I have clear proof from my Lord]. Mu'assasat al-Furqān, March 13, 2007. Arabic transcript available in *al-Majmūʿ li-qādat Dawlat al-ʿIrāq al-Islāmiyya.*

Bahaa, Ahmad. "Arjal bint fī Miṣr bidūn niqāsh ṭāliba tarfaʿ shiʿār Rābiʿa athnāʾ idhāʿat Tislam al-ayādī fī ḥuḍūr mudīr al-amn" [The bravest/manliest girl in Egypt without discussion. A student raises the four-finger slogan during the broadcast of Tislam al-Ayadi in the presence of the director of security]. September 28, 2013. YouTube video, 1:59. https://www.youtube.com/watch?v=ZEsCSa4F7yQ (accessed August 4, 2021).

Bargu, Banu. *Starve and Immolate: The Politics of Human Weapons.* Columbia University Press, 2014.

Barnett, Carolyn. "Book Review: *Dispatches from the Arab Spring: Understanding the New Middle East.*" *Middle East Law and Governance* 7, no. 1 (2015): 169–79.

Baron, Beth. *Egypt as a Woman: Nationalism, Gender, and Politics.* University of California Press, 2005.

Bayat, Asef. *Revolution Without Revolutionaries: Making Sense of the Arab Spring.* Stanford University Press, 2017.

BBC News ʿArabī. "Mā lā yuqāl—aqbāṭ fī al-shāriʿ" [What is not said—Copts in the street]. June 9, 2010. YouTube video, 30:17. https://www.youtube.com/watch?v=pwvVyYCxlLk (accessed March 23, 2021).

BBC News Arabic. "Bi'l-fīdiyū: muẓāharat iḥtijāj lil-aqbāṭ fī Shubrā ʿalā al-hajamāt" [Video: Copts protest in Shubra against the attacks]. January 4, 2011. YouTube video, 3:33. https://www.youtube.com/watch?v=FCfsl9Hiu-o (accessed May 6, 2021).

Begolly, Emerson. Conversation on October 20, 2010, between Begolly (abunancy@almanhajribat.net) and khalidabdalhakim@almanhajribat.net. http://americanjihadists.com/2011

-01-11-Begolly-Exhibits.pdf. See also http://news.intelwire.com/2011/01/look-into-troubled-mind-of-jihadist.html.

Beinin, Joel. "Egyptian Workers and January 25th: A Social Movement in Historical Context." *Social Research* 79, no. 2 (2012): 323–48.

Beinin, Joel. "The Militancy of Mahalla al-Kubra." Middle East Report Online. December 2007. https://merip.org/2007/09/the-militancy-of-mahalla-al-kubra/ (accessed January 3, 2025).

Beinen, Joel. "Workers' Protest in Egypt: Neo-liberalism and Class Struggle in 21st Century." *Social Movement Studies* 8, no. 4 (2009): 449–54.

Beinin, Joel, and Frédéric Vairel. *Social Movements, Mobilization, and Contestation in the Middle East and North Africa*. 2nd ed. Stanford University Press, 2013.

Benhabib, Seyla. *The Claims of Culture: Equality and Diversity in the Global Era*. Princeton University Press, 2002.

Benjamin, Walter. "The Task of the Translator." In *Illuminations: Essays and Reflections*, edited by Hannah Arendt, translated by Harry Zohn. Schocken Books, 1969.

Bennett, Nolan. "'The State Was Patiently Waiting for Me to Die': Life Without the Possibility of Parole as Punishment." *Political Theory* 49, no. 2 (2021): 165–89.

Bennoune, Karima. "Algerian Women Confront Fundamentalism." *Monthly Review* 46, no. 4 (1994): 26–39.

Benski, Tova, and Eran Fisher. *Internet and Emotions*. Routledge, 2014.

Bergen, Peter, and Michael Lind. "A Matter of Pride: Why We Can't Buy Off the Next Osama bin Laden." *Democracy* 3 (Winter 2007): 8–16.

Bernard-Donals, Michael, and Richard R. Glejzer, eds. *Rhetoric in an Antifoundational World: Language, Culture, and Pedagogy*. Yale University Press, 1998.

best4egypt. "Qaṣīdat al-Mīdān—ʿAbd al-Raḥmān al-Abnūdī" [Poem of the square—ʿAbd al-Raḥman al-Abnūdī]. Al-Ḥayāt al-Yawm, February 4, 2011. YouTube video, 9:57. https://www.youtube.com/watch?v=xq3tTCjMZ60 (accessed March 8, 2021).

Bigelow, Kathryn, dir. *Zero Dark Thirty*. Sony Pictures, 2012. 157 min.

Bin Laden, Usama. "Depose the Tyrants." Available in *Messages to the World: The Statements of Osama bin Laden*, edited by Bruce Lawrence, translated by James Howarth. Verso, 2005.

Bin Laden, Usama. "Iʿlān al-jihād ʿalā al-Amrīkiyyīn al-Muḥtallīn li-bilād al-Ḥaramayn" [Declaration of Jihad against the Americans Occupying the Land of the Two Holy Sites]. February 15, 2009. http://www.tawhed.ws/r?i=1502092b (accessed February 6, 2012; no longer available).

Bin Laden, Usama. Interview with Al Jazeera television. December 1998. Available in *Messages to the World: The Statements of Osama bin Laden*, edited by Bruce Lawrence, translated by James Howarth. Verso, 2005.

Bishara, Marwan. "From Hubris to Humiliation: The 10 Hours that Shocked Israel." Al Jazeera, October 7, 2023. https://www.aljazeera.com/opinions/2023/10/7/from-hubris-to-humiliation-the-10-hours-that-shocked-israel (accessed May 22, 2024).

Blair, Edmund. "Egyptian Tries to Set Himself Alight." *Reuters*, January 19, 2011. https://www.reuters.com/article/us-tunisia-egypt-immolation/egyptian-tries-to-set-himself-alight-idUSTRE70I2PT20110119 (accessed June 13, 2020).

Bleiker, Roland. "Visual Assemblages: From Causality to Conditions of Possibility." In *Reassembling International Theory: Assemblage Thinking and International Relationsm*, edited by Michele Acuto and Simon Curtis. Palgrave, 2014.

Bloch, Ernst. *Natural Law and Human Dignity*. Translated by Dennis J. Schmidt. MIT Press, 1986.

Bloch, Ruth H. "American Feminine Ideals in Transition: The Rise of the Moral Mother, 1785–1815." *Feminist Studies* 4, no. 2 (June 1978): 101–26.

Blok, Anton. "The Enigma of Senseless Violence." In *Meanings of Violence: A Cross Cultural Perspective*, edited by Göran Aijmer and Jon Abbink. Berg, 2000.

Bodenner, Chris. "'Obama Taunted Trump and Look Where It Got Us.'" *The Atlantic*, March 22, 2022. https://www.theatlantic.com/politics/archive/2016/12/obama-taunted-trump-and-look-where-it-got-us/622666/ (accessed July 1, 2023).

Bowden, Mark. *Black Hawk Down: A Story of Modern War*. Grove Press, 1999.

Bowman, James. *Honor: A History*. Encounter Books, 2006.

Brand, Laurie A. *Official Stories: Politics and National Narratives in Egypt and Algeria*. Stanford University Press, 2014.

Bromwell, Nick. *The Powers of Dignity: The Black Political Philosophy of Frederick Douglass*. Duke University Press, 2021.

Brown, Wendy L. *Manhood and Politics: A Feminist Reading in Political Theory*. Rowman & Littlefield, 1988.

Brown, Wendy. "Neoliberalism and the End of Liberal Democracy." In *Edgework: Critical Essays on Knowledge and Politics*. Princeton University Press, 2005.

Brown, Wendy. *Regulating Aversion: Tolerance in the Age of Identity and Empire*. Princeton University Press, 2006.

Brownlee, Jason, Tarek Masoud, and Andrew Reynolds. *The Arab Spring: Pathways of Repression and Reform*. Oxford University Press, 2015.

Brumberg, Daniel. "Morsi's Moment on Gaza." *Foreign Policy*, November 21, 2012. https://foreignpolicy.com/2012/11/21/morsis-moment-on-gaza/ (accessed March 2, 2021).

Btselem. "Fatalities: During Cast Lead." https://www.btselem.org/statistics/fatalities/during-cast-lead/by-date-of-event (accessed May 1, 2021).

Bubandt, Nils. "Vernacular Security: The Politics of Feeling Safe in Global, National and Local Worlds." *Security Dialogue* 36, no. 3 (2005): 275–96.

Buhite, Russell D. *Lives at Risk: Hostages and Victims in American Foreign Policy*. Scholarly Resources, 1995.

Bura'i, Sherif, ed. *Al-Judrān tahtif: jirāfītī al-thawrah al-Miṣrīyya* [*Walls Talk: Graffiti of the Egyptian Revolution*]. American University in Cairo Press, 2012. Arabic edition, Dar el-Kutub, 2012.

Butler, Judith. *Bodies That Matter: On The Discursive Limits of 'Sex'*. Routledge, 1993.

Butler, Judith. *Frames of War: When Is Life Grievable?* Verso, 2010.

Butler, Judith. *Gender Trouble: Feminism and the Subversion of Identity*. Routledge, 1990.

Butter, David. "Egypt and the Gulf: Allies and Rivals." Chatham House, April 20, 2020. https://www.chathamhouse.org/2020/04/egypt-and-gulf/sisis-debt-his-gulf-arab-backers (accessed February 25, 2021).

Cairokee and Zap Tharwat. "Ethbat makānak" [Hold your ground]. On *Matloob Zaeem*. DJ Recording, 2011. QSoft. Available on bassemyoussefshow. January 23, 2012. YouTube video, 6:05. https://www.youtube.com/watch?v=rYoCS7i0SIg (accessed May 6, 2021).

Calhoun, Cheshire. "Justice, Care, Gender Bias." *The Journal of Philosophy* 85, no. 9 (1988): 451–63.

Callahan, William A. "National Insecurities: Humiliation, Salvation, and Chinese Nationalism." *Alternatives: Global, Local, Political* 29, no. 2 (2004): 199–218.

Callimachi, Rukmini. "The Horror Before the Beheadings." *International New York Times*, October 25, 2014. https://nyti.ms/1w5TI86 (accessed November 12, 2015).

Callimachi, Rukmini. "ISIS Enshrines a Theology of Rape." *New York Times*, August 13, 2015. http://www.nytimes.com/2015/08/14/world/middleeast/isis-enshrines-a-theology-of-rape.html?_r50 (accessed December 1, 2015).

"A Call to Hijrah." *Dabiq*, no. 3 (July/August 2014). https://clarionproject.org/ (accessed December 1, 2019).

Cameron, David. "David Cameron Issues Statement on the Execution of David Haines." *5 Pillars: What Are Muslims Thinking*. September 14, 2014. http://5pillarsuk.com/2014/09/14

/david-cameron-issues-statement-on-the-execution-of-david-haines/ (accessed November 23, 2016).

Campbell, David. "Cultural Governance and Pictorial Resistance: Reflections on the Imagining of War." *Review of International Studies* 29, no. 1 (2003): 57–73.

Campbell, David. "Geopolitics and Visuality: Sighting the Darfur Conflict." *Political Geography* 26 (2007): 357–82.

Campbell, David. "Horrific Blindness: Images of Death in Contemporary Media." *Journal for Cultural Research* 8, no. 1 (2004): 55–74.

Campbell, Lisa J. "The Use of Beheadings by Fundamentalist Islam." *Global Crime* 7, nos. 3–4 (2006): 583–614.

Carr, Sarah. "Factory Workers Strike in Menufiya, Demand Bonuses." *Daily News Egypt*, March 11, 2009. https://dailynewsegypt.com/2009/03/11/factory-workers-strike-in-menufiya-demand-bonuses/ (accessed March 24, 2021).

Carr, Sarah. "Omar Effendi Workers Resume Strike Against Wage Discrimination." *Daily News Egypt*, May 7, 2009. https://dailyfeed.dailynewsegypt.com/2009/05/07/omar-effendi-workers-resume-strike-against-wage-discrimination/ (accessed March 24, 2021).

Caspar, Monica J., and Lisa Jean Moore. *Missing Bodies: The Politics of Visibility*. New York University Press, 2009.

Cattan, Henry. *An Anthology of Oriental Anecdotes, Fables and Proverbs*. Saqi Books, 2000.

Cavarero, Adriana. *Horrorism: Naming Contemporary Violence*. Translated by William McCuaig. Columbia University Press, 2011.

Cavarero, Adriana. *Inclinations: A Critique of Rectitude*. Translated by Amanda Minervini and Adam Sitze. Stanford University Press, 2016.

CBC Egypt. "Khāled al-Nabawī -ʿār ʿalaykum waṣf al-thuwwār bi'l-balṭagiyya" [Khaled al-Nabawi—Shame on you for describing the revolutionaries as thugs]. November 25, 2011. YouTube video, 6:14. https://www.youtube.com/watch?v=7kzAf2wRJSU (accessed May 11, 2021).

The Choir Project Egypt. "Ḥayāt al-Mīdān [Life of [Tahrir] Square]." February 26, 2011. YouTube video, 5:29. https://www.youtube.com/watch?v=LCBVwJ4DT10 (accessed June 22, 2021).

Çıdam, Çiğdem. *In the Street: Democratic Action, Theatricality, and Political Friendship*. Oxford University Press, 2021.

Cillizza, Chris. "Donald Trump Humiliated J. D. Vance for Fun." CNN Politics, September 20, 2022. https://www.cnn.com/2022/09/19/politics/donald-trump-jd-vance-ohio-rally/index.html (accessed May 10, 2023).

Clancy-Smith, Julia, and Frances Gouda. *Domesticating the Empire: Race, Gender, and Family Life in French and Dutch Colonialism*. University Press of Virginia, 1998.

Cohen, David. *Law, Sexuality and Society: The Enforcement of Morals in Classical Athens*. Cambridge University Press, 1991.

Cohen, Paul A. "Remembering and Forgetting National Humiliation in Twentieth-Century China." In *China Unbound: Evolving Perspectives on the Chinese Past*. Taylor & Francis, 2003.

Cohen, William B. "The Colonized as Child: British and French Colonial Rule." *African Historical Studies* 3, no. 2 (1970): 427–31.

Cole, Juan. "Christians, Muslims 'One Hand' in Egypt's Youth Revolution." *Informed Comment*, February 7, 2011. https://www.juancole.com/2011/02/christians-muslims-one-hand-in-egypts-youth-revolution.html (accessed January 12, 2022).

Coles, Romand. *Visionary Pragmatism: Radical and Ecological Democracy in Neoliberal Times*. Duke University Press, 2016.

Colla, Elliott, and Roger Owen. "The Poetry of Revolt." In *The Dawn of the Arab Uprisings: End of an Old Order?*, edited by Bassam Haddad, Rosie Bsheer, and Ziad Abu-Rish. Pluto Press, 2012.

Collins, Randall. *Violence: A Micro-sociological Theory*. Princeton University Press, 2011.

"The Complete Message from James Foley." *Dabiq*, no. 3 (July/August 2014). https://clarionproject.org/ (accessed December 1, 2019).

Connell, R. W. *Gender and Power*. Stanford University Press, 1987.

Connell, R. W. *Masculinities*. 2nd ed. University of California Press, 2005.

Connolly, William. "The Evangelical-Capitalist Resonance Machine." *Political Theory* 33, no. 6 (2005): 869–886.

Connolly, William. "Method, Problem, Faith." In *Problems and Methods in the Study of Politics*, edited by Ian Shapiro, Rogers M. Smith, and Tarek E. Masoud. Cambridge University Press, 2004.

Connolly, William. *Why I Am Not a Secularist*. University of Minnesota Press, 1999.

Cooke, Miriam. *Women Claim Islam: Creating Islamic Feminism Through Literature*. Routledge, 2000.

Cooper, Julie. E. *Secular Powers: Humility in Modern Political Thought*. University of Chicago Press, 2013.

Coptic demonstrations. January 5, 2011. YouTube video, 2:32. https://www.youtube.com/watch?v=FFtwlSljHnY (accessed January 7, 2025).

Coptic Maspero. "Aḥdāth al-aqbāṭ baʿda thawrat 25 Yanāyir" [Post-January 25th revolution Coptic events]. May 16, 2011. YouTube video, 7:16. https://www.youtube.com/watch?v=u9p3ercNn9c (accessed April 2, 2021).

Coptic Maspero. "Mā hiya al-awḍāʿ fī Miṣr al-ān liqāʾ fī Maspero 11/5/2011" [What are the conditions in Egypt now? Encounters in Maspero]. May 11, 2011. YouTube video, 8:02. https://www.youtube.com/watch?v=LCZaTufOGt8 (accessed May 20, 2021).

Cornwall, Andrea, and Nancy Lindisfarne. *Dislocating Masculinity: Comparative Ethnographies*. Routledge, 1994.

Cottee, Simon. "ISIS and the Intimate Kill." *Atlantic Monthly*, November 17, 2014. http://www.theatlantic.com/international/archive/2014/11/isis-and-the-intimate-kill-peter-kassig/382861/ (accessed May 31, 2015).

Cottee, Simon. "The Pornography of Jihadism." *Atlantic Monthly*, September 12, 2014. http://www.theatlantic.com/international/archive/2014/09/isis-jihadist-propaganda-videos-porn/380117/ (accessed December 1, 2015).

Creswell, Robyn, and Bernard Haykel. "Battle Lines: Want to Understand the Jihadis? Read Their Poetry." *The New Yorker*, June 8 and 15, 2015.

Cronin, Audrey Kurth. "ISIS Is Not a Terrorist Group: Why Counterterrorism Won't Stop the Latest Jihadist Threat." *Foreign Affairs* 94, no. 2 (2015): 87–98.

Danchev, Alex. "'Like a Dog!': Humiliation and Shame in the War on Terror." *Alternatives: Global, Local, Political* 31, no. 3 (2006): 259–83.

Dauber, Cori E. "The Shots Seen 'Round the World: The Impact of the Images of Mogadishu on American Military Operations." *Rhetoric and Public Affairs* 4, no. 4 (2001): 653–87.

Dauber, Cori E., and Mark Robinson. "ISIS and the Hollywood Visual Style." Blog post. 2015. http://jihadology.net/2015/07/06/guest-post-isis-and-the-hollywood-visual-style/ (accessed June 1, 2024).

Davies, Ray. 1972. "Celluloid Heroes." On *Everybody's in Show-Biz, Everybody's a Star*. Performed by The Kinks. Vinyl record. RCA Victor.

Day, Elizabeth. "Fedia Hamdi's Slap Which Sparked a Revolution 'Didn't Happen.'" *The Guardian*, April 23, 2011. https://www.theguardian.com/world/2011/apr/23/fedia-hamdi-slap-revolution-tunisia (accessed March 26, 2021).

Dekel, Udi, and Orit Perlov. "President Morsi and Israel-Egypt Relations: Egyptian Discourse on the Social Networks." *Institute for National Security Studies*, Insight no. 357, July 25, 2012.

Delkhasteh, Mahmood. "Humiliation: The Catalyst for Arabs' Revolutions." *Huffington Post*, February 18, 2011. https://www.huffpost.com/entry/humiliation-the-catalyst-_b_824222 (accessed January 13, 2021).

Democracy Now. "Asmaa Mahfouz and the YouTube Video that Helped Spark the Egyptian Uprising." February 8, 2011. https://www.democracynow.org/2011/2/8/asmaa_mahfouz_the_youtube_video_that (accessed February 11, 2021).

Der Derian, James. *Virtuous War: Mapping the Military-Industrial-Media-Entertainment Network*. Westview Press, 2002.

Deylami, Shirin. "Saving the Enemy: Female Suicide Bombers and the Making of American Empire." *International Feminist Journal of Politics* 15, no. 2 (2013): 177–94.

Dhākirat Maspero. "Al-Khiṭāb al-akhīr li-Mubarak—10 Fibrāyir 2011" [Mubarak's last speech—February 10, 2011]. National Media Authority (Egypt), December 7, 2015. YouTube video, 16:53. https://www.youtube.com/watch?v=9_06qCKV3bE (accessed May 27, 2021).

Diab, Mohamed. "Clash/Ishtibāk." 2016. Al-Māsa Distribution.

Diab, Mostafa. "Dina Abdel Rahman fī mawqif shujāʿ jiddan wa-mushādda kalāmiyya maʿa liwāʾ jaysh li-ithbāt ḥuqūq al-mutaẓāhirīn" [Dina Abdel Rahman takes an incredibly brave stance in a debate with a military lieutenant attesting to the rights of the protesters]. Tahrir Channel, December 31, 2011. YouTube video, 6:58. https://www.youtube.com/watch?v=1ygb-CfCw6UQ (accessed March 8, 2021).

Doooozz28. "Banāt Bilādī . . . Muḥammad el-Wadi" [The daughters of my country . . . Muhammad el-Wadi]. December 23, 2011. YouTube video, 4:17. https://www.youtube.com/watch?v=bGb-Y2StEEY (accessed April 4, 2021).

Doooozz28. "Hiya dī kull el-ḥikāya . . . Muḥammad el-Wadi" [This is the entire story . . . Muhammad el-Wadi]. January 29, 2012. YouTube video, 4:28. https://www.youtube.com/watch?v=A1nvHesyoaI (accessed March 4, 2021).

Douglass, Frederick. *The Anti-Slavery Movement*. Press of Lee, Mann & Co., 1855.

Doward, Jamie. "Egyptian Police Incited Massacre at Stadium, Say Angry Footballers." *The Guardian*, February 5, 2012. https://www.theguardian.com/world/2012/feb/05/egypt-football-massacre-police-arab-spring (accessed February 28, 2021).

Dunne, Michele, and Amr Hamzawy. "From Too Much Egyptian Opposition to Too Little—and Legal Worries Besides." Carnegie Endowment for International Peace, December 13, 2010. https://carnegieendowment.org/2010/12/13/from-too-much-egyptian-opposition-to-too-little-and-legal-worries-besides-pub-42128.

Dworkin, Ronald. *Is Democracy Possible Here?: Principles For a New Political Debate*. Princeton University Press, 2007.

Dyer, Emily. "Marginalising Egyptian Women: The Restriction of Women's Rights under the Muslim Brotherhood". The Henry Jackson Society, 2013. http://henryjacksonsociety.org/wp-content/uploads/2013/12/Marginalising-Egyptian-Women.pdf.

Eagleton, Terry. "A Short History of Rhetoric." *Rhetoric in an Antifoundational World*. Edited by Glenn Adelson, James Engell and Brent Ranalli. Yale University Press, 1998.

Egyptian Initiative for Personal Rights. "Shahādat Rashā ʿAbd al-Raḥmān ʿan kushūf al-ʿudhrīya fī al-sijn al-ḥarbī" [Testimony of Rasha ʿAbd al-Rahman on virginity tests in military prison]. February 25, 2012. YouTube video, 7:23. https://www.youtube.com/watch?v=heemiSNW94k (accessed May 4, 2021).

Egyptian Initiative for Personal Rights. "The Trap: Punishing Sexual Difference in Egypt." November 2017. https://eipr.org/sites/default/files/reports/pdf/the_trap-en.pdf (accessed March 23, 2021).

Eid, Gamal (@gamaleid). "Lā taqul irḥamū 'azīz qawm dhalla!! qul ḥākimū dīktātūr wa-illā aṣābakum al-dhull." Twitter, August 6, 2011. https://twitter.com/gamaleid/status/99646679099252737 (accessed February 10, 2021).

El Chazli, Yousef. "The Egyptian Revolution Is Not a Failure." *Counter-Argument: A Middle East Podcast*, April 27, 2023, Crown Center for Middle East Studies, Brandeis University.

el-Ghobashy, Mona. *Bread and Freedom: Egypt's Revolutionary Situation*. Stanford, CA: Stanford University Press, 2021.

Ellissy, Amr. "'Amr Ellissy fī manṭiqat maqābir al-Imām al-Shāfi'ī" [Amr Ellissy in the cemetery of Imām Shāfi'ī]. Mehwar TV, September 14, 2012. YouTube video, 22:27. https://www.youtube.com/watch?v=CvDg6JtsBgg (accessed January 7, 2025).

Ellissy, Amr. "Sikritīr Mubarak wa-ḥadīth 'an tasawwul Mubarak wa-akhlāqihi" [Mubarak's secretary and a story of Mubarak's begging and his morals]. Al Tahrir, June 16, 2011. YouTube video, 14:59. https://www.youtube.com/watch?v=IO0nOHeTmck (accessed August, 6, 2020, no longer available).

el-Baghdadi, Iyad. "Meet Asmaa Mahfouz and the vlog that Helped Spark the Revolution." February 2, 2011. YouTube video, 4:36. https://www.youtube.com/watch?v=SgjIgMdsEuk&t=75s (accessed March 1, 2020).

el-Beheri, Ahmed. "Friday Sermons to Discuss Religious Prohibition of Suicide." *Egypt Independent*, January 20, 2011. https://www.egyptindependent.com/friday-sermons-discuss-religious-prohibition-suicide/ (accessed June 13, 2020).

Elbernameg. "al-Nāshiṭ wa'l-mudawwin Wā'il 'Abbas" [Activist and blogger Wael Abbas]. Bassem Youssef, August 23, 2011. YouTube video, 15:40. https://www.youtube.com/watch?v=C_MQ773p_EU.

Elbernameg. "'Indamā ya'tī al-khiṭāb - al-ḥalqa 15 - al-juz' 2" [When the speech arrives, episode 15, part 2]. Bassem Youssef, March 1, 2013. YouTube video, 27:00. https://www.youtube.com/watch?v=6M0qc4uVp4M (accessed March 12, 2021).

Elbernameg. "I'tibruh abūk yā akhī" [Consider him your father, man]. Bassem Youssef, January 20, 2012. YouTube video, 5:51. https://www.youtube.com/watch?v=uv3ixTnfOaM (accessed May 25, 2021).

el-Gakh, Hisham. "Al-Mukālama" [The Phone Call]. February 18, 2014. YouTube video, 20:45. https://www.youtube.com/watch?v=0uwO7nB9-oA&t=1s (accessed May 4, 2021).

el-Gakh, Hisham. "Al-Ta'shīra" [The visa]. January 12, 2013. YouTube video, 10:22. https://www.youtube.com/watch?v=BQe41B8eytY (accessed May 4, 2021).

el-Gakh, Hisham. "Anā Ikhwān" [I am brotherhood]. June 29, 2013. YouTube video, 7:43. https://www.youtube.com/watch?v=ViI7vktqGPc (accessed January 7, 2025).

el-Gakh, Hisham. "Guḥā" [Guha]. December 20, 2010. YouTube video, 16:47. https://www.youtube.com/watch?v=0OEyE2SBxwY (accessed May 4, 2021).

el-Gakh, Hisham. "Mikamilīn" [We'll keep going]. Originally posted November 25, 2011. As of October 24, 2022, available on ElGakhTV. "Jadīd: Hisham el-Gakh—Mikamilīn—qaṣīdat al-Thawra al-Miṣriyya" [New: Hisham el-Gakh—"We'll Keep Going"—poem of the Egyptian Revolution.] YouTube video, 5:59. https://www.youtube.com/watch?v=2TmnX0X0R28 (accessed January 5, 2025).

El-GakhTV. "Jadīd: Hisham el-Gakh—Mikamilīn—qaṣīdat al-Thawra al-Miṣriyya" [New: Hisham el-Gakh—We'll keep going—poem of the Egyptian Revolution.] November 25, 2011. YouTube video, 5:59. https://www.youtube.com/watch?v=2TmnX0X0R28 (accessed January 23, 2021).

el-Ibrashy, Wael. "Al-Ḥaqīqa Wael el-Ibrashy: Muwājaha ma'a alladhīna ḥāwalū al-intiḥār ḥarqan fī Miṣr wa-ma'a 'ā'ilātihim, al-juz' 1, ḥalqa 22" [Interview with those who attempted self-immolation in Egypt and their families]. Dream TV, January 22, 2011. YouTube video, 15:25. https://youtube.com/W0vZdbI2Qp8 (accessed October 17, 2022).

el-Ibrashy, Wael. "Al-Ḥaqīqa Wael el-Ibrashy: Muwājaha maʿa alladhīna ḥāwalū al-intiḥār ḥarqan fī Miṣr wa-ma ʿa ʿāʾilātihim, al-juzʾ 2, ḥalqa 22" [Interview with those who attempted self-immolation in Egypt and their families]. Dream TV, January 22, 2011. YouTube video, 15:25. https://youtube.com/watch?v=276yLKAFevw (accessed October 17, 2022).

el-Ibrashy, Wael. "Al-Ḥaqīqa Wael el-Ibrashy: Muwājaha maʿa alladhīna ḥāwalū al-intiḥār ḥarqan fī Miṣr wa-maʿa ʿāʾilātihim, al-juzʾ 3, ḥalqa 22" [Interview with those who attempted self-immolation in Egypt and their families]. Dream TV, January 22, 2011. YouTube video, 14:38. https://youtube.com/0psTB6ULhIk (accessed October 17, 2022).

el-Ibrashy, Wael. "Al-Ḥaqīqa Wael el-Ibrashy: Muwājaha maʿa alladhīna ḥāwalū al-intiḥār ḥarqan fī Miṣr wa-maʿa ʿāʾilātihim, al-juzʾ 4, ḥalqa 22" [Interview with those who attempted self-immolation in Egypt and their families]. Dream TV, January 22, 2011. YouTube video, 13:12. https://youtube.com/GXbjcSVbTKM (accessed October 17, 2022).

el-Ibrashy, Wael. "Ḥiwār maʿa al-shurṭiyya ṣāḥibat ashhar ṣafʿa fī al-tārīkh wa-tasabbabat fī intiḥār Bouazzi al-Tūnisī" [Conversation with the policewoman who gave the most famous slap in history and caused the suicide of the Tunisian Bouazizi]. DreamTV, May 27, 2018. YouTube video, 15:03. https://www.youtube.com/watch?v=jtRTb6rjoJY (accessed July 1, 2021).

Ellis, John. *Seeing Things: Television in the Age of Uncertainty.* I. B. Tauris, 2000.

el-Mahdi, Rabab. "Does Political Islam Impede Gender-Based Mobilization? The Case of Egypt." *Totalitarian Movements and Political Religions* 11, nos. 3–4 (2010): 379–96.

El Nadeem Center for the Rehabilitation of Victims of Violence. "Live Testimonies on Sexual Torture in Tahrir Square and Surrounding Neighborhoods." February 1, 2013. https://elnadeem.org/2013/02/01/70/?lang=en (accessed March 15, 2021).

el-Nawawy, Alaa el-Din. Interview with Moataz Matar. "Biʾl-fīdiyū sāʾiq Mubarak al-raʾīs al-makhlūʿ kāna kathīr al-sabb wa-yakrah samāʿ al-Qurʾān - ṣaḥīfat al-wiʾām al-iliktrūniyya" [In the video, Mubarak's driver: "the removed president had a foul mouth and hated to hear the Qurʾān"—Wiʾām Online News]. Mahatet Masr Show, Mehwar 25, May 4, 2011. https://www.youtube.com/watch?v=JNB46oLRYMQ (accessed May 4, 2021).

el-Sayyed, Essam. "Sikit il-lisān wi-inkharas fī il-sikka mā itkallimish." Kullenā al-shahīd Eslām el-Sayyād. Facebook post, April 22, 2012. https://www.facebook.com/Shaheeed.MiSR.ESLAM/photos/a.172313792871525/211039922332245/ (accessed October 15, 2024).

El Shakry, Omnia, and Roger Owen. "Egypt's Three Revolutions: The Force of History Behind This Popular Uprising." In *The Dawn of the Arab Uprisings: End of an Old Order?*, edited by Bassam Haddad, Rosie Bsheer, and Ziad Abu-Rish. Pluto Press, 2012.

el-Shamy, Hasan M. *Folktales of Egypt.* University of Chicago Press, 1982.

el-Shenawi, Eman. "Four-Finger Salute: Egypt Rivals Use 'Rabaa Hand' to Turn Facebook Yellow." *AlArabiyaNews*, August 22, 2013. https://english.alarabiya.net/media/2013/08/21/Four-finger-salute-Egypt-rivals-use-Rabaa-symbol-to-turn-Facebook-yellow (accessed May 4, 2021).

el-Shobaki, Amr. "Opinion: Egypt Is not Tunisia." *Egypt Independent*, January 16, 2011. https://egyptindependent.com/egypt-not-tunisia/(accessed January 15, 2021).

Elshtain, Jean Bethke. *Women and War.* University of Chicago Press, 1987.

Elyan, Saber M. (@saberalian). "#Li-mādhā_yuḥākimū_Mursī? Li-annahu al-raʾīs al-Miṣrī al-waḥīd alladhī arāda li-#miṣr al-ʿizza waʾl-karāma baʿdamā jaʿalahā al-sābiqūn taḥyā fī al-dhull taḥta aqdām #Amrīkā." Twitter, November 4, 2013. https://twitter.com/saberalian/status/397279156234223616 (accessed February 10, 2021).

Emon, Anver. *Religious Pluralism and Islamic Law: Dhimmīs and Others in the Empire of Law.* Oxford University Press, 2012.

Emsallam, Taha(@TahaEmsallam). "Iḥdā shiʿārāt muẓāharāt #miṣr yādī al-dhull wa-yādī al-ʿār umm el-dunyā ḥākimhā ḥimār . . . nazīkīn el-maṣriyya hahaha." Twitter, July 1, 2013.

https://twitter.com/TahaEmsallam/status/351488108749000704 (accessed February 10, 2021).

"The End of Sykes-Picot." Video. Al-Ḥayat Media Center. June 29, 2014. URL no longer available.

eProductionHD. "A. Mekky Raps for the Egyptian Revolution (Jan 25th) Karāmat al-Maṣrī." Aḥmad Mekky, February 11, 2011. YouTube video, 3:30. https://www.youtube.com/watch?v=RDpWI6hluHQ (accessed June 22, 2021).

Essam, B. A. "Translation and Analysis of Diasporic Colloquial Egyptian Poems of Patriotism: A Hermeneutic Study." *Higher Education of Social Science* 7, no. 2 (2014): 139–48.

Euben, Peter. *Corrupting Youth: Political Education, Democratic Culture, and Political Theory.* Princeton University Press, 1997.

Euben, Roxanne L. "Humiliation through the Prism of Islamic Thought." In *The Oxford Handbook of Comparative Political Theory*, edited by Leigh K. Jenco, Murad Idris, and Megan C. Thomas. Oxford University Press, 2020.

Euben, Roxanne L., and Muhammad Qasim Zaman, eds. *Princeton Readings in Islamist Thought: Texts and Contexts from al-Banna to Bin Laden.* Princeton University Press, 2009.

Evans, Brad, and Henry A. Giroux. "Intolerable Violence." *Symploke* 23, nos. 1–2 (2015): 201–23.

"The Evil: Of Division and Taqlīd." *Dabiq*, no. 11 (August/September 2015). https://clarionproject.org/ (accessed December 1, 2019).

Fadl, Bilal. "Al-ʿĀ'ishūn fī al-dībāja!" [Living in the preamble!]. *Shorouk News*, December 4, 2013. https://www.shorouknews.com/columns/view.aspx?cdate=04122013&id=b5a14051-34e1-4153-a6cb-8abe7208e3e6 (accessed June 1, 2021).

Fadl, Bilal. "al-Miṣrī lil-miṣrī ka'l-bunyān . . . al-mahdūd" [The Egyptian social fabric is like an edifice . . . demolished]. In *Sitt al-ḥāja Miṣr*, 69–75. Dār al-Shurūq, 2012.

Fadl, Bilal. "Fī maḥkamat al-sayyida Nafīsa" [In the court of Mrs. Nafīsa]. *Shorouk News*, October 21, 2013. https://www.shorouknews.com/columns/view.aspx?cdate=21102013&id=37ff84f0-5f89-404c-8073-38447876e155 (accessed March 24, 2021).

Fadl, Bilal. "Man huwa al-ra'īs al-qādim?" [Who is the next president?]. *Shorouk News*, September 28, 2013. https://www.shorouknews.com/columns/view.aspx?cdate=28092013&id=ca3a7ece-b094-44e7-b32f-5cdb08882998 (accessed February 23, 2021).

Fadl, Bilal. "Qabla al-ṭūfān" [Before the flood]. *Shorouk News*, March 5, 2013. https://www.shorouknews.com/columns/view.aspx?cdate=05032013&id=5804926a-82af-45ce-969f-99e8a416b0be (accessed March 22, 2021).

Fadl, Bilal. "Tafwīḍ bi'l-baṭsh!" [Authorization to assault!]. *Shorouk News*, September 4, 2013. https://www.shorouknews.com/columns/view.aspx?cdate=04092013&id=3e101b24-967f-4a55-9b9d-8ffc0a144939 (accessed March 8, 2021).

Fahmy, Hazem. "An Initial Perspective on 'The Winter of Discontent: The Root Causes of The Egyptian Revolution.'" *Social Research: An International Quarterly* 79, no. 2 (2012): 349–76.

Faludi, Susan. *The Terror Dream: Fear and Fantasy in Post 9/11 America.* Metropolitan Books, 2007.

Fandy, Mamoun. *Saudi Arabia and the Politics of Dissent.* St. Martin's Press, 1999.

Fanon, Frantz. *The Wretched of the Earth.* Translated by Richard Philcox. Grove Press, 1968.

Faramarzi, Scheherezade. "Former Prisoner Prefers Saddam's Torture to US Abuse." Common Dreams.org, May 3, 2004. http://www.commondreams.org/cgi-bin/print.cgi?file=/headlines04/0503-02.htm (accessed January 3, 2012).

Fatayāt al-Tawḥīd. "Abkaytinī yā ummatī" [You made me cry, my mother]. *Fatayāt al-Tawḥīd Blog*, September 29, 2013. http://ftaiataltawhed.blogspot.com/2013/ (accessed March 19, 2023).

Fattah, Khaled, and K. M. Fierke. "A Clash of Emotions: The Politics of Humiliation and Political Violence in the Middle East." *European Journal of International Relations* 15, no. 1 (2009): 67–93.

Ferguson, Ann. "Cowboy Masculinity, Globalization and the U.S. War on Terror." The Center for Global Justice, October 1, 2017. https://www.globaljusticecenter.org/papers/cowboy-masculinity-globalization-and-us-war-terror (accessed January 7, 2017).

Filiu, Jean Pierre. "L'état de grâce islamiste sera fugace." *Le Progressiste*, March 21, 2012.

Filkins, Dexter. "The Death of Steven Sotloff." *The New Yorker*, September 2, 2014. http://www.newyorker.com/news/news-desk/death-steven-sotloff (accessed December 15, 2015).

Filmer, Robert. *Patriarcha; of the Natural Power of Kings*. DCK Book Binder, 1680.

Fisher, Max. "Egypt's Dictator Murdered 800 People Today in 2013. He's Now a US Ally and GOP Fold Hero." *Vox*, August 14, 2015. https://www.vox.com/2015/8/14/9153967/rabaa-sisi (accessed June 24, 2021).

5FadaFada. "Huwa fīh eih?" [What's wrong?]. *5FadaFada Blog*, June 30, 2011. http://5fadfada.blogspot.com/2011/06/blog-post30.html (accessed March 21, 2021).

5FadaFada. "Iqrā al-ḥāditha" [Listen to this]. *5FadaFada Blog*, February 25, 2011. http://5fadfada.blogspot.com/2011/02/blog-post25.html (accessed March 21, 2021).

5FadaFada. "Khāyifa" [I'm scared]. *5FadaFada Blog*, October 13, 2010. http://5fadfada.blogspot.com/2010/10/blog-post.html (accessed March 20, 2021).

Fleming, Paul J., Clare Barrington, Suzanne Maman, Leonel Lerebours, Yeycy Donastorg, and Maximo O. Brito. "Competition and Humiliation: How Masculine Norms Shape Men's Sexual and Violent Behaviors." *Men and Masculinities* 22, no. 2 (2017): 197–215.

Fodor, Éva. "A Different Type of Gender Gap: How Women and Men Experience Poverty." *East European Politics and Societies* 20, no. 1 (2006): 14–39.

"Foley's Blood Is on Obama's Hands." *Dabiq*, no. 3 (July/August 2014). https://clarionproject.org/ (accessed December 1, 2019).

Fontan, Victoria. "Polarization Between Occupier and Occupied in Post-Saddam Iraq: Colonial Humiliation and The Formation of Political Violence." *Terrorism and Political Violence* 18, no. 2 (2006): 217–38.

Foucault, Michel. *Discipline & Punish: The Birth of the Prison*. Translated by Alan Sheridan. Vintage Books, 1995.

Foucault, Michel. *Society Must Be Defended: Lectures at the Collège De France, 1975–6*. Translated by David Macey. Edited by Mauro Bertani and Alssandro Fontana. Picador, 2003.

Frank, Jason. *Constituent Moments: Enacting the People in Postrevolutionary America*. Duke University Press, 2010.

Freire, Paulo. "Fourth Letter." In *Teachers as Cultural Workers: Letters to Those Who Dare Teach*, translated by Donaldo Macedo, Dale Koike, and Alexandre Oliveira. Westview Press, 2005.

Frevert, Ute. *The Politics of Humiliation: A Modern History*. Oxford University Press, 2020.

Friedman, Thomas L. "The Humiliation Factor." *The New York Times*, November 9, 2003. https://www.nytimes.com/2003/11/09/opinion/the-humiliation-factor.html.

Friis, Simone Molin. "'Beyond Anything We Have Ever Seen': Beheading Videos and The Visibility of Violence in the War Against Isis." *International Affairs* 91, no. 4 (2015): 725–46.

"From the Battle of Al-Ahzāb to the War of Coalitions." *Dabiq*, no. 11 (August/September 2015). https://clarionproject.org/ (accessed December 1, 2019).

Frosh, Paul. "Telling Presences: Witnessing, Mass Media, and the Imagined Lives of Strangers." *Critical Studies in Media Communication* 23, no. 4 (2006): 265–84.

Fujii, Lee Ann. "The Puzzle of Extra-Lethal Violence." *Perspectives on Politics* 11, no. 2 (2013): 410–26.

Furnish, T. R. "Beheading in the Name of Islam." *Middle East Quarterly* 12, no. 2 (2005): 51–57.

Galston, William A. "Anger, Betrayal, and Humiliation: How Veterans Feel About the Withdrawal from Afghanistan." Brookings Institute, November 12, 2021. https://www.brookings.edu/articles/anger-betrayal-and-humiliation-how-veterans-feel-about-the-withdrawal-from-afghanistan/ (accessed June 22, 2022).

Gasim, Gamal. "Explaining Political Activism in Yemen." In *Taking to the Streets: The Transformation of Arab Activism*, edited by Lina Khatib and Ellen Lust. John Hopkins University Press, 2014.
Geertz, Clifford. *The Interpretation of Cultures*. Basic Books, 1975.
Georgakopoulos, Thanasis, Daniel A. Werning, Jörg Hartlieb, Tomoki Kitazumi, Lidewij E. van de Peut, Annette Sundermeyer, and Gaëlle Chantrain. "The Meaning of Ancient Words for 'Earth': An Exercise in Visualizing Colexification on a Semantic Map." *eTopoi* 6 (2016): 418–52.
Geuss, Raymond. *History and Illusion in Politics*. Cambridge University Press, 2001.
Ghanem, Hiba. "The 2011 Egyptian Revolution Chants: A Romantic-*Muʿtazilī* Moral Order." *British Journal of Middle Eastern Studies* 45, no. 3 (2018): 430–42.
Ghannam, Farha. *Live and Die Like a Man: Gender Dynamics in Urban Egypt*. Stanford University Press, 2013.
Ghatan, H. E. Yedidiah. *The Invaluable Pearl: The Unique Status of Women in Judaism*. Bloch Publishing Company, 1986.
Ghoneim, Wael. *Revolution 2.0: The Power of the People Is Greater Than the People in Power. A Memoir*. Houghton Mifflin Harcourt, 2012.
Ghoneim, Wael, and Mostafa el-Naggar. Interview with Hafez el-Marazy. "Tawthīq al-thawra al-Miṣriyya 25 January 2011—Wael Ghoneim—Mostafa el-Naggar—Bayān al-thawra" [Documenting the Egyptian revolution 25 January 2011—Wael Ghoneim—Mostafa el-Naggar—declaration of the revolution]. AlArabia TV, February 11, 2011. YouTube video, 16:00. https://www.youtube.com/watch?v=rZAHmZbDpCQ (accessed January 7, 2025).
Ghoussoub, Mai, and Emma Sinclair-Webb, eds. *Imagined Masculinities: Male Identity and Culture in the Modern Middle East*. Saqi Books, 2000.
Gilligan, James. *Violence: Reflections on a National Epidemic*. Vintage Books, 1997.
Gilmore, David D. *Manhood in the Making: Cultural Concepts of Masculinity*. Yale University Press, 1990.
The Glocal. "Maṭlūb zaʿīm li-farīq Cairokee—al-shāriʿ yughannī" [Leader Wanted by the group Cairokee—the street sings]. El-Gomhoreya TV, January 23, 2012. YouTube video, 2:22. https://youtu.be/f1NGUMY9v_I?si=05ZEUjJpay0K4HCb (accessed May 3, 2021).
Goldman, Loren. *The Principle of Political Hope: Progress, Action, and Democracy in Modern Thought*. Oxford University Press, 2023.
Graham-Harrison, Emma. "UK Attacks on Isis Met with Public Support as Anti-War Protesters Warn of Long-Term Threat." *The Guardian*, September 27, 2014. https://www.theguardian.com/world/2014/sep/27/isis-uk-attacks-support-protesters-warn-threat (accessed March 2, 2015).
Graper Hernandez, Jill. "Human Value, Dignity, and the Presence of Others." *HEC Forum* 27, no. 3 (2015): 249–63.
Griffin, Jean T. "Racism and Humiliation in the African-American Community." *Journal of Primary Prevention* 12, no. 2 (1991): 149–67.
Grossman, Dave. *On Killing: The Psychological Cost of Learning to Kill in War and Society*. Back Bay Books, 2009.
Grynbaum, Michael M. "Trump Strategist Stephen Bannon Says Media Should 'Keep Its Mouth Shut.'" *The New York Times*, January 26, 2017. https://www.nytimes.com/2017/01/26/business/media/stephen-bannon-trump-news-media.html (accessed January 4, 2023).
Guenther, Lisa. "Resisting Agamben: The Biopolitics of Shame and Humiliation." *Philosophy & Social Criticism* 38, no. 1 (2011): 59–79.
Guru, Gopal, ed. *Humiliation: Claims and Context*. Oxford: Oxford University Press, 2011.
Guweida, Farouk. *Ightiṣāb waṭan: Jarīmat nahb al-arāḍī fī Miṣr* [Raping a country: Crimes of land pillaging in Egypt]. Dār al- Shurūq, 2010.

Guweida, Farouk. "Ilā kull jallād ṭāghī" [To every tyrant executioner]. Al-Hayat Satellite Channel, September 11, 2011.

Guweida, Farouk. "Irḥal" [Leave]. Facebook post, February 1, 2011. https://www.facebook.com/GWephotographers/posts/347268671960611/ (no longer available, accessed February 1, 2021).

Guweida, Farouk. "Ka'an al-'umr mā kāna" [As if life never was]. Dār al-Shurūq, 2007.

https://www.facebook.com/255626297786057/videos/10150438309536982 (accessed February 23, 2021).

Gwynne, Rosalind W. "Usama bin Ladin, the Qur'an and Jihad." *Religion* 36, no. 2 (2006): 61–90.

"Hādhā wa'd Allāh" [This is the promise of God]. Mu'assasat al-Furqān. June 2014. Audio courtesy ISD, 34:00.

Hafez, Mohammed M. "Martyrdom Mythology in Iraq: How Jihadists Frame Suicide Terrorism in Videos and Biographies." *Terrorism and Political Violence* 19, no. 1 (2007): 95–115.

Hafez, Mohammed M. *Suicide Bombers in Iraq: The Strategy and Ideology of Martyrdom.* United States Institute of Peace Press, 2007.

Hagel, Chuck. "Department of Defense Press Briefing by Secretary Hagel and General Dempsey in the Pentagon Briefing Room." *U.S. Department of Defense*, August 21, 2014. https://www.defense.gov/News/Transcripts/Transcript-View/Article/606917 (accessed November 23, 2016).

Hallaq, Wael B. *Sharī'a: Theory, Practice, Transformations.* Cambridge University Press, 2012.

Hall, Donald E. *Subjectivity.* Routledge, 2004.

Hansen, Lene. "How Images Make World Politics: International Icons and the Case of Abu Ghraib." *Review of International Studies* 41, no. 2 (2015): 263–88.

Hansen, Lene. "Theorizing the Image for Security Studies: Visual Securitization and the Muhammad Cartoon Crisis." *European Journal of International Relations* 17, no. 1 (2011): 51–74.

Harré, Rom. "Embarrassment: A Conceptual Analysis." In *Shyness and Embarrassment*, edited by Ray Crozier. Cambridge University Press, 1990.

Hart Research Associates. NBC News/*Wall Street Journal* Survey Study #14901. September 3–7, 2014. http://newscms.nbcnews.com/sites/newscms/files/14901_september_nbc-wsj_poll.pdf (accessed January 3, 2025).

Harvey, David. *A Brief History of Neoliberalism.* Oxford University Press, 2005.

Hassan, Muhsin. "The Lost Boys of Eastleigh: Identity, Ideology, and the Appeal of al-Shabaab." Princeton University, unpublished.

Hassan, Nasra. "An Arsenal of Believers: Talking to the 'Human Bombs.'" *The New Yorker*, November 19, 2001.

Hassan, Robert. "Network Time." In *24/7: Time and Temporality in the Network Society*, edited by Robert Hassan and Ronald E. Purser. Stanford Business Books, 2007.

Hassan, Robert. "Time, Neoliberal Power, and the Advent of Marx's 'Common Ruin' Thesis." *Alternatives: Global, Local, Political* 37, no. 4 (2012): 287–99.

Hauerwas, Stanley, and Romand Coles. *Christianity, Democracy and the Radical Ordinary: Conversations Between a Radical Democrat and a Christian.* Lutterworth Press, 2008.

Heilman, Brian, and Gary Barker. *Masculine Norms and Violence: Making the Connections.* Promundo-US, 2018.

Henry, Leslie Meltzer. "The Jurisprudence of Dignity." *University of Pennsylvania Law Review* 169 (2011): 169–233.

Hermez, Sami. "On Dignity and Clientelism: Lebanon in the Context of the 2011 Arab Revolutions." *Studies in Ethnicity and Nationalism* 11, no. 3 (2011): 527–37.

Hersh, Seymour M. "The Gray Zone." *The New Yorker*, May 24, 2004, 38–44. https://www.newyorker.com/magazine/2004/05/24/the-gray-zone (accessed July 10, 2024).

Hessler, Peter. "Egypt's Failed Revolution." *The New Yorker*, January 2, 2017. https://www.newyorker.com/magazine/2017/01/02/egypts-failed-revolution (accessed March 1, 2021).

Hillis, Ken, Susanna Paasonen, and Michael Petit. *Networked Affect*. MIT Press, 2015.

Homolar, Alexandra, and Georg Löfflmann. "Populism and the Affective Politics of Humiliation Narratives." *Global Studies Quarterly* 1, no. 1 (2021): 1–11.

Honig, Bonnie. *A Feminist Theory of Refusal*. Harvard University Press, 2021.

Honneth, Axel. "A Society Without Humiliation?" *European Journal of Philosophy* 5, no. 3 (1997): 306–24.

Hooper, Charlotte. *Manly States: Masculinities, International Relations, and Gender Politics*. Columbia University Press, 2001.

Horkheimer, Max, and Theodor W. Adorno. *Dialectic of Enlightenment: Philosophical Fragments*. Translated by Edmund Jephcott. Stanford University Press, 2002.

Huckin, Thomas, "Propaganda Defined." In *Propaganda and Rhetoric in Democracy: History, Theory, Analysis*, edited by Gae Lyn Henderson and M. J. Braun. Southern Illinois University Press, 2016.

Human Rights Watch. "All According to Plan: The Rabʿa Massacre and Mass Killings of Protesters in Egypt." August 12, 2014. https://www.hrw.org/report/2014/08/12/all-according-plan/raba-massacre-and-mass-killings-protesters-egypt# (accessed July 5, 2021).

Human Rights Watch. "Deprived and Endangered: Humanitarian Crisis in the Gaza Strip." January 13, 2009. https://www.hrw.org/news/2009/01/13/deprived-and-endangered-humanitarian-crisis-gaza-strip# (accessed April 1, 2021).

Human Rights Watch. "Egypt: Bus Driver Raped by Police Faces New Risk of Torture." January 12, 2007. https://www.hrw.org/news/2007/01/12/egypt-bus-driver-raped-police-faces-new-risk-torture (accessed March 21, 2021).

Hussein, Abdel-Rahman. "Egyptian Protesters Claim They Were Tortured by Muslim Brotherhood." *The Guardian*, December 12, 2012. https://www.theguardian.com/world/2012/dec/12/egyptian-protesters-tortured-muslim-brotherhood (accessed March 3, 2021).

Hussein, Abdullah Abdelhameed. "The Slogans of the Tunisian and Egyptian Revolutions: A Sociolinguistic Study." May 19, 2012. https://www.researchgate.net/publication/341495509_The_slogans_of_the_Tunisian_and_Egyptian_revolutions_A_sociolinguistic_study.

Hussin, Iza R. *The Politics of Islamic Law: Local Elites, Colonial Authority, and the Making of the Muslim State*. University of Chicago Press, 2016.

i24NEWS Arabic. "Khawf wa-qalaq mutaṣāʿid wasṭa al-mithliyyīn fī Miṣr" [Growing fear and anxiety among gays in Egypt]. January 5, 2015. YouTube video, 1:15. https://www.youtube.com/watch?v=d8ctkRYT68A (accessed July 1, 2021).

Ibn Kathīr, ʿImād al-Dīn Ismāʿīl. *Tafsīr al-Qurʾān al-ʿAẓīm*. Vol. 1. Edited by Sāmī bin Muḥammad al-Salāma. Dār Ṭība, 1997.

Ibn Shuʿba al-Ḥarrānī, Abū Muḥammad al-Ḥasan ibn ʿAlī. *Tuḥaf al-ʿUqūl ʿan Āl al-Rasūl*. Edited by ʿAli Akbar al-Ghaffāri. Muʾassasat al-Nashr al-Islāmī, 1984.

Ibn Ṭāwūs, Raḍī al-Dīn ʿAlī. "al-Luhūf fī qatlā al-ṭufūf." In *Maqtal al-Ḥusayn ʿalayhi al-salām*. Muʾassasat al-Aʿlāmī, 1993.

Ibrahim, Mostafa. "Nadart il-nadr" [I made the promise]. In *Western Union / Fariʿ al-Haram*. Merit Publishing House, 2012.

Ibrahim, Sherif. "Ihdāʾ ilā kull ḥurr wa-sharīf wa-thār" [Dedicated to every free, decent, and revolutionary person]. Facebook post, March 24, 2011. https://www.facebook.com/groups/163887833660481/permalink/173504492698815 (accessed April 14, 2021).

Ibrahim, Sherif. "Iktub yā tārīkh" [Write this down, O history]. Facebook post, March 24, 2011. https://www.facebook.com/groups/163887833660481/permalink/173504492698815/ (accessed April 14, 2021).

Idris, Murad. *War for Peace: Genealogies of a Violent Ideal in Western and Islamic Thought*. Oxford University Press, 2019.

Ifāda Maktūba. "Amr Ismail, Ummī malhāsh fī al-siyāsa" [Amr Ismail, my mother doesn't care for politics]. Facebook post, December 8, 2016. https://ar-ar.facebook.com/Mohamed.Gamal751996/posts/738105419685204/ (accessed January 6, 2025).

Ikhwan Web. "Muslim Brotherhood Statement on Anti-Islam Film." September 13, 2012. http://www.ikhwanweb.com/article.php?id=30286 (accessed March 4, 2013).

Inhorn, Marica. *The New Arab Man: Emergent Masculinities, Technologies, and Islam in the Middle East*. Princeton University Press, 2012.

Iqtidar, Humeira. "Conservative Anti-Colonialism: Maududi, Marx and Social Equality." *Journal of the Royal Asiatic Society*, series 3, 32, no. 2 (2022): 295–310.

Ismail, Amr. "Ummī malhāsh fī al-siyāsa" [My mother doesn't care for politics]. Facebook post, October 3, 2010. https://www.facebook.com/127560617276846/videos/151820678190759/ (accessed March 22, 2021).

Ismail, Salwa. "The Egyptian Revolution Against the Police." *Social Research* 79, no. 2 (2012): 435–62.

Ismail, Salwa. *Political Life in Cairo's New Quarters: Encountering the Everyday State*. University of Minnesota Press 2006.

"Izzay" [How]. Lyrics by Nasr al-Din Nagy. Performed by Mohamed Mounir. Single. Released February 2011. Live at Ain Sokhna Concert 2012, *AlHayat TV*. YouTube video, 6:16. https://www.youtube.com/watch?v=yeclhmRVE7g (accessed January 7, 2025).

Jacob, Wilson Chacko. *Working Out Egypt: Effendi Masculinity and Subject Formation in Colonial Modernity, 1870–1940*. Duke University Press, 2011.

Jaheen, Samia. "Kilāb el-dākhiliyya wa-kīf ta'āmlū ma'a el-nāshiṭ el-siyāsī Dr. Taqādum el-Khaṭīb" [The hounds of the Interior Ministry and how they dealt with the political activist Dr. Taqadum el-Khatib]. October 27, 2012. Facebook post. https://www.facebook.com/notes/samia-jaheen/كلاب-الداخلية-وكيف-تعاملوا-مع-الناشط-السياسي-د-تقادم-الخطيب/10151048361312115/ (accessed March 21, 2021).

"Jaḥīm al-kuffār fī arḍ al-Anbār" [Hell of the infidels in the land of Anbar]. The Media Authority of the Mujahidin Shura Council in Iraq. n.d. Video courtesy ISD, 40:00.

Jamasyali. "Hitāfāt Mīdān al-Taḥrīr" [Chants of Tahrir Square]. February 13, 2011. YouTube video, 2:04. https://www.youtube.com/watch?v=eA8wa8Gz7C4 (accessed June 30, 2021, no longer available).

Janes, Regina. "Beheadings." *Representations* 35 (1991): 21–51.

Jankowski, James. *Nasser's Egypt, Arab Nationalism, and the United Arab Republic*. Lynne Rienner Publishers, 2002.

Jarvis, Lee. "Toward a Vernacular Security Studies: Origins, Interlocutors, Contributions, and Challenges." *International Studies Review* 21, no. 1 (2018): 107–26.

Jarvis, Lee, and Michael Lister. "Vernacular Securities and Their Study: A Qualitative Analysis and Research Agenda." *International Relations* 27, no. 2 (2013): 158–79.

Jenco, Leigh, Murad Idris, and Megan Thomas, eds. *Oxford Handbook to Comparative Political Theory*. Oxford University Press, 2020.

Jerzak, Connor T. "Ultras in Egypt: State, Revolution, and the Power of Public Space." *Interface: A Journal for and About Social Movements* 5, no. 2 (2013): 240–62.

Jewish News One. "Police Brutally Attack Egyptian Women, US Condemns, with 'Blue Bra Girl' Video on Qasr Al-Ainy." December 22, 2011. YouTube video, 1:49. https://www.youtube.com/watch?v=5kd4KLIibGU (accessed January 5, 2025).

Jones, Alan, trans. *Qur'ān*. Gibb Memorial Trust, 2007.

Juergensmeyer, Mark. *Terror in the Mind of God: The Global Rise of Religious Violence*. University of California Press, 2000.

Juris, Jeffrey S. "Violence Performed and Imagined: Militant Action, the Black Bloc and the Mass Media in Genoa." *Critique of Anthropology* 25, no. 4 (2005): 413–32.

Just, Roger. *Women in Athenian Law and Life*. Routledge, 1989.

Kaempf, Sebastian. "The Mediatisation of War in a Transforming Global Media Landscape." *Australian Journal of International Affairs* 67, no. 5 (2013): 586–604.

Kamel, Omar. "Maqāl maktūb bi-baṭāriyyat el-laptop" [Post on a laptop battery]. *Mudawwanat ʿUmar Kāmil*, August 2, 2012. https://omarmkamel.blogspot.com/2012/08/blog-post.html (accessed March 21, 2021).

Karatzogianni, Athina, and Adi Kuntsman, eds. *Digital Cultures and the Politics of Emotion: Feelings, Affect and Technological Change*. Palgrave Macmillan, 2012.

Karolak, Magdalena. "Online Aesthetics of Martyrdom." In *Political Islam and Global Media: The Boundaries of Religious Identity*, edited by Noha Mellor and Khalil Rinnawi. Routledge, 2016.

"Kasr al-Ḥudūd" [Breaking the Borders]. Mu'assasat al- I'tiṣām. June 29, 2014. Video, 12:22 (accessed February 15, 2025). https://videos.files.wordpress.com/6l1PQaNk/islamic-state-of-iraq-and-al-shc481m-22breaking-of-the-border22_dvd.mp4.

Kateb, George. *Human Dignity*. Harvard University Press, 2011.

Kaufmann, Paulus, Hannes Kuch, Christian Neuhäuser, and Elaine Webster. *Humiliation, Degradation, Dehumanization: Human Dignity Violated*. Springer, 2010.

Kayaoglu, Turan. "It Is Time to Reform the Management of The Hajj." Brookings Institute, July 23, 2020. https://www.brookings.edu/opinions/it-is-time-to-reform-the-management-of-the-hajj/ (accessed December 9, 2022).

Kerry, John. "Murder of James Foley." U.S. Secretary of State, August 20, 2014. https://www.state.gov/secretary/remarks/2014/08/230772.htm (accessed November 23, 2016).

Khatab, Sayed. *The Political Thought of Sayyid Qutb: The Theory of Jahiliyyah*. Routledge, 2006.

"Khaṭīb Fāṭima" [Fatima's fiancé]. Majlis Shūrā al-Mujāhidīn fī al-ʿIrāq, 2004. Video courtesy ISD, 9:00.

"Khiṭāb amīr al-jamāʿa al-salafīya lil-daʿwa wa'l-qitāl li-qimmat al-dhull al-ʿarabīya" [The address of the Emir of the Salafist Group for Preaching and Combat to the summit of Arab humiliation]. Al-Tajdīd al-Islāmī. March 28, 2005. Soundcloud, 1:30. https://soundcloud.com/altajdeed/rwk9az6w807j (accessed March 19, 2023).

Khlebnikov, Alexey. "Why Did the 2011 Egyptian Revolution Fail?" *Central European Journal of International and Security Studies* 10, no. 3 (2016): 88–117.

Khomeini, Ruhollah. *Islam and Revolution: Writings and Declarations of Imam Khomeini*. Translated by Hamid Algar. Mizan Press, 1981.

Khosrokhavar, Farhad. *Suicide Bombers: Allah's New Martyrs*. Pluto Press, 2005.

Khouri, Rami G. "Terrorists Are Also Spawned by Humiliation." *The New York Times*, June 29, 2010. https://www.nytimes.com/2010/06/30/opinion/30iht-edkhouri.html.

KH, Taha (@tahaelkhateeb). "Sa-ukhbir aḥfādī wa-awlādī annanī qātaltu wa-ḥārabtu min ail an takūna Miṣr dawla islāmiyya. wa-lākin al-ʿabīd fī bilādī yaʿshaqūn al-dhull wa'l-hawān." Twitter, July 3, 2013. https://twitter.com/tahaelkhateeb/status/352372580260392960 (accessed February 9, 2021).

Kilcullen, David. *Blood Year: Islamic State and the Failures of the War on Terror*. Hurst & Co, 2016.

Kim, Susanna. "Egypt's Mubarak Likely to Retain Vast Wealth." ABC News, February 2, 2011. https://abcnews.go.com/Business/egypt-mubarak-family-accumulated-wealth-days-military/story?id=12821073 (accessed February 25, 2021).

Kimmel, Michael. *Manhood in America: A Cultural History*. Oxford University Press, 2006.

Kimmel, Michael. "Masculinities." In *Men and Masculinities: A Social, Cultural and Historical Encyclopedia*, vol. 1, edited by Michael Kimmel and Amy Aronson. ABC-CLIO, Inc., 2004.

Kingsley, Patrick. "Canadian Pair Describe 'Shared Trauma' of Ordeal in Egyptian Prison." *The Guardian*, October 11, 2013. https://www.theguardian.com/world/2013/oct/11/canadian-greyson-loubani-ordeal-egyptian-prison (accessed March 8, 2021).

Kingsley, Patrick. "Egyptian Police 'Using Rape as a Weapon' Against Dissident Groups." *The Guardian*, April 12, 2014. https://www.theguardian.com/world/2014/apr/12/egypt-police-rape-dissidents-crackdown-16000-arrested (accessed June 30, 2021).

Kingsley, Patrick. "How Did 37 Prisoners Come to Die at Cairo Prison Abu Zaabal?" *The Guardian*, February 22, 2014. https://www.theguardian.com/world/2014/feb/22/cairo-prison-abu-zabaal-deaths-37-prisoners (accessed March 8, 2021).

Kirkpatrick, David D. "Egypt's New Strongman, Sisi Knows Best." *The New York Times*, May 24, 2014. https://www.nytimes.com/2014/05/25/world/middleeast/egypts-new-autocrat-sisi-knows-best.html (accessed May 1, 2021).

Klein, Donald C. "The Humiliation Dynamic: An Overview." *The Journal of Primary Prevention* 12, no. 2 (1991): 93–121.

Koestenbaum, Wayne. *Humiliation*. Picador, 2011.

Kraidy, Marwan M. "The Projectilic Image: Islamic State's Digital Visual Warfare and Global Networked Affect." *Media Culture & Society* 39, no. (2017): 1194–209.

Kraidy, Marwan M. "Terror, Territoriality, Temporality: Hypermedia Events in the Age of Islamic State." *Television & New Media* 19, no. 2 (2018): 170–76.

Kuch, Hannes. "The Rituality of Humiliation: Exploring Symbolic Vulnerability." In *Humiliation, Degradation, Dehumanization: Human Dignity Violated*, edited by Paulus Kaufmann, Hannes Kuch, Christian Neuhauser, and Elaine Webster. Springer, 2011.

Lane, Edward William. *An Arabic–English Lexicon*. Librairie du Liban, 1968.

Lange, Christian. "Legal and Cultural Aspects of Ignominious Parading (*Tashhīr*) in Islam." *Islamic Law and Society* 14, no. 1 (2007): 81–108.

Lawrence, Bruce, ed. *Messages to the World: The Statements of Osama Bin Laden*. Verso, 2005.

Lazare, Aaron. "Shame and Humiliation in the Medical Encounter." *Archives of Internal Medicine* 147, no. 9 (1987): 1653–58.

Lentini, Pete, and Muhammad Bakashmar. "Jihadist Beheading: A Convergence of Technology, Theology, and Teleology?" *Studies in Conflict and Terrorism* 30, no. 4 (2007): 303–25.

"A Letter to My Mother." *Al-Hussam* 19, no. 4, March 25, 1996.

Levy, Eylon. Interview with Brianna Keilar. CNN News Central. December 8, 2023. https://transcripts.cnn.com/show/cnc/date/2023-12-08/segment/10 (accessed May 23, 2023).

Levy, Gideon. "By Trying to Humiliate Gaza to Its Core, Israel Is the One Being Humiliated." *Haaretz*, December 10, 2023. https://www.haaretz.com/opinion/2023-12-10/ty-article/.premium/by-trying-to-humiliate-gaza-to-its-core-israel-is-the-one-being-humiliated/0000018c-5001-df2f-adac-fe2d3d640000 (accessed May 22, 2024).

Lewis, Bernard. *The Crisis of Islam: Holy War and Unholy Terror*. Random House, 2004.

Lewis, Bernard. "The Roots of Muslim Rage." *The Atlantic*, May 20, 2018. https://www.theatlantic.com/magazine/archive/1990/09/the-roots-of-muslim-rage/304643/ (accessed July 15, 2013).

Lewis, Shady. "Bi-lā "ishsha' wa-lā 'tūktūk'" [Without "a shack" and without a "tuktuk"]. *Almodon*, March 19, 2014. https://www.almodon.com/opinion/2014/3/19/بلا-عشة-ولا-توك-توك (accessed August 1, 2021).

Lewis, Shady. "'Ḥammām Ramsīs' wa'l-hawas bi'l-naqd" ['Hammam Ramses' and the obsession with criticism]. *Almodon*, December 24, 2014. https://www.almodon.com/opinion/2014/12/24/حمام-رمسيس-والهوس-بالنقد (accessed March 23, 2021).

Lewis, Shady. "Fawwaḍtahum lil-qatl . . . fa-qatalūka" [You authorized them to kill . . . and they killed you]. *Almodon*, February 4, 2014. https://www.almodon.com/opinion/2014/2/4/فوضتهم-للقتل-فقتلوك (accessed May 2, 2021).

Lewis, Shady. "Maʿrakat al-madāris wa'l-aṣābiʿ al-arbaʿa" [The Battle of Schools and Four Fingers]. *Almodon*, October 2, 2013. https://www.almodon.com/opinion/2013/10/2/معركة-المدارس-والأصابع-الأربعة (accessed May 24, 2021).

Lewis, Shady. "Miṣr taḥta al-wiṣāya" [Egypt under guardianship]. *Almodon*, June 11, 2014. https://www.almodon.com/opinion/2014/6/11/%d9%85%d8%b5%d8%b1-%d8%aa%d8%ad%d8%aa-%d8%a7%d9%84%d9%88%d8%b5%d8%a7%d9%8a%d8%a9 (accessed January 7, 2025).

Leys, Ruth. "The Turn to Affect: A Critique." *Critical Inquiry* 37, no. 3 (2011): 434–72.

Lia, Brynjar. *Architect of Global Jihad: The Life of al-Qaida Strategist Abu Mus'ab al-Suri*. Columbia University Press, 2008.

Li, Darryl. "A Jihadism Anti-Primer." *MERIP (Middle East Research and Information Project)*, Fall 2015. http://merip.org/mer/mer276/jihadism-anti-primer (accessed January 7, 2016).

Lindner, Evelin Gerda. *The Anatomy of Humiliation and Its Relational Character: The Case of the Victim*. 2000. www.humiliationstudies.org/documents/evelin/RelationalAnatomyHumiliationVictim.pdf (accessed December, 9, 2012).

Lindner, Evelin Gerda. "The Concept of Humiliation: Its Universal Core and Culture Dependent Periphery." University of Oslo, unpublished manuscript, 2001. http://www.humiliationstudies.org/documents/evelin/CorePeriphery.pdf (accessed January 14, 2014).

Lindner, Evelin Gerda. "Humiliation as the Source of Terrorism: A New Paradigm." *Peace Research* 33, no. 2 (2001): 59–68.

Lindner, Evelin Gerda. "Women and Terrorism: The Lessons of Humiliation." *New Routes: A Journal for Peace Research and Action* 6, no. 3 (2001): 10–12.

Lindner, Evelin, and Morton Deutsch. *Making Enemies: Humiliation and International Conflict*. Praeger Security International, 2006.

Lloyd, Vincent W. *Black Dignity: The Struggle Against Domination*. Yale University Press, 2022.

Locke, Jill. "Shame and the Future of Feminism." *Hypatia* 22, no. 4 (2007): 146–62.

Locke, John. *Second Treatise of Government*. Edited by C. B. Macpherson. Hackett Publishing, 1980.

Londoño, Ernesto, and Ingy Hassieb. "At Least 74 Dead After Egypt Soccer Match." *The Washington Post*, February 1, 2012. https://www.washingtonpost.com/world/at-least-68-dead-after-egypt-soccer-match/2012/02/01/gIQADAeTiQ_story.html (accessed February 11, 2020).

Long, Scott. "When Doctors Torture: The Anus and the State in Egypt and Beyond." *Health and Human Rights* 7, no. 2 (2004): 114–40.

Luban, David. "Human Dignity, Humiliation, and Torture." *Kennedy Institute of Ethics Journal* 19, no. 3 (2009): 211–30.

Lukes, Steven. "Humiliation and the Politics of Identity." *Social Research* 64, no. 1 (1997): 36–51.

Machiavelli, Niccolò. *The Prince*. Translated by George Bull. Penguin Classics, 2003.

Macklin, R. "Dignity Is a Useless Concept." *BMJ* 327, no. 7429 (2003): 1419–20.

Maged, Reem. "Damnā sāl wa-'irḍinā ithatak wa-sharafnā itmarmaṭ" [Our blood was shed, our honor was violated, and our dignity was trampled]. *Baladna bi'l-Masri*, OnTV September 8, 2014. YouTube video, 1:53. https://www.youtube.com/watch?v=XftfQF0-SZo (accessed February 24, 2020, no longer available).

Maged, Reem. "Ḥasan ṭifl shawāri' fī mīdān al-taḥrīr yarudd 'alā ra'īs al-wuzara' al-mukallaf Kamāl al-Ganzoury" [Hassan, a street child in Tahrir Square, responds to Prime Minister-designate Kamal al-Ganzoury]. *Baladna bi'l-Masri*, OnTV, December 1, 2011. YouTube video, 6:10. https://www.youtube.com/watch?v=yiiYJSK_5OU (downloaded February 24, 2020, longer available).

Maged, Reem. "Kaffāra yā Abū Khālid wa-'uqbāl el-barā'a līk wa-illī zayyak" [Blessings, Abū Khalid, and all the best wishes for your innocence and all those like you]. *Baladna bi'l Masri*.

OnTV, December 25, 2011. YouTube video, 7:35. https://www.youtube.com/watch?v=68AIGoHGoio (accessed March 8, 2021; no longer available).

Mahfouz, Asmaa. "Ākhir kalima qabla 25 yanāyir" [Last word before January 25]. January 24, 2011. YouTube video, 3:22. https://www.youtube.com/watch?v=hKgN6A0UWCU&t=1s (accessed July 6, 2020).

Mahfouz, Asmaa. "Asmaa Mahfouz - al-Ḥaqīqa Wael el-Ibrashy 26 Yanāyir" [Asmaa Mahfouz—"The truth" [with] Wael el-Ibrashy]. DreamTV, January 26, 2011. YouTube video, 11:06. https://www.youtube.com/watch?v=Nri0Dy2D1N8 (accessed April 5, 2021).

Mahfouz, Asmaa. "Mīʿādunā yawm al-jumʿa baʿda al-ṣalāt fī kull mayādīn Miṣr" [Our appointment is on Friday after prayers in all the city squares of Egypt]. January 26, 2011. YouTube video, 6:16. https://www.youtube.com/watch?v=gFdhE8KXm_g (accessed July 6, 2020).

Mahfouz, Asmaa (@AsmaaMahfouz). "'Ahd Mubarak mish lāqīn yāklū shūfū dhull al-nās wa-intū tiʿrafū līh Mubarak bi-yitdhall dilwaqtī." Twitter, April 14, 2011. https://twitter.com/AsmaaMahfouz/status/58449067998593024 (accessed July 22, 2019).

Maḥmood, Saba. *Politics of Piety: The Islamic Revival and the Feminist Subject.* Princeton University Press, 2005.

Mahmood, Saba. *Religious Difference in a Secular Age: A Minority Report.* Princeton University Press, 2016.

Mahmoud, Mohamed. "Meet the People Living in Graveyards in Egypt." *Middle East Eye*, December 20, 2017. https://www.middleeasteye.net/features/meet-people-living-graveyards-egypt (accessed March 12, 2021).

Makiya, Kanan, and Hassan Mneimneh. "Manual for a 'Raid.'" *New York Review of Books*, January 17, 2002. https://www.nybooks.com/articles/2002/01/17/manual-for-a-raid/.

Mamdani, Mahmood. *Good Muslim, Bad Muslim: America, the Cold War and the Roots of Terror.* Three Rivers Press, 2005.

Manion, Jennifer C. "Girls Blush, Sometimes: Gender, Moral Agency, and the Problem of Shame." *Hypatia* 18, no. 3 (2003): 21–41.

Manion, Jennifer C. "The Moral Relevance of Shame." *American Philosophical Quarterly* 39, no. 1 (2002): 73–90.

Mann, Bonnie. *Sovereign Masculinity: Gender Lessons from the War on Terror.* Oxford University Press, 2014.

Mansour, Gihan. "Shahādat Ghāda Kamāl baʿda iʿtidāʾ al-jaysh ʿalayhā 16 December" [The testimony of Ghada Kamal after the army attacked her on December 16]. *Sabahik Ya Misr*, December 17, 2011. YouTube video, 5:57. https://www.youtube.com/watch?v=Rgq4prhzots (accessed March 24, 2021, no longer available).

Marangoly George, Rosemary. "Homes in the Empire, Empires in the Home." *Cultural Critique* 26 (1993–94): 95–127.

Marei, Khaled, dir. *Asal Iswid.* Albatros Film Productions, United Brothers Cinema, 2010. Run time 130 mins.

Margalit, Avishai, and Naomi Goldblum. *The Decent Society.* Harvard University Press, 1996.

Marton, Miriam. "Terrorism and Humiliation." Paper presented at Annual Meeting of Human Dignity and Humiliation Studies, Berlin, 2005.

Maṣr Elnahārda EG. "Maṣr innahārda wa-ḥiwār ḥawla aḥdāth Tūnis" [Egypt Today and a conversation about the events in Tunisia]. Maṣr Elnahārda Channel, January 24, 2011. YouTube video, 12:01. https://www.youtube.com/watch?v=pPNwn9_K9cY (accessed April 10, 2021).

Massad, Joseph A. *Desiring Arabs.* University of Chicago Press, 2007.

Massad, Joseph A. *Islam in Liberalism.* University of Chicago Press, 2015.

Matthies-Boon, Vivienne. "Shattered Worlds: Political Trauma Amongst Young Activists in Post-Revolutionary Egypt." *The Journal of North African Studies* 22, no. 4 (2017): 620–44.

Matthies-Boon, Vivienne, and Naomi Head. "Trauma as Counter-Revolutionary Colonisation: Narratives from (Post)Revolutionary Egypt." *Journal of International Political Theory* 14, no. 3 (2017): 258–79.

Maududi [Mawdudi], Sayyid Abu al-Aʿla. *Let Us Be Muslims*. Edited by Khurram Murad. The Islamic Foundation, 1985.

Maududi, Sayyid Abu al-Aʿla. *The Meaning of the Qur'ān*. Translated by Chaudhry Muhammad Akbar. Islamic Publications Limited, 1993.

McAuley, Denis. "The Ideology of Osama bin Laden: Nation, Tribe and World Economy." *Journal of Political Ideologies* 10, no. 3 (2005): 269–87.

McFate, Jessica Lewis. "The ISIS Defense in Iraq and Syria: Countering an Adaptive Enemy." *Middle East Security Report* 27. Institute for the Study of War, May 2015. http://understandingwar.org/report/isis-defense-iraq-and-syria-countering-adaptive-enemy.

Me and Them. "ʿĀm yakād yamḍī wa-lā zilnā naṣrukh!" [Almost a year has passed, and we are still screaming!]. *Anā wa-Hā'ulā'i Blog*, December 31, 2011. http://mogradfekr.blogspot.com/2011/12/blog-post.html (accessed May 3, 2021).

Mednick, Sam, Josef Federman, and Bassem Mroue. "Hamas accepts Gaza Cease-Fire Proposal; Israel Will Continue Talks but Conducts Strikes in Rafah." Associated Press, May 7, 2024. https://abc7chicago.com/israel-and-gaza-israeli-army-tells-palestinians-to-evacuate-parts-of-rafah-ahead-expected-ground-invasion/14773061/ (accessed June 1, 2024).

Mekky, Mohamed A., Mohammed Tolba, Mohamed O. Abdel-Malek, Wael A. Abbas, and Mohamed Zidan. "Human Fascioliasis: A Re-Emerging Disease in Upper Egypt." *American Journal of Tropical Medicine and Hygiene* 93, no. 1 (2015): 76–79. https://www.ncbi.nlm.nih.gov/pmc/articles/PMC4497909/ (accessed February 23, 2021).

Mendible, Myra. "Post-Vietnam Syndrome: National Identity, War, and The Politics of Humiliation." https://www.libraryofsocialscience.com/essays/mendible-post-vietnam/.

"A Message to America/*Risāla ilā Amrīkā*" [video of James Foley]. August 19, 2014. Mu'assasat al-Furqān, 4:40. URL no longer available.

"A Message to the Refugees in the Land of Disbelief." Media Office for Wilāyat Ḥaḍramūt, 2016. Courtesy ISD.

"Message to the Wife of the Slain Infidel, Paul Johnson from the Wife of One of the Martyrs of the Arab Peninsula" [in Arabic]. *Ṣawt al-Jihād* 21 (July 28, 2004): 43. http://archive.org/stream/Sawt-aljihad-magazine/Sawt-aljihad21#page/n41/mode/2up (accessed July 28, 2013).

Miller, Susan B. "Humiliation and Shame: Comparing Two Affect States and Indicators of Narcissistic Stress." *Bulletin of the Menninger Clinic* 52, no. 1 (1988): 40–51.

Miller, William Ian. *Humiliation and Other Essays on Honor, Social Discomfort, and Violence*. Cornell University Press, 1995.

Milmartin, Chris. *The Masculine Self*. Sloan Publishing, 2006.

Mills, Charles W. "'Ideal Theory' as Ideology." *Hypatia* 20, no. 3 (2005): 165–83.

Milton-Edwards, Beverly. *The Muslim Brotherhood: The Arab Spring and Its Future Face*. Routledge, 2016.

Minh-ha, Trinh. *When the Moon Waxes Red: Representation, Gender and Cultural Politics*. Routledge, 1991.

Mitchell, Timothy. *Rule of Experts: Egypt, Techno-Politics, Modernity*. University of California Press, 2002.

Moaveni, Azadeh. "Protests in Iran: LRB 1 November 2022." *London Review of Books*, November 2, 2022. https://www.lrb.co.uk/podcasts-and-videos/podcasts/the-lrb-podcast/protests-in-iran (accessed July 15, 2023).

Moghadam, Assef. "Suicide Terrorism, Occupation, and the Globalization of Martyrdom: A Critique of Dying to Win." *Studies in Conflict & Terrorism* 29, no. 8 (December 2006): 707–29.

Moïsi, Dominique. "The Clash of Emotions: Fear, Humiliation, Hope, and the New World Order." *Foreign Affairs* 86, no. 1 (2007): 8–12.

Monks, Kieron. "Could Egypt's Revolution Be Stolen?" Al Jazeera, April 11, 2011. https://www.aljazeera.com/features/2011/4/18/could-egypts-revolution-be-stolen (accessed February 28, 2021).

Morgado, Miguel. "The Threat of Danger: Decadence and Virtù." *Perspectives on Political Science* 35, no. 2 (2006): 86–93.

Mosendz, Polly. "Beheadings as Terror Marketing." *Atlantic Monthly*, October 2, 2014. http://www.theatlantic.com/international/archive/2014/10/beheadings-as-terror-marketing/381049/ (accessed May 30, 2015).

Mosireen Collective. Egyptian resistance archive 858. Cabinet Clashes, Women's March, Blue Bra Girl (2011-12-10) at Downtown, Cairo, December 20, 2011. https://858.ma/GC/player/00:14:12.381. 3:49–4:27 (accessed January 13, 2025).

Mosireen Collective. "Sexual Torture Is Systematic: From Mubarak and SCAF to the Muslim Brotherhood (Video)." *Jadaliyya*, June 24, 2013. https://www.jadaliyya.com/Details/28836 (accessed June 4, 2021).

Mosireen Collective. "Al-Taʿdhīb al-jinsī manhajī min Mubarak lil-majlis al-ʿaskarī wa-lil-Ikhwān" [Sexual torture under Mubarak, SCAF, and the (Muslim) Brotherhood]. June 24, 2013. YouTube video, 10:33. https://www.youtube.com/watch?v=j2kMzrFHt-Y (accessed June 29, 2021).

Mosse, George L. *Nationalism and Sexuality: Respectability and Abnormal Sexuality in Modern Europe.* Howard Fertig, 1985.

Mostafa, Dalia Said. "Introduction: Egyptian Women, Revolution, and Protest Culture." *Journal for Cultural Research* 19, no. 2 (2015): 118–29.

Motaparthy, Priyanka. "The Unknown Man, and the Deaths at Abu Zaabal." *The New Yorker*, April 3, 2015. https://www.newyorker.com/news/news-desk/the-unknown-man-and-the-deaths-at-abu-zaabal (accessed June 15, 2021).

Mouffe, Chantal. *On the Political.* Routledge, 2005.

Moyn, Samuel. "Dignity's Due?" *The Nation*, November 4, 2013.

Muhammad, Agami Hassan Muhammad. "Arabic Performance Poetry: A New Mode of Resistance." *Arab Studies Quarterly* 39, no. 2 (2017): 815–41.

Muḥammad, Hadīr. "Sīrat ḥayāt al-shāʿir al-Miṣrī Hishām el-Gakh" [Biography of the Egyptian poet Hisham el-Gakh]. Almrsal.com, April 1, 2016. https://www.almrsal.com/post/282931 (accessed April 8, 2021).

Mura, Andrea. *The Symbolic Scenarios of Islamism: A Study in Islamic Political Thought.* Ashgate, 2015.

Naby, Eden. "Yazidis." In *The Oxford Encyclopedia of the Islamic World Online*, edited by John L. Esposito. Oxford University Press, 2009.

Nasrallah, Hassan. Speech on the "Innocence of Muslims." September 16, 2012. YouTube video. http://www.youtube.com/watch?v=gSed7kUksaU#! (accessed February 9, 2013; account suspended).

Naṣṣār, Mayyār. "Hind Nāfiʿ Badawī tarwī kayf ʿadhabahā rijāl al-jayh bi-waḥshiyya ṣādima" [Hind Nāfiʿ Badawī recounts how the men of the army tortured her with shocking brutality]. December 25, 2011. YouTube video. https://www.youtube.com/watch?v=p8svdG-zZnm (accessed June 30, 2021; video now unavailable).

Negm, Nawara. "Ilā al-mutaḍarrirīn . . . ḥaqqkum maʿa Mubarak mish maʿānā" [To those who have grievances . . . this is Mubarak's fault, not ours]. *Tahyyes Blog*, February 5, 2011. http://tahyyes.blogspot.com/2011/02/blog-post_05.html (accessed March 1, 2021).

Negm, Nawara. "Ilā ḥabīb al-malāyīn ba'da al-bayān al-khāmis" [To the beloved of millions after the fifth statement]. *Tahyyes Blog*, February 14, 2011. http://tahyyes.blogspot.com/2011/02/blog-post_3087.html (accessed March 2, 2021).

Negm, Nawara. "Jum'at al-istimrār wa'l-intiṣār fī maydān al-Taḥrīr" [Friday of perseverance and triumph in Tahrir Square]. *Tahyyes Blog*, February 16, 2011. http://tahyyes.blogspot.com/2011/02/blog-post_16.html.

Negm, Nawara. "Mādhā taf'al law kunta ḥarāmī?" [What would you do if you were a thief?]. *Tahyyes Blog*, May 17, 2011. http://tahyyes.blogspot.com/2011/05/blog-post_17.html (accessed June 2, 2021).

Negm, Nawara (@nawaranegm). "Morsi madhlūl dhull al-ibil wa-kullnā kidah mish 'ārifīn ni'mal lahu ḥāga 'ashān iḥnā wa-huwa khubu'āt ya'nī shwayyat al-rigāla illī ḥīlatnā mātū wa-lā ēh?" Twitter, July 31, 2012. (accessed February 15, 2021, URL no longer available).

Negm, Nawara. "Quwwitnā fī rukūbitnā" [Our strength is in being ridden]. *Tahyyes Blog*, January 22, 2014. http://tahyyes.blogspot.com/2014/01/blog-post_22.html (accessed July 1, 2021).

Nietzsche, Friedrich. *The Birth of Tragedy and the Genealogy of Morals*. Translated by Francis Golffing. Anchor Press Books, 1956.

Obama, Barack. "Statement by the President on ISIL." White House Press Office, September 10, 2014. https://www.whitehouse.gov/the-press-office/2014/09/10/statement-president-isil-1 (accessed June 7, 2015).

O'Donnell, Michael, and Sue Sharpe. *Uncertain Masculinities: Youth, Ethnicity and Class in Contemporary Britain*. Routledge, 2000.

Office of the Director of National Intelligence. Annual Threat Assessment of the U.S. Intelligence Community, February 5, 2024. https://www.odni.gov/files/ODNI/documents/assessments/ATA-2024-Unclassified-Report.pdf (accessed December 30, 2024).

Omar, Mohamed Hamdy (@mhamdyooo). "Takhayyalū lamā gīl 'āsh 'umruh fī dhull wa-mahāna wa-muṣammim innuh yikhtār linā mustaqbal min al-dhull wa'l-mahāna . . . raḥmāk yā rabbī #intikhābāt al-dam #maṣr." Twitter, May 26, 2014 (accessed February 10, 2021, URL no longer available).

Omidvar, Ahmad. "Semiotics of ISIS Poetry in the Framework of Pierce's Model (Focusing on the Poems of Ahlam Nasr)." *Journal of Research in Arabic Language: Biannual Journal of the University of Isfahan* 14, no. 2 (2022): 83–98. https://https://rall.ui.ac.ir/article_27060.html.

O'Shaughnessy, Nicholas. "Selling Terror: The Visual Rhetoric of Osama bin Laden." *Journal of Political Marketing* 1, no. 4 (2002): 83–93.

Ouf, Iman. "al-Taftīsh al-dhātī lil-sajīnāt al-Miṣriyyāt . . . taḥarrush wa-tarkība qātila min adawāt qahr al-nisā'" [Body searches of Egyptian female prisoners . . . harassment and a deadly combination of tools to subjugate women]. *Raseef22*, October 15, 2019. https://raseef22.net/article/1075202-التفتيش-الذاتي-للسجينات-المصريات-تحرش-وتركيبة-قاتلة-من-أدوات-قهر-النساء (accessed June 30, 2021).

Ould Mohamedou, Mohammad-Mahmoud. "Neo-Orientalism and the e-Revolutionary: Self-Representation and the Post-Arab Spring." *Middle East Law and Governance* 7, no. 1 (2015): 120–31.

Ouzgane, Lahoucine, ed. *Islamic Masculinities*. Zed Books, 2006.

Packer, George. "A Friend Flees the Horror of ISIS." *The New Yorker*, August 6, 2014. http://www.newyorker.com/news/daily-comment/friend-flees-horror-isis (accessed December 15, 2015).

Pape, Robert Anthony. *Dying to Win: The Strategic Logic of Suicide Terrorism*. Random House, 2006.

Paquette, Danielle, Souad Mekhennet, and Joby Warrick. "ISIS Attacks Surge in Africa Even as Trump Boasts of a '100-percent' Defeated Caliphate." *The Washington Post*, October 18,

2020. https://www.washingtonpost.com/national-security/islamic-state-attacks-surging-africa/2020/10/18/2e16140e-1079-11eb-8a35-237ef1eb2ef7_story.html (accessed September 1, 2023).

Parker, Kim, and Renee Stepler. "Americans See Men as the Financial Providers, Even as Women's Contributions Grow." Pew Research Center, September 20, 2017. https://www.pewresearch.org/short-reads/2017/09/20/americans-see-men-as-the-financial-providers-even-as-womens-contributions-grow/ (accessed July 15, 2023).

Patai, Raphael. *The Arab Mind.* Scribner, 1973.

Patterson, Orlando. *Slavery and Social Death: A Comparative Study.* Harvard University Press, 1982.

Peičius, Eimantas, Gvidas Urbonas, W. David Harrison, Aušra Urbonienė, Jolanta Kuznecovienė, Rūta Butkevičienė, Kristina Astromskė, and Ramunė Kalėdienė. "Dignity Violations and Barriers to Dignity Assurance for Terminally Ill Patients at the End of Life: A Cross-Sectional Analysis." *Medicina* (Kaunas, Lithuania) 58 (2022): 1–10. https://www.ncbi.nlm.nih.gov/pmc/articles/PMC8875998/ (accessed January 2, 2023).

Pellat, Charles. "D̲juḥā." In *Encyclopaedia of Islam*, 2nd ed, edited by P. Bearman et al. Brill, 2012.

Peteet, Julie M. *Gender in Crisis: Woman and the Palestinian Resistance Movement.* Columbia University Press, 1991.

Pew Research Center. "U.S. Muslims Concerned About Their Place in Society, but Continue to Believe in the American Dream." https://www.pewresearch.org/wp-content/uploads/sites/20/2017/07/U.S.-MUSLIMS-FULL-REPORT-with-population-update-v2.pdf. July 26, 2017 (accessed July 23, 2024).

Philpott, Daniel. "Sovereignty: An Introduction and Brief History." *Journal of International Affairs* 48, no. 2 (1995): 353–68.

Physicians for Social Responsibility. "Body Count: Casualty Figures After Ten Years of the 'War on Terror' (Iraq, Afghanistan, Pakistan)." Translated by Ali Fathollah-Nejad. Physicians for Social Responsibility, 2015. http://www.psr.org/assets/pdfs/body-count.pdf.

Pineda, Erin R. *Seeing Like an Activist: Civil Disobedience and the Civil Rights Movement.* Oxford University Press, 2021.

Pinker, Stephen. "The Stupidity of Dignity." *The New Republic*, May 28, 2008. https://newrepublic.com/article/64674/the-stupidity-dignity (accessed May 10, 2023).

Pitkin, Hanna Fenichel. *Fortune Is a Woman: Gender and Politics in the Thought of Niccolò Machiavelli.* University of Chicago Press, 1999.

Plaskin, Glen. "The *Playboy* Interview with Donald Trump." *Playboy*, March 1, 1990. https://www.playboy.com/read/playboy-interview-donald-trump-1990 (accessed July 15, 2023).

Pollock, Griselda. "From Horrorism to Compassion: Re-facing Medusan Otherness in Dialogue with Adriana Cavarero and Bracha Ettinger." In *Visual Politics of Psychoanalysis: Art and the Image in Post-Traumatic Cultures*, edited by Griselda Pollock. I. B. Taurus, 2013.

Post, Jerrold. *Military Studies in the Jihad Against the Tyrants: The al-Qaeda Training Manual.* USAF Counterproliferation Center, 2004.

Prakash, Gyan. "Writing Post-Orientalist Histories of the Third World: Perspectives from Indian Historiography." *Comparative Studies in Society and History* 32, no. 2 (1990): 383–408.

Quilliam Foundation. "Detailed Analysis of Islamic State Propaganda Video: 'Although the Disbelievers Dislike It.'" Quilliam Foundation and Terrorism Research and Analysis Consortium (TRAC), December 2014. http://www.quilliamfoundation.org/wp/wp-content/uploads/publications/free/detailed-analysis-of-islamic-state-propaganda-video.pdf (accessed October 2, 2015, site now discontinued).

Qutb, Sayyid. *Fī Ẓilāl al-Qurʾān.* Dār al-Shurūq, 1972.

Qutb, Sayyid. *Ma'ālim fī al-ṭarīq*. Dār al-Shurūq, 1991 [1964].
Ramadan, Hania Sobhy. "Education and the Production of Citizenship in the Late Mubarak Era: Privatization, Discipline, and the Construction of the Nation in Egyptian Secondary Schools." PhD thesis, University of London, School of Oriental and African Studies, 2012.
Rancière, Jacques. *The Emancipated Spectator*. Translated by Gregory Elliott. Verso, 2011.
Rawls, John. *A Theory of Justice*. The Belknap Press of Harvard University, 1999.
Reardon, Martin. "ISIL and the Management of Savagery." *Al Jazeera*, July 6, 2015. http://www.aljazeera.com/indepth/opinion/2015/07/isil-management-savagery-150705060914471.html (accessed October 17, 2016).
Reid, Donald Malcolm. *Cairo University and the Making of Modern Egypt*. Cambridge University Press, 1990.
Reinhardt, Mark. "Theorizing the Event of Photography—The Visual Politics of Violence and Terror in Azoulay's Civil Imagination, Linfield's The Cruel Radiance, and Mitchell's Cloning Terror." *Theory & Event* 16, no. 3 (2013). muse.jhu.edu/article/520028.
Reisebrodt, Martin. *Pious Passion: The Emergence of Modern Fundamentalism in the United States and Iran*. University of California Press, 1993.
Remnick, David. "Going the Distance: On and Off the Road with Barack Obama." *The New Yorker*, January 27, 2014.
Revkin, Mara, and Yussef Auf. "Egypt's Fallen Police State Gives Way to Vigilante Justice." *The Atlantic*, April 3, 2013. https://www.theatlantic.com/international/archive/2013/04/egypts-fallen-police-state-gives-way-to-vigilante-justice/274616/ (accessed March 3, 2021).
Riches, David, ed. *The Anthropology of Violence*. Oxford: Basil Blackwell, 1986.
Riabov, Oleg, and Riabova Tatiana. "The Remasculinization of Russia? Gender, Nationalism, and the Legitimation of Power Under Vladimir Putin." *Problems of Post-Communism* 61 (2) 2014: 23–35.
Rorty, Richard. *Contingency, Irony and Solidarity*. Cambridge University Press, 1989.
Rosin, Hanna. "The End of Men." *The Atlantic*, June 8, 2010. https://www.theatlantic.com/magazine/archive/2010/07/the-end-of-men/308135/ (accessed December 30, 2024).
Roy, Olivier. *The Failure of Political Islam*. Translated by Carol Volk. Harvard University Press, 1994.
Rubin, Gayle S. "Thinking Sex: Notes for a Radical Theory of the Politics of Sexuality." In *Pleasure and Danger: Exploring Female Sexuality*, edited by Carole S. Vance. Routledge & Kegan Paul, 1984.
Rushing, Sara. "What's Left of 'Empowerment' After Neoliberalism?" *Theory & Event* 19, no. 1 (2016). muse.jhu.edu/article/607286.
Ryan, Erin Gloria. "Donald Trump Is a Professional Dominatrix and the GOP Can't Get Enough of His Humiliation." *The Daily Beast*, April 13, 2017. https://www.thedailybeast.com/donald-trump-is-a-professional-dominatrix-and-the-gop-cant-get-enough-of-his-humiliation (accessed May 12, 2023).
Ryzova, Lucie. "The Battle of Muhammad Mahmoud Street in Cairo: The Politics and Poetics of Urban Violence in Revolutionary Time." *Past & Present* 247, no. 1 (2020): 273–317.
Saad, Reem. "The Egyptian Revolution: A Triumph of Poetry." *American Ethnologist* 39, no. 1 (2012): 63–66.
Ṣabāḥak Miṣrī. "Ibnat al-Shahīd Muṣṭafā 'Ibīdū: Dā'iman biḥiss anna al-ra'īs al-Sīsī ab tānī līnā" [The daughter of the martyr Mustafa Ibidu: I always felt that President Sisi was a second father to us]. Hisham 'Assy, Ṣabāḥak Miṣrī, MBCMASR 2. March 10, 2021. YouTube video, 0:56. https://www.youtube.com/watch?v=O_APaWkOw_c (accessed May 27, 2021).
Sada Elbalad. "Liqā' al-muḥāmī Farid al-Deeb ma'a Hamdi Rizq" [Interview of lawyer Farid al-Deeb with Hamdi Rizq]. June 1, 2014. YouTube video, 2:22:36. https://www.youtube.com/watch?v=Mi3FDVxF0IA (accessed May 14, 2021).

Sada Elbalad. "Muḥākamat al-qarn: Kalimat al-ra'īs al-asbaq amāma hay'at al-quḍāh" [The trial of the century: the former president's speech in front of the Judicial Council]. August 13, 2014. YouTube video, 23:09. https://www.youtube.com/watch?v=lHMbcS-0U8E (accessed March 12, 2021).

Sada Elbalad. "Nagat Attia el-Gebaly, 'Khabīr amnī yuḥadhdhir 'al-muwāṭinīn': al-sayr 'aks al-ittijāh bi'l-qurb min al-akmina yu'arriḍ ṣāḥibuhu lil-'qatl' lil-ishtibāh fīhi" [A security expert warns "citizens": [Car] owners driving in the wrong direction near hidden security stations risk being "killed" on suspicion]. January 31, 2014. https://www.elbalad.news/801799 (accessed June 22, 2021).

Salama, Mohamed Yousry (@MYousrySalama). "Ḥukūma tabda' 'ahdahā bi'l-sa'y li-iqtirāḍ 4.8 milyār dūlār min ṣandūq al-naqd al-duwalī wa-niṣf milyār min Amrīkā hiya ḥukūmat al-luḥā musta'āra!" Twitter, August 18, 2012. https://twitter.com/MYousrySalama/status/236755386437341184 (accessed February 4, 2020).

Saleh, Yasmine. "Egyptian Revolution Brings Show of Religious Unity." *Reuters*, February 18, 2011. https://www.reuters.com/article/us-egypt-christians/egyptian-revolution-brings-show-of-religious-unity-idUSTRE71H6KA20110218 (accessed January 12, 2022).

Salih, Mohammed A. and Wladimir van Wilgenburg. "Iraqi Yazidis: 'If We Move They Will Kill Us.'" Al Jazeera, August 5, 2014. https://www.aljazeera.com/news/2014/8/5/iraqi-yazidis-if-we-move-they-will-kill-us (accessed June 4, 2018).

Sanders, Lewis IV, and Mark Visonà. "The Soul of Tahrir: Poetics of a Revolution." In *Translating Egypt's Revolution: The Language of Tahrir*, ed. Samia Mehrez. The American University in Cairo Press, 2012.

Sardenberg, Cecìlia M. B. "Liberal vs. Liberating Empowerment: A Latin American Feminist Perspective on Conceptualising Women's Empowerment." *IDS Bulletin: Transforming Development Knowledge* 39, no. 6 (2008): 18–27.

Sarot, Marcel. "Theodicy and Modernity: An Inquiry into the Historicity of Theodicy." In *Theodicy in the World of the Bible: The Goodness of God and the Problem of Evil*, edited by Antti Laato and Johannes C. de Moor. Brill, 2003.

Saurette, Paul. "Humiliation and the Global War on Terror." *Peace Review* 17, no. 1 (2005): 47–54.

Saurette, Paul. *The Kantian Imperative: Humiliation, Common Sense, Politics*. University of Toronto Press, 2005.

Saurette, Paul. "Kant's Culture of Humiliation." *Philosophy & Social Criticism* 28, no. 1 (2002): 59–90.

Saurette, Paul. "You Dissin Me? Humiliation and Post 9/11 Global Politics." *Review of International Studies* 32, no. 3 (2006): 495–522.

Saxonhouse, Arlene W. *Free Speech and Democracy in Ancient Athens*. Cambridge University Press, 2008.

Sayed, Aly. "Ru'b al-ḍubbāṭ min kalām aḥad al-thuwwār li-junūd ta'mīn wizārat al-difā'" [The terror of officers from the speech of one of the revolutionaries to soldiers securing the Ministry of Defense]. February 3, 2012. YouTube video, 13:45. https://www.youtube.com/watch?v=_nWIZwCafSs (accessed March 2, 2021).

Scarry, Elaine. *The Body in Pain: The Making and Unmaking of The World*. Oxford University Press, 2006.

Schafly, Phyllis. "Christians are Better, Regardless of the Facts." The David Pakman Show. March 10, 2015, video, 9:34. https://davidpakman.com/march-10-2015/ (accessed February 18, 2025).

Schmitt, Carl. *Political Theology: Four Chapters on the Concept of Sovereignty*. Translated by George Schwab. University of Chicago Press, 2006.

Scholz, Sally J. *Political Solidarity*. The Pennsylvania State University Press, 2008.

Schwartz, Julia. "Fantasy and Morals in the Stories of Juha." Inside Arabia: Voice of the Arab People. December 2, 2018. https://insidearabia.com/fantasy-and-morals-in-the-story-of-juha/ (accessed May 9, 2023).

Schwedler, Jillian. "Against Methodological Nationalism: Seeing Comparisons as Encompassing through the Arab Uprisings." In *Rethinking Comparison: Innovative Methods for Qualitative Political Inquiry*, edited by Erica S. Simmons and Nicholas Rush Smith. Cambridge University Press, 2021.

Schwedler, Jillian. "Comparative Politics and the Arab Uprisings." *Middle East Law and Governance* 7, no. 1 (2015): 141–52.

Schwedler, Jillian. *Protesting Jordan: Geographies of Power and Dissent.* Stanford University Press, 2022.

Schwedler, Jillian. "Taking Time Seriously: Temporality and the Arab Uprisings." Paper prepared for the workshop: From Mobilization to Counter-Revolution: The Arab Spring in Comparative Perspective. Project on Middle East Political Science, May 3–4, 2016. https://pomeps.org/taking-time-seriously-temporality-and-the-arab-uprisings (accessed May 1, 2021).

Sciolino, Elaine. "Seeing Green; The Red Menace Is Gone. But Here's Islam." *The New York Times*, January 21, 1996. https://www.nytimes.com/1996/01/21/weekinreview/seeing-green-the-red-menace-is-gone-but-here-s-islam.html (accessed March 14, 2015).

"A Second Message to America/Risāla thāniya ilā Amrīkā" [video of Steven Sotloff]. 2014. Mu'assasat al-Furqān, 2:46. Intercepted and unofficially released September 2. http://www.dumpert.nl/embed/6615338/fa3276b6/ (accessed February 3, 2023).

Seedat, Fatima. 2017. "Sexual Economies of War and Sexual Technologies of the Body: Militarised Muslim Masculinity and the Islamist Production of Concubines for the Caliphate." *Agenda* 30, no. 3 (2016): 25–38.

Shaaban, Azza. "Iḥnā mish balṭāgiyya" [We are not thugs]. June 14, 2011. YouTube video, 9:11. https://www.youtube.com/watch?v=9g4zFkgCNOI (accessed March 14, 2021).

Shabakat Raṣd. "Ḥaflat saḥl li-aḥad mu'taṣimī rābi'a 'alā yad ḍābiṭ wa-junūdihi" [An assembly to drag one of the Rābi'a protesters by an officer and his soldiers]. August 14, 2013. YouTube video, 1:39. https://www.youtube.com/watch?v=HGp6YgAITaM&t=58s (accessed March 8, 2021).

"Shaḥdh al-himam li-daf' 'ādiyat al-umam" [Honing Ambitions to Repel the Aggression of the Nations]. Al-Bayan audio recording 51:15. https://archive.org/details/souheil_08/شحذ+الهمم+لدفع+عادية+الأمم+06.ogg (accessed February 16, 2025).

Shafy, Samiha. "'Horribly Humiliating': Egyptian Woman Tells of 'Virginity Tests.'" *Der Spiegel*, June 10, 2011. https://www.spiegel.de/international/world/horribly-humiliating-egyptian-woman-tells-of-virginity-tests-a-767365.html (accessed March 20, 2021).

Shahin, Hassan. "Faḍīḥatunā taluff al-'ālam min aqṣāhu ilā aqṣāhu" [Our disgrace is spreading all over the world, from one end to the other]. Interview by Yousry Fouda. OnTV, September 8, 2014. YouTube video, 4:36. https://www.youtube.com/watch?v=uLRbidftdNc (accessed March 20, 2021, no longer available).

Shalaby, Ethar, and Shereen Youssef. "Palestinian Recounts Being Stripped and Driven Away by Israeli Army." BBC Arabic, December 9, 2023. https://www.bbc.com/news/world-middle-east-67666270 (accessed May 23, 2023).

Shephard, Alex, and Laura Reston. "Trump's Political Lesson: Humiliate, or Be Humiliated." *The New Republic*, October 16, 2023. https://newrepublic.com/article/139176/trumps-political-lesson-humiliate-humiliated (accessed February 15, 2017).

Sherko, Pasar. "How Islamic State Ideology Contributes to Its Resilience." *Fikra Forum*, July 1, 2021. https://www.washingtoninstitute.org/policy-analysis/how-islamic-state-ideology-contributes-its-resilience.

Shklar, Judith N. *Ordinary Vices.* Harvard University Press, 1984.

Shoman, Hazem. "El-Barādeʿī wa-ḥukm Miṣr" [El-Baradei and the rule of Egypt]. March 27, 2011. YouTube video, 3:31. https://www.youtube.com/watch?v=r5JhW5sV4Cw (accessed May 7, 2021, no longer available).

Shulman, George. "Chasing the Whale: *Moby-Dick* as Political Theory." In *A Political Companion to Herman Melville*, edited by Jason Frank. University Press of Kentucky, 2013.

Siboni, Gabi, Daniel Cohen, and Tal Koren. "The Islamic State's Strategy in Cyberspace." *Military and Strategic Affairs* 7, no. 1 (2015): 127–44.

Siddiqui, Sohaira. "Beyond Authenticity: ISIS and the Islamic Legal Tradition." *Jadaliyya*, February 24, 2015. http://www.jadaliyya.com/pages/index/20944/beyond-authenticity_isis-and-the-islamic-legal-tra (accessed January 1, 2016).

Silver, Maury, Rosaria Conte, Maria Miceli, and Isabella Poggi. "Humiliation: Feeling, Social Control and the Construction of Identity." *Journal for the Theory of Social Behaviour* 16, no. 3 (1986): 269–83.

"Ṣināʿat al-Rijāl" [Making men]. Al-muʾassasāt al-munāṣara lil-dawla. Courtesy ISD.

Singerman, Diane. "Youth, Gender and Dignity in the Egyptian Uprising." *Journal of Middle East Women's Studies* 9, no. 3 (2013): 1–27.

Šisler, Vít. "From Kuma\War to Quraish: Representation of Islam in Arab and American Video Games." In *Playing with Religion in Digital Games*, edited by Heidi A. Campbell and Gregory P. Grieve. Indiana University Press, 2014.

Sivakumaran, Sandesh. "Sexual Violence against Men in Armed Conflict." *The European Journal of International Law* 18, no. 2 (2007): 253–76.

SocialSphereInc. *Politico* Poll, July 3–13. *Politico*, July 21, 2014. Politico.com. https://misc.pagesuite.com/pdfdownload/c9ebdcc7-8262-45cc-b70c-8e382c35f50f.pdf (accessed January 3, 2025).

Sondy, Amanullah de. *The Crisis of Islamic Masculinities.* Bloomsbury Publishing, 2014.

Statman, Daniel. "Humiliation, Dignity and Self-Respect." *Philosophical Psychology* 13, no. 4 (2000): 523–40.

Steinberg, Blema S. "Psychoanalytic Concepts in International Politics: The Role of Shame and Humiliation." *International Review of Psycho-Analysis* 18 (1991): 65–85.

Sterling, Joe. "CNN Fact Check: Obama Went on an Apology Tour, Romney and Others Say." CNN Politics, October 23, 2012. https://edition.cnn.com/2012/10/23/politics/fact-check-apology-tour/index.html (accessed December 9, 2022).

Stern, Jessica. *Terror in the Name of God: Why Religious Militants Kill.* Harper Collins, 2003.

Stern, Jessica, and J. M. Berger. *ISIS: The State of Terror.* Ecco, 2015.

Stewart, Frank Henderson. *Honor.* University of Chicago Press, 1994.

"The Story of a *Mujāhid*." *Al-Hussam*, July 28, 1995.

Strier, Roni, Zvi Eisikovits, and Eli Buchbinder. "Masculinity, Poverty and Work: The Multiple Constructions of Work among Working Poor Men." *Journal of Social Policy* 43, no. 2 (2014): 331–49.

Ṭabarī, Muḥammad ibn Jarīr. *Tafsīr al-Ṭabarī - Jāmiʿ al-Bayān ʿan taʾwīl āy al-Qurʾān.* 7 vols. Edited by Bashshār ʿAwwād Maʿrūf and ʿIṣām Fāris al-Ḥurristānī. Beirut: Muʾassasat al-Risāla, 1994.

Taddonio, Patrice. "Watch: Inside the Night President Obama Took on Donald Trump." *PBS Frontline*, September 22, 2016. https://www.pbs.org/wgbh/frontline/article/watch-inside-the-night-president-obama-took-on-donald-trump/ (accessed July 1, 2023).

Tadros, Mariz. "Challenging Reified Masculinities: Men as Survivors of Politically Motivated Sexual Assault in Egypt." *Journal of Middle East Women's Studies* 12, no. 3 (2016): 323–42.

Tadros, Mariz. "Understanding Politically Motivated Sexual Assault in Protest Spaces: Evidence from Egypt (March 2011 to June 2013)." *Social and Legal Studies* 25, no. 1: (2016): 98–99.

Tarnopolsky, Christina. "Prudes, Perverts, and Tyrants." *Political Theory* 32, no. 4 (2004): 468–94.

"Ṭāṭī ṭāṭī" [Lower, lower]. Lyrics by Abu Zeid Bayoumy. Performed by Ramy Essam. "Ṭāṭī ṭāṭī—Rāmī 'Iṣām min Maydān al-Taḥrir 27 Māyū" [Lower, Lower—Ramy Essam at Tahrir Square, May 27]. June 28, 2011. YouTube video, 2:05. https://www.youtube.com/watch?v=pC9ajdzyV_M (accessed January 6, 2025).

Tauber, Ezriel. *To Become One: The Torah Outlook on Marriage*. Shalheves, 1990.

Taylor, Charles. "Interpretation and the Sciences of Man." In *Philosophy and the Human Sciences: Philosophical Papers*, vol. 2. Cambridge University Press, 1985.

Taylor, Charles. *A Secular Age*. Harvard University Press, 2007.

Taylor, Charles. *Sources of the Self: The Making of Modern Identity*. Harvard University Press, 1989.

Ten TV. "Al-Ra'īs el-Sīsī: lammā el-balad kashafit ḍahrahā [*sic*] wa-'arrit kitfahā fī 2011 ḥaṣalit azmit sadd al-nahḍa" [President el-Sisi: When the country exposed its back and bared its shoulders in 2011, the Renaissance Dam crisis occurred]. *Bi'l-Waraqa wa'l-Qalam*, October 13, 2019. YouTube video, 1:52. https://www.youtube.com/watch?v=PWaKITUJA9I (accessed July 31, 2021).

Thucydides. *The History of the Peloponnesian War*. Translated by Richard Crawley. The Modern Library, 1982.

Tickner, J. Ann. *Gender in International Relations: Feminist Perspectives on Archiving Global Security*. Columbia University Press, 1993.

Tierney, John. "Another Man's Honor." *The New York Times*, July 25, 2006. https://www.nytimes.com/2006/07/25/opinion/25tierney.html (accessed July 24, 2023).

Tinnes, Judith. "Although the (Dis-)Believers Dislike It: A Backgrounder on IS Hostage Videos." *Perspectives on Terrorism* 9, no. 1 (2015): 76–94.

Toldo, Ahmed. "Amr Ismail, Ummī malhāsh fī el-siyāsa" [Amr Ismail, My mother doesn't care for politics]. October 3, 2010. YouTube video, 8:22. https://www.youtube.com/watch?v=RoKtFnkEylQ (accessed October 16, 2022).

Topper, Keith. *The Disorder of Political Inquiry*. Harvard University Press, 2005.

Topper, Keith. "Introduction: The Rhetorical Turn in Political Theory." In *The Oxford Handbook of Rhetoric and Political Theory*, edited by Dilip Parameshwar Gaonkar and Keith Topper. Oxford University Press, 2025.

Topper, Keith. "Resistance to Rhetoric: The Case of Hobbes." Unpublished manuscript, PDF, 2024.

Trump, Donald J. "Donald Trump's Complete Convention Speech, Annotated." *The Los Angeles Times*, July 21, 2016. https://www.latimes.com/politics/la-na-pol-donald-trump-convention-speech-transcript-20160721-snap-htmlstory.html (accessed September 15, 2016).

Trump, Donald J. "Remarks at the Collier County Fairgrounds in Naples, Florida." The American Presidency Project, October 23, 2016. https://www.presidency.ucsb.edu/documents/remarks-the-collier-county-fairgrounds-naples-florida (accessed July 1, 2023).

Trump, Donald J. "Remarks at the Southeastern Livestock Pavilion in Ocala." The American Presidency Project, October 12, 2016. https://www.presidency.ucsb.edu/documents/remarks-the-southeastern-livestock-pavilion-ocala-florida (accessed February 20, 2018).

Trump, Donald J. (@realDonaldTrump). "Iran humiliated the United States with the capture of our 10 sailors. Horrible pictures & images. We are weak. I will NOT forget!" Twitter, January 14, 2016. https://x.com/realDonaldTrump/status/687510877847851008 (accessed December 26, 2024).

Ufheil-Somers, Amanda. "The Militancy of Mahalla al-Kubra." *The Middle East Research and Information Project* (MERIP), September 29, 2007. https://merip.org/2007/09/the-militancy-of-mahalla-al-kubra/.

Usher, Sebastian. "Jihad Magazine for Women on Web." BBC News, August 24, 2004. http://news.bbc.co.uk/1/hi/world/middle_east/3594982.stm (accessed September 8, 2022).

van de Sande, Mathijs. "The Prefigurative Politics of Tahrir Square—an Alternative Perspective on the 2011 Revolutions." *Res Publica* 19, no. 3 (2013): 223–39.

Veto Gate. "Aḥad Abnā' Mubarak yuṭālib el-Sīsī bi'l-'afw 'an al-ra'īs al-asbaq" [One of Mubarak's sons demands el-Sīsī to pardon the former president]. June 1, 2014. YouTube video, 2:55. https://www.youtube.com/watch?v=YVUyDxApNdg (accessed November 20, 2020).

Villanger, Espen. "Arab Foreign Aid: Disbursement Patterns, Aid Policies and Motives." *Forum for Development Studies* 34, no. 2 (2007): 223–56.

Waldron, Jeremy. *Dignity, Rank, and Rights.* Oxford University Press, 2012.

Wall, Melissa, and Sahar el Zahed. "'I'll Be Waiting for You Guys': A YouTube Call to Action in the Egyptian Revolution." *International Journal of Communication* 5 (2011): 1333–43.

Walzer, Michael. *In God's Shadow: Politics in the Hebrew Bible.* Yale University Press, 2012.

Weber, Cynthia. *Faking It: US Hegemony in a "Post-Phallic" Era.* University of Minnesota Press, 1999.

Webster, Elaine. "Degradation: A Human Rights Law Perspective." In *Humiliation, Degradation, Dehumanization*, edited by Paulus Kaufmann, Hannes Kuch, Christian Neuhäuser, and Elaine Webster. Springer, 2010.

Welter, Barbara. "The Cult of True Womanhood: 1820–1860." *American Quarterly* 18, no. 2 (1966): 151–74.

Wengst, Klaus, and John Bowden. *Humility: Solidarity of the Humiliated.* Translated by John Bowden. SCM Press, 1988.

West, Johnny. *Karama! Journeys through the Arab Spring.* Heron Books, 2011.

White, Lucie E. "Subordination, Rhetorical Survival Skills, and Sunday Shoes: Notes on the Hearing of Mrs. G." In *At the Boundaries of Law: Feminism and Legal Theory*, edited by Martha Albertson Fineman and Nancy Sweet Thomadsen. Routledge, 1991.

Wilāyat Sinai. "al-Dhull wa'l-Mahāna fī arḍ al-Kināna" [Humiliation and Degradation in the Land of Kinana]. Khattab Media Foundation. Video courtesy ISD, 4:31.

Williams, Bernard. *Shame and Necessity.* University of California Press, 1993.

Williams, Michael. "Words, Images, Enemies: Securitization and International Politics." *International Studies Quarterly* 47, no. 4 (2003): 511–31.

Wilson Center. "ISIS: Resilient on Sixth Anniversary." June 18, 2020. https://www.wilsoncenter.org/article/isis-resilient-sixth-anniversary.

Wittgenstein, Ludwig. *Philosophical Investigations.* 2nd ed. Translated by G. E. M. Anscombe. Blackwell Publishers, 1997.

Wittgenstein, Ludwig. *Wittgenstein's Nachlass. The Bergen Electronic Edition.* Oxford University Press, 1998.

Wolin, Sheldon S. "Fugitive Democracy." *Constellations* 1, no. 1 (1994): 11–25.

Wolin, Sheldon S. "Political Theory as a Vocation." *American Political Science Review* 63, no. 4 (December 1969): 1062–82.

Woltering, Robert. "Unusual Suspects: 'Ultras' as Political Actors in the Egyptian Revolution." *Arab Studies Quarterly* 35, no. 3 (2013): 290–304.

Woman News Agency-Cairo. "Tadāwul ṣuwar 'ṣādima li-junūd Miṣriyyīn yasḥalūn nisā' mutaẓāhirāt fī Maydān al-Taḥrīr" [The circulation of "shocking" images of Egyptian forces dragging female protesters in Tahrir Square]. December 8, 2011. http://wonews.net/ar/index.php?ajax=preview&id=1478 (accessed March 24, 2021).

World Bank. "The Decline of the Breadwinner: Men in the 21st Century." In *World Development Report 2012: Gender Equality and Development.* World Bank, 2011. https://elibrary.worldbank.org/doi/10.1596/9780821388105_spread2.

"Yā ahl Miṣr hādhā huwa al-ṭarīq" [O people of Egypt, this is the Way]. Al-mu'assasāt al-munāṣara lil-dawla. Video courtesy ISD, 7:00.

Yassine, Abdessalam. *Winning the Modern World for Islam.* Translated by Martin Jenni. Justice and Spirituality Publications, 2000.

Young, Iris Marion. "The Logic of Masculinist Protection: Reflections on the Current Security State." *Signs* 29, no. 1 (2003): 1–25.

Zaman, Muhammad Qasim. "Divine Sovereignty—Some Reflections." *Journal of the Royal Asiatic Society* series 3, 32, no. 2 (2022): 377–86.

Zaman, Muhammad Qasim. "The Sovereignty of God in Modern Islamic Thought." *Journal of the Royal Asiatic Society* 25, no. 3 (2015): 389–418.

ZAP Tharwat. "Nahārnā nadā" [Our morning is dew]. English translation available in Lewis Sanders and Mark Visonà, "Soul of Tahrir: Poetics of a Revolution." In *Translating Egypt's Revolution: The Language of Tahrir,* edited by Samia Mehrez. The American University in Cairo Press, 2012.

Žižek, Slavoj. *Violence.* Profile Books, Ltd., 2009.

Zogby Research Services. "Egyptian Attitudes: September 2013." September 15, 2013. http://static.squarespace.com/static/52750dd3e4b08c252c723404/t/5294bf5de4b013dda087d0e5/1385480029191/Egypt%20October%202013%20FINAL.pdf (accessed June 16, 2021).

محمد الاحمري (@alahmarim). Wa-hākadhā 'azīz qawm dhalla Miṣr thalāthūn 'āman saraqa wa-ṭawāri' wa-sujūn wa-khiyānat Ghazza wa-saraqat 70 milyār dūlār li-dhā sa-yaḥtajj al-shurakā' li-ṭardika." Twitter, February 9, 2011 (accessed June 15, 2019, URL no longer available).

محمد الهاشمي الحامدي (@MALHACHIMI). "Dukhān al-shawāri' fī Miṣr laysa min qanābil al-ghāz/wa-innamā min qulūb tamla'uhā al-karāhiyya/wa-'uqūl admanat al-sharr/wa-nufūs ushribat thaqāfat al-dhull wa'l-istibdād/wa-takhshā nasā'im al-ḥurriyya." Twitter, December 1, 2013. https://twitter.com/MALHACHIMI/status/407212045033955328 (accessed March 2, 2020).

الخطاري (@Truthcaller). "Lā yamil al-'abīd min al-tadhallul li-sayyidihim bi'l-raghm min an-nahu ṭaradahum wa-rakalahum bi-qadamihi!! Ya'shaqūn ḥayāt al-dhull #maṣr gharrid bi-ṣūra." In the picture: "Waqafnā ganbak nargūk tuqaf ganbinā mish 'āyizīn ḥurriyya mish 'āyizīn wa-ẓāyif sībūna na'kul 'aysh." Twitter, March 25, 2014 (accessed July 30, 2019, URL no longer available).

الخطاري (@Truthcaller). "Muṣṭafā Ḥusayn wa-Aḥmad Ragab—wa-kilāhumā min al-muṭabbilīn lil-Sīsī—dhallū 'alā bāb qaṣr al-ṭāghiya wa-harabū min al-ḍarb! Man a'āna ẓāliman dhalla #miṣr." Twitter, June 10, 2014 (accessed July 30, 2019, URL no longer available).

احمد الزايد (@AHM_RGL). "'Alā Allāh ba'd kull al-kharā illī wāklīnuh dah ya'raf yighayyar al-nīla al-dustūr wa-na'mil intikhābāt qabl mā nimūt . . . Allāh yikhrib bītik yā maṣr yā midawaqānā al-dhull gatik nīla." Twitter, April 2, 2010. https://twitter.com/AHM_RGL/status/11456613211 (accessed February 8, 2020).

العراب (@AhmedSalah007). "Fir'aun dās 'alīhum bi-gazmituh, qaddisūh . . . el-nabī Mūsā a'ṭā lahum ḥurriyyit'hum, 'abadū el-'igl . . . qiṣṣit 7000 sana 'ubūdiyya . . . wa-kull man tarabbā 'alā el-dhull fī #Maṣr yaṣbaḥūn #sha'b-'abīd." Twitter, July 3, 2013 (accessed February 9, 2021, URL no longer available).

بلا اقنعة (@truth4ever1). "Hal sawf tughlaq sifārat Isrā'īl fī Miṣr wa-hal sawf tulghā mu'āhadat al-dhull ma'a al-kayān al-ṣahyūnī? Hādhā huwa al-mu'ashshir 'alā man sawf yaḥkum Miṣr fī al-marḥala al-qādima. 'Amār yā Miṣr." Twitter, July 4, 2013. https://twitter.com/truth4ever1/status/352649670234873856 (accessed February 8, 2020).

تسلم الايادي (@masriaawi). "Taqbīl yad #al-murshid fī rābi'a ha-ya'īshū 'abīd wa-yamūtū 'abīd itrabbū 'alā al-dhull lil-murshid #Miṣr #al-taḥrīr #al-iskandarīya." Twitter, July 5, 2013 (accessed February 18, 2020, URL no longer available).

دراسات عسكرية (@samyalhasan). "Man raḍaʿa thady al-dhull dahran ** raʾā fī thawrat al-shuʿūb al-ʿarabīya kharāban wa-sharran #Miṣr #sūriyā." Twitter, August 22, 2013 (accessed June 4, 2019, URL no longer available).

عبد الرحمن (@Abdelrahman_3). "Shafīq min abṭāl ḥarb Uktūbir, hādhā al-jīl al-rāʾiʿ alladhī intashala Miṣr min dhull al-hazīma ilā karāmat al-naṣr wa'l-ʿubūr #ḥamlat-daʿm-Shafīq-raʾīsan-li-Miṣr." Twitter, September 9, 2013. https://twitter.com/abdelrahman_3/status/377058240367837184 (accessed June 10, 2019).

محمد البلال (@mohdgnibi). "'Abd Allah bin 'Abd al-ʿAzīz yadhill el-Sisi wa-yastadʿīhi li-ṭāʾiratihi al-khāṣṣa lil-ḥadīth maʿahu thumma yughādir, hadhā huwa el-Sisi al-dhalīl alladhī ightaṣaba al-ḥukm fī Miṣr ayyi mahāna wa-ayyi dhull." Twitter, June 21, 2014 (accessed July 29, 2019, URL no longer available).

INDEX

Page numbers followed by n indicate notes.

GPSR Authorized Representative: Easy Access System Europe - Mustamäe tee 50, 10621 Tallinn, Estonia, gpsr.requests@easproject.com

www.ingramcontent.com/pod-product-compliance
Lightning Source LLC
Chambersburg PA
CBHW020844270326
41928CB00006B/539
9780691183688